Cuba and Puerto Rico

Cuba and Puerto Rico

Transdisciplinary Approaches to History, Literature, and Culture

EDITED BY
Carmen Haydée Rivera
and Jorge Duany

University of Florida Press
Gainesville

Publication of this work made possible by a Sustaining the Humanities through the American Rescue Plan grant from the National Endowment for the Humanities.
Copyright 2023 by Carmen Haydée Rivera and Jorge Duany
All rights reserved
Published in the United States of America.

28 27 26 25 24 23   6 5 4 3 2 1

Library of Congress Cataloging-in-Publication Data
Names: Rivera, Carmen Haydée, editor. | Duany, Jorge, editor.
Title: Cuba and Puerto Rico : transdisciplinary approaches to history, literature, and culture / Carmen Haydée Rivera and Jorge Duany [editors].
Description: Gainesville : University of Florida Press, [2023] | Includes bibliographical references and index. | Summary: "In this first systematic comparative study of Cuba and Puerto Rico from both a historical and contemporary perspective, contributors highlight the interconnectedness of the two archipelagos and encourage a more nuanced and multifaceted study of the relationships between the islands and their diasporas"—Provided by publisher.
Identifiers: LCCN 2022031536 (print) | LCCN 2022031537 (ebook) | ISBN 9781683403302 (cloth) | ISBN 9781683403333 (paperback) | ISBN 9781683403456 (pdf) | ISBN 9781683403494 (epub)
Subjects: LCSH: Popular culture—Cuba. | Popular culture—Puerto Rico. | Cuban literature—History. | Puerto Rican literature—History. | Cuba—History. | Puerto Rico—History. | BISAC: HISTORY / Caribbean & West Indies / Cuba | HISTORY / Caribbean & West Indies / General
Classification: LCC F1776 .C787 2022 (print) | LCC F1776 (ebook) | DDC 972.91—dc23/eng/20220722
LC record available at https://lccn.loc.gov/2022031536
LC ebook record available at https://lccn.loc.gov/2022031537

University of Florida Press
2046 NE Waldo Road
Suite 2100
Gainesville, FL 32609
http://upress.ufl.edu

Contents

List of Figures vii
Acknowledgments ix
Introduction: "Two Wings of a Bird" 1
   Carmen Haydée Rivera and Jorge Duany

Part I. Cuba and Puerto Rico: Historical Perspectives

1. Passive Puerto Rico and Revolutionary Cuba? Myths, Realities, and the Optics of History 31
   Lillian Guerra

2. Nuclearized Wings: The Binary Roads of Cuba and Puerto Rico at the Takeoff of the Cuban Revolution (1959–1963) 43
   Silvia Álvarez Curbelo

3. The Repeating Island? Cuban–Puerto Rican Counterpoints between the Cold War and the Reencounter 62
   Francisco A. Scarano

4. Local Eyes into Caribbean Rural Life: Anthropological Informants in Cuba and Puerto Rico in the Post–World War II Era 79
   Jorge L. Giovannetti-Torres

5. The Harlem of the Club Las Dos Antillas: Race, Space, and Politics in Early Antillean New York 100
   Jesse Hoffnung-Garskof

Part II. Puerto Rican and Cuban Literary Expression

6. Exploding the Limits of Bodies and Islands: The Literary Works of Yolanda Arroyo Pizarro and Legna Rodríguez Iglesias 121
   Monica Simal

7. Puerto Rico *en Areíto*: Translation, Ethnic and Cultural Studies, and Other Collaborations among Cuban and Puerto Rican Migrant Intellectuals 136
   Laura Lomas

8. Psychological and Physical Space in Puerto Rican and Cuban Twentieth-Century Theater 158
   Maida Watson

9. *Hechos* and *desechos*: Environmental Degradation and Violence in Mayra Montero's *Tú, la oscuridad* 176
   Mary Ann Gosser Esquilín

10. Caribbean Dialogues by María Zambrano 192
    Madeline Cámara

11. "The Two Ephemeral Wings of the Angel of Love": Archipelagic Fantasies in the Narrative of Lourdes Casal and Manuel Ramos Otero 209
    Yolanda Martínez-San Miguel

Part III. Manifestations of Cuban and Puerto Rican Culture

12. Listening to Our New Possessions: Music and Imperial Writings on Puerto Rico and Cuba, 1898–1920s 233
    Hugo R. Viera-Vargas

13. The Musical Impact of the Mariel Boatlift on the Latin Music Scene of New York City and Interethnic Collaboration among Puerto Ricans and Cubans 256
    Benjamin Lapidus

14. Allora and Calzadilla: Noise and the Politics of Sonic Decoloniality 267
    Alan West-Durán

15. The Narratives and Life Projects of *Orientales* from Cuba in Puerto Rico and Florida: An Initial Comparative Study 280
    Blanca Ortiz-Torres and Mario A. Rodríguez-Cancel

16. Becoming Cuba-Rican: A Personal Testimony 295
    Jorge Duany

List of Contributors 313

Index 317

Figures

5.1. Members of the Club Las Dos Antillas   106

5.2. Racial Segregation in East Harlem and Yorkville, ca. 1900   111

5.3. Buildings with Members of the Political Club Las Dos Antillas   112

12.1. Orchestra Verdadera Juventud, conducted by Juan Madera   243

12.2. "A group of 'jíbaros' who formed Orquesta Brava of Aguadilla . . ."   244

12.3. "Music of the Poor"   245

12.4. "Native Musicians, Porto Rico"   246

Acknowledgments

Carmen Haydée Rivera: I would like to thank my coeditor, Jorge Duany, for his abundant, incisive, and inspiring research on Puerto Rico and Cuba and, especially, for his collaboration on this project. Working together with Jorge has always been a highlight for me in our professional relationship that spans over two decades. Gratitude also goes to the English Department at the University of Puerto Rico, Río Piedras, for facilitating my work on this collection of essays and, in particular, to former Department Chair, Dr. Nancy Vicente, for her unwavering and heartfelt support and friendship. Thanks to Stephanye Hunter for welcoming this volume to the University of Florida Press. Finally, to my family, *toda mi gratitud por su amor y apoyo constante, en y fuera de Puerto Rico.*

* * *

Jorge Duany: I would like to thank the staff members of the Cuban Research Institute at Florida International University for their constant support throughout the years: Sebastián Arcos, Aymee Correa, Paola Salavarria, Katherine Dieguez. In addition, I would like to recognize my coeditor, Carmen Haydée Rivera, for taking the initiative of putting together this collection and inviting me to collaborate with her. It is also a pleasure to acknowledge the encouragement of Stephanye Hunter, editor-in-chief of the University of Florida Press. Both Carmen Haydée and I would like to thank Emily M. Hinnov for copyediting the manuscript and Eleanor Deumens for overseeing its publication. As always, I am grateful to my immediate family members for their steadfast nurturance: my wife Diana Johnson, my daughter Patricia, and my son Jorge Andrés.

Introduction
"Two Wings of a Bird"

CARMEN HAYDÉE RIVERA AND JORGE DUANY

Why dwell on the ties between Cuba and Puerto Rico? To begin, both are archipelagos located in the Larger Antilles and were conquered by Spain after 1492. Although Cuba is about twelve times larger than Puerto Rico, they share a tropical climate, a summer rainy season, a stark contrast between coastal plains and inner highlands, vulnerability to hurricanes and storms, and other environmental threats such as rising sea levels and temperatures.[1] In both places, Spanish warfare, slavery, disease, migration, and biological intermixture decimated the Aboriginal populations by the mid-sixteenth century. Most of the contemporary inhabitants of Cuba and Puerto Rico, like the rest of the Caribbean, are descendants of immigrants, primarily from Europe and Africa.

The two Caribbean archipelagos were subjected to more than four centuries of uninterrupted Spanish colonialism (except for eleven months during the British occupation of Havana in 1762–63), which imposed the Spanish language and Catholic religion on local populations.[2] In turn, these populations were largely the product of the blending among Indigenous groups (especially Taínos), Spanish settlers, and enslaved Africans. As a result, Cuban and Puerto Rican cultures are closely intertwined, including their linguistic, literary, food, musical, and religious practices. Even the flags of the two countries have an identical format, only with inverted colors (three horizontal red or blue stripes alternating with two white stripes), with a white star on a red or blue triangle. Exiles from the islands adopted the two flags in New York City in 1895 as part of their common struggle against Spanish rule.

Cuba and Puerto Rico were Spain's two remaining colonies in the Americas, after the independence of the mainland Spanish American republics in the 1820s. As Spain lost its American empire in the nineteenth century, the United States expanded its economic, political, and military power in the Caribbean. During the first third of the twentieth century, Cuba and Puerto Rico consolidated their primary economic role as sugar exporters for the U.S. consumer market. Both archipelagos sent substantial portions of their populations to the United States during the second half of the century, though migratory movements began much earlier. Smaller numbers of Cubans also moved to Puerto Rico and other countries after 1959. Today, Puerto Ricans are the second largest population of Latin American origin in the United States (after Mexicans), while Cubans are the third largest. Both groups have contributed to the hybrid cultures of Latinxs in the United States, particularly in New York and Florida.

Within Latin America and the Caribbean, Cuba has traditionally been deemed exceptional. Given its strategic location between the New and Old Worlds, and between the Northern and Southern hemispheres, Cuba has long enjoyed a privileged position in international affairs, disproportionate to its land mass and population size. Its capital, Havana, became one of the leading shipping and trading entrepôts of the Americas during the sixteenth century, especially after the *flota* (convoy) system established in 1561 required all Spanish ships to rendezvous in that port city on their way back to Spain. The Gulf Stream, which begins in the Gulf of Mexico and crosses the North Atlantic Ocean, helped to make Havana the American hub of Spanish colonial navigation. Because of Cuba's commercial and military significance, the Spanish Crown hailed it in 1634 as the "key to the New World and rampart of the West Indies" (Martínez-Fernández). Cuba was also known as Spain's "ever-faithful isle" from the early nineteenth century until the mid-nineteenth century (Queen María Cristina belatedly bestowed that title on Puerto Rico as well in 1897). However, Cuban insurrectionists waged the Ten Years' War of liberation from Spain between 1868 and 1878, which ended in a truce (followed by a smaller revolt in 1879–80), only to reengage in the third and final war of independence in 1895–98.

The United States invaded Cuba on 22 June 1898, four months after the USS *Maine* mysteriously exploded in Havana harbor, thus beginning what Secretary of State John Hay (qtd. in Thayer 33) called a "splendid little war," which lasted only fifteen weeks (the so-called Spanish-American War). The United States established a provisional military government in Cuba between 1898 and 1902, when the country became formally independent. However, the Platt Amendment to the Cuban Constitution allowed the United States to intervene in Cuban affairs to protect U.S. interests. U.S.

troops occupied the archipelago again between 1906 and 1909 to prevent a civil war and returned in 1912 to quell an Afro-Cuban rebellion. A third U.S. military intervention took place from 1917–22 to safeguard U.S. sugar investments. In effect, the nascent Cuban republic became a protectorate of the United States, until the Platt Amendment was repealed in 1934.

After a popular uprising against the dictator Gerardo Machado, a reformist government was briefly in power between 1933 and 1934. Sergeant-turned-coronel Fulgencio Batista ruled Cuba indirectly from 1935, until he was elected president in 1940. A short democratic interlude followed between 1940 and 1952, during which a new constitution was approved. Batista staged a coup d'état on 10 March 1952, which returned Cuba to military rule, suspending elections and canceling the constitution. On 26 July 1953, Fidel Castro launched a guerrilla movement that took power on 1 January 1959. The Cuban Revolution, which Castro declared socialist in May 1961, has provoked the exodus of about 1.7 million Cubans to the United States and Puerto Rico, and hundreds of thousands more to other countries, over the past six decades. By 2019, nearly 2.4 million persons of Cuban origin lived in the United States, compared to less than 11.2 million in the archipelago (U.S. Census Bureau; Oficina Nacional de Estadística e Información). Today, Cuba is the only Communist country in the Western Hemisphere and one of four in the world (together with China, Laos, and Vietnam).

On the other hand, Puerto Rico's prolonged colonial history with Spain and current colonial ties to the United States are often judged an anomaly in a postcolonial world. The archipelago was a neglected military outpost of the Spanish empire for most of the period between 1493 and 1898. As one of Spain's first and last overseas possessions (along with Cuba), Puerto Rico experienced one of the longest periods of Spanish hegemony in the Americas. On 25 July 1898, however, U.S. troops invaded the archipelago during the Spanish-Cuban-American War, and the United States has since dominated Puerto Rico militarily, politically, and economically.

The U.S. Supreme Court paradoxically defined Puerto Rico in 1901 as "foreign to the United States in a domestic sense" because it was neither a state of the American union nor an independent republic (see Burnett and Marshall). The Court also ruled that the archipelago was "a territory . . . belonging to . . . but not a part of" the United States (*Downes v. Bidwell*), meaning that Congress would determine which parts of the U.S. Constitution applied to Puerto Rico. In another 1904 case, the Court declared that Puerto Ricans were not "aliens" for immigration purposes and could not be denied entry into the U.S. mainland (*Gonzales v. Williams*).

Congress granted U.S. citizenship to all residents of Puerto Rico in 1917 but did not extend to them all constitutional rights and obligations, such as having Congressional representation or paying federal income taxes. To this day, moving from Puerto Rico to one of the fifty states of the American union means acquiring the full benefits of U.S. citizenship for former island residents.

Puerto Rico became a U.S. Commonwealth (or Estado Libre Asociado) in 1952, with limited autonomy in local matters, such as elections, taxation, economic development, education, health, housing, culture, and language. Still, the federal government remained in control of most State affairs, including citizenship, migration, customs, defense, currency, transportation, communications, foreign trade, and diplomacy. For practical purposes, Puerto Rico continues to be a colony because it lacks sovereignty and effective representation in the federal government. (Like the District of Columbia and other territories such as Guam and the U.S. Virgin Islands, Puerto Rico elects a delegate—called, in Puerto Rico's case, a resident commissioner—to the U.S. House of Representatives, but such delegates can vote only in committee.) The archipelago's political status—with its lack of legal barriers to migrate to the United States—has facilitated the stateside relocation of more than 2.3 million Puerto Ricans since 1898. By 2019, more than 5.8 million people of Puerto Rican origin lived in one of the fifty states of the American union, compared to less than 3.2 million in the archipelago (U.S. Census Bureau). Puerto Rico is a prime example of a "transnational nation" or a "nation on the move," whose population is split between the home territory and its metropole (Duany, *The Puerto Rican Nation on the Move*). In addition, the archipelago is one of the few remaining colonies in the world, along with several islands in the Caribbean and the Pacific.

Focusing on key aspects of history, literature, and culture in this collection of essays as they pertain to Cuba and Puerto Rico allows for a comparative analysis that highlights the concept of intersectionality—the interconnectedness among social categories such as nation, race, class, and gender—in nuanced ways. These topics of critical investigation are by no means exclusive, nor do they rule out other approaches to both countries, but they provide an appropriate starting point from which to draw the similarities and differences that contribute to academic discussions in archipelagic studies.[3]

Two Wings, One Bird

Lola Rodríguez de Tió's famous 1893 poem "A Cuba" ("To Cuba"), published in her collection *Mi libro de Cuba* (*My Book of Cuba*), juxtaposes a symbiotic relation between Cuba and Puerto Rico during crucial moments of historical and political unrest in both archipelagos. When the book was published, the Puerto Rican independence advocate was exiled with her family in Cuba, never to return to live in Puerto Rico. In her poem, Rodríguez de Tió wrote: "Cuba y Puerto Rico son / de un pájaro las dos alas / reciben flores o balas / sobre el mismo corazón" ("Cuba and Puerto Rico are / two wings of a bird / they receive flowers or bullets / in the same heart"). She also expressed her longing that the two countries would become a "patria sola" ("single motherland"). Generations of Cubans and Puerto Ricans have recited these verses as an expression of the solidarity between the two peoples, their shared cultural traditions, and the unfinished political project of self-determination.

Rodríguez de Tió's view of the interconnectedness between Cuba and Puerto Rico through common political, cultural, literary, and linguistic traits, and her staunch advocacy for sovereignty for both countries, prompted a patriotic poetic rendition that has been praised as an emblem of an era of revolutionary zeal and political activism. Yet historical events that contrasted with Rodríguez de Tió's views played a defining role in the development of these two archipelagos and the divergent realities they face today. This development is, in many ways, affected by both archipelagos' relations to the United States for over a century and the geopolitical and migratory processes that have ensued therein.

Considerable differences in how each archipelago evolved after their cession by Spain to the United States through the 1898 Treaty of Paris, as well as similarities conceived from various demarcations and disciplines, may also shed light on the ways in which Puerto Rico and Cuba remain the subject of continuous scrutiny and critical study. It is precisely these relations that prompts the publication of this collection of essays addressing how history, literature, and culture have informed the multiple interpretations of the archipelagos' significance in their larger hemispheric positioning. In this sense, the essays contained in this volume propose an in-depth and long-term analysis of Puerto Rico and Cuba and their diasporic communities in the United States.

In conducting a systematic comparison between Cuba and Puerto Rico, the significant differences between the two countries should not be minimized. Even during the Spanish colonial period, each archipelago played a distinct role within the Spanish empire. After the Spanish conquest and colonization of Mexico and Peru in the early sixteenth century, Cuba—and especially Havana—acquired a pivotal position within Spain's Atlantic commercial system. Meanwhile, Puerto Rico languished as a marginal port of call, outside the main sea routes between the Americas and the Iberian peninsula. Furthermore, Cuba developed the largest sugar plantation system in the world during the nineteenth century (after the demise of the plantation economy in neighboring Saint-Domingue, later Haiti). Meanwhile, Puerto Rico remained largely a frontier settler colony subsisting primarily on a combination of mixed farming, cattle raising, and smuggling at least until 1815. To satisfy the growing demand for labor, Cuba imported nearly one million African slaves during the Spanish colonial period, but Puerto Rico only received about 43,000, according to recent estimates (*SlaveVoyages*). The free colored population grew rapidly in both countries throughout the nineteenth century, especially in Puerto Rico, where it surpassed 41 percent of the entire population by 1860 (qtd. in Díaz Soler 123n55; see also Kinsbruner 29). Finally, Cuba embraced a militant revolutionary tradition, particularly during the insurrection against Spain in the last third of the nineteenth century, while the dominant political movement in Puerto Rico sought to assert autonomy from Spain by peaceful means, which it achieved in 1897. Aside from the 1868 Grito de Lares uprising, which was quickly squelched by Spain, armed struggle did not characterize the movement for self-government on the island.[4]

Enter the twentieth century. Although the United States occupied both Cuba and Puerto Rico during the War of 1898, Cuba became an independent nation (at least in name) in 1902 while Puerto Rico became an "unincorporated territory" (a colony except in name) of the United States. Although the Platt Amendment to the Cuban Constitution thwarted the sovereignty of the young Cuban republic, it acquired its own constitution, elected president, legislature, armed forces, diplomatic corps, and national symbols such as a flag and anthem. The political and economic hegemony of the United States over Puerto Rico was much more direct and extensive than over Cuba. Moreover, a nationalist ideology was more entrenched in Cuba than in Puerto Rico throughout the first half of the twentieth century. The political trajectories of the two countries bifurcated even more widely after 1959, with the triumph of the revolution led by Castro, particularly with his adoption of socialism in 1961, and Puerto Rico's growing integration within the U.S. political and economic orbit under Governor Luis

Muñoz Marín (1948–64), especially after the establishment of the Estado Libre Asociado in 1952. As Cuba distanced itself from the United States, Puerto Rico grew closer.

During the Cold War, Cuba and Puerto Rico represented two opposite models of political and economic development. Socialist Cuba became a single-party system increasingly reliant on a Soviet-type central planning of the economy, after the nationalization of most of the means of production and the mass media in the 1960s. Puerto Rico adopted a predominantly two-party system (representing autonomist and annexationist forces that alternated in power since 1968) and experienced considerable economic growth under the government-led industrialization strategy between the late 1940s and early 1970s. Critics decried each model's dependence on massive subsidies by one of the two superpowers, the Soviet Union and the United States. Whereas the revolutionary government curtailed civil liberties and human rights in Cuba, the Commonwealth government generally guaranteed them in Puerto Rico—despite constant harassment and persecution of the independence movement by both federal and local authorities. Cuba thus became an anti-capitalist paradigm of national sovereignty and social equality, while Puerto Rico was upheld as a "showcase of democracy" and an example of what the free market could do for small developing countries.

The Cuban Revolution of 1959 affected Puerto Rico in many ways.[5] The breakup of diplomatic relations between the United States and Cuba in 1961, and the U.S. trade embargo of Cuba established in 1962, created economic opportunities for Puerto Rico, such as an expanded market for U.S. tourism and the rum industry. Furthermore, Puerto Rico was a key site of U.S. military operations during the Cold War, especially in the offshore islands of Vieques and Culebra, as well as counterintelligence activities. Thus, Puerto Rico became a bastion of anti-Communism in the Caribbean and Latin America. For decades, the archipelago functioned as a major U.S. military enclave, largely designed to contain the Cuban "threat" to security and stability in the Western Hemisphere.

To this day, the Cuban revolutionary government has unconditionally supported Puerto Rico's independence advocates—often citing Rodríguez de Tió's mantra of interisland solidarity—particularly at the United Nations and the Movement of Non-Aligned Countries. Since the early 1960s, Cuban authorities established close ties with the Pro-Independence Movement (MPI or Movimiento Pro-Independencia) created in 1959 and later transformed into the Puerto Rican Socialist Party (PSP, 1971–93), and more recently the Hostosian National Independence Movement (2004 to the present). In turn, the Marxist-Leninist ideology espoused by the Cuban government increasingly radicalized pro-independence activists in Puerto Rico. Similarly, the Cuban Revolution inspired Puerto Rican militants in the United States, such as the Young Lords and the Pro-Independence Movement, during the 1960s and 1970s.

The Cuban Revolution also triggered the resettlement of more than thirty-six thousand exiles to Puerto Rico between 1959 and 2019. The exiles quickly established themselves as a "middleman minority" in San Juan, specializing in key sectors of the Puerto Rican economy such as retail trade, professional services, the mass media, and construction. Linguistic, cultural, and even religious similarities eased the socioeconomic adaptation of Cubans in Puerto Rico. By 1970, a swath of Cuba's prerevolutionary elite had reconstituted itself in San Juan (see Cobas and Duany). Cuban refugees tended to reinforce the conservative ideology of Puerto Rico's middle and upper classes. Some right-wing clandestine exile groups, such as Alpha 66 and Omega 7, endorsed the use of violence against the Cuban government and the pro-independence movement in Puerto Rico, particularly between the 1960s and 1980s (see Quiroga, Atiles-Osoria, Arboleya Cervera et al.). More broadly, the presence of an influential and prosperous Cuban exile community in San Juan nurtured the fear of "another Cuba," contributed to the popular rejection of independence as a viable option for Puerto Rico, and often supported its full annexation to the United States (see Maldonado Denis).

A Brief Literary Counterpoint

The literary histories of Cuba and Puerto Rico have been tightly interwoven, especially since the nineteenth century. Several anthologies have documented the literary parallels between Cuba and Puerto Rico (as well as the Dominican Republic) since the Spanish colonial period, including Romanticism, the depiction of local manners and customs (*costumbrismo*), indigenism, Naturalism, Modernism, Creolism (*criollismo*), and Afro-Antillealism (*negrismo*), as well as more recent trends such as colloquial poetry and coming of age narratives (see, for example, Colón Zayas, Bobes et al., and Rodríguez; see also Paravisini-Gebert). The next section focuses on the literary production of Cubans and Puerto Ricans in the United States.

Studies of Puerto Rican and Cuban letters in the United States tend to follow a distinct trajectory alongside migration patterns of nationals from both archipelagos, dating back to the mid-nineteenth and early twentieth centuries.[6] Among the earliest Antillean migrants to seek refuge in the United States, primarily in New York City, were leading intellectual figures such as the Cuban José Martí (preceded by Félix Varela and José María Heredia) and the Puerto Ricans Segundo Ruiz Belvis, Eugenio María de Hostos, Ramón Emeterio Betances, Sotero Figueroa, Arturo Alfonso Schomburg, and Lola Rodríguez de Tió herself, among others. The so-called Pilgrims of Freedom[7] were for the most part Puerto Rican and Cuban revolutionary exiles with separatist ideals, in staunch defense of independence for both countries. They convened in New York City at the turn of the twentieth century and continued to advocate for independence from Spain as they helped form alliances with like-minded comrades who found their way to the United States. These expatriates mostly wrote in Spanish and founded several organizations, newspapers, and literary magazines that embodied their revolutionary ideals. At the same time, they maintained close ties to their countries of origin in their journalistic and literary writing, and in their correspondence with family members and other political and intellectual leaders of the time.

The "Pilgrims of Freedom" became the precursors of community chroniclers, such as Bernardo Vega and Jesús Colón, who contributed to established newspapers and literary magazines in New York City, while they also founded some of their own. Vega and Colón migrated from Puerto Rico to the United States at the beginning of the twentieth century, in 1916 and 1917, respectively. They formed part of several organizations with Puerto Rican, Cuban, and other Latin American members, and became highly active in trade unions and proletarian causes. Both writers published many articles and essays in popular newspapers and magazines of the time, including *Gráfico*, *Alma Boricua*, *Pueblos Hispanos*, *Liberación*, and the *Puerto Rico Herald*. Colón also published opinion pieces in English in venues such as the *Daily World*, *Mainstream*, and the *Daily Worker*.

Vega's writing and Colón's collected works would appear as single publications years later. Colón gathered a sample of his writing in his 1961 collection *A Puerto Rican in New York and Other Sketches*. On the other hand, the first edition of the *Memorias de Bernardo Vega: Contribución a la historia de la comunidad puertorriqueña en Nueva York* appeared posthumously in 1977, twelve years after Vega's death, edited by César Andreu Iglesias and later brought to publication by José Luis González. In 1984, Juan Flores published an English translation of the work as *Memoirs of Bernardo Vega: A Contribution to the History of the Puerto Rican Community in New York*.

Another posthumous collection of essays by Colón, edited by Edna Acosta-Belén and Virginia Sánchez Korrol, appeared in 1993 as *The Way It Was and Other Writings*. Vega and Colón's works, as well as those by the "Pilgrims of Freedom," have been widely published and anthologized, and serve as the foundational narratives that influenced a wide array of literary representations that followed.

Among the early Puerto Rican writers to publish their works in the diaspora were Pedro Juan Labarthe (*The Son of Two Nations: The Private Life of a Columbia Student*, 1931) and later Piri Thomas (*Down These Mean Streets*, 1967), who relied on biography and memoir to focus on growing up Puerto Rican in the first half of the twentieth century in New York City. Other writers such as Edwin Torres (*Carlito's Way*, 1975), Edward Rivera (*Family Installments*, 1982), Rodney Morales (*The Speed of Darkness*, 1988), and Abraham Rodriguez (*The Boy Without a Flag*, 1992) followed. Nicholasa Mohr provided her perspective as a young Latina in the United States in her semi-autobiographical novel *Nilda* (1973), among many other publications, including children's books. Judith Ortiz Cofer's numerous publications, among them *Silent Dancing: A Partial Remembrance of a Puerto Rican Childhood* (1990), and Esmeralda Santiago's *When I Was Puerto Rican* (1992) also highlight childhood experiences from the island to the diaspora. Other writers, such as Luisita López Torregrosa in *The Noise of Infinite Longing: A Memoir of a Family—and an Island* (2004), include depictions of a young adult in the diaspora and her subsequent travels through many countries on her journalistic appointments for the *New York Times* and *National Geographic*. Giannina Braschi takes writing to another level in her surrealistic and highly innovative fiction that blends literary genres, languages, and historical worldviews in works like *Yo-Yo Boing!* (1998) and *United States of Banana* (2011). These writers often went beyond the merely experiential to consider other thematic concerns, both in fiction and nonfiction, which included race relations, gendered conditioning, cultural identity, language merging, and historical-political relations between the United States and Puerto Rico. Their works help to portray a larger, multifaceted, and heterogeneous picture of the Puerto Rican diaspora, from those born and raised on the island who later migrated to the United States to those born and raised in the United States with Puerto Rican parents.

A landmark in the literary history of the Puerto Rican diaspora was the foundation of the Nuyorican Poets Café in 1973, led by Miguel Algarín and Miguel Piñero. Nuyorican poetry—a portmanteau derived from the blending of "New York" and "Puerto Rican"—not only explored new nomenclatures of identity formation and questioned the status quo but also brought together a group of young poets highly influenced by the Civil Rights and gay liberation movements in the United States and the independence movement in Puerto Rico. In 1975, Algarín and Piñero published *Nuyorican Poetry*, the first anthology that showcased some of the best performances and set the stage for many other collective and independent publications by these and other poets in the years to come. Poets such as Jorge Brandon, Pedro Pietri, Jesús Papoleto Meléndez, Tato Laviera, Víctor Hernández Cruz, and Sandra María Esteves were among the first to perform at the Nuyorican Poets Café. Other poets such as Willie Perdomo, and later Caridad "La Bruja" de la Luz and María Teresa "Mariposa" Fernández, joined the poetry slams organized by the café. In very innovative and provocative ways, these and other writers like them[8] revolutionized poetic literary form and deliverance by bringing to the forefront a kind of performance poetry that sought to combine different artistic elements (including music) in a more inclusive open mic scenario that welcomed, promoted, and awarded interethnic cultural exchanges.

In recent years, a host of new Puerto Rican memoirists, novelists, poets, and dramatists in the diaspora have included Raquel Salas Rivera, Aya de León, Denise Frohman, Migdalia Cruz, Quiara Alegría Hudes, Tony Medina, Justin Torres, José Rivera, Willie Perdomo, Urayoán Noel, and Lin-Manuel Miranda, and graphic novelists Gabby Rivera and Edgardo Miranda-Rodríguez, among many others. These writers continue to experiment with literary forms and characterization in ways that demonstrate how diasporic Puerto Rican writing has evolved. The continued use of social media and the Internet, which highly influence the writing of contemporary authors in ways that were not part of the literary scene in the early to mid-twentieth century until their prevalence in the 1990s onward, reveals how other forms of expression and representation helped carve a new poetics of literary creativity in a continuum that spans over a century of literary production. And this continuum evolves and branches out to other communities and countries with the emergence of new voices in diaspora, on the archipelago of Puerto Rico, and around the world, both in physical presentations by the artists and through cyberspace.

Similarly, critics have often studied Cuban American literary history in direct relation to processes of immigration (and exile), mostly after 1959. Isabel Alvarez Borland traces the development of this literary legacy through four distinct periods of immigration in her seminal 1998 work *Cuban-American Literature of Exile*. Alvarez Borland distinguishes two main groups of writers that emerged from the Cuban exodus in the United States, describing the first-generation writers as "the Golden Exiles":[9] those who left Cuba as adults, fully educated and formed individuals, who may have already had literary careers of their own. Alvarez Borland divides the second-generation writers into two subcategories: the "one-and-a half" generation (7), born in Cuba and experiencing immigration to the United States in their adolescence, and "Cuban-American ethnic writers" (8), those who left Cuba as infants or who were born in the United States to first-generation Cuban exiles.

Alvarez Borland begins her discussion with "the Golden Exiles" who left Cuba immediately after the Cuban Revolution and Castro's takeover (1959–62), though she carefully acknowledges (and other studies show) that Cuban immigration began much earlier. Most of these writers considered their exile as temporary and continued to write in Spanish, recording their displacement with indignation and anger toward Castro and the traumatic events that caused what they considered a forced dispersal from their homeland. In this category, Alvarez Borland places exiled writers such as Guillermo Cabrera Infante, Severo Sarduy, Hilda Perera, Heberto Padilla, Antonio Benítez Rojo, and Reinaldo Arenas, among others.[10] Their works reveal profound feelings of loss, betrayal, and nostalgia for former lives, with overtly political content and bitter anti-Castro sentiment.

The second and third waves of the Cuban exodus to the United States, the "Freedom Flights" of 1965–1973 and the 1980 Mariel boatlift respectively, not only changed the demographics of those fleeing the archipelago but also transformed the thematic content and language use of the literature produced during these periods and set the foundation for the publication of literary works by Cuban Americans in the years that followed.[11] The one-and-a-halfers, a 1960s term coined by sociologist Rubén Rumbaut and adopted by writers such as Gustavo Pérez Firmat, refer to immigrants who experienced Cuban childhood and adolescence and, upon migration, young adulthood and adulthood in the United States. These authors include Pérez Firmat himself, Roberto G. Fernández, José Kozer, Pablo Medina, and Lourdes Gil. According to Alvarez Borland, they managed their experiential transitions from Cuba to the United States alongside complex acculturation processes and many opted to write about their experiences in bilingual or predominantly English-language texts, though some of their works may have still retained Spanish as their primary literary language.

Alvarez Borland also traces the works of those she refers to as "Cuban-American ethnic writers," the authors whose exile occurred during early childhood, with little to no recollection of their lives in Cuba, and those who were born in the United States. These writers moved farther away from the thematic concerns of first-generation exiles in their construction of a bicultural identity without the plight of antirevolutionary or anti-Castro sentiment as driving forces, though they may refer to their Cuban heritage and share a common diasporic background. English became the primary language of their literary works with predominantly American reading audiences in mind. In this category, Alvarez Borland places writers such as Oscar Hijuelos and Cristina García, to which other critics would later add Richard Blanco, Ana Menéndez, and Vanessa Garcia.[12]

A cursory look at the publishing industry and book market today, especially with the incursion of e-books and digital readers, reveals that Puerto Rican and Cuban American authors not only form part of a larger Latinx literary heritage that spans over a century but that their works have also made their way into the larger corpus of American letters studied in major academic curricula in and out of the United States, particularly through translation, and especially due to increased author recognition and prestigious awards. Their multimodal texts stretch the boundaries of nationalist discourses, genres, and disciplines in ways that continue to invigorate contemporary literature. Their works offer opportunities for intercultural and transdisciplinary studies that critically examine intersectionality, multidimensional literary modalities, and innovative linguistic shifting in a rich array of literary output that enhances the reading experience in American literature.

Cuba and Puerto Rico: Historical Perspectives

By concentrating on historical antecedents and comparative analyses of key figures and events, the idiosyncrasies of both countries come to the forefront and provide contrastive discourses with which to examine the islands' socioeconomic and political development. Part I of this collection includes essays on various historical aspects of both archipelagos, especially their political and economic transformations after World War II.

In the opening chapter, "Passive Puerto Rico and Revolutionary Cuba? Myths, Realities, and the Optics of History," Lillian Guerra debunks the conventional stereotypes of the two archipelagos in the U.S. imperial imagination: those of "Cubans' inclination to chaos and revolution as well as Puerto Ricans' alleged apathy and political passivity." Guerra traces how these twin myths were popularized during the first half of the twentieth century to justify the territorial, military, political, and economic expansion of the United States. Yet the author shows that Cubans and Puerto Ricans adopted their own strategies of resistance to U.S. hegemony and negotiated significant autonomous spaces, albeit with distinct inflections, such as the Commonwealth formula in Puerto Rico or the Cuban Revolution. Despite their divergent political paths since the second half of the twentieth century, both "Puerto Ricans and Cubans have needed to break the monopoly on ideas, debates, and terms for understanding reality that a given political elite holds and enforces to keep its monopoly on power." Today, the two archipelagos face similar dilemmas, including extreme reliance on the public sector (more extensive in Cuba than in Puerto Rico) and the need to explore alternative modes of self-sustained economic growth.

Silvia Álvarez Curbelo focuses on the ideological repercussions of the Cold War in "Nuclearized Wings: The Binary Roads of Cuba and Puerto Rico at the Takeoff of the Cuban Revolution (1959–63)." Álvarez Curbelo dwells on the complex figure of Puerto Rico's Governor Luis Muñoz Marín, who at first enthusiastically embraced the lofty goals of the Cuban Revolution but became increasingly disillusioned with its radicalization in the early 1960s. In turn, Fidel Castro unleashed his fury on Muñoz Marín, Costa Rican President José Figueres, Venezuelan President Rómulo Betancourt, and other former allies. Analyzing Muñoz Marín's main speeches during this period, especially his 1959 Godkin Lectures at Harvard University, Álvarez Curbelo unveils his growing concern with a nuclear holocaust, his antipathy toward radical political movements, and his efforts to promote Puerto Rico as a "democratic left" alternative to the Cuban Revolution. While rejecting Cuban communism and Puerto Rican nationalism, Muñoz Marín argued that Puerto Rico could serve as a prototype of prosperity and social justice for Latin America and the Caribbean. He thus became one of the leading architects of one of the two main narratives of the Cold War in the region: what he dubbed "democratic development as an antidote to the conflicts of the bipolar world."

In "The Repeating Island? Cuban and Puerto Rican Counterpoints between the Cold War and the Reencounter," Francisco Scarano underlines "the convergences and similarities between these two nations, even in very recent times," despite their "remarkably disparate [political] trajectories" since the nineteenth century. Scarano points out several "unusual similarities" between contemporary Cuba and Puerto Rico, such as the short-lived experimentation with import-substitution industrialization in both countries, or their dependence on metropolitan largesse (from the Soviet Union, in Cuba's case, or the United States, in Puerto Rico's case). The ultimate failure of each country's development model, while embedded in different contexts and for distinct reasons, had a similar outcome: the decline in the living standards of most of the population in the last few decades. Scarano ends his chapter with a celebration of the cultural convergence between the two archipelagos (which he calls a "reencounter") in the post–Cold War period, especially popular musical exchanges, which reaffirm the notion of the "two wings of a bird."

Jorge L. Giovannetti-Torres discusses two analogous ethnographic projects in his chapter on "Local Eyes into Caribbean Rural Life: Anthropological Informants in Cuba and Puerto Rico in the Post–World War II Era." He examines Sidney W. Mintz's life history of the sugarcane worker Anastacio (Taso) Zayas Alvarado, and Carl Withers's unpublished manuscript on the Cuban town of Mayajigua, based on his key informant Juan Manuel Picabia y Niebla, also known as Manolo. Canvassing unpublished letters, interviews, and reports by both informants, Giovannetti-Torres identifies several recurring themes in rural Cuban and Puerto Rican societies during the 1940s and 1950s, including similar sexual norms, gender relations, health conditions, folk healing remedies, and other cultural practices. By playing close attention to Taso's and Manolo's narratives, Giovannetti-Torres privileges "voices from below to illustrate a parallel grassroots history of Cuba and Puerto Rico in the post–World War II era. Two informants pictured societies that were about to undergo dramatic changes." The rise and eventual fall of the Batista dictatorship (1952–58) in Cuba and the inauguration of the Estado Libre Asociado in Puerto Rico (1952) would sharpen the counterpoints between the two countries and accelerate the rate of social and political transformation in each archipelago.

Closing the section on historical perspectives, Jesse Hoffnung-Garskof turns to the Cuban and Puerto Rican diasporas and analyzes their multiracial origins in "The Harlem of the Club Las Dos Antillas: Race, Space, and Politics in Early Antillean New York." Las Dos Antillas was one of several revolutionary exile clubs in the United States, established in the late nineteenth century, which served as the cauldron of a political alliance between Cubans and Puerto Ricans, both Black and White. Furthermore, the Cuban Revolutionary Party, founded in New York in 1892, which added a Puerto Rican section in 1895, was devoted to promoting the independence of the two countries. Hoffnung-Garskof centers on the emergence of a racially inclusive ideology among Afro-descendant members of the Cuban nationalist movement, along with their Puerto Rican allies, who tended to settle in what would later become the Spanish Harlem neighborhood of New York City. This chapter draws upon the minutes and other archival materials on Las Dos Antillas to reconstruct "a multiracial coalition in the broader experience of 'migrating while Black' in a city with a very small Black population" in the late nineteenth century. This experience of coalition building among mostly working-class Caribbean migrants gives new meaning to the expression "two wings of a bird."

Puerto Rican and Cuban Literary Expression

Part II of this collection focuses on the critical analysis of literary works, whether autobiographical or fictionalized, of Puerto Rican and Cuban/Cuban American authors. Discussions of the literary history of Puerto Rican and Cuban writers in the United States and the study of their works are a fundamental part of the American literary tradition. This is not to say that the experience of island or stateside Puerto Ricans and Cubans is homogeneous; the heterogeneity of this experience is captured through the multifaceted cultural and linguistic tropes and techniques present in their writing. But there is much to say about the value of a body of work that, as critic Ilan Stavans has noted in the introduction to *The Norton Anthology of Latino Literature*, dates to the beginning of the cultural encounters in the Americas, where writings in the Spanish language existed well before any permanent English settlement. With continued acknowledgments, awards, and recognition, the works of stateside Puerto Rican and Cuban/Cuban American writers (and those living in both archipelagos) enhance critical perspectives on American literature in and out of academia.

The experience of migration and exile in the United States informs much of the discussion in this section of our book. Cuban novelist Leonardo Padura's comments on Cuban exile, in many ways, relate to Puerto Rican migration as well:

> La experiencia del exilio ha sido una calle de doble sentido. Todos hemos sido tocados por su drama en alguna parte—o en muchas—de nuestras sensibilidades e historias individuales: los que partieron, desde el desarraigo; los que permanecimos, desde una sensación de pérdida. . . . Y aunque pocos de ellos optarían en algún momento por

regresar a vivir a Cuba, el hecho de que muchos arrastren a la isla consigo los define y, curiosamente, los fortalece. . . . Aunque no emprendan el vuelo de regreso, saben de dónde son y por eso son como son: cubanos en un exilio en el que tantos han reconstruido sus vidas y en el que a tantos se les ha ido la vida. (44–45)

(The experience of exile has been a two-way street. We have all been touched by its drama in some part—or in many—of our sensitivities and individual histories: those who left, from their uprooting; those of us who stayed, from a sense of loss. . . . And although only a few of them would choose at some point to return to live in Cuba, the fact that many drag the island with them defines them and, curiously, strengthens them. . . . Even if they do not embark on the flight back home, they know where they are from and that is why they are who they are: Cubans in an exile where many have reconstructed their lives and where so many of their lives have withered away.)

In "Exploding the Limits of Bodies and Islands: The Literary Works of Yolanda Arroyo Pizarro and Legna Rodríguez Iglesias," Monica Simal examines two novels by a Puerto Rican and a Cuban American writer, to raise the possibility of addressing language as a new form of territoriality that unites contemporary Latin American and Latino literature. Simal identifies recurring themes in "narratives that reflect a migrant community within a new space that is imperial, global, and fragmented." The comparative analysis of Arroyo Pizarro's novel *Los documentados* (2005) and Rodríguez Iglesias' *Mi novia preferida fue un bulldog francés* (2017) allows Simal to demonstrate that "it is precisely within the territory of language that resistance to and escape from gendered, racialized, and imperialized dynamics are possible in the Caribbean."

In "Puerto Rico *en Areíto*: Translation, Ethnic and Cultural Studies, and Other Collaborations among Cuban and Puerto Rican Migrant Intellectuals," Laura Lomas underscores the long tradition of solidarity in the struggle for the islands' independence. Lomas focuses on the cultural and political significance of *Areíto*, the most widely circulated magazine of the progressive Cuban and Latin American diaspora during the mid-1970s and early 1980s. The magazine, founded by the New York–based Afro-Cuban exile Lourdes Casal and others, expressed a version of *Latinidad* (Latinness) that endorsed national self-determination and decolonization. This chapter reflects on the practice and representation of collaboration between Cubans and Puerto Ricans in *Areíto* to grasp how twentieth-century projects built upon and transformed nineteenth-century modes of solidarity within the struggle for Cuban and Puerto Rican independence.

In the following chapter, Maida Watson examines the construction of "Psychological and Physical Space in Puerto Rican and Cuban Twentieth-Century Theater." Building on Bertolt Brecht's theory of the epic theater, Antonin Artaud's Theatre of Cruelty, and the Theatre of the Absurd, Cuban and Puerto Rican playwrights during the second half of the twentieth century rejected the dominance of realistic drama and staged plays where psychological space played a key role. In the three works studied by Watson (René Marqués's *Los soles truncos*, José Triana's *La noche de los asesinos*, and Rolando Ferrer's *Lila, la mariposa*), the contrast between psychological and physical space serves not only to portray the characters' individual tragedies but also to criticize their ideological and political circumstances. The various theatrical techniques used to create the counterpoint between psychological and physical space in these plays thus fulfill both artistic and political purposes.

Yolanda Martínez-San Miguel's chapter, "'The Two Ephemeral Wings of the Angel of Love': Archipelagic Fantasies in the Narrative of Lourdes Casal and Manuel Ramos Otero," provides a revealing twist to the phrase "Cuba and Puerto Rico are / two wings of a bird." Martínez-San Miguel proposes a reinterpretation of Rodríguez de Tió's classic text through a "juxtaposed reading" of two short stories, "Página en blanco y staccato" (1987) by the Puerto Rican Ramos Otero and "Los fundadores: Alfonso" (1972) by Casal. These stories "project a queered imaginary of Cuban and Puerto Rican nationalities" by decentering the Hispanophile and Creolist definitions of national identity, highlighting the Black and mulatto elements of that identity, and creating Asian and queer characters emblematic of the Hispanic Caribbean. Both Casal and Ramos Otero sought to compensate for the dearth of Afro-Asian voices within the historical archives as well as the creative literature of their countries during the 1970s and 1980s. Martínez-San Miguel concludes her essay with a discussion of how archipelagic and diasporic themes present in these tales undermine traditional nationalist narratives about Cuba and Puerto Rico.

Mary Ann Gosser Esquilín explores yet another angle of the "two wings of a bird" trope in her essay, "*Hechos* and *desechos*: Environmental Degradation and Violence in Mayra Montero's *Tú, la oscuridad*." Montero is a well-known Cuban-born writer who has lived in Puerto Rico since 1972.

Gosser Esquilín reads Montero's work *Tú, la oscuridad* (1995) as the first "environmentalist novel" of the Caribbean, to quote Lizabeth Paravisini-Gebert, primarily concerned with the ecological deterioration of Haiti (and more broadly the island of Hispaniola) as a synecdoche for the body of the Antillean bird, of which Cuba and Puerto Rico are the two metaphoric wings. As Gosser Esquilín writes, "to the linguistic, political, and racial differences that separate these islands, especially after 1959, Montero adds the pressing ecological concerns to shine a distinctive and focused Caribbean light." This chapter shows how Montero's fictional work sounds the alarm about environmental threats in Haiti, such as the disappearance of native amphibians, and their implications for the rest of the region and the world. Haiti's experience resonates with both Cuba and Puerto Rico, particularly the endangerment of several endemic species of frogs such as the *coquí*, the beloved emblem of Puerto Ricans.

Manifestations of Cuban and Puerto Rican Culture

The cultural exchanges between Puerto Ricans and Cubans in the United States as well as in their home countries form part of a long legacy of fusion and creativity in artistic expression. In this globalized era of technological advances, interconnectivities, and "ethnoscapes" (a term coined by Arjun Appadurai),[13] a full appreciation of diasporic Puerto Ricans and Cubans involves an understanding of bicultural histories, transnational identities, and linguistic hybridity. It implies coming to terms with migrants and exiles, and the generations that followed in diaspora, who form part of communities in constant transition, where the concept of cultural affirmation at once reflects but also complicates lived experience and literary representation, whether on the islands or in the United States.

Part III concentrates on the musical, literary, and artistic manifestations of Puerto Rican and Cuban culture at home and in the diaspora. Hugo R. Viera-Vargas opens this section with his essay, "Listening to Our New Possessions: Music and Imperial Writings on Puerto Rico and Cuba, 1898–1920s." Viera-Vargas elaborates the notion of a "sonic colonial discourse" in both archipelagos, developed by U.S. travelers (including journalists and government officials) who often served as colonial agents, during the first three decades of the twentieth century. The author argues that through "a racialized form of hearing," many of these travelers constructed Cuba and Puerto Rico as musically different. Whereas most U.S. travelers perceived Cuba as closer to U.S. and European standards of musical practice and therefore more "civilized," they tended to regard Puerto Rico as more "primitive" in its musical traditions. According to Viera-Vargas, such perceptions helped to justify the distinct treatment of the newly acquired territories by the United States: the swift independence (though constrained by the Platt Amendment) of Cuba, together with the continued colonial presence in Puerto Rico to date.

Madeline Cámara's chapter, "Caribbean Dialogues by María Zambrano," unravels the strong links that the Spanish philosopher established with Cuban and Puerto Rican lettered women between 1940 and 1953, when she lived and worked intermittently in both archipelagos. These friendships among women generated an indispensable sustaining network in Zambrana's daily life as an exile after the Spanish Civil War, and at the same time constituted discursive communities during the decades in which modernity was reinforced. Cámara pays close attention to Zambrana's interaction with Lydia Cabrera and Josefina Tarafa in Cuba, as well as Elsa Fano, Nilita Vientós Gastón, and Inés María Mendoza in Puerto Rico. Cámara demonstrates the intellectual affinity between Zambrana and Mendoza, who would marry Muñoz Marín in 1946 and become Puerto Rico's First Lady in 1948. Like Mendoza and Muñoz Marín, Zambrano envisioned Puerto Rico as a potential site of hemispheric solidarity against European fascism during the 1940s.

In his chapter, Benjamin Lapidus assesses "The Musical Impact of the Mariel Boatlift on the Latin Music Scene of New York City and Interethnic Collaboration among Puerto Ricans and Cubans." Although Cubans and Puerto Ricans have interacted musically throughout history, the 1980 Mariel exodus reinforced their collaborations. As Lapidus notes, few academic works have focused on the musical contributions of the Mariel exodus. Existing scholarship on Cuban music in the United States has centered on the period before and immediately after 1959 and has overlooked leading musicians who brought the newest Cuban musical information to the United States in the late twentieth century. Lapidus discusses the musical dimensions of the Mariel boatlift by examining some of the dancers and musicians who arrived in New York City at that time. The activities of these and other musicians had long-term repercussions for music scenes in New York and the United States, not only as performers but often as teachers for subsequent generations of Cuban and non-Cuban musicians. These interactions produced hybrid forms of Cuban and Puerto Rican genres such as rumba, charanga, son, and salsa, and contributed significantly to the growth of Latin jazz. Mariel immigrants served as key points of connection for musicians and dancers who arrived in the early 1990s during the era of the *balseros* (rafters) and would fit into established networks of Cuban and Puerto Rican musicians.

Alan West-Durán's contribution, "Allora and Calzadilla: Noise and the Politics of Sonic Decoloniality," discusses the joint work of the U.S. visual artist Jennifer Allora and the Cuban-born Guillermo Calzadilla (A & C), both based in Puerto Rico. West-Durán considers several of A & C's videos and installation-performances, which document the peace movement that led to the 2003 withdrawal of the U.S. Navy from Vieques, the island-municipality off the eastern coast of the main island of Puerto Rico. A & C's video *Returning a Sound* (2004) celebrates the success of this grassroots movement, while raising questions about the island's future. According to West-Durán, "*Returning a Sound* can be read as 'noise,' as a political statement that interrupts normal political discourses, especially those that are conventionally patriotic, and certainly counters the noise of militarization." More broadly, A & C's Vieques videos "deal crucially with the issue of sovereignty, be it at the real, symbolic, political, or spatial level."

In "The Narratives and Life Projects of *Orientales* from Cuba in Puerto Rico and Florida: An Initial Comparative Study," Blanca Ortiz-Torres and Mario A. Rodríguez-Cancel analyze the experience of Cubans from the eastern provinces of Cuba, who have moved to Puerto Rico and the United States in the past two decades. The participants in Ortiz-Torres and Rodríguez-Cancel's interviews usually perceived themselves as different from Cubans from other regions, especially from *habaneros/as* (natives of Havana), and those living in the United States. They often expressed feeling like foreigners in their own country of origin, since their migratory process typically started by moving to Havana. The theme of discrimination has been central for most of the participants in their transit from Havana to Puerto Rico and Florida. Their narratives include nostalgia for their homeland, appreciation for the welcoming response from Puerto Ricans, and the possibility of personal and professional growth while living abroad. Even though some felt uprooted, their interactions with Puerto Ricans facilitated their adaptation and many now identify as Puerto Rican. Ortiz-Torres and Rodríguez-Cancel point to the need for further research with a larger sample, which would help to document the particularities and subjectivities of migrants from eastern Cuba to Puerto Rico and the United States.

In the last chapter of this collection, "Becoming Cuba-Rican: A Personal Testimony," Jorge Duany reflects upon his hyphenated cultural identity as part Cuban and part Puerto Rican. After leaving Havana as a child, Duany lived first in Panama City and then in San Juan. He pursued his university studies in the United States, then returned to Puerto Rico and lived most of his adult life there. In this chapter, Duany places himself within the context of the Cuban community in San Juan, where he was raised and which he explored for his doctoral dissertation. This autobiographical account allows him to better understand the privileged but ambivalent position of Cubans in Puerto Rico as a "middleman" or trading minority, which sometimes puts them at odds with members of Puerto Rican society. In 2012, Duany became the director of the Cuban Research Institute at Florida International University in Miami, where he has reencountered his Cuban roots in a city he calls "the crossroads of nomads." Duany's testimony reminds us that the journeys of the Cuban and Puerto Rican diasporas are complex and diverse, and take migrants on many roads back and forth and beyond their homelands.

Though studies on U.S. Latinx and Caribbean topics abound, they have usually focused on one of the migrant-sending countries and/or on individual disciplines rather than adopting comparative, regional, and transdisciplinary approaches. This collection of essays features contributions from multiple academic disciplines (including history, literary criticism, anthropology, musicology, and psychology) that traverse and intersect with one another in the larger discussion of their fields as they relate to both archipelagos. The collection showcases the breath and diversity of recent scholarship, conceptual approaches, and academic debates in Cuban, Cuban American, and Puerto Rican studies. The topics under discussion in the essays range from the natural history of Cuba and Puerto Rico to the regional impacts of the Cold War, to the cultural identities of Cubans and Puerto Ricans in the United States. Literary criticism on the works of Cuban American and Puerto Rican authors, as well as the analysis of political coalitions, interisland sororities, environmental issues, and the musical impacts of migration on the archipelagos, encourage a more nuanced and multifaceted study of the connections between the two countries and their diasporas. The collection, thus, brings together a comparative, extended discussion of varied issues in one volume hitherto absent in the extant scholarship. In many ways, revisiting the relevance of Lola Rodríguez de Tió's poem demonstrates how both Puerto Rico and Cuba remain vital concerns of archipelagic and diaspora studies and still require incisive critical and comparative approaches, even beyond the scope of this project. This collection is a major step in that direction.

Notes

1. For a discussion of the impact of contemporary climate change in Cuba and Puerto Rico, see Fain et al.

2. The following paragraphs are based on Duany's introduction to *Blurred Borders*, 4–7. Although both Cuba and Puerto Rico are conventionally referred to as "islands," they are actually archipelagos. Cuba consists of more than 4,000 islands and keys surrounding the main island, the largest of which is the Isle of Youth (formerly known as the Isle of Pines) south of Havana. Puerto Rico has over 140 islands and keys, aside from the main island, the largest of which are Vieques and Culebra, east of Ceiba and Fajardo, and Mona, an uninhabited island west of Mayagüez.

3. A recent work by Melissa Fuster examines the similarities and differences in the culinary traditions of Cuba, Puerto Rico, and the Dominican Republic.

4. For more comparative historical information on Cuba and Puerto Rico, see Duany, "Ethnicity in the Spanish Caribbean"; Bergad; and Álvarez Curbelo. Franklin Knight (184–6, 190–1) has conducted a classic analysis of Cuba and Puerto Rico during the nineteenth century in the context of the rise of slave societies. Joaquín Freire has highlighted the contribution of Puerto Ricans to Cuba's independence struggle from Spain. For a polemical essay arguing that Cuba was "sick" because of its radical revolutionary tradition, while Puerto Rico remained loyal to Spain, see Arana Soto. Noel Luna has a more sober conversation with Arcadio Díaz Quiñones regarding the literary and cultural practices of the two countries. Julia Sagebien and Ramón Coto-Ojeda have examined the possibilities of commercial relations between Cuba and Puerto Rico in a post-embargo era. More recently, Hans-Jürgen Burchardt and Johanna Leinius have compiled a series of comparative essays on the colonial legacies of Cuba, Puerto Rico, and the Philippines.

5. The following two paragraphs are based on Duany, *Puerto Rico*, 81–82.

6. For more information on the migratory processes of Puerto Ricans to the United States and the establishment of communities, especially in New York City as the primary site of settlement in the late nineteenth and early twentieth centuries, see Sánchez Korrol, Acosta-Belén et al., and Matos-Rodríguez and Hernández, among other sources.

7. Félix Ojeda Reyes coined the term to refer to six political figures from Puerto Rico who were forced into exile, some of whom participated in Cuba's insurrection against Spain: Ramón Emeterio Betances, Eugenio María de Hostos, Lola Rodríguez de Tió, Juan Rius Rivera, Sotero Figueroa, and Francisco Gonzalo ("Pachín") Marín. For more details on the "Pilgrims of Freedom" in New York City, see Acosta-Belén and Santiago 45–53.

8. An important poet writing outside the locus of the Nuyorican Poets Café is Martín Espada, whose award-winning publications date back to 1982, with distinguished recognitions including the Before Columbus Foundation American Book Award, a Pushcart Prize, an International Latino Book Award, and a Guggenheim Fellowship.

9. The Golden Exiles, also known as the Historical Exiles, refer to educated, professional, and entrepreneurial Cuban immigrants who fled Cuba to the United States after Castro's takeover and formed important Cuban immigrant enclaves and businesses in several cities, most notably Miami, though other Cubans had already arrived in the

United States beforehand (see Duany, "Cuban Migration"). Alvarez Borland (4–5) contends that Cuban exile literature dates to the nineteenth-century Cuban independence movements from Spain, with several writers (such as María Mercedes Santa Cruz y Montalvo, countess of Merlin, José María Heredia, Gertrudis Gómez de Avellaneda, and José Martí) already depicting the theme of exile in their works.

10. Though Arenas' exile came much later as part of the 1980 Mariel exodus, his writing elaborates an explicitly antagonistic view of the revolutionary process, with harsh anti-Castro sentiment throughout his works, which prompts Alvarez Borland (10) to place him within this first generation of Cuban exile writers. Padilla and Benítez Rojo also left the island in 1980, but not through the Mariel boatlift.

11. Though Alvarez Borland discusses a fourth period of Cuban immigration to the United States in her study, those arriving after 1994, the first three periods are foundational for Cuban American letters and serve as a reference point for literary discussions of publications that appeared in later years. Additional critics, such as Ofelia García, Silvia Burunat, Carolina Hospital, Eliana Rivero, and Iraida López, have written eloquently about and anthologized Cuban American literature.

12. For a more recent example of Alvarez Borland's work, see Alvarez Borland and Bosch. For a recent anthology of second-generation Cuban American writers, see López and Rivero.

13. In his seminal work *Modernity at Large*, Arjun Appadurai defines the concept of "ethnoscape" as the movement of people and global cultural flows that destabilize hegemonic notions of community formation and cultural identity (33–34).

Works Cited

Acosta-Belén, Edna, and Carlos E. Santiago. *Puerto Ricans in the United States: A Contemporary Portrait*. 2nd ed. Lynne Rienner Publishers, 2018.

Acosta-Belén, Edna et al. *"Adiós Borinquen Querida": The Puerto Rican Diaspora, Its History, and Contributions*. Center for Latino, Latin American, and Caribbean Studies, U at Albany, SUNY, 2000.

Algarín, Miguel, and Miguel Piñero, editors. *Nuyorican Poetry: An Anthology of Puerto Rican Words and Feelings*. Morrow, 1975.

Alvarez Borland, Isabel. *Cuban-American Literature of Exile: From Person to Persona*. UP of Virginia, 1998.

Alvarez Borland, Isabel, and Lynnette M. F. Bosch, editors. *Cuban-American Literature and Art: Negotiating Identities*. State U of New York P, 2009.

Álvarez Curbelo, Silvia. "Caribbean Siblings: Sisterly Affinities and Differences between Cuba and Puerto Rico in the Nineteenth Century." *The Routledge Hispanic Studies Companion to Nineteenth-Century Spain*, edited by Elisa Martí-López. Routledge, 2021, pp. 4–18.

Andreu Iglesias, César, editor. *Memorias de Bernardo Vega: Contribución a la historia de la comunidad puertorriqueña en Nueva York*. Ediciones Huracán, 1980.

Appadurai, Arjun. *Modernity at Large: Cultural Dimensions of Globalization*. U of Minnesota P, 1996.

Arana Soto, Salvador. *Cuba y Puerto Rico no son . . . o la enfermedad de Cuba*. L. D. Paret, 1963.
Arboleya Cervera, Jesús, with Raúl Alzaga Manresa and Ricardo Fraga González. *La contrarrevolución cubana en Puerto Rico y el caso de Carlos Muñiz Varela*. 2nd ed. Callejón, 2016.
Atiles-Osoria, José M. "Pro-State Violence in Puerto Rico: Cuban and Puerto Rican Right-Wing Terrorism from the 1960s to the 1990s." *Socialism and Democracy*, vol. 26, no. 1, 2012, pp. 127–42.
Bergad, Laird W. "¿Dos alas del mismo pájaro? Notas sobre la historia socioeconómica comparativa de Cuba y Puerto Rico." *Historia y Sociedad*, vol. 1, 1988, pp. 143–53.
Bobes, Marilyn et al., editors. *Los nuevos caníbales: Antología de la más reciente cuentística del Caribe hispano*. Vol. 1. Isla Negra, 2000.
Burchardt, Hans-Jürgen, and Johanna Leinius, editors. *(Post-)colonial Archipelagos: Comparing the Legacies of Spanish Colonialism in Cuba, Puerto Rico, and the Philippines*. U of Michigan P, 2022.
Burnett, Christina Duffy, and Burke Marshall, editors. *Foreign in a Domestic Sense: Puerto Rico, American Expansion, and the Constitution*. Duke UP, 2001.
Cobas, José A., and Jorge Duany. *Cubans in Puerto Rico: Ethnic Economy and Cultural Identity*. UP of Florida, 1997.
Colón, Jesús. *A Puerto Rican in New York and Other Sketches*. International Publishers, 1982.
———. *The Way It Was and Other Writings*. Edited by Edna Acosta-Belén and Virginia E. Sánchez Korrol. Arte Público P, 1993.
Colón Zayas, Eliseo, editor. *Literatura del Caribe: Antología. Siglos XIX y XX—Puerto Rico, Cuba, República Dominicana*. 3rd ed. Plaza Mayor, 2006.
Díaz Soler, Luis M. *Historia de la esclavitud negra en Puerto Rico*. 3rd ed. Editorial de la Universidad de Puerto Rico, 1970.
Downes v. Bidwell. U.S. Supreme Court. 182 U.S. 244, 1901.
Duany, Jorge. *Blurred Borders: Transnational Migration between the Hispanic Caribbean and the United States*. U of North Carolina P, 2011.
———. "Cuban Migration: A Postrevolutionary Exodus Ebbs and Flows." *Migration Information Source*, July 6, 2017, https://www.migrationpolicy.org/article/cuban-migration-postrevolution-exodus-ebbs-and-flows. Accessed 13 Sept. 2022.
———. "Ethnicity in the Spanish Caribbean: Notes on the Consolidation of Creole Identity in Cuba and Puerto Rico, 1762–1868." *Ethnic Groups*, vol. 6, 1985, pp. 99–123.
———. *The Puerto Rican Nation on the Move: Identities on the Island and in the United States*. U of North Carolina P, 2002.
———. *Puerto Rico: What Everyone Needs to Know*. Oxford UP, 2017.
Fain, Stephen J. et al. *Cuba, Puerto Rico, and Climate Change: Shared Challenges in Agriculture, Forestry, and Opportunities for Collaboration*. International Institute of Tropical Forestry, U.S. Department of Agriculture, 2020, https://data.fs.usda.gov/research/pubs/iitf/iitf_gtr_49.pdf. Accessed 10 Sept. 2021.
Freire, Joaquín. *Presencia de Puerto Rico en la historia de Cuba*. Instituto de Cultura Puertorriqueña, 1966.

Fuster, Melissa. *Caribeños at the Table: How Migration, Health, and Race Intersect in New York City*. U of North Carolina P, 2021.
García, Ofelia, and Silvia Burunat, editors. *Veinte años de literatura cubanoamericana: Antología, 1962–1982*. Bilingual P, 2008.
Gonzales v. Williams. U.S. Supreme Court. 192 U.S. 1, 1904.
Hospital, Carolina, editor. *Cuban American Writers: Los Atrevidos*. Linden Lane P, 1988.
Kinsbruner, Jay. *Not of Pure Blood: The Free People of Color and Racial Prejudice in Nineteenth-Century Puerto Rico*. Duke UP, 1996.
Knight, Franklin W. *Slave Society in Cuba during the Nineteenth Century*. U of Wisconsin P, 1970.
López, Iraida H. *Impossible Returns: Narratives of the Cuban Diaspora*. UP of Florida, 2015.
López, Iraida H., and Eliana S. Rivero, editors. *Let's Hear Their Voices: Cuban American Writers of the Second Generation*. SUNY P, 2019.
Luna, Noel. "Cuba y Puerto Rico no son: Conversación con Arcadio Díaz Quiñones." *Encuentro de la Cultura Cubana*, vol. 26–27, 2002–3, pp. 209–22.
Maldonado Denis, Manuel. "Efectos de la Revolución Cubana en la política puertorriqueña." *Revista de Ciencias Sociales*, vol. 8, no. 3, 1964, pp. 271–78.
Martínez-Fernández, Luis. *Key to the New World: A History of Early Colonial Cuba*. U of Florida P, 2018.
Matos-Rodríguez, Félix V., and Pedro Juan Hernández. *Pioneros: Puerto Ricans in New York City, 1892–1948*. Arcadia Publishing, 2010.
Oficina Nacional de Estadística e Información, República de Cuba. *Anuario estadístico de Cuba 2019: Población*. 2020, www.onei.gob.cu. Accessed 14 Jan. 2020.
Ojeda Reyes, Félix. *Peregrinos de la libertad: Documentos y fotos de exiliados puertorriqueños del siglo XIX localizados en los archivos y bibliotecas de Cuba*. Instituto de Estudios del Caribe/Editorial de la Universidad de Puerto Rico, 1992.
Padura, Leonardo. "Cubanos en el exilio: Desarraigo y resistencia." *The New York Times*, 20 Jan. 2019, https://www.nytimes.com/es/2019/01/20/espanol/opinion/revolucion-cubana-leonardo-padura.html. Accessed 14 Jan. 2020.
Paravisini-Gebert, Lizabeth. "Caribbean Literature in Spanish." *The Cambridge History of African and Caribbean Literature*, edited by F. Abiola Irele and Simon Gikandi. Cambridge UP, 2000, pp. 670–710.
Quiroga, José. "The Cuban Exile Wars: 1976–1981." *American Quarterly*, vol. 66, no. 3, 2014, pp. 819–33.
Rivero, Eliana S. *Discursos desde la diáspora*. Aduana Vieja, 2005.
Rodríguez, Néstor E., editor. *Isla escrita: Antología de la poesía de Cuba, Puerto Rico y República Dominicana*. Amargord, 2018.
Rodríguez de Tió, Lola. "A Cuba." *Mi libro de Cuba*. Imprenta La Moderna, 1893, pp. 3–6.
Sagebien, Julia, and Ramón Coto-Ojeda. *From Cold Warriors to Business Associates: Cuba-Puerto Rico Relations in the Last Half of the 20th Century*. Canadian Foundation for the Americas (FOCAL), 1999, https://www.focal.ca/pdf/cuba_Sagebien_Cuba%20Puerto%20Rico%20relations%20Cold%20Warriors%20Business%20Associates_February%202000.pdf. Accessed 15 Sept. 2021.

Sánchez Korrol, Virginia E. *From Colonia to Community: The History of Puerto Ricans in New York City*. U of California P, 1994.

SlaveVoyages. "Transatlantic Slave Trade—Estimates" and "Intra-American Slave Trade—Estimates." Undated, https://slavevoyages.org/assessment/estimates. Accessed 14 Sept. 2021.

Stavans, Ilan, editor. *The Norton Anthology of Latino Literature*. W. W. Norton & Co., 2010.

Thayer, William Roscoe. *The Life and Letters of John Hay*. Vol. 2. Houghton Mifflin, 1915.

U.S. Census Bureau. *Explore Census Data*. 2019, https://data.census.gov/cedsci/. Accessed 14 Jan. 2020.

Vega, Bernardo. *A Contribution to the History of the Puerto Rican Community in New York*. Edited by César Andreu Iglesias and translated by Juan Flores. Monthly Review P, 1984.

I

Cuba and Puerto Rico
Historical Perspectives

1

Passive Puerto Rico and Revolutionary Cuba?
Myths, Realities, and the Optics of History

LILLIAN GUERRA

Cuba and Puerto Rico are the societies of Latin America whose histories are most intimately connected to the political development of the United States as an imperial superpower in the twentieth century. When the United States invaded both these islands in 1898, they not only became pivotal to the growth of U.S. economic control in the region, but the events of 1898 forever transformed the political destinies and national identities of all three societies. For many in the United States, the acquisition of colonies abroad was not only unprecedented but a total reversal of what it meant to be an "American." Yet framing the debate over empire were longstanding and intensifying beliefs in racial hierarchy and in the inferiority of all non-European peoples that proved deeply appealing to Americans who liked to think of themselves as an exceptional country endowed with a divine mission. Fifty years earlier, John O'Sullivan, a newspaper editor whose sister had married Cuba's wealthiest slaveowner and sugar planter (Cristóbal Madan), called that divine mission "Manifest Destiny" (Chaffin 12-15; Stephanson 28-111). After 1898, imperial expansion did not discernably improve the economic conditions of the lower classes in the United States, but it did provide a kind of ideological glue through the racialized, gendered power that millions of European immigrants with little in common shared in celebrations of U.S. imperial "Whiteness" (LaFeber 159-87; Slotkin 164-83; Kaplan 219-35).

In a six-volume work called *Winning the West*, published in 1888, Teddy Roosevelt first shamelessly launched the historical argument that militarism, masculinity, and "the urge to conquer" formed the essence of U.S.

national character. Less than ten years later, when the Republican Party included imperial expansion in its 1896 political platform and in 1898, when Roosevelt himself led the charge to exclude "the victors from the victory" in Cuba's last War for Independence from Spain, as Louis A. Pérez has written, Roosevelt's argument became a self-fulfilled prophecy (Pérez, *The War of 1898* 81–107). Indeed, U.S. imperialism was not just a set of policies that derailed and distorted Cuba and Puerto Rico's futures but a hegemonic cultural movement that *made* Americans White and proud, uniting them against the foil of savage lands, tropical political pathologies, and semi-barbaric peoples whose seductive cultures had dangerously "degenerated" their races, possibly to the point of no return. Accordingly, two myths long explained away the strategies of resistance that Cubans and Puerto Ricans deployed in contesting the United States' respectively neocolonial and colonial methods of rule: Cubans' inclination to chaos and revolution as well as Puerto Ricans' alleged apathy and political passivity.

These contrarian national essences arose, imperial thinkers contended, from deficiencies of character and culture that made Cubans and Puerto Ricans either too hot-blooded, immature, scatterbrained, or simply too lazy, prone to political whimsy, and corruptible for successful self-rule. So pervasive were these tenets in defining U.S. images of Cuba and Puerto Rico that even the critics of U.S. policies abroad relied on them, reiterating and reinforcing many of the very same racist, culturally condescending, and arrogant values that justified those policies (Pérez, *Cuba in the American Imagination*; del Moral; Krenn; Michaels; Hopkins 383–36). As anyone who has examined the historical record of the United States' New Imperial Age can attest, from official speeches to political cartoons, it is impossible to avoid references to these twin myths of Cuba and Puerto Rico that the U.S. government, media, and popular culture produced over the first fifty or more years of the twentieth century. Yet these myths were not merely narcissistic, fictional stories whose constant repetition made them into truths for most Americans. These myths about Cuban unreliability and Puerto Rican incompetence justified the violations of the U.S. Constitution and its own national birth in anti-imperialist revolution; they made average Americans *believe* that the freedom and sovereignty of the United States depend on restricting the freedom and repressing the sovereignty of other aspiring nation-states.

The Indian Wars (1877–92) had clearly set the legal and political precedents for treating Puerto Ricans like a "conquered people": like Native Americans, Washington officials stripped them of all sovereignty and defined Puerto Ricans as a domestically dependent population who were neither foreigners nor equal citizens, owing allegiance to the U.S. government but having no automatic guarantees of legal protection from it in return. Endowed with only partial citizenship in 1917—one that bars islanders from voting in presidential elections and denies voting representatives in Congress—Puerto Rico's original "incorporation" premised on loyalty vested in presumptions of gratitude and benevolence still holds true today (Burnett and Marshall; Sparrow; Erman). Thus, Puerto Ricans, who had just won autonomy from Spain in February 1898 and held their first island-wide, multiparty elections for a provincial assembly based on universal male suffrage, saw their political emergence abruptly aborted and their history reversed (Clark; Guerra, *Popular Expression*). The economic dependence of Puerto Ricans on the politically directed nature of their island's colonial development as an "unincorporated territory" partly explains why Puerto Rico today remains twice as poor as Mississippi, the poorest state of the United States (Dietz, *Economic History of Puerto Rico*; *Puerto Rico*).

In Cuba, the U.S. military intervention, sequential military occupations of 1898–1902 and 1906–9, and century-long commitment to Plattist approaches, have forever altered what kind of nation would be possible in Cuba. In 1898, the United States deliberately reversed the achievements of three wars for independence and the ostensibly centuries-long fight of slaves and their descendants to empower and put into positions of leadership those who would otherwise have remained at the political margins. Preventing poor and illiterate foot soldiers, Black, mulatto, and even female officers of the Liberating Army of Cuba from radically altering the social order and economic organization of power—in the plantation as well as its attending ideologies of inequality—was precisely the point of U.S. intervention (Foner; Pérez, *The War of 1898*; Guerra, *The Myth of José Martí*). Shoring up what would have been the *losing* side of Cuba's independence—the Spanish, conservative elites, the interests of the "propertied classes" whose property had once included slaves—was Washington and Wall Street's primary goal.

However, to say that the imperial strategies and policies of the United States succeeded is to ignore the fundamental ways in which Cuba and Puerto Rico are not dissimilar but alike; it is also to deny how U.S. efforts to "Americanize" Cuba and Puerto Rico have ironically resulted in a counter-colonization of U.S. politics, culture, and territory. Today, more Puerto Ricans live in the mainland of the United States than on the island, constituting a population of more than 5.8 million versus less than 3.2 million on the island; Puerto Ricans are also the second largest Latino group after Mexicans. Cubans in the United States number less than 2.4 million, compared to 11.3 million in Cuba, yet what they lack in numbers they make up for in political and economic power as well as myriad other ways—for better or for worse, I would say (Duany; Pedraza). Still, the numbers are not the strongest evidence of the Cubanization and Puerto Ricanization of the United States.

Today, the identity and politics of many in the United States (particularly in the Trump White House) may harken back to the racial hatreds and "might-makes-right" principles that consistently defined U.S. nationalism and U.S. policies abroad in the wake of an imperial metamorphosis in 1898. Nonetheless, just as many Americans have anti-imperial values, egalitarian viewpoints, and everyday means of living and surviving, the relentless fictional mantra of a meritocratic "American Dream" resonates with and perhaps owes their origins to the Cuban and Puerto Rican example. I say "example" in the singular because Cuba and Puerto Rico have far more in common than differences today. Those commonalities derive from the many related lessons that Cubans and Puerto Ricans drew or were forced to draw from their engagements with the United States.

Like the case of Puerto Rico, the United States set up a triangular relationship in Cuba between U.S. investors and their political backers in Washington and competing political elites and the popular classes. Unlike Puerto Rico, however, the United States faced in Cuba a highly politicized, well-organized, and mobilized population that had fought three guerrilla wars for independence: these wars left an ideologically diversified spectrum of politically conscious and activist groups in their wake that was not divided by class but by cross-class, competing visions of nation that, thanks to the United States, increasingly clashed. The site of struggle was control over a State that would implement a particular vision of nation. This created a paradox: from the beginning, elites in Cuba and the popular classes would press for the United States to simply *get out* of the island to consolidate local control. Within a decade, however, Cuba's political elites would come to rely on the threat of a U.S. invasion to justify repression of their critics and opponents and maintain control of the State as well as a political status quo. This siege reality and mentality, born of the Platt Amendment to the Cuban Constitution of 1901, would have a long shelf life, becoming in the wake of the Cuban Revolution of 1959 and the U.S.-directed invasion at the Bay of Pigs, the linchpin of Fidel Castro's one-party rule. But neither the context of the Cold War nor Castro's obstinate commitment to retaining control at all costs form the origin of this long-ingrained strategy. Political elites learned to use U.S. interventionism as leverage against the demands for change from below in the first decade of the Republic (Pérez-Stable; Pérez, *Cuba*; Guerra, *The Myth of José Martí*).

To be more precise, it was in 1908–12 when veterans of the independence wars founded the Partido Independiente de Color (PIC, Independent Party of Color) that political elites turned to the threat of U.S. intervention and used it to unite against change. Representing a multiracial, cross-class coalition of peasants, middle-class progressives, and cigarmakers for equal rights, the PIC organized under Black leadership to demand that the State uproot the continuing disproportionate power of Spaniards and White elites in the economy, public sector jobs, and government. After the party was declared illegal by the Morúa Law of 1909, its newspaper raided and leaders jailed in 1910, the PIC rose in what was supposed to be a brief, symbolic protest that prohibited attacks on people but proposed attacks on property, particularly the property of Spaniards, to remind Cubans of what they had fought three decades to achieve. They chose the ten-year anniversary of the withdrawal of U.S. troops and Cuban independence from the United States, 20 May 1912, for the protest (Helg; de la Fuente 23–98; Guerra, *The Myth of José Martí* 193–242).

In reply, the Cuban government carried out a viciously racist campaign of repression and terror that left some 4,000 Blacks dead in the name of defending an "anti-racist" and "race-blind" nation. Thereafter, officially sanctioned antiblack violence made Black autonomous activism—that is, activism without White leadership—both treasonous and taboo. The fact that only sixteen members of the government's forces died (including eight Afro-Cubans murdered by their White comrades on suspicion of sympathizing with the rebels and others killed by friendly fire) in what became known as the *Guerra Racista* or the "Race War of 1912" reveals the depth of that taboo (Helg 225). As Aline Helg demonstrates, the PIC did not stage a "black uprising against whites but an armed protest to force the relegalization of their party. The violent reaction they prompted, however, was little short of a race war" (Helg 226). For President José Miguel Gómez, who ordered the army's indiscriminate machine-gunning of Blacks and allowed hundreds of murders by White vigilantes, many of them Spanish loyalists, the prospect of Black mobilization clearly represented a higher order threat to the monopoly on power that Cuba's liberal and conservative White political establishment wanted to retain. Such a reaction to their own citizens' demands for accountability and representation as well as Black veterans' clear, legitimate claim for inclusion reduce any justification of that reaction in the name of "sovereignty" to the dung heap of lies, not history. Perhaps predictably, Cuba's current regime, while condemning the severity of the 1912 government's response, concurs with the logic of this lie. Indeed, José Miguel Gómez's enormous mausoleum in Havana, originally built in the 1920s but restored amid the revival of Black efforts to mobilize culturally and politically under Raúl Castro, stands as only one highly visible example.

Arguably, aside from ensuring the long-term marginalization of Blacks and Blackness from the structures of power in Cuba, the political system and State might have paid the greatest, most enduring cost. For decades, popular-class Cubans saw the State as acting only in its own interests, as a State for itself, not for the people. Not until the 1940s and 1950s did the awesome power of Cuba's civil society reconstitute itself into the moral crusade against impunity and stagnation that brought down not only the neocolonial dictator Fulgencio Batista but U.S. Plattist policymaking permanently (Ehrlich; Guerra, *Heroes, Martyrs, and Political Messiahs*). In the Cuban Republic structured and backed by the United States, the neocolonial government's repression of citizens' demands for a democratic State, accountable to them alone, catalyzed revolution and radical politics. Today, revolution and radical politics have produced a nationally sovereign government that maintains itself in power largely by repressing citizens' demands for a democratic State, accountable to itself alone. As a foil and a specter, the United States is an indispensable foundation to the national narrative, policies, and most importantly, claims of legitimacy of the Cuban State—from 1898 to this day. The lesson here is not only an appreciation for the ironies of a history shaped by a foreign power's presence and, post-1959, absence. Rather, the lesson lies in what enables a political elite to gain and sustain its monopoly of control under conditions where engagement of the United States as a threat or an ally serves that cause.

For Puerto Rico, negotiation of rights and spaces for activism occurred throughout the first half of the twentieth century, in a context where neither U.S. colonial rulers nor their mostly conformist political counterparts tolerated nationalist mobilization. This was because the mainstreaming of its leaders or message of liberation—let alone their triumph—*would have displaced both* and rendered fear-mongering over the fate of "tiny" Puerto Rico's economy irrelevant. Few Puerto Ricans need to be reminded of the systematic silencing that Pedro Albizu Campos and his fellow Nationalist Party endured from the 1930s to the 1940s. However, what remains critically forgotten and foundational to the rise of Puerto Rico's two-party, locally managed colonial State from the 1950s to the present is the collaborative reliance on violence to smother any alternative (Denis). Like Cuba, political sovereignty would be framed within the rigid bounds of a historical taboo.

In 1947, both houses of the U.S. Congress passed the Law for the Election of the Governor of Puerto Rico for a four-year term of office, effective immediately; for the first time in 450 years of colonialism, Puerto Ricans would decide who their governor would be, with Luis Muñoz Marín winning 61 percent of the vote (Scarano 727). From 1947–50, Muñoz Marín campaigned aggressively for what he called the "definitive resolution of the status question in Puerto Rico" and the creation of a new industrialization model that would jump-start "development" and "modernization" in Puerto Rico. By 1950, President Harry Truman had signed the bill into Law 600 and called for a referendum to be held among the Puerto Rican people in favor of or against the holding of a Constitutional Convention to write a constitution for Puerto Rico as a "Free Associated State," thereby enshrining Puerto Rico's invented, still colonial but new semiautonomous limbo status with control over its budget and access to federal subsidies for impoverished citizens (Scarano 719–29; 732–36).

To guarantee victory for the new colonial pact, Muñoz Marín, who was still at the head of the Puerto Rican Senate, passed Law No. 53, which became known as the "Law of the Muzzle" or "Gag Law" (*Ley de la Mordaza*) in 1948. This law decreed that the State had the right to arrest any citizen on the mere suspicion of conspiring against public security. The *Ley de la Mordaza* specifically claimed that it was "incompatible to be a public servant of the government . . . and advocate the overthrow of the Government of Puerto Rico or the United States [in Puerto Rico] through force and violence *or* to be a member of any group, society, assembly, or organization that advocates such an overthrow" (Scarano 729–30). In other words, the law decreed that discrimination or firing of any civil servant, bureaucrat, or government employee for harboring pro-independence views was legal. It also endorsed the surveillance, persecution, and imprisonment of anyone who might be part of an organization that favored independence. During the course of the debate of the law, it was clear that leaders (especially Muñoz Marín, who wrote it) intended for it to be used against members of the Nationalist Party and communists, conflating one with the other although they were not the same thing. Silenced and criminalized, the Nationalist Party staged a revolt in late October 1950, days before the referendum, declaring the independence of Puerto Rico in Jayuya on the 30th. A rash of armed uprisings against local officials and armed authorities in Arecibo, Utuado, Naranjito, and Mayagüez soon followed, as did a direct attack on La Fortaleza, the Governor's Palace (Scarano 731–32). Nationalists later staged an assault on Blair House, the temporary residence of President Truman to draw attention to the Puerto Rican cause for independence and protest its exclusion from the post–World War II international agenda of decolonizing Africa and Asia.

The response of local authorities under the governorship of Muñoz Marín was all-out war. Muñoz Marín called out the National Guard. Thousands of Puerto Ricans suspected of being nationalists, communists, or independence sympathizers were arrested and imprisoned for violating *la Ley de la Mordaza*. Heavily armed units carrying submachine guns militarily occupied the towns of Arecibo, Utuado, Jayuya, Naranjito, and Mayagüez. U.S. naval aircraft bombed the towns of Utuado and Jayuya, where nationalist support was strongest. Most critical of all, Albizu Campos—who claimed absolutely no role in the affair—was dragged from his home on November 2 and charged with "having inspired" the Nationalist Assault on Blair House. Critically important was that once again, the U.S. government could not find any evidence that Albizu Campos was responsible in any direct way for nationalist acts of violence (Denis 191–208; Junta Pedro Albizu Campos).

Thus, Albizu Campos was not charged with any criminal act or having any connection to illegal possession or acquisition of weapons that the nationalists had planned to use. Instead, he was charged with violating the *Ley de la Mordaza*, that is, for "having expressed himself in ways contrary to the Insular Government on different occasions and by diverse means." In February 1951, a federal court found Albizu Campos guilty and sentenced him to seventy-nine years of imprisonment in the federal penitentiary in Atlanta. Five months later, in June 1951, 76.5 percent of the Puerto Rican electorate voted in favor of Muñoz Marín's plan for establishing the Free Associated State of Puerto Rico. Later, Muñoz Marín would release Albizu Campos on grounds of poor health only to rejail him a few months later, when the nationalists famously opened fire on Congress, wounding five. Silenced once again, Albizu Campos died in prison less than ten years later. His, like the crime of Cuba's Independent Party of Color, was one of striving for legitimate pluralism and the right to dramatically transform the State through the political process. In both cases, sovereignty rested on the willingness of citizens to surrender to a vision of nation singularly defined by leaders.

To revolutionize their respective States, Puerto Ricans and Cubans have needed to break the monopoly on ideas, debate, and terms for understanding reality that a given political elite holds and enforces to keep its monopoly on power. In both cases, the United States' cooperation, even its enmity, ironically and paradoxically has made central contributions to the stagnation leaders in Cuba and Puerto Rico glossed as stability and legitimacy.

However, it would be inaccurate to assess the kinds of States that "passive" Puerto Rico and "revolutionary" Cuba produced in the last half of the twentieth century as unstable or illegitimate. Cubans who supported Fidel Castro's Revolution—even those who did so unconditionally—were no more "brainwashed" than Puerto Ricans who supported Muñoz Marín and Operation Bootstrap unconditionally. Poor and working-class Cubans or Puerto Ricans who saw their living standards improve or transform under Fidel or Muñoz Marín's Popular Democratic Party leadership—in less than one generation—supported their governments because these leaders, more than any before, demonstrated a commitment to subverting the accumulated injustices of history. For at least one to two generations, they appeared to achieve this goal. Both Cuba and Puerto Rico's economic model for redeeming the masses relied on essentially the same factors: a dominant public sector (that, albeit in Cuba, was near total); direct government planning and management of the economy; and an enormous dependence on massive subsidies from a foreign power, the Soviet Union in Cuba's case and the U.S. federal government in that of Puerto Rico.

By the 1980s, James Dietz found, more than 80 percent of island Puerto Ricans relied on federal transfer payments to get by, creating the illusion of "food-stamp prosperity," that is, a system in which the federal government makes up for what mainland U.S. corporations do not provide: a living wage (Dietz, *Economic History of Puerto Rico* 298–300). Today, that reality of dependency on food stamps and other essential subsidies in an economy that neither provides enough jobs nor sufficient salaries has not changed but deepened. In Cuba, the vast majority of citizens rely on wartime rations for the vast majority of their calories. After thirty years of Communist Party–controlled State capitalism, an estimated 80 percent of the population relies on woefully underpaid government jobs. Both measures are means of control: that is, the Cuban Communist Party prefers to reduce the potential for prosperity among citizen-entrepreneurs whose activity the collapse of the Soviet Union forced to legalize in 1991–92 because economic power would likely translate into the negotiation of its sixty-year monopoly on rule (Mesa-Lago and Pérez-López; Mesa-Lago et al.; Ritter and Henken).

Undoubtedly, the United States' unyielding pursuit of its economic interests and continued political hegemony in the post-1948 period we call the Latin American Cold War, limited the liberating potential of both political projects, Muñoz Marín's Free Associated State/Operation Bootstrap and Castro's Communist Party–led socialism/State capitalism. Yet the totalizing discourse of anti-communism versus communism and the tangible support of the United States on behalf of those allies who enforced its interests surely contributed to Castro's "popularity" and the Free Associated State's legitimacy: after all, there was or appeared to be nothing else. Until the 1990s, to criticize Operation Bootstrap–style capitalism in Puerto Rico made one a communist, a terrorist, or a self-deceiving nationalist. To criticize socialism, the Castro brothers' rule, or the political policies of repressing dissent in communist Cuba from the 1960s to the present still makes one a counter-revolutionary, a traitor, or an unconscious agent of U.S. imperialism.

Arguably, Cubans and Puerto Ricans today think more intensely about the legacies and lessons of their history because they must. Most Cubans and Puerto Ricans cannot take the past for granted because it explains key aspects of their everyday lives. After more than one hundred years after the United States invaded Puerto Rico and Cuba and after more than one hundred years of struggling for a second independence, the destinies of island Cubans and island Puerto Ricans could not be more tied to the wealth, power, and, unfortunately, political whim of the United States.

What Cubans and Puerto Ricans are above all is avid historians; it is consciousness of their history and the propensity to think about history as a regular factor in their daily lives that forms the strongest common cultural denominator. In the wake of 2017's obliterating hurricanes, Puerto Ricans who participate in the informal economy and support *tomas*, illegal occupations of unused land or "land rescues," do so because they have inherited the values of their ancestors, the *jíbaros*, peasants who became proletarians in the century after 1898. Under the Spanish, the *jíbaros* fled, resisted, and actively undermined an economy that did not serve them and required them to contribute their labor without any possibility of ever becoming owners. Under U.S. rule, they organized labor unions, participated in virtually annual strikes, forced the political elite of the Free Associated State and the U.S. government to take their poverty, their demands for dignity, and their aspirations for prosperity seriously. Meanwhile, island Cubans who subvert their one-party State and its grip on the economy through the black market, joke-telling, creating networks of trade, and the illegal exchange of ideas over the Internet, as well as other forms of "unarmed day-to-day guerrilla warfare," mimic the passive resistance of slaves, the active resistance of rebels, and the multiple generations of cross-class heirs to their legacy. Today, the Cuban Communist State's popularity and legitimacy, like that of Puerto Rico's Free Associated State, are as illusory and theatrical as those that the United States helped to construct in the past. Today, Cubans and Puerto Ricans have weathered decades of near constant economic crisis and outmigration to the United States in search of individual hope and ambitions. Those who remain search for a collective sense of truth and freedom that will propel the nation to found a new breed of State, one that will displace and replace their elites and command not only greater national independence before the United States but, more importantly, accountability to the citizenry. The recent history of Cuba and Puerto Rico is not a history of exceptions; it is still a history of consistent patterns of behavior and a history of the rules by which the United States has enabled that behavior. Breaking the rules by rebelling and protesting injustice and conformity are not just equally Cuban and Puerto Rican traditions; they are also deeply American.

Works Cited

Burnett, Christina Duffy, and Burke Marshall, editors. *Foreign in a Domestic Sense: Puerto Rico, American Expansion, and the Constitution.* Duke UP, 2001.
Chaffin, Tom. *Fatal Glory: Narciso López and the First Clandestine U.S. War against Cuba.* U of Virginia P, 1996.
Clark, Truman R. *Puerto Rico and the United States, 1917–1933.* U of Pittsburgh P, 1975.
de la Fuente, Alejandro. *A Nation for All: Race, Inequality and Politics in Twentieth-Century Cuba.* U of North Carolina P, 2001.
del Moral, Solsirée. *Negotiating Empire: The Cultural Politics of Schools in Puerto Rico, 1898–1952.* U of Wisconsin P, 2013.
Denis, Nelson A. *War Against All Puerto Ricans: Revolution and Terror in America's Colony.* Nation Books, 2015.
Dietz, James. *Economic History of Puerto Rico: Institutional Change and Capitalist Development.* Princeton UP, 1986.
———. *Puerto Rico: Negotiating Development and Change.* Lynne Rienner Publishers, 2003.
Duany, Jorge. *Blurred Borders: Transnational Migration between the Hispanic Caribbean and the United States.* U of North Carolina P, 2011.

Ehrlich, Ilan. *Eduardo Chibás: The Incorrigible Man of Cuban Politics*. Rowman & Littlefield, 2015.

Erman, Sam. *Almost Citizens: Puerto Rico, the U.S. Constitution, and Empire*. Cambridge UP, 2019.

Foner, Philip S. *The Spanish-Cuban-American War and the Birth of American Imperialism, 1895–1902*. 2 vols. Monthly Review P, 1972.

Guerra, Lillian. *Heroes, Martyrs, and Political Messiahs in Revolutionary Cuba, 1946–1958*. Yale UP, 2018.

———. *The Myth of José Martí: Conflicting Nationalisms in Early Twentieth-Century Cuba*. U of North Carolina P, 2005.

———. *Popular Expression and National Identity in Puerto Rico: The Struggle for Self, Community, and Nation*. UP of Florida, 1998.

Helg, Aline. *Our Rightful Share: The Afro-Cuban Struggle for Equality, 1886–1912*. U of North Carolina P, 1995.

Hopkins, A. G. *American Empire: A Global History*. Princeton UP, 2018.

Junta Pedro Albizu Campos. *Nervio y pulso del mundo: Nuevos ensayos sobre Pedro Albizu Campos y el nacionalismo revolucionario*. Talla de Sombra Editores, 2014.

Kaplan, Amy. "Black and Blue on San Juan Hill." *Cultures of United States Imperialism*, edited by Amy Kaplan and Donald Pease. Duke UP, 1993, pp. 219–35.

Krenn, Michael L., editor. *Race and U.S. Foreign Policy in the Ages of Territorial and Market Expansion, 1840–1900*. Garland Publishers, 1998.

LaFeber, Walter. *The American Age: United States Foreign Policy at Home and Abroad, 1750 to the Present*. 2nd ed. W. W. Norton and Company, 1994.

Mesa-Lago, Carmelo, and Jorge F. Pérez-López. *Cuba's Aborted Reform: Socioeconomic Effects, International Comparisons, and Transition Policies*. UP of Florida, 2005.

Mesa-Lago, Carmelo, et al. *Voices of Change in Cuba from the Non-State Sector*. U of Pittsburgh P, 2018.

Pedraza, Silvia. *Political Disaffection in Cuba's Revolution and Exodus*. Cambridge UP, 2007.

Pérez, Louis A., Jr. *Cuba: Between Reform and Revolution*. Oxford UP, 1995.

———. *Cuba in the American Imagination: Metaphor and the Imperial Ethos*. U of North Carolina P, 2008.

———. *The War of 1898: The United States and Cuba in History and Historiography*. U of North Carolina P, 1998.

Pérez-Stable, Marifeli. *The Cuban Revolution: Origins, Course, and Legacy*. Oxford UP, 1993.

Ritter, Archibald R. M., and Ted A. Henken. *Entrepreneurial Cuba: The Changing Policy Landscape*. First Forum Press, 2014.

Roosevelt, Theodore. *Winning the West*. 4 vols. Cosimo Classics, 2020.

Scarano, Francisco A. *Puerto Rico: Cinco siglos de historia*. 4th ed. McGraw-Hill, 2015.

Slotkin, Richard. "Buffalo Bill's 'Wild West' and the Mythologization of the American Empire." *Cultures of United States Imperialism*, edited by Amy Kaplan and Donald Pease. Duke UP, 1993, pp. 164–84.

Sparrow, Bartholomew H. *The Insular Cases and the Emergence of American Empire*. UP of Kansas, 2006.

Stephanson, Anders. *Manifest Destiny: American Expansion and the Empire of Right*. Hill and Wang, 1995.

2

Nuclearized Wings

The Binary Roads of Cuba and Puerto Rico at the Takeoff of the Cuban Revolution (1959–1963)

SILVIA ÁLVAREZ CURBELO

It is worth starting with visions, though, because they establish hopes and fears. History then determines which prevail.

John Lewis Gaddis (*The Cold War: A New History*)

I'm afraid there will never be a post-nuclear world for us to live in unless we can somehow attain a post-nationalist world.

Luis Muñoz Marín
(*Statement before the U.S. Senate Foreign Relations Committee, March 10, 1958*)

The year 1959 was born with the victory of the Cuban Revolution to which Luis Muñoz Marín, governor and architect of the process of economic and political modernization of Puerto Rico in the postwar period, had given significant backing.[1] It ended with the defeat in the U.S. Congress of a bill to augment the autonomous powers of the Estado Libre Asociado (the Commonwealth of Puerto Rico), which constituted an intimate and public defeat for the aging governor. During that year, he also delivered the Godkin Lectures at Harvard University and decided to run for governor once again, although in his inner self he longed to retire from day-to-day executive duties and renew writing like in his younger years as a journalist and poet (Rosario Natal). When he spoke at Harvard, it had only been two days since a young Fidel Castro had received a massive welcoming at the Harvard football stadium, the only place in Cambridge that could accommodate the hero of Sierra Maestra in his last stop of a triumphant twelve-day tour of the United States and his admiring American followers.

Carlos Gil Ayala notices "una melancolía, una aflicción por algo dejado afuera, algo dejado, algo abandonado" ("a melancholy, an affliction for something left out, something left, something abandoned") (122) in the lectures that often have the tone of a public confession. In an enclosed setting and formal atmosphere, so different from the vibrant location and youthful enthusiasms that had received Castro, Muñoz Marín developed a reflection that encompassed many of the proposals he had sustained since the end of World War II (Reina Pérez, "Llegó la hora" 21-22). For many years he had declined the invitation to be a Godkin speaker. Then, in what he thought would be his final years at the governorship, he felt compelled to tell the story of Puerto Rico as a breakthrough from the constraints of nationalism and colonialism.

It was not easy to put into writing two decades of personal ideological negotiations. The complex narrative of the lectures recovers the resonances of the demise of independence as the lasting solution for poverty-stricken Puerto Rico and his adjustments to Cold War–driven discourse codes; the appeals to fight communism—which he precociously viewed as a mutant form of Russian nationalism—in the name of an "armed" democracy; the accolades for having overcome the worn out formulas of political status for Puerto Rico (classic independence and statehood) with a new concept in the constitutional architecture of the United States; and the sight of the glorious banner of the island flying as a prototype of democratic development for Latin America and the rest of the developing world. However, the lectures—which he never consented to publish—contain another lingering image: that of a "perplexed world," the possibility of yet another eclipse of civilization, as he had felt two decades before, when Europe was plunged into the darkness of war.

After the defeat of the Axis Powers, Muñoz Marín, then Senator in the Puerto Rican Legislature, painted a sobering picture of a world that needed to reconfigure its horizons. On the one hand was the persistent danger of the "fascist seduction" incarnated by militant nationalisms; on the other, the emergent nuclearization of history. It was a contradictory coexistence. Nationalisms propelled the world toward fragmentation and tribalism. Nuclear power commanded a unifying logic. As early as 1946, the contouring of this new world determined much of Muñoz Marín's thoughts about Puerto Rico and its future (Álvarez Curbelo, "Las lecciones de la guerra").

For Muñoz Marín, the nuclear artifact represented an unexpected gain. Albeit its destructive nature, the bomb had created a single world and a cosmopolitan temporality ("Nuevos caminos" 496). It was time to admit that "todas las decisiones básicas se toman fuera del control de la mayor parte de las comunidades a las que han de afectar profundamente más allá de todo documento de soberanía, más allá de toda delimitación nacional o racial, o lingüística o cultural" ("all basic decisions are taken outside the control of most communities that are to be profoundly affected notwithstanding a sovereignty document and national, racial, linguistic or cultural delimitations") ("Nuevos caminos" 498). The nuclear world—he added—required an interdependence that made obsolete the prewar protectionist political and economic borders and the national discourses that had underpinned them. But this new reality did not preclude that colonial domination—in Puerto Rico and elsewhere—had to be solved. What was important for Muñoz Marín was the manner of solving it: "No podemos proceder fútilmente, dentro de lo que, a nosotros con abandono romántico, nos gustaría que fueran las realidades. No podemos ser en la vida pública poetas a medias. Tenemos que ser poetas buenos, o por lo menos, prosistas competentes." ("We cannot proceed futilely, with romantic abandonment, to see reality as we want it to be like. We cannot be half-poets in public life. We have to be good poets, or at least competent prosaists") ("Nuevos caminos" 501). In a strange way, the doomsday weapon could spell the obsolescence of the romantic myth of nationalism, which could lead to fascism, and allow what Muñoz Marín called "creative statesmanship" ("Nuevos caminos" 503).

The successful testing of an atomic bomb by the Soviet Union in 1949, the triumph of the Chinese Revolution that same year, and the takeover of Eastern Europe by communist regimes added complexity to Muñoz Marín's reflection but did not cancel its principal tenet. As the binary Cold World carved new spheres of influence and demanded alignments, it expedited a particular exit from colonialism and from fascist-prone nationalisms in the case of Puerto Rico. The U.S. Congress ratified the Commonwealth formula in 1952 and the following year the United Nations eliminated Puerto Rico from its list of colonial territories.

In the Puerto Rican leader's thinking, atomic power emerged as a Faustian figure in a second sense: "una bomba multitudinariamente mortal, figura de muerte que eventualmente... si no mata al mundo antes, podrá descubrirse en el uso de producir abundancia a las grandes multitudes" ("a massively deadly bomb, a death figure that eventually... if it does not kill the world before, can be used to produce abundance for large populations") ("Nuevos caminos" 496). It could be an instrument for doom or prosperity. President Dwight Eisenhower's "Atoms for Peace" speech to the

United Nations in 1953 fueled hopes that the peaceful use of nuclear energy could bring a solution to hunger, disease, and other secular scourges (Eisenhower). When Harvard University's alumni recognized Muñoz Marín's international leadership in 1955, the governor paid tribute to the U.S. president for his quest to channel nuclear energy for the benefit of humanity instead of its destruction. On that occasion, he linked the issue of a nuclear peace to the three modernization operations undertaken by Puerto Rico—Operation ELA (Commonwealth), Operation Bootstrap, and Operation Serenity—with its common denominator: democratic social justice ("Harvard 1955").

At a lecture given two years later at the French University of Strasbourg, entitled "The Nation State and the International World," Muñoz Marín proposed the figure of the "perplexed world" as a starting point for his reflection on contemporary world affairs ("Strasbourg"). He expressed that he was speaking as a citizen of Puerto Rico, a border and small place, but above all as a citizen of the world. As such he wanted to convene his "perplexed compatriots" of all latitudes.

In Strasbourg, Muñoz Marín reiterated the need for a "creative statesmanship" demanded by nuclear times. He encouraged his audience to "imagine" freedom, by accepting the plurality of economic, political, and social forms it could take. He only had one caveat: a free society had to guarantee individual freedom and individual dignity. Moreover, if the forms of freedom could be multiple, the same principle applied to self-determination. Puerto Rico was proof that anticolonialism did not have to depend on narrow nationalism to garner spiritual and material energies to become a modern society. In his appreciation of the Puerto Rican "experiment," Carl Friedrich, one of Muñoz Marín's closest advisors, would expand on this point by suggesting Puerto Rico as "a new model for future developments in the sphere of the liberation of colonial peoples" (17). With the successful Soviet launching of the Sputnik satellite on 4 October 1957, the atomic age conflated with the space age. With awe, many awarded sinister possibilities to the Soviet satellite that circled the planet every hour and a half. In his annual allocution to Puerto Rican soldiers stationed in various parts of the world, Muñoz Marín spoke again of the perplexed world: "Nunca el hombre se había sentido tan perplejo y tan acosado por fuerzas caóticas como en nuestro tiempo" ("Man has never felt so perplexed and as harassed by chaotic forces as in our time") ("Mensaje de Navidad").

The space/arms race boosted the negative sign of the bipolar nuclearized world inasmuch as it was ideologically codified. Muñoz Marín embraced yet another argument. For the governor, the race between the superpowers was a strategic waste: the decisive battlefield was not in the faraway confines of space nor in any armed conflict happening in this planet. Rather, the real battle was being fought "in the depths of the mind." In an important declaration, he thinks the world is in an undesirable cul-de-sac and subtly blames the two powers:

> Aliento la esperanza de que podamos superar en el futuro esta era de tensiones y ansiedades que agobian a los pueblos del mundo. Sería aterrador pensar que nos hallamos en un callejón sin salida cuando está en juego el destino del hombre sobre la Tierra. Urgen en estos tiempos difíciles que la sensatez prepondere sobre la confusión, que los diálogos sustituyan a la Guerra Fría y el entendimiento mutuo ocupe el lugar de la hostilidad frenética. La verdad es que el enemigo común de los dos bandos en que se divide el mundo son las armas nucleares que poseen ambos bandos. ("Mensaje del Día del Veterano")

> (I hope that we will be able to overcome in the future this era of tensions and anxieties that overwhelm the peoples of the world. It is terrifying to think that we are at a dead end when man's fate on Earth is at stake. In these difficult times, there is an urgency that wisdom prevails over confusion, that dialogues can replace the Cold War, and that mutual understanding can take the place of frantic hostility. The truth is that the common enemy of both sides are the nuclear weapons that both sides possess.)

On the other hand, although he was wary of its entropic logic, Muñoz Marín watched technological advancement with fascination. He enthusiastically greeted the inauguration of Puerto Rico's public television under the jurisdiction of the Department of Education (then called Department of Public Instruction). For him, the WIPR-TV project met two important social purposes: that of education and the peaceful, humanizing, and productive use of technology: "Vivimos en una época en que la ciencia, aunque en artefactos de guerra parece amenazar al hombre, lo acercará, si procede con buen saber, a la paz y, en la paz, a una civilización más alta." ("We live in a time when science, although it seems sometimes to threaten man, will bring humankind closer, if it proceeds with good knowledge, to peace and, in peace, to a higher civilization") ("Mensaje WIPR-TV").

Along the same lines, Muñoz Marín invited the Puerto Rican Legislature to be abreast of world events because the island's future was unfolding according to the "great drama" of civilizations. Science, technology, and nuclear energy appear in that address as the axes of a universal drama. On nuclear power, he stated:

> Ante esta nueva fuerza, amiga o enemiga según la sabiduría con que se use, el drama del mundo adquiere una dimensión más honda: es lucha, y lucha mortal, entre la maravillosa dinámica del hombre contemporáneo por apoderarse de las fuerzas de la naturaleza y multiplicarlas, y su lento y pesado armatoste intelectual-político que se manifiesta en la estrechez de sus ideas nacionales. ("Mensaje a la Legislatura 1958")

> (Faced with this new strength, friendly or hostile according to the wisdom with which it is used, the drama of the world takes on a deeper dimension: it is a struggle, and a mortal one, between the wonderful dynamics of contemporary man to harness the forces of nature and multiply them, and his slow and heavy intellectual-political contraption that manifests itself in the narrowness of national ideas.)

Within this cosmic drama, nationalistic outbursts were not of much value because "la única soberanía total que queda en la Tierra es la que en un día ominosamente cercano podrá tener la ciencia nuclear para acabar con todos nosotros—la soberanía total del exterminio" ("the only total sovereignty left on Earth is that which, on an ominously close day, nuclear science can have to wipe all of us out—the total sovereignty of extermination") ("Conferencia de Intercambios"). Even though Muñoz Marín tried to modulate his nuclear anxieties, many of his close friends and political associates—such as Juan Manuel García Passalacqua—described his 1959 Godkin Lectures as his "end-of-the-world mediations."

Months later, in one of his last speeches of 1959, Muñoz Marín devoted himself to imagining the coming decade. It would be "una época llena de peligros y, a la vez, una época rica en posibilidades de grandes logros. ¿Qué podemos hacer para no existir meramente durante ella, sino para abrir brecha en sus peligros?" ("a time full of dangers and, at the same time, a time rich in possibilities of great achievements. What can we do to not merely exist within it, but rather to open new ground in the face of such dangers?") ("Asociación Nacional de Relaciones Intergrupales"). Much of the speech was devoted to what he described as "una amenaza que cubre al mundo a manera de tienda de campaña, siempre en peligro de caerse" ("a threat that covers the world as a tent, always in danger of falling") ("Asociación

Nacional de Relaciones Intergrupales"). He was worried for the young people living in the nuclear age "que no habrán dormido una sola noche sin que sea posible que su casa, su ciudad, su país, su mundo, acaso no exista la mañana siguiente" ("that will not have slept a single night without thinking that it was possible that their homes, their cities, their countries, their world, may not exist the next morning") ("Asociación Nacional de Relaciones Intergrupales"). Would the United States, with its strong sense of isolationism, be able to lead the way in the global drive to conquer hunger, freedom, and dignity? asked Muñoz Marín. The answer to this question was crucial to determine how humanity would face the urgent problems of the next decade: "el final del colonialismo, las crecientes ambiciones de todos en todas partes; la necesidad de cerrar la brecha económica; las consecuencias sociales del desarrollo económico; el creciente sentido de identificación con el grupo que implica grandes potencialidades para el desarrollo o la destrucción" ("the end of colonialism; everyone's increasing ambitions in all places; the need to close the economic gap; the social consequences of economic development; the growing sense of identification with a group that implies greater potential for development or destruction") ("Asociación Nacional de Relaciones Intergrupales").

Ironically, when he felt the perplexity of the world at its fullest, Muñoz Marín found in John F. Kennedy's campaign for the presidency a new source of hope and optimism. He also found renewed energy to champion his idea of democratic development as an antidote to the conflicts of the bipolar world. The 1960 elections in Puerto Rico were the last ones in which Muñoz Marín would appear as a candidate for governor. After the defeat suffered in his pursuit to enhance the powers of the Commonwealth, he felt frustrated and tired. But, perhaps because his main rival in the election was not a party but the all-powerful Catholic Church, the fighting spirit returned to the fatigued warrior and he carried out one of his best electoral campaigns. At dawn on 9 November, his joy was double. Not only had he succeeded, but Kennedy, whom he had supported since his days as a young senator from Massachusetts, had won the presidency of the United States. Curiously, Muñoz Marín was elected despite the Catholic Church's opposition; Kennedy, in spite of his Catholicism.

Since his initial interventions with international resonance, the imperative for development was linked in Muñoz Marín to democracy, the futility of narrow-minded nationalism, and the inescapable nuclearization of the world. This was especially true regarding Puerto Rico's neighboring countries in the Caribbean, Central and South America.

Latin America's development agenda had already been the main topic in a 1958 speech delivered by Muñoz Marín before the American Legion convention. He contrasted what the United States was trying to do in Latin America and other less-developed areas of the world and the role they had played in the postwar process of modernization in Puerto Rico. In the latter case, the United States had been respectful of the people's democratic will expressed in elections and referenda; in the former, the United States often aligned with dictators and the most reactionary political and social forces:

> In the vast continents of Asia, Africa and South America, these countless millions are rebelling today not only against poverty and any remaining vestiges of colonialism, but also against their own feudal dictatorships as they would rebel against the Communist dictatorships if Russia were less ruthless. In Hungary they tried it, but they never had a chance. This revulsion against authoritarianism is a portent which the United States often misreads. ("American Legion")

The governor contested the "wisdom" of the policy that backed "Our S.O.B.'s"[2] because most of the time the United States' enemies would eventually win the battle of public opinion by posing as "friends of the oppressed." The wave of the future was not tyranny; it was freedom, human dignity, and the hope of a decent life. Accordingly, Puerto Rico was a "psychological outpost" in the underdeveloped world. Referring to the military concept of outpost, Muñoz Marín used the example of the Puerto Rican–based 65th Infantry Regiment to state that it is not the mercenaries hired by the dictatorships who come to the defense of democracy but those who have already conquered democracy ("American Legion").

Muñoz Marín was aware that a new generation had entered the Puerto Rican political arena, inspired by the ongoing Cuban Revolution that he himself supported. In the midst of a flurry of protests led by the Cuban-inspired Movimiento Pro Independencia (MPI, Pro-Independence Movement), the Federación Universitaria Pro Independencia (FUPI, Pro-Independence University Federation), and the traditional bastions of the Partido Independentista Puertorriqueño (PIP, Puerto Rican Independence Party), and the Partido Nacionalista (Nationalist Party), the first U.S. Governors' Conference outside the mainland was held in Puerto Rico.

Muñoz Marín celebrated the milestone but dedicated his keynote address to reflect upon the global "circumstances" surrounding the meeting and the need to strengthen Pan-American union from a concept common to both issues: the frontier. On the one hand, the world was at a crossroads among the conquest of space, the peaceful use of atomic energy, and the abyss of a nuclear final showdown. The circumstances required political imagination and dynamism, as evidenced by two supranational bodies: the North Atlantic Treaty Organization (NATO) and the newly born European Common Market. The era of nationalism represented an anachronism in the Cold War. The fate of the world—certainly, Puerto Rico's—was in the development of new forms of federalism ("United States Conference of Governors").

It was also a frontier moment for relations with Latin America. It was urgent—said Muñoz Marín—for the United States to overcome the negative purpose of containing communism and instead establish a pragmatic relationship between the Americas, nurtured by a determination to abolish poverty in the southern half of the hemisphere by 1999. A few months later, he advised the United States to exercise moral leadership and lead peoples—not just governments—against tyranny. The moral compass is lost if we face a despotic regime only when it supports a non-capitalist economic system but not when despotism serves capitalist interests, he claimed ("Federal Bar Association").

The governor's strategy of presenting Puerto Rico as a model of democratic development and himself as a mediator between the Americas contained much political realism and self-interest. As part of his management of the Commonwealth brand, it was key for Muñoz Marín to give Puerto Rico a place in the world. On the other hand, as someone knowledgeable in hemispheric history, the Puerto Rican politician was convinced that, with few exceptions, U.S. policy toward Latin America and later toward other emerging regions was often counterproductive and ineffective.[3]

Both objectives were present in the inaugural message offered by Muñoz Marín on the occasion of the Third Meeting of the Inter-American Cultural Council of the Organization of American States that also took place in San Juan. The main theme of the message was the mutual misgivings between the United States and Latin America and how Puerto Rico's example could clear many of them. By holding the United States accountable for many of these disagreements, he contrasted the cases of Venezuela and Cuba. The U.S. prejudice that Latin Americans did not understand that the concept of freedom "se desvanece ante el juicio que procede de la observación de cómo el pueblo cubano, caso a puño limpio, desbarató una dictadura armada hasta los dientes, y de cómo el pueblo venezolano, ha establecido, por el proceso ordenado e iluminado de las urnas, un gobierno de gran tolerancia, sabiduría y progreso" ("fades in the face of the observation of how the

Cuban people, in a clean fight, broke down an armed dictatorship to the teeth, and how the Venezuelan people have established, by the orderly and enlightened process of the ballot boxes, a government of great tolerance, wisdom, and progress") ("Consejo Interamericano Cultural"). In a world where we do not know "qué hacer con las bombas amontonadas ni con las fuerzas nucleares desatadas sobre el destino de la humanidad" ("what to do with the bombs piled up or with the nuclear forces unleashed on the fate of humanity"), we should not add to our griefs and risks "la fuerza corrosiva del prejuicio" ("the corrosive force of prejudice") ("Consejo Interamericano Cultural").

On the verge of a new decade, Muñoz Marín seemed pressed by history. Political changes and in cultural mindsets had to take place soon: "it is most important that we do not wait until the first Latin American country has a Communist revolution before launching a program which will fire the imagination and hopes of Latin Americans as the Marshall Plan did for the Europeans in 1947" ("Federal Bar Association").

During 1961 and 1962, Muñoz Marín would play an important role as Kennedy's *consiglieri* on Latin American affairs. Days before the inaugural ceremony in Washington, he met with the president-elect in New York. Photographs of the meeting show both politicians in comfort and complicity, which boded well for Muñoz Marín's new effort to influence the direction of U.S. policy toward Latin America. There, the governor shared with the young president-elect what he understood as the basis for a revamped U.S. regional policy, using Puerto Rico's success as a prototype.

A transcript of contemporary notes taken by a Muñoz Marín aide of the hour-long meeting is preserved ("Notas al dictáfono"). Three elements stand out in the conversation with Kennedy: first, his view that any plan regarding Cuba should not include an outright military invasion and by no means entail the restitution of the Batista regime; secondly, a commitment to overthrow the Dominican dictator Rafael Trujillo; and finally, a promise by Kennedy to take into account the views of the Democratic Left to balance the less nuanced positions of the CIA and other right-wing elements in the U.S. government.

During his inaugural message as governor in January 1961, Muñoz Marín subtly commented on the Cuban situation:

> Ha de ocupar una parte importante de nuestro propósito ayudar a que se entienda que la gran transformación, la gran revolución que los pueblos de América Latina tienen ante sí pueda realizarse como

debe realizarse a plenitud en términos de democracia y libertad personal y amistad y respeto mutuo entre todos los pueblos de nuestro Hemisferio Americano. ("Mensaje Inaugural 1961")

(It must occupy an important part of our purpose to help in the understanding that the great transformation, the great revolution before the peoples of Latin America, can be fully accomplished in terms of democracy and personal freedom, and friendship and mutual respect, among all the peoples of our American Hemisphere.)

The governor insisted on attaching a democratic meaning to the concept of revolution. Latin America, he said, needed a revolution, but in the best sense of the word, that is, "el de la visión y la transformación honda basada en la visión profunda de las necesidades de los pueblos" ("a vision and profound transformation based on an equally deep vision of the needs of the people") ("Homenaje en su cumpleaños"). The revolution will take place and there must be one, says Muñoz Marín, but "el problema es si esa revolución ha de ocurrir en términos de tiranía comunista o en términos de libertad, de democracia y de respeto al ser humano" ("the problem is whether that revolution is to happen in terms of a communist tyranny or in terms of freedom, democracy, and respect for the human being") ("Homenaje en su cumpleaños"). Muñoz Marín was expressing one of the core uncertainties of the Cold War, as defined by historian John Lewis Gaddis: "It is worth starting with visions, though, because they establish hopes and fears. History then determines which prevail"(3).

Cuba is constantly in Muñoz Marín's mind and it is the subject of many communications with fellow members of the Democratic Left circle as well as with influential voices in the new Kennedy administration. Muñoz Marín admits that Democrats of the two Americas "no estamos de acuerdo con los métodos de la Revolución Cubana, ni mucho menos podemos estar de acuerdo con las alianzas soviéticas que se han buscado los líderes de la revolución" ("we do not agree with the methods of the Cuban Revolution, let alone agree with the Soviet alliances sought by the leaders of the revolution") ("Homenaje en su cumpleaños"). But they were not ready to disqualify the revolution yet: "estamos en completa simpatía . . . con todo lo que sea la corrección enérgica de injusticias, corrección que ha representado en Cuba por más de 100 años el sueño de los cubanos de establecer una gran república para un pueblo que en su corazón y en su espíritu merece una gran República" ("we are in complete sympathy . . . with all that constitutes a vigorous correction of injustices, a rectification that for more than 100 years has been the aspiration of Cubans: to establish a great republic for a people who in their heart and spirit deserve a great Republic") ("Homenaje en su cumpleaños").

However, the U.S. confrontation with the new Cuban regime intensified soon. On 17 April 1961, in an operation funded by the CIA and approved since March 1960 by then-president Eisenhower, an exile force invaded Cuba at the Bay of Pigs.[4] On the first day of the operation, Muñoz Marín addressed the Young Presidents' Organization meeting in San Juan. He was confident of President Kennedy's statements that there would be no U.S. direct military intervention in Cuba. Muñoz Marín's hope was that, after a while, the dictatorship would fall without external intervention: "History shows that the Cuban people love freedom militantly and that no dictatorship has been able to prevail for long in their midst" ("Young Presidents").

His reflection that day revolved once again around the concept of revolution in times of nuclear power:

> The atom was parted, and its powers released. So were its furies. The moon is encircled, and we will soon put a man on it. No previous century, not tens of centuries, can match these mere decades for an explosion of man's energy, discovery, and power for evil and good. This is the epoch of revolution—essentially a good revolution. It is our job as free men not to slow it down but to deepen it. ("Young Presidents")

The governor urged the young entrepreneurs gathered in San Juan not to make the mistake of turning the principle of free enterprise into a fetish: "Let us not commit the error of thinking that private enterprise is democracy" ("Young Presidents"). The time was ripe for revolution and that mistake could be fatal:

> A very serious revolution is developing throughout Latin America and all the underdeveloped areas of the world. The question is, will that revolution be violent and in the direction of Soviet philosophy? Or will it be peaceful and in the direction of Western democratic thinking? ("Young Presidents")

Muñoz Marín believed that Cuba's radicalization had causes that preceded the revolutionary guerrillas of the Sierra Maestra in the 1950s. For many years, the United States had courted or given the appearance that it admired dictatorships. "The problem," says Muñoz Marín, "is that when these dictatorships fall, the people who succeed them do not forget who the friends of their oppressors were... To some extent, this happens in the Cuban situation. Fidel Castro has made the most of it" ("Young Presidents").

Two days later, the Bay of Pigs invasion was crushed on land, sea, and air. It was a major humiliation for Kennedy. With the U.S. military fiasco and the hardening of positions in relation to Cuba, Muñoz Marín tried to salvage his reformist alternative out of the blunder. The Puerto Rican governor did not want to derail from what was much more critical to him: to advance the agenda of democratic development that could become the fulcrum of a new regional policy by the United States. In March 1961, Kennedy had announced a ten-year plan for Latin America, which was ratified at the Inter-American Conference held in Punta del Este, Uruguay, and had many of the elements for which Muñoz Marín had advocated since the early days of former President Harry Truman's Point Four Program.[5]

Of the three items on the urgent agenda that Muñoz Marín had presented to Kennedy at the meeting sustained shortly after the elections, one had been fulfilled at least in principle: the announcement of a plan for Latin America that was basically aligned with the positions of the Democratic Left on development; another, U.S. support for the end of the Trujillo dictatorship in the Dominican Republic, which would be accomplished in a sinister way with Trujillo's execution on 30 May 1961, although the return to democracy in that country did not have the outcome that Muñoz Marín would have wanted. The Cuban situation would be the biggest challenge and in the long run a failure for U.S. politics and Muñoz Marín, personally.

Many saw the designation of Teodoro Moscoso, the architect of Operation Bootstrap in Puerto Rico, as the first administrator of the Alliance for Progress, as a validation of an international development model. The same month, the governor and his wife Inés Mendoza were the guests of honor at a dinner at the White House. The renowned Catalonian cellist Pablo Casals, at that time living in exile in Puerto Rico, agreed to play at the event despite his long-held promise not to step on continental U.S. soil due to U.S. support of Francisco Franco's dictatorship. That evening, Casals performed his composition *The Song of the Birds*, an anthem to peace and world harmony (Reina Pérez, *El arco prodigioso*).

From Washington, Muñoz Marín traveled to Dallas where he was the keynote speaker at the Associated Press Managing Editors Forum on Latin America. He titled his message: "Crisis in Latin America." The governor began his remarks by telling his audience that he had been a journalist much of his life. He deplored that of the five W's (What, Where, Who, When, and Why) that condensed the profession's credo, U.S. journalists did little to take care of the last one: the Why. To understand why things were happening the way they did in Latin America, reporters had to do more interpretative journalism. He thought that many Americans were obsessed with Fidel Castro and the Cuban Revolution when the substantive issues were elsewhere: "The issues are poverty, ignorance, disease, and tyranny—the four modern horsemen of the Apocalypse" ("Associated Press"). The Alliance for Progress—he promised—would deliver not only abundant but enlightened aid.

Muñoz Marín was optimistic in the early months of 1962. In his annual message to the Puerto Rican Legislature, he welcomed the prominent role of Puerto Rico and Puerto Rican-born officials in the Kennedy administration and operation of the Alliance for Progress with the promise that all aid would be provided to governments that responded to genuinely democratic principles ("Mensaje a la Legislatura 1962"). However, the initiative's launching had not been easy. Two sources of mistrust still had to be won: the federal bureaucracy and public opinion in Latin America. Muñoz Marín expressed concern, especially regarding the latter, at a conference on community services sponsored by the powerful AFL-CIO trade union:

> What deeply troubles me is the seeming lack of emotional commitment in Latin America toward this great and historical venture. The Alliance cannot be purely an economic undertaking, a transfusion of capitals and skills. To succeed, it must stir the hearts of men, it must inspire them to dream and hope, and then to work hard and purposefully. It must have strong ideological content. ("AFL-CIO Message")

Muñoz Marín thought that only one group was capable of operating the Alliance in an effective manner: the Democratic Left. First, in a suggestive fashion, he pointed out to his audience what "Left" meant: "Left usually means left of reaction, left of feudalism, left of exploitation" ("AFL-CIO Message"). Then he defined what the Democratic Left was for him:

> I would call the Democratic Left in Latin America the group which seeks social advances and higher living standards for all the people in a framework of freedom and consent. It is not necessarily based on class, and often includes important elements of the middle class and even a few enlightened members of the wealthy oligarchies ... Only the Democratic Left has the dynamic ideological base to compete with the totalitarian Left: the Communists, the Castroists, and the Fascists. ("AFL-CIO")

Muñoz Marín's version of democratic development seemed to be taking root in two countries that had suffered from long military dictatorships. Venezuela, where his friend Rómulo Betancourt was president since 1959, proclaimed a Democratic Constitution on 23 January 1961. Another friend, Juan Bosch, was campaigning to become president of the Dominican Republic, an election he would win in December 1962.

However, none of the above would constitute that year's distinctive mark. In October 1962, for thirteen days that shook the world during the Cuban Missile Crisis, the lives of those in power; of those who knew little of nuclear dilemmas but heard the alarming news; of young people who entered college that year; of the *braceros* embarking to work in the fields of New Jersey or of the peasants and factory workers in Puerto Rico, were on hold waiting for the end of days.

The Cuban Missile Crisis[6] that broke out in the last two weeks of October 1962 illuminated the fragile threads that sustained the perplexed world. The nuclear-based bipolarity in the march of world affairs was confirmed and again the human quest for peace, development, and freedom bowed to national arrogances. The "Great Barbarian," as Muñoz Marín called nuclear power, was awake and the Archangel Saint Gabriel was tuning his apocalyptic trumpet as Soviet ships approaching Puerto Rico on their way to Cuba turned around and the nuclear catastrophe was averted. During those alarming days, Puerto Rico—a strategic outpost of the United States with nuclear installations in its soil—plunged into a deep existential crisis. The "Red Threat" that for years had been personified as a Soviet tank and lately as a bearded warrior mutated into a bodyless enemy that left little room to maneuver.

Muñoz Marín made few public expressions in those two weeks. His support of President Kennedy's 22 October speech, which announced the U.S. position in the face of the Soviet challenge and the imposition of a blockade on Cuba, yields some clues. The governor congratulated the president on the moral courage and intellectual lucidity of his statement (*El Mundo*, 25 Oct. 1962). More than Puerto Rico, the target of this communication to Kennedy was Latin America. Anticipating that the course of democratic development in the region could be in jeopardy, he advocated that all Latin America recognize its own interest in supporting the course of action undertaken by the United States (*El Mundo*, 25 Oct. 1962). For him, it was the only path toward peace.

A few days after the Armageddon cliffhanger was prevented, René Marqués, the laureate Puerto Rican writer, addressed a letter to Muñoz Marín.

The author of the iconic play *La Carreta* (*The Oxcart*) had been one of the signatories of the Extermination Document drafted by a group of Puerto Rican intellectuals and artists in 1961 that opposed nuclear proliferation. In his letter, Marqués argued that now, more than ever, it was necessary for Puerto Rico to support Brazil's efforts at the United Nations to declare Latin America a nuclear-free zone. Because of its geography, history, culture, and language, Puerto Rico was part of that regional desire (*El Mundo*, 2 Nov. 1962). For Marqués, Puerto Rico was living the threat of total extermination without wanting it, asking for it, nor having, as a people, voted democratically for that form of collective suicide. It was a futile request. Marqués was speaking in moral terms; Muñoz Marín resorted to the language of expediency. Among the most significant limitations of Commonwealth status were foreign relations and military affairs, both areas under federal jurisdiction.

Despite not having the fatal outcome that many expected, the Missile Crisis heralded other tragedies and outcomes. Kennedy's assassination in November 1963, the little interest in the Alliance for Progress on the part of the Johnson administration, the coup against Juan Bosch in the Dominican Republic with the support of the United States, and the beginning of a new cycle of military dictatorships in Latin America, starting with Brazil in 1964, affected Muñoz Marín strongly. His alternatives to nuclear extermination failed to stop the siren songs of right-wing authoritarianism and of the socialist revolution preached from Cuba. The arms race and repressive anticommunism hijacked his scheme of democratic development. I believe that these portents, while the Third World became a proxy fighting ground in the Cold War, must have weighed on his decision to decline another nomination for governor of Puerto Rico in 1964.

Notes

1. Fragments of this essay appear in Álvarez Curbelo, "Un mundo perplejo."

2. The phrase refers to U.S. support for Latin American dictatorships during the twentieth century. President Franklin Delano Roosevelt is generally credited with describing Nicaraguan dictator Anastasio Somoza in this manner: "Somoza may be a son of a bitch, but he's our son of a bitch."

3. For an account of Muñoz Marín's participation in the anti-dictatorship causes of Latin America during the 1920s, see Rosario Natal.

4. See Kornbluh; Jones; Ackerman; National Archives for chronologies, documents, and interpretations of the event that sealed Cuba's isolation in the hemisphere and also became the first major crisis of the Kennedy administration.

5. For an excellent interpretation of the Alliance for Progress, see Smith.
6. For a collection of key documents about the Cuban Missile Crisis, see Chang and Kornbluh.

Works Cited

Ackerman, Holly, editor. "Bibliography on Moderate Cuban Politics, 1952–1965," http://scholar.library.miami.edu/cubamoderate/index.html. Accessed 3 Dec. 2020.

Álvarez Curbelo, Silvia. "Las lecciones de la guerra: Luis Muñoz Marín y la Segunda Guerra Mundial." *Luis Muñoz Marín: Ensayos del centenario*, edited by Fernando Picó. Fundación Luis Muñoz Marín, 1999, pp. 30–64.

———. "Un mundo perplejo: La discursiva de Luis Muñoz Marín en tiempos nucleares, 1946–1963." *Tiempos binarios: La Guerra Fría desde Puerto Rico y el Caribe*, edited by Manuel R. Rodríguez Vázquez and Silvia Álvarez Curbelo. Callejón, 2017, pp. 117–62.

Chang, Laurence, and Peter Kornbluh, editors. *The Cuban Missile Crisis, 1962: A National Security Archive Documents Reader*. New Press, 1992.

Eisenhower, Dwight D. "Address by Mr. Dwight D. Eisenhower, President of the United States of America, to the 470th Plenary Meeting of the United Nations General Assembly, Tuesday 8 December 1953 2:45 p.m.," https://www.iaea.org/about/history/atoms-for-peace-speech. Accessed 21 Dec. 2020.

Friedrich, Carl. J. *Puerto Rico: Middle Road to Freedom*. Rinehart & Company, 1959.

Gaddis, John Lewis. *The Cold War. A New History*. Penguin Books, 2005.

Gil Ayala, Carlos. "La brecha del terror: Luis Muñoz Marín y las Conferencias Godkin." *Cavilando el fin del mundo: Apología y confesión en las Conferencias Godkin 1959 de Luis Muñoz Marín*, edited by Pedro Reina Pérez. Alamo West Caribbean Publishing, 2005, pp. 79–128.

Jones, Howard. *The Bay of Pigs*. Oxford UP, 2008.

Kornbluh, Peter. *Bay of Pigs Declassified: The Secret CIA Report*. New Press, 1998.

El Mundo. "Muñoz apoya bloqueo." 25 Oct. 1962, p. 18.

———. "Pide Puerto Rico sea Zona Libre de Armas Nucleares." 2 Nov. 1962, p.17.

Muñoz Marín, Luis. "Address by Governor Luis Muñoz Marín at the Inauguration of the United States Conference of Governors in San Juan, Puerto Rico." Archivo Fundación Luis Muñoz Martín (AFLMM), Sección V: Luis Muñoz Marín Gobernador, Serie 9: Discursos, 3 Aug. 1959.

———. "Address by Governor Luis Muñoz Marín before the AFL-CIO National Conference on Community Services." AFLMM, Sección V: Luis Muñoz Marín Gobernador, Serie 9: Discursos, 3 May 1962.

———. "Address of Governor Luis Muñoz Marín at the Federal Bar Association Dinner in Honor of the Justices of the United States Supreme Court, Washington, D.C." AFLMM, Sección V: Luis Muñoz Marín Gobernador, Serie 9: Discursos, 26 Sept. 1959.

———. "Discurso del gobernador Luis Muñoz Marín en la reunión de la Asociación Nacional de Relaciones Intergrupales." AFLMM, Sección V: Luis Muñoz Marín Gobernador, Serie 9: Discursos, 13 Oct. 1959.

———. "Discurso del gobernador Luis Muñoz Marín en ocasión del homenaje en su cumpleaños." AFLMM, Sección V: Luis Muñoz Marín Gobernador, Serie 9: Discursos, 18 Feb. 1961.

———. "Lecture Given by Governor Luis Muñoz Marín at Strasbourg University in France." AFLMM, Sección V: Luis Muñoz Marín Gobernador, Series 9: Discursos, 3 Aug. 1955.

———. "Mensaje del gobernador Luis Muñoz Marín a la Asamblea Legislativa de Puerto Rico." AFLMM, Sección V: Luis Muñoz Marín Gobernador, Serie 9: Discursos, 22 Jan. 1958.

———. "Mensaje de Navidad del gobernador Luis Muñoz Marín a los puertorriqueños que prestan servicio en las Fuerzas Armadas en Alemania." AFLMM, Sección V: Luis Muñoz Marín Gobernador, Serie 9: Discursos, 18 Dec. 1957.

———. "Mensaje del gobernador Luis Muñoz Marín en el Día del Veterano." AFLMM, Sección V: Luis Muñoz Marín Gobernador, Serie 9: Discursos, 11 Nov. 1958.

———. "Mensaje del gobernador Luis Muñoz Marín en la Conferencia sobre Intercambios de Personas en América." AFLMM, Sección V: Luis Muñoz Marín Gobernador, Serie 9: Discursos, 14 Oct. 1958.

———. "Mensaje del gobernador Luis Muñoz Marín en la inauguración de la estación WIPR-TV del Gobierno de Puerto Rico." AFLMM, Sección V: Luis Muñoz Marín Gobernador, Serie 9: Discursos, 6 Jan. 1958.

———. "Mensaje Inaugural del gobernador Luis Muñoz Marín." AFLMM, Sección V: Luis Muñoz Marín Gobernador, Serie 9: Discursos, 2 Jan. 1961.

———. "Notas al dictáfono." AFLMM, Sección V: Luis Muñoz Marín Gobernador, Serie 9: Discursos, 17 Feb. 1961.

———. "Nuevos caminos hacia viejos objetivos." *Puerto Rico: Cien años de lucha política*, edited by Reece Bothwell, vol. 3. Editorial Universitaria, 1979, pp. 456–76; 498–505.

———. "Palabras del gobernador Luis Muñoz Marín en la sesión inaugural de la Tercera Reunión del Consejo Interamericano Cultural." AFLMM, Sección V: Luis Muñoz Marín Gobernador, Serie 9: Discursos, 22 Nov. 1959.

———. "Remarks by Governor Luis Muñoz Marín at Harvard University." AFLMM, Sección V: Luis Muñoz Marín Gobernador, Series 9: Discursos, 16 June 1955.

———. "Speech by Governor Luis Muñoz Marín before the Associated Press Managing Editors Forum on Latin America at Dallas, Texas." AFLMM, Sección V: Luis Muñoz Marín Gobernador, Serie 9: Discursos, 17 Nov. 1961.

———. "Speech of Governor Luis Muñoz Marín before the National Convention of the American Legion, Chicago, Illinois." AFLMM, Sección V: Luis Muñoz Marín Gobernador, Serie 9: Discursos, 4 Sept. 1958.

———. "Speech of Governor Luis Muñoz Marín to the Young Presidents' Organization Meeting at San Juan." AFLMM, Sección V: Luis Muñoz Marín Gobernador, Serie 9: Discursos, 17 Apr. 1961.

———. "Statement of the Honorable Luis Muñoz Marín, Governor of the Commonwealth of Puerto Rico before The U.S. Senate Foreign Relations Committee." AFLMM, Sección V: Luis Muñoz Marín Gobernador, Serie 9: Discursos, 10 Mar. 1958.

National Archives and Records Administration (NARA). "Military Resources: Bay of Pigs Invasion & Cuban Missile Crisis," https://www.archives.gov/research/alic/reference/military/cuban-missile-crisis.html. Accessed 3 Dec. 2020.

Reina Pérez, Pedro. "Llegó la hora." *Cavilando el fin del mundo: Apología y confesión en las Conferencias Godkin 1959 de Luis Muñoz Marín*, edited by Pedro Reina Pérez. Alamo West Caribbean Publishing, 2005, pp. 21–52.

Reina Pérez, Pedro, editor. *El arco prodigioso: Perspectivas sobre Pablo Casals y su legado en Puerto Rico*. Facultad de Estudios Generales/Fundación Luis Muñoz Marín/Instituto Ramón Llull, 2009.

———. *Cavilando el fin del mundo: Apología y confesión en las Conferencias Godkin 1959 de Luis Muñoz Marín*. Alamo West Caribbean Publishing, 2005.

Rosario Natal, Carmelo. *La juventud de Luis Muñoz Marín: Vida y pensamiento, 1898–1932*. Edil, 1989.

Smith, Peter H. *Talons of the Eagle: Dynamics of U.S.-Latin American Relations*. Oxford UP, 1999.

3

The Repeating Island?
Cuban–Puerto Rican Counterpoints between the Cold War and the Reencounter

FRANCISCO A. SCARANO

> I've never mixed music with politics, but politicians can learn a lot from us because of the brotherhood that exists among musicians.
>
> Geño Acosta Ithier

The record of what we conceive as repetitive in the insular Caribbean is well known. For María Dolores González Ripoll, this includes "[the] values shared by different human groups, a culture open to influences, a banal and raucous image to be sold to tourism, an Antillean identity fragmented by geography and history or a sense of loss, of stolen roots" (González Ripoll 257–58; my translations throughout). From literature, Antonio Benítez Rojo proposes the figure of a "repeating island," a metaphor that captures the fundamental paradox of the region: a geographical area, relatively small and fragmented politically by imperial powers, that history—and the institutions of slavery, the plantation, and colonialism—managed to mend (Benítez Rojo). For those who pursue the repetitiveness of the Caribbean from the fields of anthropology and history, the search usually begins with interrelated ecologies and geographies, and ends with the common experience of a lasting colonial subordination. Key economic and social institutions emerge from all this, none more important than the enslavement of Africans and their descendants. Common experiences, framed by slavery, nurtured recurrent cultural sensibilities and forms, often expressed in philosophy, literature, music, and the arts. This overlap of geographies, histories, and cultures has made it possible to think about the societies of the archipelago as a sociocultural region, with traits and histories that distinguish it from other regions of the world (Mintz).

Although the coining of the phrase "repeating island" is relatively recent, neither the image nor the experiences to which it alludes are new, as the late Cuban essayist and novelist Benítez Rojo well understood. The Caribbean has thus been conceived at successive moments of introspection throughout history as a plurality of societies and cultures that, while occupying homologous spaces and coming from similar historical-social trunks, share trajectories and destinations (Gaztambide; Sheller). Amerindians and immigrants, colonizers and colonized, masters and slaves, bureaucrats and peasants, workers and philosophers—everyone, at some point, has lived it and thought this way. Under European rule, people were aware of the inherent repetitiveness of the archipelago, created by force through successive invasions and conquests. In the early colonial centuries, the notion that the islands were like precious stones in other people's crowns that, by rubbing bayonets, would shine the same or more in their own, inspired more than one imperial adventure. Just changing owners was enough to appropriate them and remake them in the image and likeness of their new masters; that is, repeat them to blows on the imperial anvil. The territories and societies built there were therefore like the gold of their ancestral rivers: malleable, subject to easy transmutation.

Then, well into the twentieth century, and as the old empires were reduced to one, young and hesitant, the Caribbean was conceived of as the American Sea, both in the literal sense, as the sea of the hemisphere, and in the most metaphorical, as a maritime backyard of the (North) American colonizer. The United States conceptualized repetitiveness as a strategic advantage for its defense in more recent times, especially during World War II and at the time of the Caribbean Commission (1946–60), when showcases were not yet necessary to exhibit the successes and hide the mistakes of master ideologies in the arsenal of the Cold War (Thorning). Closer to our day, the gaze of the ancient colonizers, whose tiredness begat a handful of new nations, began to view the Caribbean, especially from the outside, as the region where the colonial and postcolonial overlapped and blurred. Material now for a great First-World academic enterprise, that fascinating Caribbean repeats itself and, in doing so, agitates and confuses the certainties of modernity (Martínez-San Miguel).

In their struggles against those who oppressed them, some natives of these lands filled the Caribbean repetitiveness with an indigenous character.

The so-called Carib Indians, some of them descendants of the vanquished and displaced Taínos and Ciboneys, did this when they sailed in their canoes in the waters of the region, keeping alive in their memories the *conucos* (small parcels of land) and *bateyes* (central plazas) they left behind in Haiti, Borikén (now Puerto Rico), or Cubanacán (Cuba). Or the runaway slaves, Caribbean globetrotters par excellence, when they exchanged one island refuge for another to make greater sense of their forged freedom on the run (Chinea).

Centuries later, recognizing that their experiences and history reflected those of their Antillean brothers, joined together not only by language but by a certain idiosyncrasy, the forgers of the homelands in the Spanish Antilles and in Santo Domingo dreamed of a confederation led by Cuba. This idea was not lost, but postponed, when Cuban rebels with their allies—including thousands of Caribbean people, less well known than Máximo Gómez or Juan Rius Rivera, but no less important—launched their turn-of-the century cry against Spain before drowning in the overwhelming tide of an ill-anticipated imperial project (Arroyo-Martínez).

Two Birds and the Same Bullet?

From this collaboration for a *Cuba Libre* was born, it is worth remembering, the emblematic poem of the [Hispanic] repeating island, from the pen of the Puerto Rican resident in Cuba, Lola Rodríguez de Tió, which in its initial stanzas exclaims:

> Cuba and Puerto Rico are
> two wings of a bird,
> they receive flowers and bullets
> in the same heart.
> How much of an illusion
> that a thousand dyes swirl,
> dreams Lola's muse
> with fervent fantasy,
> of this land and mine:
> to make a single homeland!
>
> (Rodríguez de Tió)

These ideas have rhetorically anchored many of the comparisons between the two islands, the last two Spanish possessions in the Americas, sometimes to confirm the poet's intuition—to certify an inherent repetitiveness, attentive to its full and combined national possibilities—or to deny it, or at least qualify it.

Despite its charm and simplicity, doña Lola's metaphor has had its detractors. For Laird Bergad, significant details of the economic and social history of the two countries contradict the parallel. Nineteenth-century Cuba experienced an intense slave trafficking that spurred a dizzying growth in the number of slaves. The enslaved population exceeded 400,000 in 1841, more than 40 percent of the island's total (Murray). In Puerto Rico, on the other hand, free peasants made up most of the population throughout the Spanish colonial period, even in times of sugar-slave boom, when slaves never exceeded 12 percent of the population. And, unlike Cuba, the coffee economy flourished in the Puerto Rican mountainous interior during the last third of the nineteenth century, outpacing the coastal sugar complex in value and labor force. As the coffee plantations expanded, small and medium-sized farms owned by Creoles intermixed with large farms owned by a preponderance of Majorcans and Corsicans (Bergad).

The cultural and political contrasts between the two island nations are also very stark. Luis Martínez-Fernández and Salvador Arana Soto rightly argue that the character of Puerto Ricans and Cubans, especially in terms of political culture and behavior, could not differ more. The first author includes the Dominican Republic in a comparative study of political cultures, arguing that the three island nations show "remarkably disparate trajectories" mainly due to the historical divergences of the nineteenth century that placed them on "markedly dissimilar paths that produced different political models and political struggles" (Martínez-Fernández 9, 10). The second author writes in the early 1960s, just as the revolutionary process began in Cuba and ten years after the inauguration of Commonwealth status (Estado Libre Asociado, in Spanish) in Puerto Rico. He affirms from that vantage point that the metaphor of the "two wings of a bird," despite its popularity among Puerto Ricans (mainly independence supporters), was "far from" applicable to a scenario in which one nation began a socialist revolutionary experiment, while the other was at the cusp of a fleetingly successful paradigm of colonial capitalism (Arana Soto).

In short, some scholars have stated that the histories, societies, cultures, and politics of Cuba and Puerto Rico may be inherently dissimilar, largely because the subordination of the islands to two successive empires did not engender equivalent social structures or political cultures. And because different mentalities, sensibilities, and institutions germinated in them,

Cuban and Puerto Rican cultures would never be as parallel or even as similar as Rodríguez de Tió claimed amid the personal and political turmoil that led her to write her famous verses.

This, at least, is alleged by those who prefer to accentuate the differences between the two Hispanic Antilles. For them, with the possible exception of Arana Soto, who incorporated in his criticism of the bird and its two wings the convulsed Cuban Revolution and the recently launched Puerto Rican Free Associated State, the history of both nations before 1950 is reason enough for denial. About the Cuban–Puerto Rican comparison in the second half of the twentieth century and the first decade of the twenty-first, what remains to be said but that repetition was implausible? If Cuba had a socialist-nationalist revolution, which made it a society of tight institutional, political, and personal frameworks, with an autocratic government, increasingly on the defensive, and in Puerto Rico the colonial situation deepened despite the creation of feeble institutions of self-government and liberal-democratic political practices, absent true decolonization, what chances of flight would such disparate two wings bring to the ill-fated bird?

I would like to revisit the Cuban–Puerto Rican comparison to underline the convergences and similarities between these two nations, even in very recent times. Not to assume an uncompromising position—to affirm or deny the historical-cultural parallel, as most authors have—but to deny it in affirmation and affirm it in denial; that is, to underscore repeated experiences, historical convergences, and unusual similarities, even in very recent times, while pointing out the profound and unavoidable differences.

I am interested in identifying in the last half of the twentieth century some trends that illuminate the repetitiveness about which Benítez Rojo so eloquently wrote. Similarities or differences cannot be taken at face value or in the abstract, but must be placed in specific global, regional, and local—that is, historical—contexts. Such contextual specificity reveals the logic behind mechanisms of cultural production and agency that appear to work in concert even as they imprint historical processes with their uniqueness.

The Frost of the Cold War

The context I will focus on is the Cold War (1945–91), when, in Braudelian terms, historical time accelerated and a juncture of global conflict opened with unsuspected projections and consequences (Braudel). This contest between East and West turned Cuba and Puerto Rico into models or paradigms of two systems in voracious planetary struggle and, in due course, created *the illusion* of a permanent deviation of two histories that until then had appeared parallel. In the midst of the Cold War, in the 1960s and 1970s, to observe closely the situation of the two countries was to recognize, painfully, the extent to which the war context had thwarted the dreams of integration expressed by José Martí and Francisco "Pachín" Marín from New York during a period of insurgent optimism, a feeling expressed in the paired flags of inverted colors of the two countries (Díaz Quiñones; Lomas).

Anyone who, having lived intensely those moments of ideological warfare, set their eyes on both nations, will remember the irreconcilable contrast between them. In Cuba, many of those who expressed their solidarity with Puerto Rico did so in condemnation of a Yankee imperialism that, as Fidel Castro proclaimed in 1966, on the occasion of the Cuban delegation's return to the Central American Games held on that sister island, had tried to "destroy Puerto Rican nationalism . . . destroy Puerto Rico's culture, . . . destroy all the characteristics of the Puerto Rican people. And even today, unfortunately, the people of Puerto Rico are not independent: even today Puerto Rico is what is called a Free Associated State, which has nothing free or associated" (Castro Ruz). In Puerto Rico, around the same time public opinion was polarized around revolutionary Cuba, and while some on the right viewed the revolution as little less than the devil's boiler, others on the left proclaimed the patriotic ideal of building "another Cuba." A conservative attitude, however, predominated, tenaciously opposed to Cuban revolutionary processes. Then-Governor Luis Muñoz Marín himself took advantage of every opportunity to proclaim Puerto Rico's "peaceful revolution" an antithesis of that which unfolded hundreds of miles to the west of his island.

This evident Antillean Manicheanism from the 1960s to the 1980s had deep roots in economic, social, and political phenomena—but most of all, I would like to suggest here, in *political ideological* ones stemming from the Cold War. I mean that *formally political* processes—on the one hand, the intense Puerto Rican bipartisanship around the status issue, within a liberal-electoral framework and a prevalent attitude of accommodation to the U.S. metropole; and, on the other hand, the authoritarian Cuban one-party system in the service of a socialism understood now, above all, as a state monopoly—rang very different notes. The dense frost produced by the Cold War, which distorted everything, disguised socioeconomic and cultural practices, processes, and structures of surprising parallelism. There was a vital connection between them, especially if seen in a comprehensive optics and in the medium-term *duration* (the conjunctural historical time) conceived by Fernand Braudel.

How can we sustain the idea that Puerto Rican colonial capitalism and Cuban bureaucratic socialism were not so far away from each other, despite everything? We must begin this seemingly counterintuitive exercise by noting an essential fact: many of the differences exhibited after 1959 had existed before. As far as political economy is concerned, the two societies had been diverging since the end of World War II and what the Cuban Revolution did, if anything, was to widen a preexisting gap. Import substitution industrialization (ISI), to which many countries, especially Latin American countries, were driven during World War II and later years, was prolonged and expanded in the early years of the Revolution. In Puerto Rico, which also had a brief period of ISI, a new development model was imposed, precisely in 1947. Unusual at first, the blueprint would be copied in Asia and Latin America in the decades to come. It consisted of industrialization by invitation, or offshore export manufacturing, a paradigm that, in a somewhat amended version, suggested the *maquiladoras* of later times (Ward and Devereux; Dietz, *Economic History*). At some point during the 1940s, then, the economies of the two Caribbean nations had begun to diverge.

But how significant and real was this divergence, especially if observed in a broader time frame? Operation Bootstrap (Manos a la Obra, in Spanish), a model of industrialization based on generous concessions to foreign capital, increasingly turned Puerto Rico into an economy that produced what it did not consume and consumed what it did not produce. It was a kind of plantation economy for late modernity, which instead of sugar and molasses produced clothing, shoes, and electronic components. Increasingly integrated into the metropolitan economic area and with a migration deficit of almost a third of its population in a span of just two decades between the 1940s and 1960s, the Puerto Rican national economy was modernized and consumption increased in great strides. Meanwhile, the agricultural sphere shrank quite drastically (Dietz, *Puerto Rico*). In contrast, in Cuba after 1959, at least for a few years, the country continued to pursue ISI while promoting domestic consumption at the expense of savings (as in Puerto Rico, where savings rates were negative throughout the period) (Mesa-Lago). In the first revolutionary five-year period, the Cuban economy took a turn toward industrialization to meet internal needs and, at the same time, toward strict statization, allowing the State to distribute more resources to the population than before. Conveniently for redistributive projects, a large share of the wealthiest Cubans emigrated. The professional sectors followed them into exile, leaving behind goods and bank accounts readily disposable by the State.

In the mid-1960s, however, both models began to falter. Or more than faltering, they went into crisis. The Puerto Rican model failed because it had been imitated in other countries where labor was cheaper and the Cuban model failed because, in addition to the U.S. blockade, the search for ISI along with policies of extreme government control were unsustainable in the medium and long term. It is perhaps odd that at this crossroads two seemingly different economies, framed in deeply dissimilar political systems, ended up, at approximately the same juncture, seeking formally equivalent "solutions": deepening their dependence on metropolitan subsidies and, based on them, sustaining the second phase of their economic growth during the Cold War.

In the Puerto Rican case, this phase (1965–1982) involved the forging of a heavy industrial sector (led by transnational companies, manufacturing pharmaceutical, electronic, and other products), which expanded foreign control over the economy, and the development of consumption levels for the most affluent classes and even for a rising American-style "middle class." The unequal distribution of income, however, guaranteed the perpetuation of a large sector of the population mired in poverty. Although this sector was now defined by the loosest criteria used by the U.S. government, its indigence remained a scourge on the social body and on the very model of colonial capitalist development. Its poverty was what some call "dichotomic": more noticeable and disparate the more it clashes with rising levels of consumption by the new middle and affluent classes. One fact is disturbingly revealing: at the beginning of the federal (U.S.) food stamp program in 1976, two-thirds of Puerto Rican families qualified to receive them.

Meanwhile, Cuba would see, albeit to a much lesser degree than Puerto Rico, a wavering yet gradual rise in living standards (until the late 1980s) within a system that distributed social wealth equitably—more than any other country in the world, some economists argue—but strictly limited consumption and insufferably reduced the scope of individual decisions, all framed in a political economy that directed a significant portion of the social product toward the military establishment. Cuban economic stabilization was part of a deepening of the formal ties between that nation and those of the Soviet-led Eastern Bloc, a relationship that perhaps alleviated the most extreme misery but did not solve the problem of external dependence and more likely than not aggravated it. The agricultural sector maintained an important role, so Cuba had a much greater balance than Puerto Rico between the different constituent sectors of the economy and the workforce. Interestingly, throughout the 1960s and 1970s the State was the fastest-growing employer in both countries (Ibarra and Máttar).

Thus, in the 1970s, at uncertain times in the Cold War, both Caribbean nations seemed formally, structurally similar, but politically disparate. With growing populations of migrants in the United States, both Cuba and Puerto Rico appeared to stabilize economically and socially at the expense of higher levels of external dependence than ever before.[1] Two poles emerged in the debates of that period, one that condemned Puerto Rico's colonial status and another that excoriated the new colonial dependence lived in Cuba. Truths, exaggerations, and falsehoods populated both camps. Those who saw polarization as a product of a planetary contest—part of a struggle for hegemony, not within a nation but globally—fully understood the rules of the game. The Cold War turned these Caribbean nations into showcases of capitalism and socialism for poor countries, models of consumer society, on the one hand, and a classless society, on the other. Neither of the two monikers captured the complex realities in progress and in this, as in economic ups and downs, parallels and coincidences were significant.

Although quite distinct in terms of human hardship, the rows of food stamps in Puerto Rico and the rationing queues in Cuba (more ubiquitous and sadder than the former, no doubt), answered to a similar logic. Again, they did not *mean* the same nor were they internalized and suffered equally, because in their effect on the scope of action and the possibilities of individual freedom, these two systems of food distribution were almost the inverse of each other. The Cuban system severely restricted individual initiative, while the Puerto Rican one often multiplied the chances of deciding what, when, and how to consume. More importantly, the Cuban case emblematized the reduction in food consumption by the population and in the quality of food products, whereas the Puerto Rican case had an opposite effect. In both cases, however, large sections of the population exacerbated their dependence on, and subordination to, the functions of the State. Although in Puerto Rico the framework of State operation was much smaller than in Cuba, under Puerto Rican populism (1940–68) bureaucratic and semi-State operations experienced such a pace of growth that at the height of the 1960s and 1970s they made up the largest source of employment in the country. In the political economy of both nations, therefore, the State occupied a key space.

By virtue of their historic struggle, the two irreducible ways of understanding freedom in the twentieth century had sought to turn Puerto Ricans and Cubans into pieces on a world chess board—stellar protagonists of the most spectacular world competition of the second half of the century. It would be up to the people themselves, however, through their cultural, intellectual, sporting, and leisure productions to make sense of, and in the end question and contradict, these roles.

These efforts to craft their own destiny evolved with a significant degree of autonomy from the geopolitical game of the moment. Thus, for example, Cubans did not bend to the designs of their powerful neighbor to the north, which constantly harassed the island, and at the same time refused to Sovietize beyond appearances. Puerto Ricans rejected myriad pressures to dilute linguistically and culturally with the metropole, and by the 1970s more than a third of the population of self-described Puerto Ricans resided in the fifty states of the American union. These were by far two of the most significant milestones of resistance in the Hispanic Antilles during the Cold War. To be sure, music and sports were two of the most solid platforms of identity creation and reinforcement, from which Cubans and Puerto Ricans expressed their individuality, their sensibilities anchored in a profound past, and their intention to rearticulate the threads of their parallel histories.

In addition to the economy in its most formal aspects, the other key to the Cuban–Puerto Rican convergence of this period was, therefore, culture. I cannot in this essay analyze all the ways in which cultural and identity production in Cuba and Puerto Rico responded to similar dynamics and logics, even in the years of greatest formal and political divergence. Suffice it to say that in those moments when the Antillean world had become more Manichean under the strictures of the Cold War, the Spanish Caribbean parallel continued to manifest itself in struggle as well as in enjoyment, much as it had for another generation almost a century earlier. One thinks, for example, of the way Cubans and Puerto Ricans converged in the sounds and rhythms of salsa—a syncretism of Afro-Cuban, Afro-Puerto Rican, and African American musical forms—to give the world the most vibrant version of tropical music in the last decades of the twentieth century (Quintero Rivera). Or of the enormous development undertaken in literature and the visual arts, with writers and artists engaged in redefining the canons inherited from the neocolonial era (in Cuba) and classical colonial era (in Puerto Rico).

After 1989, the global conflict of the Cold War receded and so did the spaces of obvious difference between the two Caribbean nations. This is what I call the "reencounter" phase, one that is still ongoing in 2022. More "natural" encounters between Cubans and Puerto Ricans now began to take place, involving individuals, groups, and institutions of improbable prominence during the Cold War years.

The Thaw and Its Effects

What did the twilight of the Cold War bring to the Caribbean's former "model nations"? When the Soviet Union disintegrated and the Eastern Bloc went into eventual disarray, the consequences for Cubans were disastrous. The island nation underwent one of the worst crises in its history; the worst, no doubt, of the twentieth century. While international conditions undermined the pillars on which socialist Cuba had relied for at least two decades, the euphemistically called "Special Period" (1991–95) shook up the certainties of Cuban socialism and launched a radical reexamination of some of its core principles of social organization, such as social and racial parity. Cuba underwent a phase of sudden and profound changes in all orders. The initial economic dislocations generated sharp and long-lasting repercussions in all facets of life (Hernández-Reguant).

In Puerto Rico, by contrast, the end of the Cold War did not provoke readjustments so sudden and profound, although the reduced paradigmatic value of Commonwealth status eventually produced, in the medium and longer term, historically transformative results. The United States gradually dismantled its military facilities on the island, which lost value in its strategic plans for the Caribbean. The successful fight to forbid the U.S. Navy's use of the embattled Puerto Rican island of Vieques for naval exercises and target practice was a turning point, whose significance only became clear a couple of decades later. A ceasefire at the island's firing range in 2003 was immediately followed by the closure of the nearby Roosevelt Roads naval station (2004), one of the largest U.S. naval bases outside the North American continent. With it, the process of strategic redefinition that had been unfolding for decades reached its peak.

Meanwhile, the fiscal conservatism prevailing in the U.S. Congress after 1994 prompted a reconsideration of tax concessions enjoyed by large manufacturing firms installed in Puerto Rico under Section 936 of the federal Internal Revenue Code. Beginning in the 1970s, Section 936 corporations, which were exempt from most federal and Commonwealth taxes on their Puerto Rican earnings, grew to become the backbone of the island's dominant industrial complex. The decision to gradually phase out their tax advantages between 1995 and 2005 jeopardized the Puerto Rican industrial promotion model and eventually prompted many of the advantaged corporations to leave the island. The number of island manufacturing plants declined and wages in that sector took a significant hit (Feliciano and Green). Thus, in the final years of the twentieth century and the early years of the next, as its economic development landscape became unsettled, Puerto Rico lost much of its value as a "showcase of democracy." In the future it would not depend as much as its neighbors (especially Cuba) on tourism or on the expansion of capital-intensive manufacturing to promote growth, as it had between the 1970s and 1990s (Córdova Iturregui).

The reorientation of the Cuban economy mainly toward tourism in mixed-capital enterprises (foreign and State-owned) and, secondly, toward the development of industries based on scientific findings, such as pharmaceuticals and biotechnology, defined a new economic policy juncture. Cuba's transformation into a major tourist destination signaled the abandonment of comprehensive development projects and the commitment of national development to the forces that turn "tropical paradises" into new-type plantations (Patullo). Other changes—the decline of the agricultural sector, especially the sugar industry, dollarization, small business proliferation, a marked reduction in State employment, and many more—also pointed to the economic redefinition of Cuban socialism after 1991, a readjustment that could better accommodate the country to the global capitalist system, paradoxically without requiring the lifting of the U.S. blockade. Recall here what some analysts have noted about U.S.-Cuban relations at this juncture: that beginning in the 1990s, and especially after 2000, the blockade did not prevent Cuba from importing a growing share of its food from its neighbor to the north and that cooperation between the two countries on matters such as immigration and navigation had largely been regularized, despite the absence of formal diplomatic relations between the two countries (until 2015). Paradoxically, the "even colder war" stage between these two countries, which broke out in the 1990s, was accompanied by a series of important bilateral agreements of great economic significance to both sides, but especially to a Cuba that had been blocked off from traditional supply sources of food, medicine, and other essential goods.[2]

The Reencounter

If the collapse of the Soviet world-system marks Fukuyama's wrongly labeled "end of history," it stands to reason that the time would be conducive to Cuban–Puerto Rican convergence (Wallerstein; Fukuyama). And that is precisely what the new global realignment triggered in the once-paradigmatic Caribbean nations. As we have seen, both Caribbean countries revisited tourism as a source of foreign exchange and new jobs. Cuba achieved this adjustment more thoroughly, largely because of the size of its territory, but also because there the policy of tourism development was more aggressive. Biotechnology industries expanded in both islands, a development that relied heavily on the provision of highly trained scientists and workforce, that is, on the fruits of investments made in human capital, through education, during the Cold War. In structural terms, therefore, the parallels between the two countries once again turned out to be more significant than the divergences.

Even in the most difficult years of the Special Period and despite the prohibition on travel to Cuba to which the U.S. government subjected its citizens, including Puerto Ricans, contacts between Cubans and Puerto Ricans not only grew in frequency; they also changed in tone. Absent now were the ideological assessments and conflicting rhetoric that had permeated these contacts during the Cold War. In this new climate, cooperation and friendship were the order of the day. Exchanges between musical and sporting groups were perhaps the most important because they gained instant notoriety with a broad slice of island citizens. Encounters between musicians were particularly impactful because they spread their message through mass media and cultural markets, both within and outside national borders.

The communion between Cuban and Puerto Rican musicians and producers, intense and fruitful, rediscovered and once again exploited the metaphor of the bird and its two wings. Two examples should suffice to calibrate their intent. The first consists of a collaboration of great performers of danceable popular music, an area that has always shown an acute awareness of the Cuban–Puerto Rican parallel. Beginning in 1994, Puerto Rican musicologist Geño Acosta Ithier produced a series of collaborations (*De aquí pa'llá* [1994], *De allá pa'cá* [1996], and *Son de Cuba y Puerto Rico* [2007]) in which famous musicians from both nations performed the genres and songs that best united them: classics from the dance repertoires and the golden eras of the *son*, bolero, salsa, and Latin jazz. The "here" (Puerto

Rico) and the "there" (Cuba) of this dyad were clearly defined; it was undoubtedly a Puerto Rican initiative. On the first of the albums, musicians from Puerto Rico performed the Cuban repertoire. In the second, Cuban artists reciprocated the gesture, performing the Puerto Rican repertoire. However, despite the clarity of their underlying motives, the titles of the albums were purposefully ambiguous, allowing listeners to conceive of the intended convergence of cultural identities. The title *Son de Cuba y Puerto Rico* refers to the rhythmic *son* that links the best-known danceable genres of both nations, but also evokes the phrase "Cuba and Puerto Rico *son*" (are), the opening line in Rodríguez de Tió's poem.

In an interview with journalist Jaime Torres Torres, Acosta Ithier revealed what he understood as the essence of his project and left no doubt that his intentions were to rearticulate the two nations through music. The promoter's passion for the creative genius of both countries still provoked what the journalist understood as a possible suspension of nationality and cultural self for the sake of a common identity: "I have never mixed music with politics, but politicians can learn a lot from us because of the brotherhood that exists among musicians," Acosta Ithier said. The journalist added: "His pride in Caribbean music is so great that sometimes it is not easy to distinguish whether Geño Acosta is Cuban or Puerto Rican" (Torres Torres). If integration was now the objective, then the recording project, as a cultural production, had made its creator the person, no matter what nation he came from, who through the effort to integrate managed to disguise, yet not completely erase, his national identity.

The second example came from a new cultural register: Latin hip hop. In 2006, Melisa Rivière, then a doctoral student of anthropology at the University of Minnesota, directed and produced a collaboration by Puerto Rican *reggaetonero* Tego Calderón and the Cuban hip hop group Anónimo Consejo. The leitmotif of the album, entitled *Son dos alas: Anónimo Consejo Featuring Tego Calderón*, is the usual one, but the metaphor now serves to entwine the two Caribbean nations, not because of their shared sensibilities, but because of the racism practiced in both places against Blacks and their resistance to their marginalization. The exchange between Cubans and Puerto Ricans described a shared exclusion; the challenge to both societies was now set in motion.[3]

In this moment of reencounter, therefore, when the Cold War no longer distorted motives and upset meanings, issues such as shared racism would be approached directly. Not only had the perennial "cultural integration" been revealed openly, but also the shared conflict, the result of parallel, confluent, but at the same time unique histories. The uncovering had only been possible in the post–Cold War era. The icy planetary conflict that for almost half a century disguised the similarities, both structural and cultural, between Cuba and Puerto Rico had been superseded. In this new awareness of the repetitiveness of experiences and expressions, it would be possible to capture, once again—thanks to the clarity of the optics that had allowed the temporary distraction of empires—the interplay of external forces and the "local possibilities of innovation and adaptation" which, according to Jean Benoist, are necessary counterpoints in Caribbean history (Benoist 78).

Notes

This chapter is a translated version, with minor changes, from Scarano, "Epílogo: ¿Una isla que se repite?" Translated by Jorge Duany.

1. It is interesting to observe that these "external communities" of Cubans and Puerto Ricans in the United States, which in the beginning were very different, over time acquired somewhat analogous profiles. As more immigrants arrived, the parallel became clearer. On the one hand, the Cuban immigrant community, which originally was essentially upper and middle class, with a high proportion of White people, became more representative of island society, both in terms of class and race. On the other hand, as a result of a growing number of professionals and other members of the middle and upper classes, especially in the 1970s and thereafter, Puerto Rican communities in the United States also became more representative of the socioeconomic and racial profile of the sending society.

2. In 2000, Cuba was the 200th market for U.S. food imports in the world. Four years later, after receiving $400 million in supplies in a year, the island had risen to number twenty-five on the list. In 2005 and 2006, this amount was reduced to $350 million and $340 million, respectively, and, in the second of these years, Cuba finished thirty-fourth among importers of U.S. agricultural products. U.S.-Cuba Trade and Economic Council (http://cubatrade.org).

3. Tego Calderón Featuring Anónimo Consejo, *Son dos alas*, https://www.youtube.com/watch?v=EnYAhrOKWJA, accessed 15 Oct. 2020.

Works Cited

Arana Soto, Salvador. *Cuba y Puerto Rico no son: O, la enfermedad de Cuba*. Luis D. Paret, 1963.

Arroyo-Martínez, Jossianna. "Betances, Haití y la Confederación Antillana (Parte II)." *8ogrados*, 26 Aug. 2018, https://www.8ogrados.net/betances-haiti-y-la-confederacion-antillana-parte-ii/. Accessed 15 Oct. 2020.

Benítez Rojo, Antonio. *The Repeating Island: The Caribbean and the Postmodern Perspective*. Translated by James E. Maraniss. Duke UP, 1989.
Benoist, Jean. "La organización social de las Antillas." *África en América Latina*, edited by Manuel Moreno Fraginals. Siglo XXI, 1985, pp. 77–102.
Bergad, Laird W. "¿Dos alas del mismo pájaro? Notas sobre la historia socioeconómica comparativa de Cuba y Puerto Rico." *Historia y Sociedad*, vol. 1, 1988, pp. 143–53.
Braudel, Fernand. *La historia y las ciencias sociales*. Alianza, 1974.
Castro Ruz, Fidel. "Discurso pronunciado por el comandante Fidel Castro Ruz, Primer Secretario del Comité Central del Partido Comunista de Cuba y Primer Ministro del Gobierno Revolucionario, en el resumen del Acto de Bienvenida a la delegación deportiva cubana que asistió a los X Juegos Centroamericanos y del Caribe, celebrado en el Estadio Latinoamericano el 29 de junio de 1966," 1966, http://www.cuba.cu/gobierno/discursos/1966/esp/f290666e.html. Accessed 15 Oct. 2020.
Chinea, Jorge L. "A Quest for Freedom: The Immigration of Maritime Maroons into Puerto Rico, 1656–1800." *Journal of Caribbean History*, vol. 31, nos. 1–2, 1997, pp. 51–87.
Córdova Iturregui, Félix. *La eliminación de la sección 936: La historia que se intenta suprimir*. Gaviota, 2020.
Dietz, James L. *Economic History of Puerto Rico: Institutional Change and Capitalist Development*. Princeton UP, 1986.
———. *Puerto Rico: Negotiating Development and Change*. Lynne Rienner, 2003.
Díaz Quiñones, Arcadio. *Sobre los principios: Los intelectuales caribeños y la tradición*. Colección Intersecciones. Universidad Nacional de Quilmes Editorial, 2006.
Feliciano, Zaida M., and Andrew Green. "US Multinationals in Puerto Rico and the Repeal of Section 936 Tax Exemption for U.S. Corporations." National Bureau of Economic Research, NBER Working Paper Series, Working Paper 23681, 2016. http://www.nber.org/papers/w23681. Accessed 17 Oct. 2020.
Fukuyama, Francis. *The End of History and the Last Man*. Free P, 1992.
Gaztambide, Antonio. "La invención del Caribe en el siglo XX: Las definiciones del Caribe como problema histórico y metodológico." *Revista Mexicana del Caribe*, vol. 1, 1996, pp. 74–96.
Hernández-Reguant, Ariana, editor. *Cuba in the Special Period: Culture and Ideology in the 1990s*. Palgrave Macmillan, 2009.
Ibarra, David, and Jorge Máttar. "The Cuban Economy." *CEPAL Review*, no. 66, 1998, pp. 29–37.
Lomas, Laura. "'El negro es tan capaz como el blanco': José Martí, 'Pachín' Marín, Lucy Parsons, and the Politics of Nineteenth-Century Latinidad." *The Latino Nineteenth Century*, edited by Rodrigo Lazo and Jesse Alemán. New York UP, 2016, pp. 301–22.
Martínez-Fernández, Luis. "Political Culture in the Hispanic Caribbean and the Building of U.S. Hegemony, 1868–1945." *Revista Mexicana del Caribe*, vol. 6, no. 11, 2001, pp. 7–55.
Martínez-San Miguel, Yolanda. *Coloniality of Diasporas: Rethinking Intra-Colonial Migrations in a Pan-Caribbean Context*. New Caribbean Studies. Palgrave Macmillan, 2014.
Mesa-Lago, Carmelo. "The Economy and International Economic Relations." *Cuba in*

the World, edited by Cole Blasier and Carmelo Mesa-Lago. U of Pittsburgh P, 1979, pp. 169–98.

Mintz, Sidney W. "The Caribbean as a Socio-Cultural Area." *Journal of World History*, vol. 9, no. 4, 1966, pp. 912–37.

Murray, D.R. "Statistics of the Slave Trade in Cuba, 1790–1867." *Journal of Latin American Studies*, vol. 3, no. 2, 1971, pp. 131–49.

Patullo, Polly. *Last Resorts: The Cost of Tourism in the Caribbean*. 2nd ed. Monthly Review P, 2005.

Quintero Rivera, Ángel G. *La danza de la insurrección: Para una sociología de la música latinoamericana. Textos reunidos de Ángel G. Quintero Rivera*. CLACSO, 2020.

Rodríguez de Tió, Lola. "A Cuba." *Mi libro de Cuba*. Imprenta La Moderna, 1893, pp. 3–6.

Scarano, Francisco A. "Epílogo: ¿Una isla que se repite? Contrapuntos cubano-puertorriqueños entre la Guerra Fría y el reencuentro." *Cuba: Contrapuntos de cultura, historia y sociedad/Cuba: Counterpoints on Culture, History, and Society*, edited by Francisco A. Scarano and Margarita Zamora. Callejón, 2007, pp. 385–402.

Sheller, Mimi. *Consuming the Caribbean: From Arawaks to Zombies*. Routledge, 2003.

Thorning, Joseph F. "The American Mediterranean." *World Affairs*, vol. 120, no. 2, 1957, pp. 46–48.

Torres Torres, Jaime. "Une lo mejor de Cuba y Puerto Rico." *El Nuevo Día*, 1 Apr. 2007.

Wallerstein, Immanuel. *World-Systems Analysis: An Introduction*. Duke UP, 2004.

Ward, Marianne, and John Devereux. "The Road Not Taken: Cuban Pre-Revolutionary Living Standards in Comparative Perspective." *The Journal of Economic History*, vol. 72, no. 1, 2012, pp. 104–32.

4

Local Eyes into Caribbean Rural Life
Anthropological Informants in Cuba and Puerto Rico in the Post–World War II Era

JORGE L. GIOVANNETTI-TORRES

Hoy tengo poco de qué escribir, tengo que hacerlo, pero no tengo suficientes datos para hacerlo, así que tengo que tratar de hacerlo sin posibilidades de cubrir el trabajo de tres hojas[,] o páginas, mejor dicho.
(Today I have little to write, I have to do it, but I do not have enough data to do it, so I must try to do it without the possibility of covering the work of three sheets, or better said, pages.)
Juan Manuel Picabea y Niebla, 12 August 1949

Sid me dices que estas preparando unos datos sobre Jauca[.]
Me alegro mucho que en esta obra yo ayude en algo.
(Sid you tell me that you are preparing some data about Jauca[.] I am very happy that in that work, I help in some way.)
Anastacio (Eustaquio) Zayas Alvarado, 1 May 1950

I begin with two statements from the Other; or rather, from two local members of Caribbean societies studied by U.S. anthropologists. In both cases, the individuals address the foreign ethnographer; the first is a written report and the second a letter. It transpires from their statements that these locals were not just passive Others answering a questionnaire or being observed in the field. They were conscious contributors to the anthropological enterprise.

Juan Manuel Picabea y Niebla, also known as Manolo, was the informant and assistant to Carl Withers, a barely known anthropologist who did fieldwork in the town of Mayajigua in the Cuban province of Sancti Spiritus between January and August 1948 (Giovannetti, "An Unfinished"). Anastacio (Eustaquio) Zayas Alvarado, known as don Taso, was the key Puerto

Rican informant to the well-known Sidney W. Mintz during his first fieldwork in Puerto Rico between March 1948 and August 1949, from where both started a collaboration and friendship that later resulted in Taso's life history, *Worker in the Cane* (Mintz). In the epigraphs, at one end of the anthropological enterprise, Manolo is under pressure and laments not having enough data to produce three pages of fieldnotes aimed at contributing to Withers' rural community study. At the other end, Taso's letter recognizes the processing of data about his town and expresses pride about the role he played in what will be the final written product (the *obra* or work), Mintz's Ph.D. dissertation and eventual chapter in *The People of Puerto Rico* (Steward et al.).

The voices of informants and intermediaries such as Manolo or Taso often remain silenced in the ethnographies they facilitate and the publications they "help" to produce. This may happen for reasons ranging from ethics and Institutional Review Board considerations to disciplinary culture and the aims and whims of the anthropologists as authors. Taso himself is perhaps one of the few exceptions in Caribbean anthropology where the informant's voice took center stage. But this was only after Mintz produced the community study of Barrio Jauca in Santa Isabel, Puerto Rico, for his degree (Mintz, "Cañamelar") and subsequent circumstances led him to work toward Taso's life history. But overall, other than Taso, and more recently, the Saamaka healer Tooy (Price), Caribbean informants and community intermediaries (or gatekeepers) are rarely center staged in the final anthropological product.[1] This happens in spite of their role facilitating numerous studies within the exponential growth in U.S. anthropological interest in the region over the last seventy-five years. We might as well ask whether many of the ethnographies about the Caribbean that we read would be different, or if they would even exist, without locals helping the foreigners or providing them with access to ground information.

This chapter prioritizes the voices of two Caribbean informants from Cuba and Puerto Rico with two modest objectives that hopefully can open windows into future research. First, I will mine the sources available through which the views and ideas of these informants emerge, muting or bypassing the anthropologists, attempting to get as close as possible to a local grassroots appraisal of their respective rural worlds. Second, I will trace a counterpoint between various themes and issues in both places as expressed by the informants, teasing a comparative discussion about rural life and culture in two countries with similar trajectories and on the verge of dramatic social and historical changes.

In the late 1940s and early 1950s, both Cuba and Puerto Rico were about to take almost opposite sociopolitical directions. The dictatorship of Fulgencio Batista in Cuba (1952–58) created the conditions for a revolutionary movement that would transform that nation and lead to a rupture with the United States. In Puerto Rico, the consolidation of the Popular Democratic Party and Operation Bootstrap—the government-led industrialization program—altered the island's economy and society and increased the entanglement with the northern neighbor. In each of these contexts, Manolo and Taso can provide insights into the social life of rural areas *before major change*, when Cuba and Puerto Rico were under seemingly stable and similar conditions. The remnants of Spanish colonialism, after 1898 both islands endured U.S. intervention and insertion in their economic and political sphere, were exploited under the early twentieth-century heyday of sugar cultivation and dumped during the Great Depression but kept at arm's reach as neocolonial and colonial outposts during World War II. The timespan of the materials produced by these two informants covers the postwar years, during a time of transition, shedding light into how this was experienced from below.

From an anthropological standpoint, there are certainly disciplinary considerations about the analytical exercise performed below, and the sources used: questions on the history of fieldwork in the Caribbean; dilemmas on the relations between ethnographer and informant; issues on ethnographic authority or anthropological writing. I recognize these issues and their importance.[2] But to focus on the Cuban and Puerto Rican counterpoint that aligns with this book's main theme, I will only be able to provide basic background information about the anthropological encounters that make my exercise possible. Then I will move to a counterpoint between Manolo and Taso on specific themes, including gender relations, sexuality, masculinity, sex work, health and medicine, and the popular understandings around these matters.

The Informants and the Stories They Leave

As I noted above, one of the informants included in this article is well known, at least within Caribbean anthropology, for his collaboration was with no other than Sidney W. Mintz, who became a leading scholar in the field. Don Taso was Mintz's principal collaborator in Barrio Jauca of Santa Isabel, his southern coast field site for "The Puerto Rico Project" organized from Columbia University by Julian Steward in the 1940s.[3] After Mintz's fieldwork turned into a Ph.D. dissertation and was in the process of publication as a book chapter, he and Taso remained in contact and Taso's conversion to Pentecostalism triggered Mintz's interest to work on his friend's life history during the 1950s. The second informant, from Cuba, was Juan Manuel Picabea y Niebla, or Manolo. He is essentially unknown and was once dubbed a "Cuban nobody."[4] Manolo was the main collaborator of Carl Withers, who was also unknown for several reasons, including that his first community study titled *Plainville, U.S.A.* was written under a pseudonym (West). Like Mintz, Withers had studied anthropology at Columbia University, but never finished the Ph.D. That did not stop him from anthropological pursuits, including a proposal to do a community study in Cuba that ended up being his fieldwork in Mayajigua, which led to meeting Manolo there (Giovannetti, "An Unfinished" 204–5).

While Taso's insights emerge from his long interviews and the published life history in English and its Spanish translation, Manolo's views come mostly out of the daily reports to Withers. These accumulated reports from April 1948 to August 1951 became "The Manolo Manuscript," a total of 1,515 single-spaced typewritten pages of daily events, chronicles, tales, and other musings by its author (Brown and Giovannetti 181–84). In other words, Taso's account of rural Puerto Rico is an oral one published by Mintz, while Manolo's is a written and unpublished one handed to Withers. We do have written materials from Taso, in the way of sixty letters he wrote to Mintz between 1950 and 1958, mostly personal in nature, but providing some insight into 1950s Puerto Rico.[5] One consequence of the nature of their respective accounts is that Taso's is more one-dimensional, from him, outward, about his environment, or addressed to Mintz as his interlocutor. Manolo's account has some multidimensionality, as he reports things others experienced and things that were told to him in Mayajigua and other rural locations. His reports tell us about events and his views about them, while he uses the opportunity to insert some autobiographical and personal stories.

Other important differences should be noted at the outset. Mintz met Taso as he was pursuing his Ph.D. from Columbia in the 1940s, and Withers met Manolo after *not* obtaining his Ph.D. from Columbia. The informants and the anthropologists also show an inverse age difference. While Taso was in his forties when he started to collaborate with Mintz (in his twenties), Manolo was in his twenties, when he began working for Withers (in his forties). Here, collaboration and work are important distinctions in the two cases, since Manolo received payment for his reports. The informants' class background and labor experiences were also different, with Taso being a laborer in the sugar industry and Manolo doing errands for his father, working in clerical jobs, and writing for *El Mundo* newspaper. Taso's oral history is accompanied by that of his wife, Elisabeth, whose own version of events was also recorded by Mintz. Manolo's written accounts, on the other hand, transcribed what other friends told him.

These precisions are important considerations methodologically, as one approaches the sources left by these informants to reach an understanding of the historical period I want to examine. This became more evident to me as this essay took shape, and while I do not neglect the methodological considerations that can generate plenty of intellectual discussion (or a different article), I want to put them aside in the interest of focusing on life in rural areas of agricultural production in both Cuba and Puerto Rico. This comparative look from below, I insist, adds to our understanding of the Hispanic Caribbean in the mid-twentieth century and the sociocultural transformations that followed.

One final note on the "selection" of protagonists for this essay and the sources used, which is as personal as it is important. I am Puerto Rican, but it is only recently that I have given some research attention to my country of birth, after studying other Caribbean territories, especially Cuba for several years. Having said that, to study social sciences in Puerto Rico (which is different from being a specialist on Puerto Rico) meant becoming familiar with Taso's life history. The comparison that follows probably emerged only because by the time I encountered the "Manolo Manuscript" years ago, elements of Taso's history were immediately retrieved from my mind. A hypothetical opposite history would probably generate an equivalent affinity if a scholar of Cuba familiar with Manolo's writings suddenly read *Worker in the Cane* (Mintz). That would happen precisely because of the significant commonalities and parallels that I believe exist in the two cases, the ones that made possible the comparative and sequentially related vignettes that follow. Hopefully, this essay will encourage similar research exercises by scholars interested in Cuban and Puerto Rican rural life and culture.

Taso and Manolo: A Counterpoint

One of the captivating aspects of reading Taso's life history in the 1990s, as I did the first time as an undergraduate student, was learning about the stories of elopement and relations with the opposite sex in Puerto Rico during the mid-twentieth century. Therefore, in 2007, when I read Manolo's reports on these topics for the same historical period, but in a different Hispanic Caribbean country, it sparked my (comparative) curiosity.

One initial story in the case of Puerto Rico is the elopement of Taso's sister, Tomasa. Taso narrated that a general understanding was that "by eight-thirty or nine [in the evening] a girl had to be in her house—if from then on she didn't appear, she had probably eloped with her sweetheart" (Mintz, *Worker* 46). The practice was well known in rural Puerto Rico during the early twentieth century and while the way the girl's nocturnal absence was interpreted was changing at the time of the interview with Mintz, the dilemmas to the family could be many. For example, in the context of discussing jealousy from his wife, Elisabeth (or doña Elí), Taso mentioned that "there are so many cases in which a man has carried off a girl, and for whatever reason they haven't made him marry her. And after a while he carries off another girl, and then they make him marry that one, and then this one here is left" (Mintz, *Worker* 103). Doña Elí had her own take on the practice of elopement. "Because here," she said, "they have the custom that when a youth carries off a señorita, he has to carry her far, far from her family, because he is stealing her, he is a fugitive" (Mintz, *Worker* 107). If the man was marked as a "fugitive," the elopement also marked the woman as "ruined" or *dañada* (Mintz, *Worker* 93).

In Cuba, the characterization of women was similar. According to Manolo's report for 17 September 1949, an unmarried woman presumed to have had a sexual encounter was perceived as "useless" or *echada a perder*, or spoiled (Picabea, "Manuscript" 1236). Manolo used the word *rapto* (literally abduction) for elopement when writing about a couple whose sexual desires were too strong to wait until marriage. Since they had already rented and furnished their future home, they went there and "el hecho de RAPTO ocurrió precisamente como a las tres de la tarde y todavía al otro día por la tarde, no había *resollado* ninguno de ellos, con lo que quiero decir que no habían tenido noticias de ninguno, que habían mantenido la casa cerrada y ellos acostados" ("the ABDUCTION happened just around three in the afternoon and still the next day in the afternoon, none of them had shown signs of life, meaning that there was no news about any of them, they had kept the house locked and remained lying down") (Picabea, "Manuscript" 1104).

The report emphasizes that the couple was beyond the family's surveillance (the lack of "news" about the couple) as sufficient for the presumption that they had sexual intercourse. Using hearsay in the town, Manolo's reporting on the event acquired a more scandalous character when he described the sexual encounter as an "excessive" one produced by "enormous heat" that neither she nor he could control (Picabea, "Manuscript" 1104). The excessive time presumably engaged in sexual intercourse was such, according to the stories collected by Manolo, that it triggered comparison of the man with the Carey turtle (*Eretmochelys*) for its endurance in the mating ritual (Picabea, "Manuscript" 1104–5).

In the Puerto Rican countryside, the connection between wildlife and sexual behavior was also present. Taso's response when asked how men knew what they were supposed to do with women was that it "could be from watching the animals, or whatever" (Mintz, *Worker* 78). "That is something so common here; it's a thing a child is accustomed to seeing," he responded when pressed about his experience. But in Cuba, the connection between sex and wildlife apparently went beyond watching if we read the written reports from Mayajigua. On 6 June 1949, Manolo documented an anecdote about a man bitten by a mare: "Parece que como [es]to e[s] tan corriente en Mayajigua, donde muchos, gran numero de jovenes y de hombres sostienen y han sostenido relaciones sexuales con las lleguas [*sic*], el hombre pudo pensar que el viejo trato de hacerlo y que la llegua se viro y lo mordió" ("It seems that because this is so common in Mayajigua, where many, a great number of youngsters and men have or have had sexual relations with mares, the man [telling the anecdote] may have thought that the old man tried to do it and the mare turned around and bit him") (Picabea, "Manuscript" 1094).

In subsequent reports of November 1949, Manolo wrote about this practice of satisfying sexual impulses with mares, in a story of some young friends he encountered who told him that they were going to *pizar lleguas por ahí* (literally, "step on mares out there"). Upon discussing the specific mares to be chosen for the deed, one belonging to a certain Mr. "Cabreales" was discarded because, according to one of them, *esa llegua tira muchas patadas* ("that mare throws many kicks"). Other criteria included fear of guards (vigilantes) because if found, that would imply *un rollo*, or a problem (Picabea, "Manuscript" 1400).

Since "our business," Manolo wrote, "is to inquire about everything," he kept asking his friends more details about these sexual practices with animals, including people's concerns of being discovered. When noting that it would be "ugly" if someone sees them, one of the youngsters stated that it was preferable to "run in order not to be seen." Another friend who was nearly caught in the act stated that "for him" it would be "bochornoso que un hombre mayor, que una persona mayor o un hombre que tuviese hijas, lo encontrase pisando lleguas y que por eso corrió" ("embarrassing that an older man, an old person, or a man who had daughters, found him stepping mares and for that reason ran away"). The specific concern of being discovered by an "older man" or a "man who had daughters" was related to the implications that such a "repugnant" act would have if the young man ever wanted to address the older man as the potential suitor for his daughter (Picabea, "Manuscript" 1401).[6]

In his writing, Manolo shared some thoughts about why these *aventuras amorosas con lleguas* (literally, "love adventures with mares") were taking place (Picabea, "Manuscript" 1402), which allows me to move to another important topic that emerges in the two Hispanic Caribbean rural settings. Manolo concluded: "Es posible que el motivo de que ocurran estas cosas tan inmorales en Mayajigua, pudiera deberse al hecho de que no hay casas de mujeres públicas, (de putas), que pudieran ser[v]irles de [h]embra a esos individuos solteros que actualmente tienen que utilizar los animales [h]embras" ("It is possible that the motive for the occurrence of things that are so immoral in Mayajigua, may be because of the fact that there are no houses of public women [of whores], who could serve as females to these single individuals who currently have to use female animals" (Picabea, "Manuscript" 1403). Setting the animal connection aside, despite the absence of a specific "house for public women," other reports by Manolo indicate that sex work was common in Mayajigua. It was common as well in rural Puerto Rico, as Taso's account indicates. A discussion about how "the most ancient profession in the world" was practiced in the Hispanic Caribbean countryside becomes inevitable in any reading of the two local accounts considered here.

In the case of Jauca, we learn that for Taso and other adolescents, their first sexual experience was often with sex workers. When asked about the moment when he did more than kissing with a woman, he said: "That type of woman. I was working. I was working at the time, and my mother was already dead. They gave a dance here, and they brought—someone here—they brought women—from Salinas. They would bring them from Ponce and from Santa Isabel. And after that I backed away a little from that..." (Mintz, *Worker* 78). Taso's reference to "those dances" and "that kind of dance" (Mintz, *Worker* 79) seems to indicate a subtle distinction from other dances ("commercial dances"), to which he refers in his life history, where more formal courtship took place (Mintz, *Worker* 65–67, 71–77, 89, 99).

Courtship dances seem to be equally common in Mayajigua, according to Manolo's entry for 25 August 1948: "En los bailes se tiene la oportunidad de besar la novia o la compañera si esta se deja y no lo vé el [v]ocal de turno o uno de los directivos de la sociedad, porque si lo vé, lo requiere y le hace pasar una pena de marca mayor" ("In the dances one has the opportunity to kiss the girlfriend or partner if she allows for it and is not seen by the usher on duty or any of the directors of the association [hosting the dance], because if noticed, he is called upon and is imposed a high-level penalty") (325).

Another detail that emerges from Taso's account on sex workers is their mobility between nearby towns (Ponce, Salinas, Santa Isabel), something that apparently happened in other rural areas of Puerto Rico. In Barranquitas, for example, another member of the "Puerto Rico Project," Robert Manners, documented a man who brought a woman from San Juan for "nothing more" than a "good lay" (195), and sex workers who were reported as moving across towns with salespersons in a truck coming from Bayamón (395–96).[7]

In Cuba, Manolo reported that underage sex workers moved from Mayajigua to work in the nearby town of Chambas in the province of Ciego de Ávila. The traffic of sex workers was also in direction to Mayajigua, as Manolo wrote on 16 December 1949:

> Resulta ser que un mulato llamado Pedro Julio López[,] que vive en el barrio de Guayabar más acá de la carpintería de Martín Alfonso, desde hace algún tiempo se está dedicando a traer putas para su casa y servirles de chulo.-
>
> Ya ha traído varias y siempre que las trae, tiene buenos resultados porque siempre aquí se carece de eso y cuando cae una nueva, la gente le cae.-
>
> Pero últimamente ha traído una muchacha rubia que no sé desde cuando la tiene ahi [sic], pero sé que es de Ciego de Avila [sic] y que la tenía en su casa, paseándose con ella por todo el pueblo de brazo como si fuera su esposa. (Picabea, "Manuscript" 1459)

(It turns out that a mulatto named Pedro Julio López, who lives in the Guayabar sector, at this extreme of Martín Alfonso's carpentry, for some time now has been dedicated to bringing whores to his house and serving as a pimp.-

Already he has brought several of them and whenever he brings them, he has good results because here there is always a dearth of that, and when a new one lands, people fall over her.

But lately, he has brought a blond girl, who I am not sure since when she has her there, but I know she is from Ciego de Avila, and that he had her in his home, strolling all around town embracing her as if she were his wife.)

According to Manolo's report of the "scandal," López and other people ended up arrested, which led Manolo to elaborate on other aspects of rural life, such as who denounced sex work and who were the bailsmen in town. A report of 21 August 1951 singles out two Mayajigua hotels as operational locations for sex workers, suggesting their arrival from other places. Manolo wrote of an individual known to him and Withers who "brought some prostitutes" overnight; they "came to town" and operated from Hotel Covadonga. Other women from "that social sphere" also stayed "every time" in a second hotel ("Hotel de los Jara") (Picabea, "Manuscript" 1508). Earlier stories recorded by Manolo include a young woman who was in Hotel Covadonga on 26 September 1948; he could "comprehend [she] was not a decent person," and he later confirmed "what she was," namely a sex worker. Manolo "was not sure that [she] was from [Mayajigua], but [she] had her mother here" (Picabea, "Manuscript" 478). Another case involved a sex worker from out of town who stayed temporarily in the house of a local sex worker in Mayajigua, creating a scandal with desiring customers screaming outside the house (Picabea, "Manuscript" 484).

The mobility of sex workers across Cuba's rural space may have many reasons that I cannot examine here, but one entry by Manolo for 17 September 1949 suggests how sex workers were marginalized and forced to be on the move. The story is not from Mayajigua, but from Esmeralda (in Camagüey), a town in the same north-central corridor of Cuba where Manolo lived for some time. He wrote:

> en La Esmeralda no pueden vivir en cualquier parte las mujeres que ejercen la prostitución, sino que tienen un barrio apartado que es el que se les ha asignado debido que a que hace poco tiempo, por las calle[s] 12, 10 y "J," habitaban estas mujeres, pero luego fueron desalojadas de allí por habitar también familias decentes que se ponían en muy mala situación con la presencia de ese elemento pervertido que afeaba el ambiente.

(in La Esmeralda women involved in prostitution cannot live wherever, but rather they have a separate sector that has been assigned to them because lately these women were living around 12, 10, and "J" streets, from where they were evicted due to the decent families that also live there and ended up being in a bad situation with the presence of this perverted element that made the surroundings uglier.)

Manolo commented on a woman mentioning that if her practice as a sex worker had been visible in her neighborhood, she "would have been cast by the authorities of the place where she lives to the neighborhood of the women that exercised prostitution" (Picabea, "Manuscript" 1235). In other words, while sex work itself was reason enough to move in search of customers, moral standards in certain towns may have also led to their physical relocation or laboring mobility between towns.

Given the activities of sex workers documented in the Cuban and Puerto Rican countryside, it must not be surprising that Manolo and Taso also shared stories about the health risks and concerns related to sexual practices. In Puerto Rico, Taso addressed the issue when asked about his dislike of birth control techniques and Mintz noted his nonverbal expressions: "Yes. Particularly those things that men used here in the time of the prostitutes. Then there was a spread of disease, a series of great sicknesses of those women, and the men sought means of protecting themselves from them. And then the thought of using one with one's woman [he shows distaste]" (Mintz, *Worker* 164). The elaboration of Taso's narrative by Mintz certainly points to the prevalence of venereal diseases, particularly gonorrhea, in Barrio Jauca and the limited incursion of modern medicine between the 1930s and 1940s (Mintz, *Worker* 98).

For Cuba, on 14 June 1949, Manolo documented a conversation where he was told about a man considered a womanizer and the most *putañero* (whoremonger) in Mayajigua, meaning that he was "always with whores and he had dedicated his life to them." He had "caught more than twenty-five gonorrhea [diagnoses] in Mayajigua," according to what Manolo reported, adding that "Gonorrhea is a very widespread sexual disease in my country, and I don't know how it is called scientifically" (Picabea, "Manuscript" 1057).

Venereal disease was a concern particularly for those who were single, based on what Manolo wrote on this group on 25 August 1948. "The sexual life of single men is a complicated life," he concluded, because of their "need" to find women. Including himself, he added that "we fear the prostitutes because of the diseases that ninety percent of them have" (Picabea, "Manuscript" 326, 324). Manolo further elaborated on how single men maneuvered the balance between their "need" and the risks, preferring to have sex with married women (with other kind of risks) rather than sex workers. But among the men who still opted to have relations with sex workers, "the majority have to use preservatives to avoid getting a disease" but remain unsatisfied and thus "many" do not use protection and "caught the diseases" (Picabea, "Manuscript" 325).

Health was, then, an important concern for men in the Cuban and Puerto Rican countryside, as it related to their sexual practices. But a reading of Taso's life history and correspondence, as well as Manolo's reports, suggests that general preoccupations over health were paramount in both locations. Their stories documented numerous illnesses and maladies in the 1940s and 1950s, as well as the different strategies to deal with them through modern medicines or by other means.

For example, Taso's first memory of being ill was with *perniciosa* (literally, pernicious), an unidentified affection that included "sudden high fever, convulsions, and blood" in the urine (Mintz, *Worker* 39–40). He also suffered from malaria (*paludismo*) and a toothache (Mintz, *Worker* 40–41). Taso told the story of his sister Tomasa, who died after being exposed to the smoke of roasting coffee, suffering fever and what was described as *pasmo* (shock). While Taso mentions that "they began to give her medical treatment" for *pasmo*, he does not specify who "they" were, whether a family member or a medical doctor (Mintz, *Worker* 51). One of the remedies involved boiling *comején* (termite residue) and drinking the resulting hot water. Tomasa died and the doctor's diagnosis was puerperal fever, but Taso was skeptical because she had been fine after delivery.

Pregnancy was also problematic for Elisabeth, Taso's wife, who got very ill, not after, but during her pregnancy, with incrementing weakness. The experience of Taso, walking miles, free riding, searching for public passenger cars, to get either a doctor, or medicament, is truly heartbreaking.

> And because her condition was so bad, I took the prescription that Tole brought and went immediately to seek the medicine. I went to Salinas and could not find it; I went to Guayama but they did not have it there; then I came back toward Ponce. I borrowed money in Salinas from our boss on my way through, and went on to Ponce. And in the

new pharmacy there I got the medicine. I tied it up in a little sack—
that is, in a handkerchief. (Mintz, *Worker* 156–57)

The odyssey continued since "it was impossible" for Taso to get a public car. He took a bus, then walked, took a partial free ride, walked again another portion, and took another free ride with a truck driver from Ponce (Mintz, *Worker* 156–57). If there is a lasting lesson from Taso's story for the generations that followed, that is the fragility of life at the time. In his world, death was ubiquitous.

Taso's letters to Mintz between 1950 and 1958 mentioned a "measles epidemic" (21 May 1950), an illness called "blindness" that the family had (17 December 1950), sore throat and eyesight problems (23 April 1951), fevers (23 September 1951), and blood in the urine (called "hemorrhage"), which needed to be checked in the Ponce hospital (12 April 1954, 10 September 1955, 13 November 1955). One of the letters refers to the upcoming graduation of Ana Livia Cordero from Columbia Medical School and the hopes that Puerto Ricans would have a "Doctor working inexpensively [*barato*] for the poor" (5 August 1951). It is perhaps not to be taken lightly that almost every single one of the sixty available letters from Taso referred to health, either wishing "Good Health" or reporting about it.[8]

In Mayajigua, illnesses and disease were also a daily affair and pregnant women were susceptible to numerous health conditions. In his report of 27 June 1949, entitled "Women who died," Manolo tells the story of a woman who died of cardiac arrest after giving birth. He provides different versions of the story, from the woman dying after giving natural birth to her death being a product of a Cesarean section, assisted by two doctors in town. Regarding the latter, Manolo observed: "I believed this immediately, because it has happened many times," that women die during the procedure (Picabea, "Manuscript" 1089).

Manolo writes about numerous health conditions suffered or known by people in the town, including *albúmina* (albumin), the common cold, fevers, *embolia cerebral* (stroke), tuberculosis, and more. Like Puerto Rico's unidentified and presumably locally named *perniciosa*, Mayajigua had local designations for maladies that, although presented as medical conditions, had social causes and explanations. That is the case of one "illness" called *fuego*, literally fire, and another one named *padrejón* (hysteria in men), not to mention the *bicio de hacerse la paja* (masturbation addiction), which caused the death of a twelve-year-old (Picabea, "Manuscript" 600). About "fire," Manolo wrote on 23 May 1949, that women:

muchas veces dicen también que padecen de una enfermedad conocida general y v largamente por "FUEGO," la cual consiste en que la mujer siempre tiene deseos de sostener relaciones sexuales, [si]n que ningún hombre la satisfaga ni puede aguantarse con un hombre solo[,] es decir, consu marido, ya que a todas las horas deldía se encuentran como se dice vulgarmente "calientes," lo que quiere decir que se encuentran deseosas de tener marido, de sostener relación[e]s sexuales.

(often say that they suffer of an illness generally and widely known as "FIRE," consisting in that the woman is always desiring to have sexual relations, with no men being able to please her or being able to hold out with only one man, meaning her husband, because at all hours in the day they are "hot," as it is commonly said, which means that they find themselves desiring to have a man, to have sexual relations.)

Manolo clarified in the note that the condition was experienced only by "married women," which led him to believe that in some cases it was "only a lie to justify their immorality" (Picabea, "Manuscript" 1019). A particular case of unfaithfulness that took place in Hotel Covadonga was credible because the woman was having "injections against this illness" (Picabea, "Manuscript" 1120).[9]

About *padrejón*, Manolo reported on 26 February 1949 that it was something "curious," explaining that "a person, a man it has to be, not sure if due to nerves or what, for whatever motive it may be, befalls a hiccup in the pit of the stomach." It was like "heart beatings," but stronger, often caused by "suffering or a great and enduring upset." He made the distinction that for women, it was called *estérico* (hysterical), emphasizing that "numerous persons" of both sexes have it. Manolo wrote to Withers that he had it but had been unable to heal because it was not easy to him to find someone to help with it (Picabea, "Manuscript" 779).

Considering the information presented here for Cuba and Puerto Rico in the mid-twentieth century, one may ask: how did people in these rural locations deal with health challenges? While acknowledging the one-dimensionality of Taso's experience in contrast with Manolo's multidimensional narrative, one difference between the two localities appears to be the availability of treatment for health conditions. In Barrio Jauca, Taso often spoke about having to go and search for the doctor elsewhere, but

Mayajigua had around three doctors in town (Dr. Kindelán, Dr. Aguilera, Dr. Valdesuno) about which Manolo writes (Picabea, "Manuscript" 361).[10] Other than registered midwives, Taso does not refer explicitly to any other alternative medical practitioners. He mentions numerous remedies but prescribed or administered almost exclusively by female household members (mothers, wives) (Mintz, *Worker* 40, 42). Manolo, on the other hand, writes extensively about *curanderos* and *curanderismo* (folk medicine) in Mayajigua as a viable option even when there were doctors in town.

Among the remedies mentioned by Taso, one was a "syrup with lots of quinine" called *Tónico Ferruginosa*, which his mother gave him during the mornings "before the coffee." A second remedy was a "tea," a "terrible thing," he said, which involved boiling nine grams of green coffee (*café macho*) with a plant called *rascamoños* (*Launaea arborescens*). Another remedy "used was a purgative called Carabaña" (Mintz, *Worker* 41–42). Taso also tells that "women in childbirth" would not drink "common water from the rain barrels, but rather they would use what they call *moscada* [nutmeg] which they sell in the pharmacy." It was added to "the water that the women used to drink during almost the entire cuarentena [quarantine]" (Mintz, *Worker* 116–17).

The reports on remedies and *curanderismo* written by Manolo for Mayajigua are too many to share here. Suffice it to note one remedy for the already mentioned condition of *padrejón*, as detailed by Manolo in his report for 26 February 1949:

> Esto lo curan principalmente ciertas Viejas que tienen como una gracia de naturaleza para curar esto, lo curan por medio de unos resos y unas cruces que hacen sobre el estómago, esto tiene que ser por la mañana en ayunas, esto es, sin haber tomadas tomado absolutamente nada, para que haga efecto la cura.
>
> Las curanderas mandan a tomar por la mañana después de la cura, un cocimiento yo no me acuerdo de qué, pero me parece que es de anón con comino que es bueno para el estómago, también mandan a comer tres aceitunas y tomar atrás un trago de Vino Seco, esto debe hacerse durante tres mañanas, casi siempre se hace durante nueve mañanas, porque este es el tiempo que dura la curación.
>
> También mandan a tomar una llema de huebo [*sic*] con vino seco o con vino dulce, las [d]os cosas se hacen, pero las aceitunas se toman con más frecuencia que las yemas. (779)

(This is healed mainly by certain Old Ladies who have a certain natural grace to heal it, they heal it through some prayers and crosses they do over the belly; this has to be in the mornings and on an empty stomach, that is, without having drunk absolutely anything, so that the cure can have its effect.

The healers instruct to drink, in the morning, after the cure, a brewing of something I don't remember, but I believe is of Annona with cumin, which is good for the stomach, and also instruct eating three olives followed by a shot of dry wine, this must be done over three mornings, almost always it is performed in nine mornings, because that is the duration of the healing.

(They also instruct to drink an egg yolk with either dry wine or sweet wine, the two things are done, but the olives are drunk more frequently than the yolks.)

The detailed measurements and structure of *curanderismo* remedies merit a thorough analysis for which there is no space here, and hopefully future studies could explore the "Manolo Manuscript" for this purpose. The described action of the *viejas curanderas* (crosses and prayers) also opens the window for a discussion on popular religion, one topic about which both Taso and Manolo have plenty of material, from Taso's conversion to Pentecostalism to Manolo's discussions of Catholic traditions. That is also beyond the scope of this analysis.

Final Thoughts

In this chapter I have used two men's accounts to present a Cuban and Puerto Rican counterpoint from below. Therein lie the accomplishment and limitations of the exercise. To the extent that it was possible, I circumvented the authoritative voice of the anthropologists with whom these men collaborated, highlighting their own voices. However, that these accounts are from men who had much to say about women, as either sex workers or healers, is a limitation. Where are the voices of women, and how different would their perspective be on the matters discussed here? To this silence, I add that other than Taso and Manolo, we have access to very few anthropological or historical works on Cuba and Puerto Rico, providing access to voices from below. That the two cases are from more than half a century ago is as revealing as it is concerning because of the limitations on existing grassroots insights on twentieth-century transformations in Cuba and

Puerto Rico. Can we do a similar critical exercise with, say, the sources left by Oscar Lewis, Ruth Lewis, and Susan Rigdon from their anthropological studies of revolutionary Cuba? What about voices from below in Puerto Rico since the sweeping transformations of Operation Bootstrap?[11]

With questions like these in mind, my exercise here can serve as an invitation to others in various directions. Most comparative work departs, or is presented, from data at the mainstream and macrolevel of history, economics, and politics, be it for the study of social movements, economic depressions, or electoral politics, all seen from above. My invitation is consistent with decades of Caribbean historiography, to mine further whatever grassroots sources are available in Caribbean history. The goal is to provide narratives from below as genuinely as possible, nourished by micro-indicators at the base level of societies, be it oral accounts or surviving writings from the subaltern. As the saying goes in Puerto Rico, *allá abajo vive gente* ("people are living down there").

Other than what transpires from the counterpoint I have presented, how can these data from below contribute to our knowledge of Caribbean societies such as Cuba and Puerto Rico? Take my own example from when I wrote an article using Mintz's fieldnotes, which indicated that the work of *paleros* (diggers) in the sugarcane industry was racially exclusive, performed by Blacks (Giovannetti, "Not Twenty Feet Away" 375). Yet, Taso's lengthy description of this job is completely silent on race (Mintz, *Worker* 134–36). This silence does not outright invalidate one or the other, but it does tell us about what is important for each of them, and therefore what remains documented in the sources left to us. Demographic and labor statistics would surely provide another version, but the issue is that even if such data confirmed racial exclusivity or not among *paleros*, Taso's narration suggests an angle to measure the importance of this information.

The nuances from below can also be captured in Taso and Manolo, allowing for detailed analysis of micro-aspects of life that would otherwise be elusive, and yet important for our understanding of Caribbean societies. For example, when Taso says "in the time of the prostitutes" he is implicitly indicating a "time" in which this work was more prevalent than in the time he is being interviewed (Mintz, *Worker* 164). That gives some leads to the researcher about State policies against sex work highlighted in other studies for that period (Flores Ramos).

For Cuba, Manolo says that one man was hanging out with a sex worker "all around town, embracing her as if she were his wife," a statement that conveys subtle public behaviors that establish who is who ("as if"). Wives could be embraced in public, not sex workers. In another example, I think about Manolo's discussion of the *fuego* illness as one suffered only by married women, stating that he never heard of a *muchacha* (girl) suffering from it (Picabea, "Manuscript" 1019). Here, *muchacha* alone signifies *señorita*, or unmarried, an important semantic precision for people researching that historical period.

One final detail is important when dealing with oral histories, people's versions of what happened around them, or their reproduction of popular stories or events. Some of what these informants reported may seem scandalous, or could be easily considered as local gossip, as is the case of some of the content in the "Manolo Manuscript." As such, many may not consider these materials worthy of historical and sociological analysis, which is not my opinion. John Thompson reminds us that a scandal "involves the transgression of certain values, norms, and moral codes" (39). In other words, what people consider scandalous or what they gossip about is that which they consider important to the societies in which they live—otherwise, why comment about it? Following Thompson's proposition, contentions around which activities are accepted, forbidden, condemned, or socially contested provide a barometer of the "scandal sensitivity" in Cuba or Puerto Rico (Thompson 40–41). Thus, those more scandalous issues that occupied Taso, and particularly Manolo, are useful in deciphering the values, norms, and overall cultural understandings in the Hispanic Caribbean countryside.

This chapter has privileged voices from below to illustrate a parallel grassroots history of Cuba and Puerto Rico in the post–World War II era. Two informants pictured societies that were about to undergo dramatic changes, providing us with a glimpse at the rural worlds that were transformed by Puerto Rico's political and economic processes in the 1940s and by the Cuban Revolution in the 1950s. In the first decades of the twenty-first century, the "two wings of a bird" have experienced major transformations at the macro-level of politics and economy. The Puerto Rican political model built in the 1940s has collapsed and Cuba has experienced changes with the gradual end of the Castro era. It may be worth looking at the current social and cultural undercurrents that take shape at the lower levels of both countries at this juncture, where the contemporary equivalents of ordinary people like Taso and Manolo are living, experiencing wider sociopolitical changes, contesting social and cultural norms, and, almost surely, also political forces.

Acknowledgments

Research over the years with the archival sources used here was possible thanks to a visiting scholarship at the Program of Latin American Studies at Princeton University, the Faculty Resource Network Program at New York University, the INAS program at the University of Puerto Rico (PR Award PO31S100037), the Franklin Research Grant from the American Philosophical Society, and a Project Development Grant from the American Council for Learned Societies. I am grateful to my colleagues Juan José Baldrich, Ismael García Colón, Yarimar Rosa-Rodríguez, Frances Sullivan, Manuel Valdés-Pizzini, and Manuel Martínez-Nazario for exchanges and support in researching and writing this essay.

Notes

1. Some works in Cuban historiography that have been used, not without controversy, as examples of voices from below are Miguel Barnet's *Biografía de un cimarrón* and Daisy Rubiera Castillo's *Reyita, sencillamente*. In *Saamaka Dreaming*, Richard and Sally Price tell us that "the people known to outsiders as 'Saramaka' requested to be recognized as 'Saamaka,' their own pronunciation of their name" (Price and Price 231).

2. This chapter forms part of a larger long-term project that examines rural life in Cuba and Puerto Rico during the post–World War II era in connection with social science intellectual history, particularly anthropological projects in the region.

3. The only surviving records of the "Puerto Rico Project," as a project or unit, were held at the Research Institute for the Study of Man and transferred around 2008 to New York University.

4. The "Cuban Nobody" reference emerges from various attempts by Withers to deal with Picabea y Niebla's accumulated reports ("The Manolo Manuscript"). Given that the manuscript is an archival resource at NYU, readers interested in his writing can consult the translation of a small portion of his reports we published in 2016 in the journal *Sargasso* (Picabea y Niebla, "Religion, Ethnicity, and Race"). Another reference is an article by Olivia Gomes da Cunha.

5. These materials are held in the Sidney Mintz Papers (MS#581), Special Collections, Johns Hopkins University, Baltimore, MD.

6. It is always challenging to make societal generalizations from what individual informants say. But the methodological distinction I have established here raises another layer of complexity for the purposes of comparison. To be sure, both Taso and Manolo are legitimate grassroots sources from their respective societies. But when one of them (Taso) speaks from his own experience and the other (Manolo) writes from his viewpoint, but also about what other people said to him or experienced, it limits how much one can say comparatively about both societies. Such assertions would need complementary sources, which cannot be included here because of the essay's intended focus on the

informants and their narrative, which is an initial and important step for subsequent comparisons.

7. This last statement is revealing about the endogenous world of Mayajigua as a small town.

8. See the letters in Sidney Mintz Papers (MS#581), Box 6, folder 12-X-Y-Z, Special Collections, The Johns Hopkins University, Baltimore, MD.

9. The condition of "fire" is mentioned earlier in the "Manolo Manuscript," in similar terms, in Manolo's entry for 25 April 1949 (p. 923) titled "Sobre Fiestas Mayajiguences."

10. A fourth doctor is mentioned, Dr. Juárez Medina, but he was retired by the time Manolo reported and not practicing (Picabea, "Manuscript" 361).

11. For Cuba, some inroads with the Lewis materials can be found in the work of Lillian Guerra. For Puerto Rico, the two books edited by Barbara Tasch Ezratty (*Puerto Rico* and *Puerto Rico, Changing Flags*) provide important voices for different periods. Moving to other Caribbean territories, in Jamaica, the oral accounts collected by Erna Brodber (*Life in Jamaica*) for the early twentieth century have been invaluable sources for many scholars and for her own publications (*The Second Generation*; *Standing Tall*).

Works Cited

Barnet, Miguel. *Biografía de un cimarrón*. 1966. Editorial Letras Cubanas, 2001.
Brodber, Erna. *Life in Jamaica in the Early Twentieth Century: A Presentation of 90 Oral Accounts*. 1980. Institute of Social and Economic Research, 1990.
———. *The Second Generation of Freemen in Jamaica, 1907–1944*. UP of Florida, 2004.
———. *Standing Tall: Affirmations of the Jamaican Male, 24 Self-Portraits*. Sir Arthur Lewis Institute for Social and Economic Studies, 2003.
Brown, Emilyn, and Jorge L. Giovannetti. "A Hidden Window into Cuban History: The Carl Withers Manuscript Collection at New York University." *Caribbean Studies*, vol. 37, no. 2, 2009, pp. 169–92.
Ezratty, Barbara Tasch, editor. *Puerto Rico: An Oral History, 1898-2008, 110 Years of Life in La Isla*. Read Street Publishing, 2010.
———. *Puerto Rico, Changing Flags: An Oral History, 1898–1952*. Omni Arts, 1986.
Flores Ramos, José. *Mujer, familia y prostitución: La construcción del género bajo la hegemonía del PPD, 1940–1968*. Oficina de la Procuradora de la Mujer, 2007.
Giovannetti, Jorge L. "An Unfinished Ethnography: Carl Withers's Cuban Fieldwork and the Book That Never Was." *Corridor Talk to Culture History: Public Anthropology and Its Consequences*, edited by Regna Darnell and Frederic W. Gleach. U of Nebraska P, 2015, pp. 195–229.
———. 2018. "'Not Twenty Feet Away': The Caribbean—and Race—in Sidney W. Mintz's Puerto Rican Fieldwork." *Critique of Anthropology*, vol. 38, no. 4, 2018, pp. 368–86.
Gomes da Cuhna, Olivia Maria. "Exactly As People Tell, or An Ethnography of the (In) Visible Things of Mayajigua." *History and Anthropology*, vol. 26, no. 5, 2015, pp. 576–96.
Guerra, Lillian. "Former Slum Dwellers, the Communist Youth, and the Lewis Project in Cuba, 1969–1971." *Cuban Studies*, vol. 43, 2015, pp. 67–89.

Mintz, Sidney W. *Cañamelar: The Contemporary Culture of a Rural Puerto Rican Proletariat*. 1951. Columbia University, PhD dissertation.

———. *Worker in the Cane: A Puerto Rican Life History*. 1960. W. W. Norton & Company, 1974.

Picabea y Niebla, Juan M. "The Manolo Manuscript." Carl Withers Manuscript Collection, Series 6: Unpublished Manuscripts, boxes 12–13, New York, University Archives, New York University, 1948–1951.

———. "Religion, Ethnicity, and Race in Rural Cuba: A Pre-Revolutionary Amateur Ethnography." Translated and edited by Jorge L. Giovannetti and Don E. Walicek, with an introduction by Jorge L. Giovannetti and Juleisa Avilés Acarón. *Sargasso: Translation & Difference*, nos. 1–2, 2015–2016, pp. 105–27.

Price, Richard. *Travels with Tooy: History, Memory, and the African American Imagination*. U of Chicago P, 2008.

Price, Richard, and Sally Price. *Saamaaka Dreaming*. Duke UP, 2017.

Rubiera Castillo, Daisy. *Reyita, sencillamente*. Prolibros-Instituto Cubano del Libro, 1997.

Steward, Julian H., et al. *The People of Puerto Rico: A Study in Social Anthropology*. U of Illinois P, 1957.

Thompson, John B. "Scandal and Social Theory." *Media Scandals: Morality and Desire in the Popular Culture Marketplace*, edited by James Lull and Stephen Hinerman. Columbia UP, 1997, pp. 34–64.

West, James. *Plainville, U.S.A.* 1945. Columbia UP, 1947.

Zayas Alvarado, Anastacio. Letter to Sidney W. Mintz, May 1, 1950, Sidney W. Mintz Papers (MS#581), box 6, folder 12-X-Y-Z, Special Collections, The Johns Hopkins University.

5

The Harlem of the Club Las Dos Antillas
Race, Space, and Politics in Early Antillean New York

JESSE HOFFNUNG-GARSKOF

On the first Sunday in April 1892, two cigarmakers named Rosendo Rodríguez and Augusto Benech hosted a group of twenty-three men at a meeting at an apartment on Third Avenue, near Ninety-Ninth Street in Manhattan. Both of the hosts were stalwart members of La Liga, an immigrant educational society for Cubans and Puerto Ricans of "the class of color," founded in Greenwich Village several years before, as were many of those they invited. The attendees were a mixed group, mostly cigarmakers, a few typesetters, some journalists, and a handful of professionals. The minutes recorded neither their occupation nor racial status. Rodríguez took the floor to explain that they had called the meeting for the purpose of creating a political club. The men responded enthusiastically. Because some were Cuban and others Puerto Rican, they decided to call their association the Club Las Dos Antillas (The Two Antilles). Club members then elected Benech to serve as secretary and Rodríguez as president. They named the Cuban General Antonio Maceo (then living in Costa Rica) and the Puerto Rican doctor Ramón Emeterio Betances (then living in Paris) as honorary presidents. They collected contributions from the members, adding up to three dollars and forty cents. And they voted to approve the principles and bylaws of the Cuban Revolutionary Party (PRC, for its Spanish acronym). These were the crucial steps necessary to claim membership in the Party. Rodríguez was therefore able to join the presidents of the five other affiliated clubs in the city on the Party's New York Advisory Council. He was the only Black cigarmaker on the Council when it met, five days later, to elect the first Party Delegate. He cast the vote of the Club Las Dos Antillas for the poet and journalist José Martí.[1]

Of the scores of Cuban and Puerto Rican revolutionary clubs that operated within the United States in this period, the Club Las Dos Antillas is probably the one that historians in the United States are most likely to recognize by name. This is because Arturo Alfonso Schomburg, a young typesetter who arrived from San Juan in 1891, became the secretary of the club several months after the founding meeting. Benech stepped down from that post when he was elected president of another club, the Club Guerrilla de Maceo, becoming the second Black cigarmaker on the Advisory Council.[2] Most of the surviving records from dozens of PRC clubs that operated across the United States and greater Caribbean are located in the National Archive of Cuba (ANC, for its Spanish acronym), and are not consistently available for consultation. The minutes book and membership list for the Club Las Dos Antillas, however, remained in Schomburg's possession. Schomburg later became an important collector, historian, and public intellectual, and the club records are now available, both in the original and in a typescript transcription and translation, at the archive that bears his name, the Schomburg Center for Research in Black Culture, located in Harlem. As scholarly interest in Schomburg has grown over the past two decades, the existence of the Club Las Dos Antillas has been noted in dozens of articles and books (Sinnette; Schomburg; Arroyo; Valdés).

Yet, despite a general familiarity with the club, there still is much to learn about its members. Who were they? How did they come to be in East Harlem in 1892? Why, and in that context, did they gather with one another? And what were the political commitments and compromises that led them to join the coalition that propelled Martí to leadership in the independence movement? This chapter cannot answer all of those questions. But its focus on Afrodescendant participants nevertheless helps reframe longstanding scholarly debates over the racial ideals expressed by many in the Cuban nationalist movement: the promise that the revolution would avoid class and racial conflict by assuring the inclusion of all Cubans in a just social order, and the hope that a shared national project would erase all racial distinctions. Scholars and activists have expressed a healthy skepticism about such ideals, noting the ways that subsequent generations of Cuban politicians, celebrating their supposed fidelity to Martí, used them to constrain discussion of persistent racial inequalities and to stifle independent racial activism (Helg; Ferrer; de la Fuente; Alberto and Hoffnung-Garskof). By examining the political movement in which these ideas emerged, we can better understand why Afro-Antilleans like Schomburg and his comrades threw their weight behind Martí within the revolutionary coalition in the first place, and on what terms (Mirabal 61–138; Guerra 23–46).

Given the overwhelming volume and easy availability of Martí's own writings, scholars working on the independence movement have typically, and sensibly, approached the question of race textually. For New York, Nancy Raquel Mirabal, Lillian Guerra, and José Fusté have put Martí's writings, and those of other White Cuban revolutionaries, in conversation with a remarkable set of publications written by Afrodescendant migrants, most notably the newspaper *Doctrina de Martí*. Rafael Serra, the editor of *Doctrina de Martí*, who would later become one of the most successful Black politicians in early republican Cuba, attended the first meeting of the Club Las Dos Antillas. He was a mentor to the organizers of Las Dos Antillas. Sotero Figueroa, an Afrodescendant Puerto Rican typesetter and author who was a close collaborator of both Serra and Martí, was also a mentor. The large body of writings produced by Serra and Figueroa are thus extremely relevant to the politics of the club. Yet, as Gerald Poyo has shown, those texts, like Martí's, were the artifacts of an uneven and often uncertain project of coalition building, not a natural unfolding of pristine ideologies. To understand the texts, it is important to understand the ins and outs of the politics in particular times and places. Thinking through the history of this political club can thus serve a complement to the work of Thomas Orum, Melina Pappademos, and Michael Zeuske on the evolution of Black political activism in Cuba in the first republic (Orum; Pappademos; Zeuske).

This chapter uses information from the minutes book of the Club Las Dos Antillas to sketch out the political alliances at work in the PRC in these meetings in East Harlem. I focus on the addresses of the leaders and members of the club, to consider how the neighborhood where they lived, along upper Third Avenue, may have helped to shape their revolutionary activity. I have located those addresses on a map, created with the help of a team of students, a data librarian, and a cartographer, that also reveals important details about the shape of racial segregation in the neighborhood. Although it is important to recognize the limits of what this map can teach us about race and space in East Harlem (Hoffnung-Garskof, "Cuban Racial Politics"), it nevertheless adds a useful new dimension for thinking about why, how, and where the founders of the Club Las Dos Antillas came together. The analysis situates their efforts to build and participate in a multiracial coalition in the broader experience of "migrating while Black" in a city with a very small Black population (the 1880 and 1890 censuses counted less than 2 percent of New York City's population as "colored" or "mulatto") and a country rapidly descending into the nadir of race relations. The map also offers a new approach to the very early history of the neighborhood that would come to be known as Spanish Harlem, or El Barrio.

Party Building

Read carefully, the club minutes reveal quite a bit about the process of party building among Cuban and Puerto Rican exiles over the spring and summer of 1892. The Cuban Revolutionary Party grew through collaboration between working-class leaders like Rodríguez and Benech and an inner circle of "disciples" that had formed around Martí. Several prominent, White Spanish-speaking New Yorkers, closely associated with Martí, attended the first meeting of Las Dos Antillas, in Rodríguez's home. The wealthy lawyer Gonzalo de Quesada, Martí's personal secretary, as well as a leading Puerto Rican publisher and a wealthy Cuban manufacturer, all went at least once to the apartment on Third Avenue, though they lived in other neighborhoods. They remained on the membership rolls throughout the life of the club. But having lent their support and prestige to its creation, and having promised to pay regular dues, none of them would return for subsequent meetings. An exception to this rule nevertheless supports the interpretation that these men were patrons or intermediaries, who served as ties between the club and party leadership (or factions seeking to assert leadership). The young medical doctor Buenaventura Portuondo, an important member of Martí's inner circle with close ties to Serra, returned for just three meetings between March and July 1895. At that time, the Spanish-Cuban war had begun, Martí had departed for Cuba, and the party was beginning to reconfigure. His last appearance in the minutes was the meeting when the club voted for a new party delegate, following Martí's death in battle in May 1895.[3]

The inner circle of supporters and patrons supporting and overseeing the creation of Las Dos Antillas also included Martí's closest Afrodescendant allies. As already noted, Serra attended the first meeting. So did Sotero Figueroa and another Afrodescendant Puerto Rican typesetter and author, Francisco ("Pachín") Gonzalo Marín. Veterans of the Autonomist Party in Puerto Rico, the pair had quickly risen to prominence in the movement over the previous months, writing essays for Martí's newspaper, *Patria*, making speeches at party gatherings, and circulating among the various clubs formed in New York in this period. Along with a third typographer, the White-presenting Modesto Tirado, Figueroa and Marín returned to subsequent meetings. They drafted and printed a constitution for the club and offered guidance on how to interpret these bylaws. Over subsequent years, Figueroa and Marín appear several more times in the minutes, usually at meetings held jointly with the Club Borinquen, in which they were officers.[4] This was one of a group of clubs that were crucial to the influence that Serra and Figueroa wielded in the party (Guerra 69–70; Hoffnung-Garskof, *Racial Migrations* 217–60).

In addition to this group of patrons and mentors, the minutes also help to distinguish a second group that was much more crucial to the functioning of the club. The elected leadership of the club, the president, vice-president, treasurer, and secretaries, and at-large representatives, were responsible for organizing meetings, running elections, and fundraising—the key functions of the party clubs. Most of the minutes document leadership meetings, which generally included only six or seven participants. This core changed slightly over time but consistently included Rodríguez, Schomburg, Silvestre Pivaló, Isidoro Apodaca, Francisco Araúz (sometimes identified as Araujo), Eligio Valdez, and Federico Pacheco. General meetings did not necessarily attract much larger crowds, typically drawing ten to fifteen attendees. Members without any official position were expected merely to pay dues and to come to occasional meetings scheduled for elections or celebrations. Indeed, the problem of mobilizing more adherence from the general membership was a frequent topic of the smaller leadership meetings. Members liked to make donations to the party at large public events in the cigar workshops, basking in the cheers of comrades. As a result, many were in arrears on their regular dues to the club. The money reached the party coffers either way, but only money that passed through the club helped empower President Rodríguez in his interactions on the Advisory Council. After Martí's death, some in the party leadership threatened to remove the presidents of clubs who did not meet fundraising targets.[5]

Women do not appear in the list of members or as elected officers, and their presence at meetings was almost never acknowledged. But other evidence makes it clear that several of the women married to men in leadership positions also played an important role in this political community. For most of the 1890s, Josefa Blanco, a midwife, lived with her husband Isidoro Apodaca a few doors down from Rosendo Rodríguez. Birth records from the period reveal that Blanco delivered many babies to the wives of members of the Club Las Dos Antillas, some Cuban, some Puerto Rican, and some African American, in the apartment buildings along upper Third Avenue. She was likely also a source of primary health care for women and children. Along with a second Black Cuban midwife, Gertrudis Heredia, she led a women's group affiliated with La Liga. Blanco and Heredia also created and led a political club for the women in their community, the Club José Maceo, in 1896.[6] Schomburg's minutes record the participation of a Puerto Rican woman named Pilar Cazuela (who also used the last name Umpierre) at a meeting in 1896. She donated a rifle and two hundred cartridges. In the minutes she is identified with the surname of her husband, Silvestre Pivaló, who was the club treasurer.[7] She was also an officer in the Club José Maceo, along with Blanco and Heredia. It may well be that Pilar Cazuela, Josefa Blanco, Leonora Araúz, and others who shared (and did domestic labor in) the apartments on upper Third Avenue were physically present during the meetings of the Club Las Dos Antillas, though not recorded as attendees.

What is notable about the Club Las Dos Antillas and the Club José Maceo, like a handful of other clubs affiliated with La Liga—the Club Guerrilla de Maceo, the Club Alfonso Goulet, and the Club Manuel Bergues Pruna—is that in each case the leadership group primarily consisted of migrants of African descent. The evidence for this comes from various sources. Schomburg's self-identification as "Negro" is well known. The photographs that Serra published of Rodríguez, Apodaca, Blanco, and Cazuela, along with his accounts of activities at La Liga, offer the distinct impression that they were also people of color. Furthermore, United States census takers and other bureaucrats identified many of these individuals as "black," "colored," or "mulatto," including on the birth certificates signed by Josefa Apodaca. La Liga, the training ground for this cadre of worker-organizers, called itself a society for the "advancement of the intellect and elevation of the character" of "men of color, born in Cuba and Puerto Rico" ("hombres de color nacidos en Cuba y Puerto Rico") (Serra 145). Some of them also participated in local committees to support the Black civil rights struggle in Cuba.[8] When wealthier, conservative, White Cubans identified La Liga, *Doctrina de Martí*, and the political clubs that grew out of them derisively as the "democratic black" element of the movement, Serra and Figueroa vehemently denied the racial label. They pointed to a handful of White teachers at La Liga to insist that it be remembered as racially mixed, "since they do not do it the honor and justice it deserves, calling it simply an

Arturo Schomburg   Rosendo Rodriguez

Rafael Serra   Isidoro Apodaca

Josefa Blanco de Apodaca

Sotero Figueroa   Pilar Cazuela de Pivaló

Figure 5.1. Members of the Club Las Dos Antillas. Photo courtesy of New York Public Library Digital Collections.

association of Cubans and Puerto Ricans" ("era una sociedad mixta, ya que no se le hace el merecido honor y la justicia de llamarese secamente 'Sociedad de cubanos y puertorriqueños'").[9] (See Figure 5.1.)

For similar reasons, most accounts of Las Dos Antillas, including its own records, made no mention of the racial status of its leaders or members. The official ideology of the Cuban Revolutionary Party, expressed most famously in Martí's 1893 essay, "Mi raza" ("My Race"), was that political movements should not be organized by race. In response to a highly charged debate in Cuba over the creation of an island-wide civil rights organization, Martí wrote "all that specifies, separates, or encloses is a sin against humanity" ("todo lo que especifica, separa o encierra es un pecado contra la humanidad"). Even as he disavowed the leading scientific theories of Black inferiority, he warned of the risks of "black racism," arguing that the "black who isolates himself, provokes the white to isolate himself" ("negro que se aísla, provoca a aislarse al blanco"). Yet, Martí seems to have made strategic exceptions for his own close allies, who created independent Black organizations that were formally open to all. La Liga, far from being an institution that "divided men," was the institution that best combined the fundamental principle of unity with its necessary precondition, justice. There, "with neither flattery for one group, nor humiliation for the other, but rather with their gazes meeting at the same level, the children of those who committed injustice" gathered to exchange ideas with "the children of those who suffered from the injustice" ("sin lisonja de unos ni humillación de otros, sino con las miradas á nivel, los hijos de los que fueron injustos y los de los que padecieron de la injusticia").[10]

In the construction of his coalition, Martí relied on the Black and Brown organizers affiliated with La Liga, men and women like Rodríguez, Benech, Schomburg, Blanco, and Cazuela, to mobilize Black and Brown workers into party clubs. Yet Martí's newspaper, *Patria*, was scrupulous in its treatment of these clubs, leaving unspoken that the movement continued to operate against a backdrop in which racial separation, while not absolute, was still a regular feature of Cuban social and political life. Antilleans were fond of Lola Rodríguez de Tió's poem "A Cuba," which configured Cuba and Puerto Rico as two wings of a bird. But no one spoke of the prominent role that Afrodescendant Puerto Ricans played in political networks shared with the Afrodescendant Cubans among whom they settled. Census takers identified one elected officer—Vice President Leopoldo Acosta—as White.[11] And many of the remaining members appear in no surviving photographs and on no documents including racial assignations.

If a substantial proportion of those members were perceived and counted as White, Las Dos Antillas was a very unusual political club indeed—even in a movement characterized by a great deal of interracial mobilization—a club led by Black men that had a meaningfully multiracial membership.

Party Buildings

In thinking through this possibility, the context of the neighborhood provides important clues. Most of the members and nearly all of the leaders of Las Dos Antillas and José Maceo clubs lived in the immediate vicinity of Third Avenue and Ninety-Ninth Street. This makes sense. These revolutionaries worked long hours in cigar workshops all over the city, likely using the elevated train lines to reach the factories. Their political organizations seem to have been organized, partly, along geographic lines, much like elite Cuban social networks that formed downtown several decades earlier (Pérez 91–92). But, in contrast to the wealthy White families that clustered around East Thirteenth Street, the Cuban and Puerto Rican households on upper Third Avenue were renters. Their settlement patterns must be considered not only in terms of their relationship with each other but also against the backdrop of racial segregation in New York City.

Tracking racial segregation in the city turns out to be more intricate a research question than it might seem. Prior to the great migration of the early twentieth century, no majority Black neighborhoods existed in New York. Even in neighborhoods that were reputationally Black, like Southern Greenwich Village, Black residents were a small share of the population, generally between 5 and 10 percent. The color line is therefore impossible to discern at the level of census tracts or enumeration districts, or even city blocks. But it functioned nonetheless, at an extremely local level (Logan et al.). The journalist Jacob Riis wrote in 1890: "The color line must be drawn through the tenements to give the picture its proper shading. The landlord does the drawing, does it with an absence of pretense, a frankness of despotism, that is nothing if not brutal" (Riis).[12]

To see how landlords drew this line in Harlem, before the Great Migration, I began with the digitized versions of the 1900 manuscript census on FamilySearch.org. Two undergraduate students, Alexandrea Sommers and Jacob Sigman, surveyed all the enumeration districts located east of the park and north of Seventieth Street to identify districts with one or more residents born in Cuba or Puerto Rico or one or more residents enumerated as Black. Drea and Jacob then returned to those districts and created a spreadsheet, copying out names and racial identifiers for every person living in any building that had at least one resident listed either as Cuban, Puerto Rican, or Black. Then, by importing an insurance map from the time period into Google Earth, data librarian Nicole Scholtz and I were able to locate all of these addresses and trace the outlines of buildings and associate them with our data. We could then represent buildings according to the percentage of people enumerated as Black. We also located the buildings where members of the Club Las Dos Antillas and the Club José Maceo lived, addresses listed in the minutes book or found in other documents. Finally, map artist Adrian Kitzinger transformed our work into a grayscale drawing.[13]

The result shows some very interesting features of the neighborhood in the period when the Club Las Dos Antillas and the Club José Maceo were active. Although by the 1920s, Harlem would become the most famous example of a new kind of large, overwhelmingly Black neighborhood in the urban north, in 1900 it still followed a pattern of highly localized segregation identified by Logan et al. in their analysis of the 1880 census. The 5,471 persons that census takers identified as Black, and whose information we collected, lived in buildings that were, on average, more than 86 percent Black and in households that were, on average, more than 98 percent Black. Yet, this remained a majority White district. Although a few of the Black residents of the district were live-in domestic employees in White households, and some lived in one or two-family units, most lived in tenements, buildings that, in many instances, housed between seventy and 180 Black residents.

These buildings, with dozens of African American neighbors, were the most immediate context for the creation of the Club Las Dos Antillas. The first meeting took place in an apartment at 1758 Third Avenue, a building that was home to nearly 150 African Americans.

Rodríguez still lived there in 1900, with his adopted African American son. The Cuban couple Francisco and Leonora Araúz also lived there with their daughter, who had been born in Jamaica. They also hosted club meetings at their home on several occasions.[14] That same building appears in club records as the residence of at least three other members. Other club officers, notably Isidoro Apodaca and Josefa Blanco and Pilar Cazuela and Silvestre Pivaló, lived in several nearby tenements. Eligio Valdez, Jacobo Calvo, and Benito Majariaga (all identified as men of color in other sources) lived in another such building, farther west along Ninety-Seventh Street.[15] This is consistent with a broader settlement pattern, across the city.

Afro-Latinx migrants generally faced the same limited options as African Americans in the housing market, paying higher rents for lower quality apartments according to a color line brutally imposed by the despotism of New York landlords (Hoffnung-Harskof, *Racial Migrations* 102–6). (See Figures 5.2 and 5.3.)

The need to negotiate the segregated housing market and then to share neighborhood and living space with African Americans was thus something almost the entire leadership of Las Dos Antillas shared with one another, but not with most of their White-presenting compatriots. Since the 1870s, Cuban migrants of color built social and political ties with one another and with African Americans in the context not only of segregated housing shared with African Americans but also of Black fraternal organizations and Black churches. They also frequently had romantic relationships with and married African Americans (Hoffnung-Harskof, *Racial Migrations* 106–11, 228–37). The Black Puerto Ricans who arrived in the city beginning in the late 1880s joined this social and political network. Looking at the map of East Harlem, we can imagine, without straying too far into the realm of speculation, that Black Cubans and Puerto Ricans engaged with one another and with African Americans at the Thomas Barbershop (across the street from the Apodaca household)—a distribution point for the city's leading African American newspaper, the *New York Age*.[16] Perhaps they mingled with African Americans at the Cuban Restaurant and Oyster House at 1758 Third Avenue, the building where the club was founded and held most of its meetings. According to a notice in *Doctrina de Martí*, this large, predominantly Black apartment building was a "a suitable place to do a good business with Cuban and American clienteles."[17]

Yet it is also notable that a few in the leadership of the Club Las Dos Antillas, and a substantial number of members, lived on what looks like the opposite side of the color line in this same neighborhood. The three vice presidents, Francisco Acosta, Leopoldo Acosta, and Leopoldo Núñez, each appear to have lived, while members of the club, in buildings in the neighborhood that had no Black residents enumerated on the 1900 census. So did Federico Pacheco, who served as president for a brief span and was a regular fixture as an at-large representative. This would seem to support a view of the club as racially integrated, beyond the occasional visits of sympathetic professionals like the physician Buenaventura Portuondo. Perhaps the extremely localized pattern of segregation allowed a multiracial working-class migrant community made up of Cubans and Puerto Ricans to form along upper Third Avenue despite the despotism of the color line.

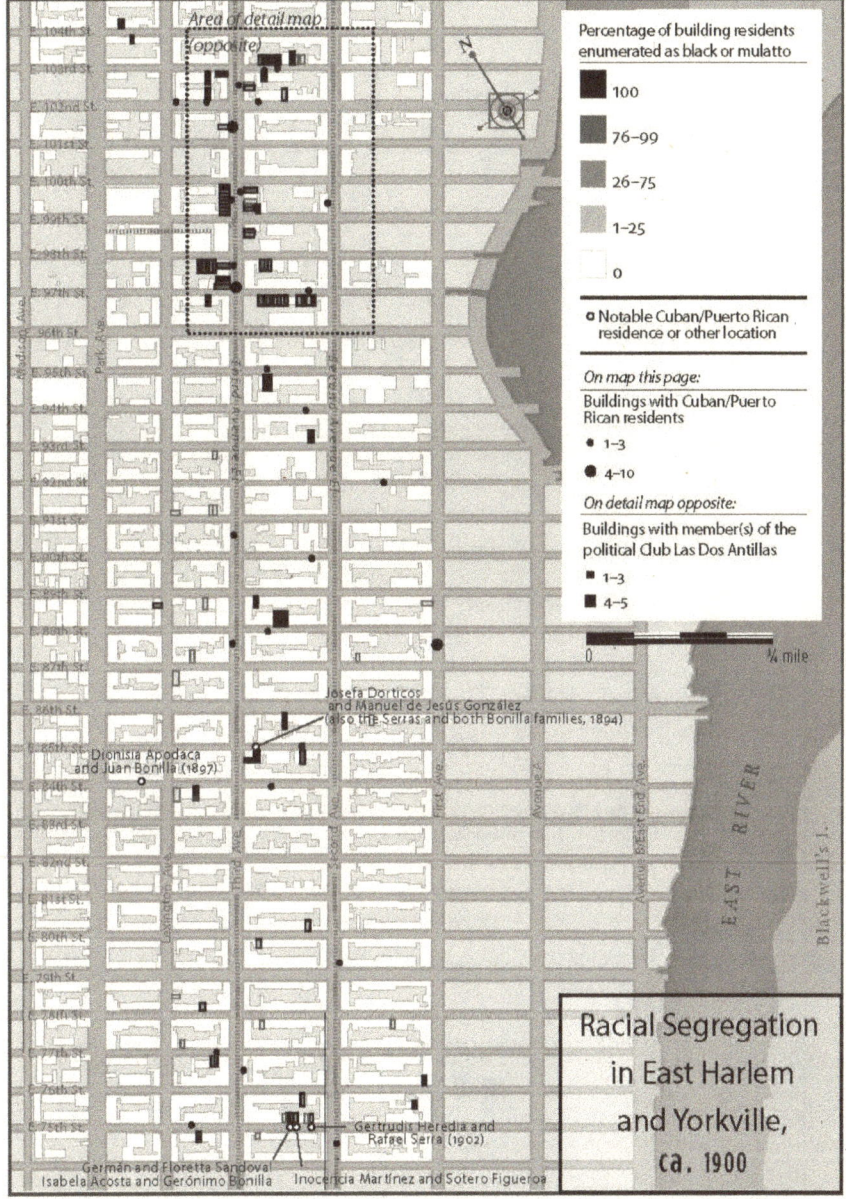

Figure 5.2. Racial segregation in East Harlem and Yorkville, ca. 1900. Map from *Racial Migrations: New York City and the Revolutionary Politics of the Spanish Caribbean* (Princeton UP, 2019), by Jesse Hoffnung-Garskof.

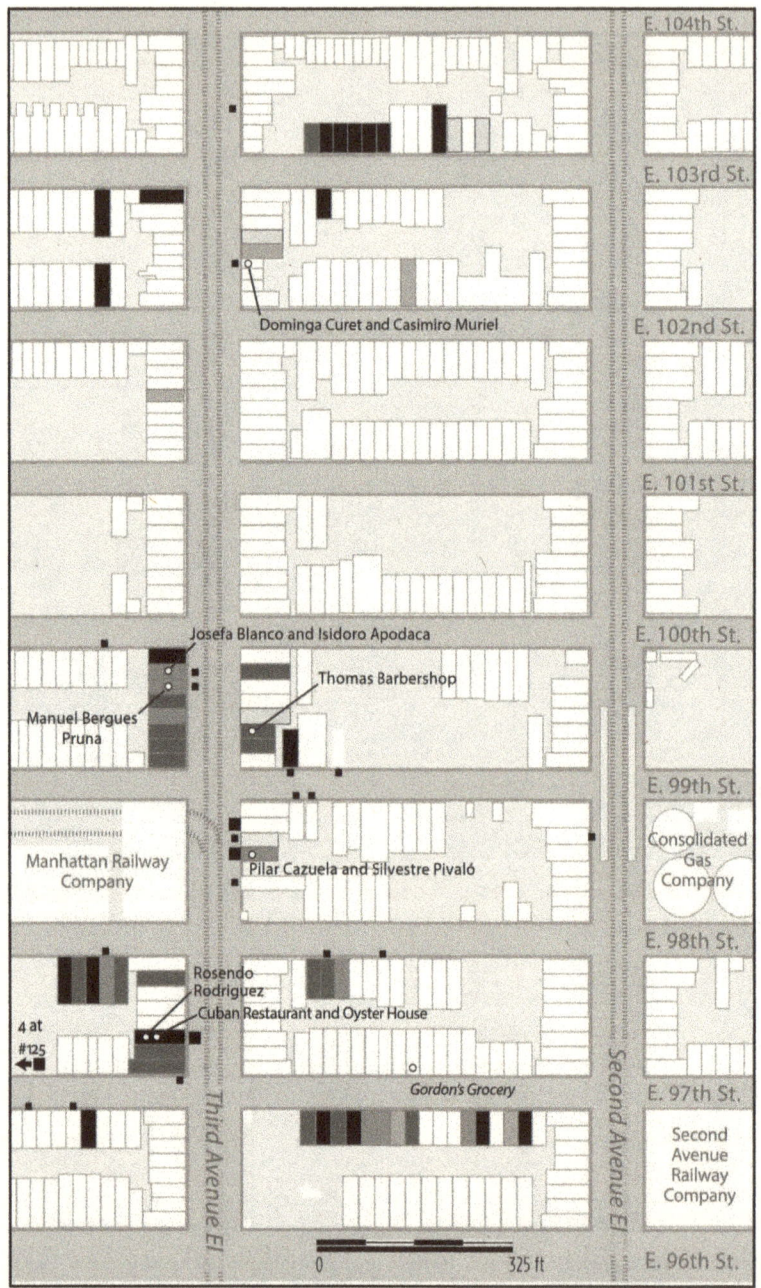

Figure 5.3. Buildings with members of the political club Las Dos Antillas. Map from *Racial Migrations: New York City and the Revolutionary Politics of the Spanish Caribbean* (Princeton UP, 2019), by Jesse Hoffnung-Garskof.

It is important to be cautious, however, about treating building composition as a proxy for the racial status of residents. It is true that very few White New Yorkers and very few Cuban migrants who identified as White, lived in buildings shared with African Americans, while Cuban and Puerto Rican migrants of color almost all did (Hoffnung-Garskof, *Racial Migrations*). Yet, several members of Las Dos Antillas who were regularly identified as Black in other sources lived in buildings that our map shows as all-White. For instance, both the Pivaló-Cazuela family and the Puerto Ricans Dominga Curet and Casimiro Muriel lived in the small two-family house at 1851 Third Avenue in 1900. According to Riis, most White renters in the city refused to occupy apartments where Black people had previously lived. Perhaps this building was an exception. Or maybe the census takers who canvassed the neighborhood transposed the data collected at 1851 Third Avenue and the data collected at the larger structure next door at 1853, which was home to three Black families and three White families. In any event, this was also the address of club Vice President Leopoldo Núñez, for whom we have no other racially identifying information. Though on our map he seems to live in a White space, it is hard to be confident that Núñez, the landlord at 1851 Third Avenue, or his comrades in the Club Las Dos Antillas thought of him as White. For the same reason it does not seem certain that club officer Federico Pacheco would have thought of himself as White, though he lived in a building on East Ninety-Seventh Street that was later enumerated as entirely White. By the time of the 1900 census, "Fred Pacheco," a Puerto Rican cigarmaker enumerated as Black, was living at a different address in Brooklyn.[18]

The case of the Cuban Marcelino Piedra, a member of the Club Guerrilla de Maceo, points to still greater uncertainty about using the 1900 census to establish the racial composition of households, or indeed the racial status of individuals. In 1900, Piedra lived in a one-family home on East Seventy-Fifth Street, with Piedra's U.S.-born wife Hannah, Hannah's sister, and several lodgers, all of whom census workers also counted as White. So, the building appears all White on our map. His immediate neighbors on East Seventy-Fifth, Germán Sandoval and Gerónimo Bonilla, were leaders of several of the most important Black Cuban institutions in the city and members of the Club Guerrilla de Maceo. If Piedra understood himself to be White, as the census taker suggests, that would be evidence that the Club Guerrilla de Maceo was substantively multiracial. Yet this census return is only one data point.

Marcelino's 1884 marriage certificate identified him as "Cuban-brown." On the 1910 census, Marcelino was counted as White and Hannah as Black. On their death certificates, both Marcelino and Hannah were classified as Black. This suggests that neither living in a building enumerated as wholly White nor even being individually enumerated as White necessarily indicates a lack of African ancestry or a day-to-day experience of Whiteness.

Conclusion

At the risk of undermining confidence in the map that is the center of this chapter, it is important to be clear that it is not a literal depiction of the local residential color line as experienced by Antillean migrants, or really anyone. That objection aside, the map does provide a useful tool for making sense of the Las Dos Antillas minutes book. A highly localized color line did exist in this neighborhood, whether or not its boundaries were as fixed or impermeable as they look on our map. Considering all available evidence, almost all of those who took on leadership roles in the Club Las Dos Antillas and José Maceo both identified and were identified as *de color*. These clubs were partnerships, in the first instance, between Black Cubans and Black Puerto Ricans. Inconsistencies, ambiguities, and outright errors aside, the map shows that this group lived in the heart of the African American colony along East Harlem's Third Avenue and its surrounding blocks, holding meetings in apartment buildings that they shared with scores, sometimes hundreds, of African American neighbors. They engaged in nationalist coalitions and became supporters of Martí even as they took part in the experience of migrating while Black in a segregated city.

At the same time, it seems likely that some club members (although perhaps fewer than a literal reading of the map would suggest) lived in the same neighborhood in buildings generally reserved for White people. Others reported more than one address to club record keepers and seem to have resided, at different moments, on both sides of the local color line. In other words, it seems that some club members were perceived by White landlords and neighbors in ways that allowed them to rent in Whites-only apartments but nevertheless chose to settle very close to comrades who lived in predominately Black buildings. Sometimes they even chose to live in those same buildings. That working-class migrants from the two Antillean islands settled in this kind of a cluster, straddling (and at times confounding) the local divide between White and Black does not suggest the existence of a national community that was free of racism. But it may be an important starting place for understanding the later settlement of the area that would eventually be known as El Barrio. Black Puerto Rican journalist and organizer Jesús Colón noted, decades later, that when he first arrived in the city "the few Puerto Ricans around lived in the heart of the Negro neighborhood together with the Negro people in the same buildings; many times as roomers in their homes" (Colón 44). And that settlement pattern can help explain how the Club Las Dos Antillas could be both an independent Black political organization and a mixed-race club, and how the politics of cross-racial nationalism that emerged around Martí, sometimes rendered as "raceless," could comfortably coexist with race-conscious politics centered on the concerns of Afrodescendants from the two Antilles.

Notes

1. Club Las Dos Antillas, "Libro de Actas," 3 Apr. 1892. See also "Los clubs," *Patria*, 10 Apr. 1892; "Proclamación Provisional, Del Partido Revolucionario Cubano," *Patria*, 10 Apr. 1892.

2. Club Las Dos Antillas, "Libro de Actas," 24 July 1892. Club Guerrilla de Antonio Maceo, "Libro de Actas," 29 Aug. 1892, Fondo Partido Revolucionario Cubano, legajo 44 B 1, ANC.

3. Club Las Dos Antillas, "Libro de Actas," 14 Mar. 1895, 26 Mar. 1895, 28 July 1895.

4. Club Las Dos Antillas, "Actas," 9 Apr. 1892, 24 July 1892, 6 Oct. 1895, 18 Mar. 1896, 26 July 1896.

5. The problem of dues collection and low attendance had been grave since the nationwide economic collapse in early 1893. Party leadership did not pressure Rodríguez and other club presidents about this issue until after the departure of Martí and the beginning of the war. Club Las Dos Antillas, "Actas," 21 May 1895, 27, 30 Aug. 1895.

6. "Gacetillas," *Doctrina de Martí*, Jan. 15 1897.

7. See, for instance, Certificate and Record of Birth for María Isidora Gomero, 4 Apr. 1893, Municipal Archives of New York (MACNY); Certificate and Record of Birth for Juan Gualberto Pivaló, 12 July 1893, MACNY; Certificate and Record of Birth for Isidoro Muriel, 4 Apr. 1897, MACNY; Certificates and Record of Birth for Miguel Olave, 10 Apr. 1899, MACNY.

8. Silvestre Pivaló was a veteran of the Ten Years' War in Cuba (1868–78) and a member of the Committee to Support *La Igualdad*. Juan Bonilla, "A Sr. Enrique Cos," 25 Jan. 1891, Fondo Adquisiciones, caja 45, número 3579, ANC.

9. Héctor de Saavedra, "A Domingo Figarola y Caneda," 9 Feb. 1897, Fondo Academia de la Historia Cubana, Caja 167, Signatura 557, ANC. This document is also cited in Guerra. "Aclaraciones oportunas," *Doctrina de Martí*, 16 Sept. 1896. "Para que se sepa," *Doctrina de Martí*, 15 July 1897.

10. "Mi raza," *Patria*, 16 Apr. 1893; "Los lunes en La Liga," *Patria*, 26 Mar. 1892.

11. Leopoldo Acosta. 1900 US Federal Census, Manhattan, ED 909, Sheet 11, line 20. Consulted on FamilySearch.org.

12. On rental markets as a site of racial exploitation, see Connolly.

13. On the need to include the names of student and librarian collaborators, see Boyles et al. For other considerations of this issue, see Anderson et al.; Braunstein. The student workers on this project were paid for their labor.

14. Club Las Dos Antillas, "Libro de Actas," 29 Aug. 1895, 22 Apr. 1896.

15. Unfortunately, this building, west of Lexington Avenue, was outside the range of our initial survey, so it does not appear on the map.

16. "Where the Age Can Be Had," *New York Age*, 19 Nov. 1892.

17. *Doctrina de Martí*, 2 Oct. 1896.

18. 1900 US Federal Census, Brooklyn, Enumeration District 141, Page 3, line 70. In 1910, however, a Puerto Rican named Fred Pacheco worked as an attendant at the Binghamton State Hospital and was enumerated as White. 1910 US Federal Census, Binghamton, NY, Enumeration District 35, page 25, line 52. Both were consulted on FamilySearch.org. For work on the counting of Puerto Ricans in U.S. censuses in the mainland and the archipelago, see Carlo-Becerra; Loveman and Muniz; Duany 236–60.

Works Cited

Alberto, Paulina L., and Jesse Hoffnung-Garskof. "'Racial Democracy' and Racial Inclusion: Hemispheric Histories." *Afro-Latin American Studies: An Introduction*, edited by Alejandro de la Fuente and George Reid Andrews. Cambridge UP, 2018, pp. 264–316.

Anderson, Katrina, et al. "Student Labour and Training in Digital Humanities." *Digital Humanities Quarterly*, vol. 10, no. 1, Feb. 2016. www.digitalhumanities.org/dhq/vol/10/1/000233/000233.html

Arroyo, Jossianna. *Writing Secrecy in Caribbean Freemasonry*. Palgrave Macmillan, 2013.

Boyles, Christina, et al. "Precarious Labor and the Digital Humanities." *American Quarterly*, vol. 70, no. 3, 2018, pp. 693–700. Project MUSE, doi:10.1353/aq.2018.0054.

Braunstein, Laura. "Open Stacks: Making DH Labor Visible." *Dh+lib*, 7 June 2017, https://acrl.ala.org/dh/2017/06/07/open-stacks-making-dh-labor-visible/.

Carlo-Becerra, Peter L. *Which Is "White" and Which "Colored"? Notes on Race and/or Color among Puerto Ricans in Interwar New York City*. 2012. State University of New York at Binghamton, Ph.D. dissertation.

Colón, Jesús. *A Puerto Rican in New York and Other Sketches*. Mainstream Publishers, 1961.

Connolly, N.D.B. *A World More Concrete: Real Estate and the Remaking of Jim Crow South Florida*. U of Chicago P, 2014.

de la Fuente, Alejandro. "Myths of Racial Democracy: Cuba, 1900–1912." *Latin American Research Review*, vol. 34, no. 3, 1999, pp. 39–73.

Duany, Jorge. *The Puerto Rican Nation on the Move: Identities on the Island and in the United States*. U of North Carolina P, 2002.

Ferrer, Ada. *Insurgent Cuba: Race, Nation, and Revolution, 1868–1898*. U of North Carolina P, 1999.

Fusté, José I. "Translating Negroes into Negros: Rafael Serra's Transamerican Entanglements between Black Cuban Racial and Imperial Subalternity, 1895–1909." *Afro-Latin@s in Movement: Critical Approaches to Blackness and Transnationalism in the Americas*, edited by Petra R. Rivera-Rideau et al. Palgrave Macmillan, 2016, pp. 221–45.
Guerra, Lillian. *The Myth of José Martí: Conflicting Nationalisms in Early Twentieth-Century Cuba*. U of North Carolina P, 2005.
Helg, Aline. *Our Rightful Share: The Afro-Cuban Struggle for Equality, 1886–1912*. U of North Carolina P, 1995.
Hidalgo Paz, Ibrahim. *Cuba, 1895–1898: Contradicciones y disoluciones*. Centro de Estudios Martianos/Centro Juan Marinello, 1999.
Hoffnung-Garskof, Jesse. "Cuban Racial Politics in Nineteenth-Century New York: A Critical Digital Humanities Approach." *American Historical Review*, vol. 126, no. 1, 2021, pp. 109–39. doi.org/10.1093/ahr/rhab007.
———. *Racial Migrations: New York City and the Revolutionary Politics of the Spanish Caribbean*. Princeton UP, 2019.
Logan, John R., et al. "Emergent Ghettos: Black Neighborhoods in New York and Chicago, 1880–1940." *American Journal of Sociology*, vol. 120, no. 4, 2015, pp. 1055–94.
Loveman, Mara, and Jeronimo O. Muniz. "How Puerto Rico Became White: Boundary Dynamics and Intercensus Racial Reclassification." *American Sociological Review*, vol. 72, no. 6, 2007, pp. 915–39. SAGE Journals, doi:10.1177/000312240707200604.
Mirabal, Nancy Raquel. *Suspect Freedoms: The Racial and Sexual Politics of Cubanidad in New York, 1823–1957*. New York UP, 2016.
Orum, Thomas T. *The Politics of Color: The Racial Dimension of Cuban Politics during the Early Republican Years, 1900–1912*. New York UP, 1975.
Pappademos, Melina. *Black Political Activism and the Cuban Republic*. U of North Carolina P, 2011.
Pérez, Lisandro. *Sugar, Cigars, and Revolution: The Making of Cuban New York*. New York UP, 2018.
Poyo, Gerald E. *With All, and for the Good of All: The Emergence of Popular Nationalism in the Cuban Communities of the United States, 1848–1898*. Duke UP, 1989.
Riis, Jacob. *How the Other Half Lives*. Charles Scribner and Sons, 1890, http://www.bartleby.com/208/13.html.
Schomburg, Arthur Alfonso. *Arthur A. Schomburg: A Puerto Rican's Quest for His Black Heritage*, edited by Flor Piñero de Rivera. Centro de Estudios Avanzados de Puerto Rico y el Caribe, 1989.
Serra, Rafael. *Ensayos políticos, sociales y económicos*. Imprenta de A. W. Howes, 1899.
Sinnette, Elinor Des Verney. *Arthur Alfonso Schomburg, Black Bibliophile and Collector: A Biography*. Wayne State UP, 1989.
Toledo, Josefina. *Sotero Figueroa, editor de Patria: Apuntes para una biografía*. Editorial Letras Cubanas, 1985.
Valdés, Vanessa Kimberly. *Diasporic Blackness: The Life and Times of Arturo Alfonso Schomburg*. State U of New York P, 2017.
Zeuske, Michael. "Clientelas regionales, alianzas interraciales y poder nacional en torno a la 'Guerrita de Agosto.'" *Illes i imperis*, Jan. 1999, pp. 127–56.

II

Puerto Rican and Cuban Literary Expression

6

Exploding the Limits of Bodies and Islands
The Literary Works of Yolanda Arroyo Pizarro and Legna Rodríguez Iglesias

MONICA SIMAL

> Tuve un padre marinero que se convirtió en árbol. Voy a verlo y el árbol ni siquiera mueve las ramas. Genéticamente, algún día yo también me convertiré en árbol. Lo llevo en la sangre.
>
> (I had a sailor dad that turned into a tree. I am going to see it and the tree does not move its branches. Genetically, someday I will also turn into a tree. I have it in my blood.)
>
> Legna Rodríguez Iglesias, *Mi novia preferida fue un bulldog francés*

How can we imagine and think about the Caribbean in present times after the work of Édouard Glissant, Derek Walcott, and Antonio Benítez Rojo, among others? How can we depart from their thinking to continue problematizing the Caribbean's enunciations, imaginaries, and spatial complexities? If the Caribbean extends beyond a geographical entity, if the islands and continental coasts erode a pretended fixed insularity, if places like New York and Miami can also be part of the Caribbean, then the Caribbean seems to be "defined" as a way of being. It is the way in which we occupy and transform a space. It is a way of thinking and of being thought. It is an illusion and a dilemma, resistance, and *vaivén* (coming and going); it is the catastrophe and also the calm. If its definition cannot be prescriptive and Caribbeanness has no fixed marks, then how can we approach the fictional works of writers such as Yolanda Arroyo Pizarro (Puerto Rico, 1970) and Legna Rodríguez Iglesias (Cuba, 1984)?

I propose in this chapter that these writers are precisely "defined" by an exercise of demarcation that goes beyond their insular territories: Cuba and Puerto Rico. Their literature exemplifies the plural and conflicted condition of the act of representing Caribbeanness. They resist labels and yet at the same time contain some. Nonetheless, they are continually fugitive because they have mastered the art of escaping. Their lack of definition is their best definition, and it is precisely this that makes them *caribeñas*. Arroyo Pizarro and Rodríguez Iglesias have created characters that move between the local and the global and whose races, gendered identities, and diasporic conditions are constantly shifting.

I argue that Arroyo Pizarro and Rodríguez Iglesias posit a radical escape through their writing. Arroyo Pizarro claims *cimarronaje* (maroonage)—that is, her Afro-Caribbeanness and Afro-feminism—as her literary praxis. In the case of Rodríguez Iglesias, she resists through her playful and ideological use of language. If Arroyo Pizarro claims a literary *cimarronaje* and her writing is a call for activism and resistance—a literary getaway if you will—then for Rodríguez Iglesias, the escape is also the written/tattooed body and her refusal to be encapsulated by a fixed linguistic display. I analyze the novels *Los documentados* (2005) by Arroyo Pizarro and *Mi novia preferida fue un bulldog francés* (2017) by Rodríguez Iglesias precisely due to the impossibility of their homogenization. These narratives expose complex relations between race and identities in literature and show the impossibility of speaking of a single model used to define not only Puerto Rican and Cuban contemporary literary production but also the Hispanic Caribbean. I am most interested in examining how Arroyo Pizarro and Rodríguez Iglesias position themselves in the current sociopolitical global order.

In *Aquí América latina: Una especulación,* Josefina Ludmer examines "el territorio de la lengua" ("the territory of language") as "uno de los centros de la fábrica de realidad y (como la isla urbana y la nación profanada) uno de los instrumentos conceptuales para pensar los años 2000 en América Latina" ("one of the centers in the fabrication of reality and [as the urban island and the profane nation] one of the conceptual instruments to think about the 2000s in Latin America") (189). Walter Mignolo, interested in the effects of coloniality on peoples' lives, coined the term "coloniality of Being" to refer to the colonial experience and its impact on language. He explains that "languages are not just 'cultural' phenomena in which people find their 'identity'; they are also the location where knowledge is inscribed" (669). Parting from these critical notions, I approach the novels of these two Caribbean writers to examine to what extent they convene a new form of territoriality or transterritoriality by being aware of the power behind language. Arroyo Pizarro and Rodríguez Iglesias seem to complicate the (im)possibility of addressing the territory of language as a new form of territoriality that (re)unites contemporary Caribbean writers.

I propose then an analysis of the novels *Los documentados* and *Mi novia preferida fue un bulldog francés* as examples of new cartographies that put bodies and stories in circulation. How and from where do they speak? How do their acts of telling stories disavow official discourses and/or national narratives? How do they decolonize hegemonic centers to propose *other* spaces? Can we indeed find a new form of territoriality or transterritoriality in narratives that reflect a migrant community within a new space that is imperial, global, and fragmented? *Los documentados* and *Mi novia preferida fue un bulldog francés* will allow me to answer these and other questions and also to demonstrate that it is precisely within the territory of language that resistance to and escape from gendered, racialized, and imperialized dynamics are possible in the Caribbean.

Documenting the Human Drama

Among other literary works in which she reflects on gendered and racialized identities, Arroyo Pizarro is the author of novels such as *Carapazones* (2010) and *Violeta* (2013), as well as short story collections such as *Lesbianas en clave caribeña* (2013), *Lesbofilias* (2014), and *Las negras* (2016). She won the PEN Club prize in 2006 with her first novel *Los documentados* (2005), which will be examined in the following pages.

The novel narrates the arrival of groups of Dominican and Haitian migrants to the coasts of Puerto Rico, specifically at Playa Tereque in Camuy. The narrator-witness is a deaf girl who, from atop a tree, each night meticulously writes down everything concerning the arrival of these migrants. She notes how the men, women, and children escape and run for their lives before they are detained by the U.S. Immigration and Customs Enforcement (ICE). They run for their freedom "en su carrera interminable de querer alcanzar la felicidad, fuera donde fuera, ignorando límites territoriales y fronteras de aguas asesinas" ("in their endless race to achieve happiness, wherever that may be, ignoring territorial limits and borders of murderous waters") (27). While the girl, Kapuc, writes down this reflection, the headlines of local newspapers announce with capital letters: "AUTORIDADES DESCUBREN NUEVO ARRIBO DE INDOCUMENTADOS A LAS COSTAS DEL PAIS"; "SE AHOGAN TRES ILEGALES EN CAMUY"; "difícil legalizar el status de los que llegan en yola" ("AUTHORITIES

DISCOVER NEW ARRIVAL OF UNDOCUMENTED MIGRANTS ON OUR COASTS; "THREE ILLEGALS DROWN IN CAMUY"; "it is difficult to legalize the status of those who arrive in *yola* (yawls)") (131).

These Caribbean bodies are displayed in a discourse that responds to "una lógica de repudio y exclusion" ("a logic of repudiation and exclusion") (Bustamante 131). Arroyo Pizarro tries to resist and denounce that logic from her literature. For her main character, Kapuc, it is evident that the migrants were not running toward death but toward life. They are chasing an illusory dream, but a dream after all. This contrasts sharply with the anti-immigrant media portrayal of them, and Kapuc's chronicles then become a counternarrative, a reaction against the official narrative that appears on radio and television. Her action of recording/documenting from the top of a tree, far from being the eye of a powerful surveillance system (a guard in a panoptic tower), is rather what enables resistance through writing. She testifies and legitimizes the human drama with words that seem prophetic: "Yo voy escribiendo todo lo que atestiguan mis ojos. Quizás algún día será productivo revisitar esta crónica" ("I am writing everything that my eyes witness. Perhaps one day it will be productive to revisit this chronicle") (10). The disabled girl empowers herself by being on top of her dear tree and documents meticulously the lives of these migrants. In doing so, she rescues each one from silence. Although she does not know their names, much less their personal stories, her desire to keep a sort of diary of these "illegal" arrivals is a way of reacting to the collectivization and homogenization that, from the media, claim these bodies, silencing and politicizing their lives. She restores their existence as suffering beings, damaged by systems that failed to protect them and from which they must flee.

In the novel, Arroyo Pizarro describes Antillean, inter-island immigration as "un viaje puente, en donde personas de Haití, Cuba y algunos orientales utilizan las costas de Santo Domingo como resorte para luego llegar a territorio puertorriqueño" ("a bridge journey, where people from Haiti, Cuba, and some Orientals use the coasts of Santo Domingo as a means to later reach Puerto Rican territory") (129). The novel transcends literature by exposing this humanitarian crisis that many countries are experiencing today: the plight of thousands of displaced people who leave their places of origin and find themselves in other precarious situations. The novel then exemplifies what Josefina Ludmer describes as "literatura posautónoma" ("post-autonomous literature"), erasing the differences between reality and fiction in its pages (135). According to Ludmer, the public imagination is equivalent to a "fábrica de realidad" ("a reality factory"). Based on this logic, fiction is everywhere, and it is therefore impossible to distinguish it from reality. The territory of language "(c)ontiene la literatura pero la desborda" ("contains literature but overflows it") and that is why all those words heard, read, and remembered form part of this territory, in addition to everything that is put into circulation through the media: radios, newspapers, magazines, the Internet, telephones, translations, encyclopedias (189).

Arroyo Pizarro, like her character, uses this novel to document the reality of the migrants coming to Puerto Rico to use the island as a bridge to the United States. Her novel is a fight against invisibility and vulnerability. In the migrants' search for shelter in other lands, the country that badly welcomes them ends up damaging them again with exclusionary policies that are both xenophobic and racist. *Los documentados* problematizes official narratives regarding migration to Puerto Rico from other Caribbean islands, as well as criticizes the stereotypes used by Puerto Ricans to talk about racialized Others. By displaying a Caribbean that rejects its own inhabitants based on racial and ethnic prejudices, Arroyo Pizarro questions the very nature of the borders of the Caribbean islands. Her novel can be read as an inclusive and heterogenous fictional archipelago that exposes the precariousness of migrant bodies as well as the official narratives that frame them. Both textual projects, Kapuc's and Arroyo Pizarro's, function as a recording apparatus against oblivion. Words are mechanisms to save personal stories, to restore individualities, and to reconstitute humanity.

Although all emigration implies a familial and cultural breakdown and the search for opportunities in another country, for Arroyo Pizarro it is important to question whether what is occurring is a new form of territorialization or rather a cultural and identity continuation. In this way she distances herself from what Néstor García Canclini proposed in his book *Ciudadanos y consumidores* (*Citizens and Consumers*), where he equates migration with deterritorialization. The novel extends a network, a bridge that touches all the Caribbean islands. These pages attempt to establish an archipelago, a community that naturally and culturally connects its inhabitants. It is more productive then to read this novel with the archipelagic lens in mind. Arroyo Pizarro "make[s] visible discontinuous and multifocal experiences that are sometimes historically connected but have been disconnected by national, international, transnational, hemispheric, and global frameworks" (Martínez-San Miguel and Stephens 70). The narrator comments: "(V)ienen de lugares tan distantes como Dominicana y Haití, lugares alejados de mi tierra por tan sólo unas cuantas horas de travesía caótica...; lugares de un olor tan distintivo como antillano del mismo archipiélago pero de otro distinto litoral, desde donde el pavor únicamente se aferra a quienes se quedan enterrados en la tierra natal" ("They come from places as distant as the Dominican Republic and Haiti, places far from my homeland for only a few hours of chaotic journey...; places with a smell as distinctive as Antillean from the same archipelago but from a different coastline, from where dread only clings to those that remain buried in their native land") (82). Arroyo Pizarro celebrates these interconnected individualities the same way she celebrates nature itself. Like the mangroves, like the beaches, like the archipelagos, the human condition has been in communion with that same nature and with those same landscapes for centuries.

If "the real force of the Caribbean island archipelago movement is a metamorphosis that emphasizes invention and creation" (Martínez-San Miguel and Stephens 8), this metamorphosis clearly operates in the novel when the arts are highlighted as a way to reconstitute invisible identities and also as a powerful force that interconnects them. Kapuc finds her counterpart in Samuel, the Dominican boy who has reached the shores of Camuy. He also draws and writes to document the human drama, although he does so from the other shore. When he reflects on his clandestine arrival in Puerto Rico, he comments:

> por fin piso una arena que se conecta con la arena del otro lado de la orilla, pero que es otra, que es otra que me dejará comer más a menudo, que me dejará esculpir. Que me permitirá buscar a mi padre y tener cuantas hermanas y hermanos me plazca, y en donde se harán realidad todos mis sueños. No tengo nada conmigo, excepto mis notas, mi crónica, mis números que cada madrugada daban testimonio de todos mis compatriotas que hasta acá se embarcaban. Extraño a Samaná, pero más extraño esto. Quiero esto. Quiero vivir esto. (50)

> (I finally step on sand that connects with the sand on the other side of the shore, but that is another, that is another that will let me eat more often, that will let me sculpt. That will allow me to look for my father and have as many sisters and brothers as I please, and where all my dreams will come true. I have nothing with me, except my notes, my chronicle, my numbers that every morning bore witness to all my compatriots who until here embarked. I miss Samaná, but I miss this more. I want this. I want to live this.)

Los documentados exposes how "las políticas de la lengua son hoy políticas económicas de la globalización, políticas imperiales y también políticas de los sentimientos (afecciones)" ("the politics of language are today economic politics of globalization, imperial politics and also politics of feelings (affections)") (Ludmer 191–92). Arroyo Pizarro leads us to reflect, from the territory of language, on those policies. This is why her character Kamuc documents the arrival of these emigrants whom she will no longer call "indocumentados" ("undocumented"), but "documentado" ("documented"). The word *documented* is symbolic, and its use in the title also makes it a signifier. Arroyo Pizarro turns this novel into "an archipelagic poetics [that] also opens space to express solidarity with other peoples, places, and species who have similar struggles and experiences. Furthermore, the archipelagic links the island to the continent, thus making visible profound differences and power dynamics" (Santos Pérez xv).

Although some of the migrants, like Samuel, arrive on the "isla de las libertades y la felicidad verde" ("island of freedoms and green happiness") (108) seeking to make their dreams come true, Arroyo Pizarro opposes this idealized image of Puerto Rico by presenting a chronicle of corruption, social inequalities, and discrimination based on disability, gender, and race issues that prevail on the island. The novel exposes the involvement of many military officials and civilians who benefit economically from this human trafficking. The racist and anti-immigrant sentiments of a section of the population are revealed. Newcomers are wrongly seen as usurpers of jobs and must endure being stereotyped and rejected, in the case of the men "por ser machistas" ("for being sexist") and the women for apparently liking that type of sexist man: "y a la mayoría de las mujeres esos son los tipos que les gustan, y contaminarán [la] religión con una madeja de creencias africanas pulguientas que van desde el santerismo hasta el vodoo" ("for most of the women those are the dudes they like, and they all [men and women] will contaminate religion with a skein of flea-ridden African beliefs ranging from Santería to Voodoo") (105–6).

To delve into the texts of Arroyo Pizarro is to understand these dynamics beyond the contours of her local city. In the exordium to her book *Las negras* (2016), Marie Ramos Rosado highlights Arroyo Pizarro's concern for filling the gaps in historiography not only in Puerto Rican history but also in universal history. In this sense, the book, which collects the three stories "Wanwe," "Matronas," and "Saeta," rescues the voices of those Black women made invisible by history to counteract what Ramos Rosado points out as "óptica patriarcal" ("patriarchal optics") (17), which has given an "invisibilidad histórica" ("historical invisibility") to "las mujeres esclavas" ("slave women") (17). Arroyo Pizarro documents/testifies the stories silenced by History both in the colonial past and in the neocolonial and neoliberal present. And it is in this politics of language where Arroyo Pizarro moves from the local to the global and vice versa. These silenced stories and the mobilization they carry out cannot be understood without that "vuelta al mundo" ("round the world tour") (Ludmer) that language bestows upon them. To be understood, Arroyo Pizarro must position her narrative within an anti-systemic, anti-institutional struggle, thus overflowing the confines of the island. As a Black, lesbian feminist, Arroyo Pizarro blows up the binomial knowledge-power inherited from colonialism and Euronorthcentric thought, and her literature becomes a political praxis. Language informs her activism and vice versa; language itself is her epistemological *cimarronaje*.

La isla tatuada (the Tatooed Island)

Rodríguez Iglesias is a poet, playwright, and short story writer whose work includes poems collected in *Chupar la piedra* (2012), *Tregua fecunda* (2012), *Chicle* (2016), *Miami Century Fox* (2016), and novels such as *Mayonesa bien brillante* (2012) and *Las analfabetas* (2015). She has received multiple awards, including the Julio Cortázar Ibero-American Short Story Prize in 2011, the Casa de las Américas Prize in Theater in 2016, and the 2016 Paz Prize from the National Poetry Series in the United States. The novel I will examine, *Mi novia favorita fue un bulldog francés*, was published by Alfaguara in 2017.

In this novel, Rodríguez Iglesias presents a universe where differentiating between reality and fiction is difficult because, as Ludmer would say, the work operates within the logic of "el movimiento, la conectividad, la superposición y la sobreimpresión de todo lo visto y oído" ("the movement, connectivity, superposition and the superimposition of everything seen and heard"). According to the Argentine critic, the "idea de imaginación pública tiene que ver con que estamos sumergidos en discursos, imágenes, y que eso es con lo que se construye la realidad" ("idea of public imagination has to do with the fact that we are immersed in speeches, images, and that this is what reality is built with") (Ludmer, "La crítica"). The epigraph with which Rodríguez Iglesias opens her work already places us within that logic of reading/understanding reality through literature: "Cualquier semejanza con hechos reales pueden echarme la culpa a mí. Me tiene sin cuidado" ("You can blame me for any resemblance to real events. I do not care").

The fifteen stories that make up this novel demolish the borders of the island and the body and re-create a constellation of stories and words that are "desajustadas" ("maladjusted"). Rodríguez Iglesias questions the role of the writer in today's global society by problematizing individual space, as well as the disintegration of a physical body. For her, although a body may be ill, it can still manage to rebel against the imposition of political orders. This is why in her study of Rodríguez Iglesias' novel *Las analfabetas*, Nanne Timmer comments: "Se hace más que desacralizar la Historia oficial, se arrasa con los discursos modernos para instalar un lenguaje que cuestiona todo y juega a ser una polifonía sin fin" ("What is done is more than desecrating official history, since it destroys modern discourses to install a language that questions everything and plays at being an endless polyphony") (46). These words also can be applied to the analysis of *Mi novia preferida fue un bulldog francés*. The ludic polyphony behind the words positions Rodríguez Iglesias as an irreverent writer. Rodríguez Iglesias seems to be talking thorough her character presented as "una desajustada" ("a misfit") and that is precisely her poetic. More than that, she appears to "understand phrases, sentences, and stanzas as textual archipelagos" (Santos Pérez xvi).

In the short story "Nadie" ("Nobody"), the character says that the "núcleo familiar es decadencia" ("the nuclear family is decadence") and that the "isla es la violencia" ("the island is violence") (45), also adding:

> que lo peor de no ser nadie no es precisamente, como lo indica la lógica, suponiendo que es lógico ser, no serlo, sino saber, y encima aceptar que no eres nadie aquí y ahora. El fenómeno sucede todo el tiempo, en cualquier sociedad y en cualquier sistema, unas u otros albergan al individuo y al mismo tiempo lo echan fuera, en esa eterna circunferencia que a ratos ni siquiera sufre movimientos. (45)

> (that the worst of not being nobody is not exactly, as logic indicates, assuming that it is logical to be, not to be it, but to know, and above all to accept that you are nobody here and now. The phenomenon happens all the time, in any society and in any system, someone or another harbors the individual and at the same time casts him out, into that eternal circumference that at times does not even undergo movements.)

Rodríguez Iglesias understands the underlying forces of systems that expel and oppress. Even though she does not present them as racialized bodies, as Arroyo Pizarro does from her position as an Afro-Puerto Rican, Rodríguez Iglesias articulates these systemic expulsions as part of an imperial/global dynamic, thereby exposing a history of control and regulation of bodies forced to transit between center and periphery. Precariously positioned, these bodies must fight to occupy a space, to live, and, ultimately, even to exist.

Time and again the characters and the places in these stories literally embody the politics of repression and control. In the story "Dios" ("God"), one of the characters has to leave the country on a medical mission abroad, leaving his daughters behind. We hear one daughter confess: "Le tengo miedo al comandante que envió a mamá a una misión"; "Le tengo miedo al comandante que envía misioneros que abandonan a sus hijas." ("I'm afraid of the Commander who sent Mom on a mission"; "I am afraid of the Commander who sends missionaries who abandon their daughters") (74). The Commander is simultaneously a character as well as the system, the oppressor, the trafficker. The fear he inspires is linked directly to his position related to the aforementioned "patriarchal optics." His oversight of individual bodies is all part of a larger system of oversight intended to regulate bodies as a collective. So it is that in the eighth section of her book, entitled "Miami," Rodríguez Iglesias introduces us to the city as a commercial, bilingual place, where the Internet is easily accessed and, as a result, her character can connect with friends all over the world. Miami is a kind of "país digital" ("digital country") far away from the world where the narrator of this story lives. This is why the female narrator points it out: "donde vivo no hay eso llamado wi-fi" ("where I live there is no such thing as Wi-Fi") (87). And while it is true that this digital country is liberating, it is also complicit with the forces of repression that seek to monitor and to regulate those who inhabit it.

Now, returning once again to the story "Nadie" ("Nobody"), when the character reaches the U.S.-Mexican border and asks the officer for asylum, she tells him, "quiero ajustarme, estoy desajustada" ("I want to adjust, I am out of order") (48). The deliberate use of word play connected to "desajustada" suggests a different discourse altogether, one that is well known within the Cuban émigré community: the Cuban Adjustment Act, the border crossing, the arrival in the United States. But Rodríguez Iglesias does not stop at re-creating a history structured neatly with a beginning, development, and conclusion. Rather, the author presents us with a series of elements, of images that overlap and stumble upon each other. Her literature is an act of linguistic juggling, and once again we confront Ludmer's notion of the territoriality of language. Rodríguez Iglesias remarked in an interview: "El libro es muy clínico. Pero yo no podía dejar de expresar eso. La sociedad como un hospital, como un antro de gente enferma. Y al mismo tiempo muy ambiguo. ¿De qué está hablando? ¿Está hablando de la sífilis o está hablando de la Revolución? Políticamente es correcto y es incorrecto" ("La sociedad"). ("The book is very clinical. But I couldn't stop expressing that. Society as a hospital, as a den of sick people. And at the same time very ambiguous. What are you talking about? Are you talking about syphilis or are you talking about the Revolution? Politically it is correct and it is incorrect.") In Timmer's words, Rodríguez Iglesias' narrative proposes a "redistribución de lo sensible a través de una erótica de la escritura, como gesto vital tanto como político" ("redistribution of the sensible through an erotics of writing, a vital gesture as well as a political one") (51).

This focus on sick bodies is also evident in the story "Lepidóptero" ("Lepidoptera"). The protagonist, who suffers from cancer, recognizes himself as a mollusk, and says that his tumor resembles this animal because "lleva su casa a cuesta. Yo soy su casa" (110). "Al morir el caracol, también muere su casa" (111) ("it takes his house on his back. I am his home") (110). "When the snail dies, its house also dies") (111). Obsessed with books and poetry, he apologizes to his daughter for constantly referring to poetry. By addressing his daughter in this text, he observes: "Los poemas de José Kozer sobre lo que él considera una casa son deliciosos manjares" ("José Kozer's poems about what he considers a house are delicious delicacies") (111). The sick character leaves his library as an inheritance and warns his daughter that if books seem tedious and impenetrable to her, at the very least she should stop at a word discovered randomly in order to investigate its meaning (111). The character observes: "Cada libro es mucho más que palabras y papel. A mí, por ejemplo, me encantan las tipografías, las ilustraciones, los títulos de los poemas o los capítulos. Suele haber en las frases breves toda una ciencia de vida, otro tipo de amor, que también duele" (111). ("Each book is much more than words and paper. For example, I love fonts, illustrations, titles of poems, or chapters. In short sentences, there is usually a whole science of life, another kind of love, which also hurts.") And that is precisely the house that Rodríguez Iglesias talks about in her work: the hazardous territory of the word. And it is from her obsession with words, with those randomly short sentences, that this novel is made.

The beginning of each of the fifteen stories contains transitional and/or opening pages with phrases that function as "updates" or "posts." These "posts" occupy the whole page due to the use of a large font. The short sentences falsely pretend to be meaningless but, on the contrary, invoke sounds, images, and thoughts. The reader is assigned the task of discovering the connections among them. Often, the phrases seem dismembered and meaningless, much like the lives of the characters themselves: "Mi novia preferida fue un bulldog francés: respondía a mis regaños orinándose"; "Me duermo. Me ahogo. Trago agua. En el fondo del océano hay un Samsung Galaxy vibrando." ("My favorite girlfriend was a French bulldog: she responded to my scolding by urinating"; "I'm falling asleep. I'm drowning. I gulp water. At the bottom of the ocean there is a Samsung Galaxy vibrating.") Nevertheless, just as an atlas is filled with maps, these "meaningless" phrases illustrate the pages of the stories, producing for the reader an archipelago composed of words. Yolanda Martínez-San Miguel and Michelle Stephens reference a painting by Kathryn Chan titled *Archipelago* to reflect on a new archipelagic methodology for their book. If Chan in her artwork connects "apparently disparate pieces," Rodríguez Iglesias intends to do exactly the same in her writing. In the story "Tatuaje" ("Tattoos"), the narrator refers to the tattoos on her body as:

Así que son tatuajes nacidos del amor.
Duele porque quema.
El tatuaje y el amor. (121)
...
¿No vas a preguntarme qué es Cuba para mí?
Mira.
El mapa de Cuba me lo tatué en el noventa y nueve.
...
En las costillas, donde más duele.
Macho, la patria es la patria. (129)
(So these are tattoos born from love
It hurts because it burns
The tattoos and love.
...
Aren't you going to ask me what Cuba means to me?
Look.

I had a map of Cuba tattooed on me in nineteen ninety-nine.
. . .
On the ribs, where it hurts the most.
Dude, the homeland is the homeland.)

Lines, as words, are tattooed on an ill body, allowing readers to make sense of their interplay. Rodríguez Iglesias' character uses her body to represent the collective body of Cuba as a nation, although she does so by disavowing along the way any sacred notion of Cuba as a homeland. *Patria*, as a signifier, is void of meaning and is comprehensible instead by "reading" the tattooed contours of the island itself. Cuba is an ill-fitted, tattooed body. Even though the island is the largest within the Cuban archipelago, we cannot forget that it is also part of the Caribbean archipelago. The inked lines on a body, just as the fragmented words of the stories, are the pieces that integrate the archipelago. Rodríguez Iglesias, as Chan did with her painting, "connects the apparently disparate pieces of the multiple, translocal human displacements that define the Caribbean as a complex and random process that signifies" (Martínez-San Miguel and Stephens 2). The apparently chaotic and disconnected words of this novel are carefully assembled to map out the ethical and political position of Rodríguez Iglesias as a writer reacting against the grandiose narratives of Nation, Being, and Modernity. Rodríguez Iglesias is a modern subject conscious of her "coloniality" status (Maldonado-Torres 243). To enter this author's universe is an exercise of connecting words that unpack fixed understandings of love, family, culture, and nation. Like a disease invading the body, these words are interconnected tattoos and/or islands in Rodríguez Iglesias' archipelago.

Conclusion

Using the narrative of Latin American immigrants as a reference, Ludmer comments on what she understands as a fracture between the concepts of "territorio de la nación" and "territorio de la lengua e imperio" ("territory of the nation" and "territory of language and empire"). When immigrants leave their national territory, they make the break between their nation and language possible. Language, together with the lost nation, becomes the deterritorialized homeland, which, in turn, makes possible a transnational community. However, these writers present in their literature certain forms of (trans)nationality and (trans)territoriality that resist the dynamics that have historically demarcated the national, the local, and the Caribbean. Rodríguez Iglesias states:

> Nunca me interesa lo del espacio. Me interesa el tono universal, [aunque] sería despreciable incluso, para usar una palabra grave, no tocar el tema cubano. Pero me gusta que [la historia] no esté pasando donde se supone. Por qué, si en realidad es global. El bien y el mal es global. La historia de amor pasa donde sea, y si es una catástrofe, también. Me interesa mucho más el personaje, lo que está sufriendo ("La sociedad").
>
> (I'm never interested in space. I am interested in the universal tone, [although] it would be despicable even, to use a serious word, not to touch the Cuban theme. But I like that [the story] isn't happening where it is supposed to. Why, if it is actually global. Good and evil is global. The love story happens anywhere, and if it's a catastrophe, that happens anywhere too. I'm much more interested in the character, in what he is suffering.)

This interest in representing a universal pain, or achieving, in general, a certain universality that reaches beyond the local is what the works of Rodríguez Iglesias might have in common with those of Arroyo Pizarro. To achieve their aims, both writers have put traditional modes of representation in tension (although paradoxically they have also made use of them). Experimentation, along with a certain linguistic playfulness, remains present in their narratives in spite of the anti-systemic, violent representations of History's political and gender dynamics. I have tried not to base my approach to their work on what distinguishes them from one another and/or similarities they share, but rather to return to those modes of enunciation, to that territory of language from which the edges of our islands continue to be blown apart; to insist on that stressed relationship between the local and the global, which is continually marked by the logic of the positionality of Being. A critic once described Rodríguez Iglesias as "tsunami Legna." Maybe this is the most fitting way to talk about both of these women writers. They are tsunamis that burst the "logic" of the archipelago to re-create modes of seeing and of being seen. They write on and about bodies that are running to make sense of life itself.

Works Cited

Arroyo Pizarro, Yolanda. *Los documentados*. 3rd ed. Publicaciones Boreales, 2017.
———. *Las negras*. 4th ed. Publicaciones Boreales, 2016.
Bustamante, Fernanda. "'Correr y que no te devuelvan, correr para olvidar de dónde has partido': Una lectura de *Los documentados* (2005) de Yolanda Arroyo." *Revista Letral*, no. 22, 2019, pp. 129–50.
García Canclini, Néstor. *Consumidores y ciudadanos: Conflictos multiculturales de la globalización*. Grijalbo, 1995.
Ludmer, Josefina. *Aquí América Latina: Una especulación*. Eterna Cadencia, 2010.
———. "La crítica pura me aburre." 23 Oct. 2011. https://josefinaludmer.wordpress.com/.
Maldonado-Torres, Nelson. "On the Coloniality of Being: Contributions to the Development of a Concept." *Cultural Studies*, vol, 21, nos. 2–3, 2007, pp. 240–70.
Rodríguez Iglesias, Legna. *Mi novia preferida fue un bulldog francés*. Penguin, 2017.
———. "La sociedad es como un hospital, como un antro de gente enferma." *El País*, 1 Feb. 2018, https://www.elmundo.es/cultura/literatura/2018/01/31/5a71ee52e2704e50408b45dd.html.
Santos Pérez, Craig. "Archipelagic Poetics: A Foreword." *Contemporary Archipelagic Thinking: Toward New Comparative Methodologies and Disciplinary Formations*, edited by Michelle Stephens and Yolanda Martínez-San Miguel. Rowman & Littlefied, 2020, pp. xv–xvi.
Stephens, Michelle, and Yolanda Martínez-San Miguel, editors. *Contemporary Archipelagic Thinking: Toward New Comparative Methodologies and Disciplinary Formations*. Rowman & Littlefied, 2020.
Timmer, Nanner. "Cartografía de la no-nación: Escritura y oralidad en *Las analfabetas*, de Legna Rodríguez Iglesias." *Telar*, vol. 11, no. 17, 2016, pp. 38–53.

7

Puerto Rico *en Areíto*
Translation, Ethnic and Cultural Studies, and Other Collaborations among Cuban and Puerto Rican Migrant Intellectuals

LAURA LOMAS

Poco después de aquella fiesta, me encontré asistiendo a las reuniones mensuales que [Lourdes Casal] convocaba en su apartamento situado al norte de la ciudad, bordeando a Harlem. Eran todo un ritual, iniciada con la solemnidad de una misa política que a menudo motivaba buenas rondas.

(A little after that party, I found myself attending the monthly meetings that [Lourdes Casal] convened in her apartment situated north of the city, on the edge of Harlem. They were a full-on ritual, initiated with the solemnity of a political mass that often led to good rounds.)

Román de la Campa ("Revista *Areíto*: Herejía de una nación improbable")

Areíto, a "leftist" Cuban exile periodical, diverged radically from the dominant version of Cuban exile cultural politics, which may help explain why the magazine has received surprisingly limited attention given its long life (first series, 1974–84, and second series, 1987–95). The magazine's title, which refers to a Taíno practice of singing about a people's collective past while dancing, alludes to the publication's decolonial agenda, which is why *Areíto* and its collaborators merit further attention: many of the major Latin American and Caribbean intellectuals of the latter twentieth century published their work in its pages, and this work demonstrates a twentieth-century investment in Lola Rodríguez de Tió's late-nineteenth-century dream of independence as a single bird, with Cuba and Puerto Rico as its wings. Following the example of Rodríguez de Tió's contemporary José Martí and the late-nineteenth-century revolutionary movement's *veladas de danzón* (dance soirées), oratory, and poetry events, and writing under the aegis of Cuba's widely respected founding father and New York–based Latino community organizer, the magazine used the ligaments and conviviality of print culture to coalesce fragments of the Hispanic Caribbean diaspora toward shared goals. The editorial committee and Cuban and Puerto Rican contributors to the magazine helped foment interisland collaboration along with emerging area studies such as Latin American, Cuban, and Puerto Rican studies as they intersected with emerging interdisciplinary Latina/o/x, Black, and cultural studies, which gained an institutional footing in the mid-to-late 1970s, in the same years when *Areíto* was born.[1]

Areíto's leadership distinguished its agenda from that of right-wing media conglomerates based in Miami by affirming a critical pluralism with space for center-to-left politics, including ending the U.S. blockade against Cuba that has been in place since 1961 and promoting dialogue with the Cuban government despite the blockade. As the editors and letters to that collective note, from its first issue *Areíto* received support from readers dispersed throughout the United States and faced vociferous attacks in the conservative press in Miami because—the editors surmised—the magazine affirmed an unexpectedly wide array of political positions and transnational affiliations for Cuban exiles: "*Areíto* representa el reconocimiento y la legitimación de un pluralismo ideológico en el exilio, que indudablemente es anatema para los que controlan la prensa exiliada" ("*Areíto* represents the recognition and legitimization of an ideological pluralism in the exile community, which undoubtedly is anathema for those who control the exile press") (*Areíto*, "Editorial no. 2" 1). Román de la Campa notes that the perspective of *Areíto* was almost unimaginable as a Cuban exile publication—"ni me imaginaba una revista como tal" ("I could hardly imagine such a magazine existed")—when he first encountered its *chispas*, poetry, *testimonio*, artwork by Rapi Diego, and analysis in the University of Minnesota library's copy of the magazine in 1975 (de la Campa, "Revista *Areíto*" 138). De la Campa became involved in monthly meetings after a Puerto Rican writer, Luis López Nieves, invited him to a gathering in Queens, New York, where de la Campa met the mobilizing force behind *Areíto*, Afro-Cubana poet and social psychologist, Lourdes Casal.[2]

Like Cuba's Martí, who is quoted often in decorative epigraphs in *Areíto*, the editorial committee saw the magazine's focus as interrelated with the region's cultural and political existence, with special attention to Cuba and Puerto Rico and their diasporas in the United States. In this way *Areíto* adopted interisland collaborations resembling those among the late-nineteenth-century Puerto Ricans Sotero Figueroa, Arturo Alfonso Schomburg, and the "black Lord Byron" (as Puerto Rican cigarmaker Bernardo Vega called him), Francisco "Pachín" Gonzalo Marín, who joined Cubans Rafael Serra, Juan and Gerónimo Bonilla, and Martí in New York–based clubs to build momentum for independence, at a time when racial segregation was the law of the land, enforced by the police and vigilante racial terror, even as African-descended residents—including Afro-Latinos—were organizing in Black-identified and integrated, mixed-race forums.[3] Neither in the battlefields of Cuba nor in the brilliant solitary mind of Martí, but through collaboration and negotiation across the color line and across Caribbean national groupings did this antiracist, anticolonial politics grow (Hoffnung-Garskof, *Racial Migrations* 275).

Similar to late-nineteenth-century collaborators, Cuban exiles in Puerto Rico and in New York City self-consciously promoted Puerto Rico in *Areíto*.[4] From the magazine's inception in April 1974, Puerto Rican–based Cuban exile and economics professor at the University of Puerto Rico, Francisco Aruca, helped to foreground the interrelatedness of Cuban and Puerto Rican independence. The magazine and travel agencies based in Puerto Rico and New Jersey aimed to facilitate up-close study of contemporary and historical processes in Cuba from divergent political angles and with academic rigor. The diasporic intellectuals who participated in *Areíto* often faced racism in the U.S. heartland and found a Cuban diasporic audience that resonated with Puerto Rican migrant experiences of exploitation and exclusion.[5] *Areíto* created space for discussions of Puerto Rico's political prisoners, of the island's "colony economy" (to use Eduardo Lalo's term), and of a longstanding struggle for self-determination, alongside Cuba.[6] The magazine eulogized Puerto Rico–based Cuban activist of the Antonio Maceo Brigade, Carlos Muñiz Varela, after his assassination by right-wing Cuban groups in Puerto Rico in 1979, which marked the beginning of the end of the first phase of the magazine. Threats by Abdala and other right-leaning Cuban groups addressed to *Areíto* and to its editors (and health concerns) prompted Casal's return to Havana in December 1979, where she died due to kidney disease in February 1981.[7]

In addition to the exceptionalist project of reconnecting the Cuban diaspora and Puerto Rican allies to Cuba's revolution as an object of study, *Areíto* resignified a critique of the Hispanic Caribbean diaspora's cultural significance.[8] Support for Puerto Rico's independence coexisted with a recognition of the diaspora's future as a major cultural force inside the United States. An interview with Noel Colón Martínez during the Conference in Solidarity with the Independence of Puerto Rico, which took place in Havana in 1975, documents the long history of Puerto Rican and Cuban mutual aid, dating back to the friendship of Ramón Emeterio Betances, Eugenio María de Hostos, and Martí (*Areíto*, "Entrevista con el licenciado Noel Colón Martínez"). The interview with Colón Martínez situates the twentieth-century wave of Puerto Rican struggles for independence within the history of Puerto Rican nationalist Pedro Albizu Campos' visit to Cuba in 1927, and as an unfinished project of the Committee on Decolonization of the United Nations and the Non-Aligned Movement, which itself arose in response to the Cold War after the Bandung Conference in 1955, a coalition of African, Asian, and Latin American solidarity that gave rise to Cuba's "tricontinentalist" project (see Mahler). At the same time, a review of an art exhibit curated by Jack Agüeros, "El espíritu de independencia," at the Cayman Gallery of SoHo in New York City, describes contemporary photographs of and paintings inspired by the Puerto Rican independence movement, led among others by Albizu Campos. This reportage on New York-Puerto Rican visual art of the 1970s commented on the alienation inside late capitalist society that revolutionary Hispanic Caribbean diaspora aesthetics addresses (*Areíto*, "Reseña de Cayman Gallery"). The longstanding cross-island alliance informs *Areíto*'s portrayal of decolonization as a cultural and political project of relevance not only to Puerto Rico but also to revolutionary Cuba and the United States, as we shall see.

Beyond the pull of nostalgia for the largely inaccessible space of what de la Campa has theorized as "a severed nation," *Areíto* introduced the study of Cuban Americans and Puerto Ricans as part of Latinx diasporas and ethnic subgroups, which would by the end of the twentieth century become recognized as making up the largest minority in the United States (Lee A1). *Areíto* predicted the lasting intellectual, historical, and cultural legacy of this emergent minority group in the United States by the turn of the twenty-first century, when the magazine's first editorial foregrounded the imminent significance of "Cuban Americans" in its *raison d'être* and effectively redefined the migrant, exile, and diaspora communities as a future defining force:

Lo cotidiano nuestro se desenvuelve en el exilio. Y este pueblo que salió y sus hijos que han nacido o crecido en los Estados Unidos también nos preocupan; pues en veinte años serán un grupo minoritario más dentro de la sociedad norteamericana y ya no serán cubanos, sino "Cuban-Americans." (*Areíto*, "Editorial no. 1" 1)

(Our quotidian existence unfolds in exile. And this people that left, and their children who have been born or raised in the United States, also concern us; for, in twenty years, they will have become another minority group in North American society, and they will no longer be Cubans, but rather "Cuban-Americans.")

Against this idea of the Cuban diaspora as just "another minority group," Casal articulated the Cuban "minority" as inextricably linked to Latin America, at a time when Puerto Rican and Mexican immigrants constituted the largest demographic groups within this minority and largely failed or refused to become unidentifiable, or "to melt" in the melting pot. In her essay entitled "Recognizing Our Roots," Casal introduces a broad conception of *Latinidad* as an expression interconnecting Latinx and Latin American cultures that can play an indispensable role in promoting distinct epistemologies, critical reflection, participant observation, and activist reimagining of U.S. policy in the Western Hemisphere (39). This connection would contribute to institutional transformation by supporting contemporaneous Chicano, African American, and Puerto Rican efforts to redefine the university curriculum and expand recruitment of Black and Latinx faculty and students. The Grupo Areíto (of which de la Campa and Casal were both members) authored *Contra viento y marea*, the award-winning *testimonio* of Cuban-American experiences of immigration. This book cites the affinities Cuban diaspora interviewees felt with the U.S.-based civil rights, antiwar, and pro-Puerto Rican independence movements of the late 1960s, in which they spent their first decade as migrants, refugees, and exiles in the United States (Grupo Areíto).[9]

Situated amidst ads recruiting readers to corporate jobs and essays by leading Chicana/o, Puerto Rican, and Cuban intellectuals and artists, Casal's essays "Recognizing Our Roots" and "Memories of a Black Cuban Childhood" (in the magazine *Nuestro*) affirm the diaspora's connection and hybrid aesthetic forms, so often despised and attacked, both in the islands and in the United States. Latin American and diasporic concerns and cultural sensitivities in *Areíto* mingle in the simple act of flipping a page of *Nuestro*, subtitled *The Magazine for Latinos*. In *Areíto*, the literature of the Argentine novelist Julio Cortázar appears just a few pages away from Roberto González Echevarría's experimental fiction and his reading of Alejo Carpentier, all of which anticipate the radical U.S.-based British Latin Americanist Jean Franco's reflections on Gabriel García Márquez's Nobel Prize acceptance speech, an essay by García Márquez, the poetry of

New York–based Puerto Rican Víctor Fernández Fragoso and of New York-Cuban Dolores Prida (see González Echevarría, "'En la más alta esfera'" and "Concierto barroco"; Cortázar; Franco). This *nuestro americanismo* reconnects Puerto Rico—cut off by the U.S. invasion of 1898—to the region south of the United States.[10]

From the very first issue of *Areíto*, the twinned focus on Cuba and Puerto Rico as a gesture of "our Americanist" solidarity is directly related to the study of invisible and oppressed Cuban and Puerto Rican minorities within the urban capitalist metropolis of New York (Belnap and Fernández). The opening issue of *Areíto* calls attention to the research of Rafael Prohías, whose work Casal edited and completed for publication after his untimely death in 1973. According to an article in the first issue of *Areíto*, the most controversial section of this 300-page report on "the Cuban minority" documents the housing discrimination that Black Cubans faced from White Cubans and from White Americans in the United States (*Areíto*, "La minoría cubana en EE.UU." 7). *Areíto* thus counters the conventional interpretation of the Cuban success story and affirms a research agenda such as Prohías' that calls for an understanding of the United States, not unlike that offered by Puerto Rican writers.[11] What rankles, the article suggests, is evidence that contests the portrait of Cubans as a universally successful, White-identified model minority that feels nothing but love and gratitude for a magnanimous country for offering temporary refuge and a shot at the American Dream. According to this pioneering research, Cuban immigration to the United States does not necessarily offer economic progress nor equality of opportunity, especially if you are Black and working class.

Against the celebrated portrait of Cuban exiles and much more like a growing Puerto Rican literature, *Areíto*'s reportage on "The Cuban Minority in the U.S." calls attention to a different aspect of exile: "la otra cara de la moneda: los que no sonríen desde la portada de *Life*" ("the other side of the coin: those who do not smile from the front cover of *Life* magazine") (*Areíto*, "La minoría cubana en EE.UU." 9). Rather than hide the reality of a Black and mulatto Cuban diaspora's proletarianization, racialization, and economic exclusion, similar to other Latinx minorities and especially dark-skinned Puerto Ricans, some of whom were also of Cuban origin, *Areíto* recognized that under late-twentieth-century neoliberalism, most Cuban and Puerto Rican migrants must toil at several jobs just to survive, and often experienced exclusion because of overlapping forms of discrimination.[12]

Some Cuban exiles would eventually disparage the revolutionary antiracist cultural studies of *Areíto*. González Echevarría, for example, later characterized *Areíto*'s leadership as lacking a "strong political, philosophical, or ideological education" and he assessed the magazine's intellectual quality as "not high" (*Cuban Fiestas* 114). Yet González Echevarría—a distinguished scholar who led Yale University's Spanish Department for decades—himself published in *Areíto* and even remembers Casal fondly, as a "friend" who visited his home when they both participated in the magazine. Whether the *rondas* were good or bad—as Agustín Lara sings—the gatherings of *Areíto* contributors imagined Cuban and Puerto Rican fortunes as intertwined and they formed part of an early experimental phase of many *cubanólogos*—a term de la Campa uses to describe those who study and write about Cuba from the comfort of the U.S. academy ("Revista *Areíto*" 139)—and Puerto Rican writers like López Nieves. For this reason, the magazine, and its culture of collaboration, merit more careful study.

Writing as a Weapon and Translation as Decolonization: Revolutionary Collaborations

The collaboration among Cuban and Puerto Ricans in *Areíto* brings into focus the intertwined legacy of centuries of colonization and enslavement, which carved up Caribbean territories and cultures according to language and the geopolitical relations of Europe and North America. *Areíto* addresses the problem of language as a barrier by including "English language supplements," in which translations of Spanish-language essays appear. Analytical essays penned in English and translated into Spanish, discussing Brazil or Chile, also appeared regularly in *Areíto*. This strategy created the possibility of contact and cross-pollination at a time when access to information across Cold War capitalist-communist battle lines was proscribed both in the United States and in Cuba, and thus gives *Areíto* the feeling of contraband circulating out of bounds.

In one Puerto Rican and Cuban collaboration that *Areíto* made possible, de la Campa, as part of the magazine's contributing writers, interviews the Puerto Rican literary critic, essayist, translator, and academic Roberto Márquez about how he got started as a translator in El Barrio in New York.[13] Translation was a way for Márquez to make available the poetry of Nicolás Guillén to his Upward Bound students, mainly Afro-Latinx working-class youth in New York City. Márquez affirms how segregated barrio enclaves gifted the culture of the islands to New York—a tropicalization memorialized by Guillermo Cotto-Thorner, Frances Aparicio, and Susana Chávez-Silverman, among others—but they did not often have ready access to the cultural capital that the "newspaper or print culture more generally" represented. Similarly, the *periódico* did not often represent nor address U.S. Black and Afro-Latinx New York barrios and readers. *Areíto* counteracts this invisibility by publishing de la Campa's interview with Márquez, which exemplifies generative cross-island collaboration in the diaspora.

Puerto Rican translators who contributed to *Areíto* transform the definition of American literature and thus contribute to the decolonization of U.S. and Caribbean cultural imaginaries. Eventually becoming a distinguished professor, translator, and author, Márquez got his start by translating Guillén's poetry—some of whose work, such as *La paloma de vuelo popular* (1958) had not been available in English—as a means to fill a gap in the relevant texts available to his students but also to direct attention beyond the folklorized version of Guillén—epitomized in the early dialect poetry of *Motivos de son* (1930). This dialect poetry tended to eclipse the rest of Guillén's oeuvre and to sideline his connections to other radical Afro-Caribbean intellectuals, such as Martinican theorist of Algerian decolonization, Frantz Fanon, or the African American poet Langston Hughes. Similarly, Juan Flores translated Bernardo Vega to counteract Latinx invisibility in the United States: Flores' English version of the *Memorias de Bernardo Vega* makes an English-dominant reading public in the United States aware of Puerto Rican historical contributions to both Cuba and New York. Of relevance to our discussion here, Flores' translation demonstrates New York Puerto Ricans' indispensable ideological and material contributions—including many New York–based Puerto Ricans or Boricuas (from the Taíno name for the island of Borinquen) who gave their lives to the cause of the 1895–98 Cuban War of Independence, because they believed that an independent Cuba would subsequently contribute to Puerto Rican independence.[14] Furthermore, research on Afro-Puerto Rican Arturo Alfonso Schomburg's writing in English and Spanish reveals his contributions to a decolonizing project that valorizes the legacies of Black culture by building an archive to refute antiblack racist assumptions and stereotypes at the heart of imperial modernity. This antiblackness remained entrenched in the officially antiracist Cuban Republic, and in the post-1961 period, after the revolutionary government claimed to have eliminated racism.[15]

If the African diaspora is a call to translate, as Brent Hayes Edwards has noted, in the work of Márquez and Flores, Caribbean and African diasporas intersect and call for translation as a neglected facet of decolonization (Edwards 118). Márquez, who later published the most comprehensive and eloquent translations of Puerto Rican poetry in English, observed in *Areíto* commonalities across Caribbean literatures grounded in shared histories of colonization, enslavement, and cultural survival: "Todos van tocando lo mismo: cuestiones históricas de lo que quiere decir ser antillano; la posesión de la tierra, en todos sus niveles—espiritualmente, económicamente, políticamente, etc., y la articulación de la cultural nacional dentro de un proceso de descolonización" ("They all touch upon the same themes: historical questions about what it means to be Antillean; the possession of the land, in all of its levels—spiritually, economically, politically, etc., and the articulation of a national culture in the process of decolonization") (de la Campa, "Entrevista a Roberto Márquez" 40). Márquez continues to develop this comparative reading of an Antillean civilization that begins through his Puerto Rican insights in *Areíto*. His latest book, *A World among These Islands*, continues to explore these themes.

Referring to a body of writing by Caribbean authors destined to become renowned as founding Caribbean literary figures—Wilson Harris, Edward Kamau Brathwaite, Derek Walcott, Jacques Roumain, and René Depestre, alongside Guillén—Márquez depicts the common preoccupations of what Afro-Cuban writer Rogelio Martínez Furé calls an "Antillean civilization," made up of "national cultures in a process of decolonization."[16] These national and linguistic divisions are a legacy of colonization that continues to divide and weaken trans-Caribbean connections. Against the common Hegelian and Froudian accusation of "barbarism" and an absence of history, Márquez sees shared concerns beyond residual colonial linguistic barriers.[17] His comparative reading assembles a critical Caribbean mass that might ground collective rights to spiritual, economic, and political possession of the islands, over and against lingering European or U.S. colonial legacies or anachronistic sovereignties, a theme of urgent concern in Puerto Rico and Martinique, which persist under the legal and economic yoke of U.S. and French hegemony.

Márquez relates the work of decolonization to the transformation of language by the African-influenced diaspora cultures of the Caribbean. In the barrios where Márquez began his career as a translator, working-class Black and Latinx "Calibans" were engaging in the creative remaking and "breaking" of English, the colonizer's language, into Spanglish. It is worth noting that the journal Márquez founded, *Caliban: A Journal of New World Thought and Writing* (1975–81), was inspired by his participation in the English translation of Cuban poet and essayist Roberto Fernández Retamar's influential essay in the *Massachusetts Review*, "Caliban: Notes Towards a

Discussion of Culture in Our America," which appeared in 1974, and reappeared in book form (without the acknowledgment of the earlier version) in 1989.[18] In other words, translation triggered a debate about the decolonial aesthetics of Caribbean and "New World" literature in the United States. The goal of Márquez's journal *Caliban* was "convertir en propiedad lingüística del antiguo imperio, la historia de toda una región ("to convert the formerly imperial linguistic property into the history of an entire region)" (de la Campa, "Entrevista a Roberto Márquez" 42). Multilingual Caribbean literary texts document common decolonial questions and interests but have existed in segregated and segmented forms. Márquez's mode of reading—and *Areíto*, as stage for this conversation between Márquez and de la Campa—connect the ideologies of the Cuban Revolution and the concerns of Puerto Rican literary critics. Like the journal *Caliban* and Afro-Caribbean adaptations of the Shakespearean character to recenter the colonized's creative revolt against European masters, Márquez's translation disrupts the isolation and Eurocentric subjugation imposed upon the Hispanic Caribbean:

> al tratar la historia y cultura del Caribe en el modo segmentario que lo vamos haciendo hasta ahora, ofreciendo, por ejemplo, cursos titulados "historia cultural del Caribe" o "literatura del Caribe" que presentan solamente el Caribe hispano o el Caribe angloparlante o el francoparlante, aceptamos implícitamente categorías colonialistas. (de la Campa, "Entrevista a Roberto Márquez" 42)

> (when treating the history and culture of the Caribbean in this segmented mode as we have been doing until now, offering, for example, courses entitled "cultural history of the Caribbean" or "literature of the Caribbean" that present only the Hispanic Caribbean or the Anglophone or Francophone Caribbean, we implicitly accept colonialist categories.)

This insight deserves attention, for only in the twenty-first century have major English-language journals in Caribbean studies, such as *Small Axe*, begun to take seriously Márquez's insight in the 1970s, which emerges from a Puerto Rican and Cuban dialogue in a diasporic journal like *Areíto*. Moreover, Márquez presumes that island-based intellectuals do not have a monopoly on the Calibanic capacity to curse.

Casal forcefully articulates a similar critique of Fernández Retamar in a "rereading" of the essay "Calibán" that also appeared in *Areíto* ("Relecturas:

Calibán"). Her commentary follows Márquez in affirming the bilingual remaking of imperial languages by dark-skinned, working-class, hybrid, and hybridizing diaspora subjects not identified with European cultures nor ideologies, as the primary wellspring of revolutionary aesthetics. Resonating with Márquez's call to read across linguistic differences to study Caribbean civilization through the lens of post-plantation diasporas, Casal's essay in *Areíto* affirms that Afro-mulatto border writers in the barrios of New York may define a Cuban revolutionary aesthetics as much as or perhaps more than Latin America's New World intellectuals writing from places of class and race privilege in Latin American cultural institutions.[19]

In his interview with de la Campa, Márquez offers a reading of the relationship between history and poetic form that helps us understand the emergence of new, or even revolutionary, poetic experiments by urban, working-class, and Black-identified Puerto Ricans in a hostile Anglo- and White-dominant cultural environment. Márquez's analysis of the historical conditions of emergence of what Miguel Algarín, Pedro Pietri, Miguel Piñero, and Tato Laviera have called "Nuyorican" poetry, in English, Spanish, and Spanglish, usefully supplements Urayoán Noel's important literary history of "slam" poetry's origins, which does not mention either *Areíto* or Márquez. Márquez observes the crucial distinction among Cuban, Haitian, Jamaican, and Puerto Rican migrants in that these other migrants never assume the mantle of "Nuyo-Cuban," "New York-Haitian," nor "New York-Jamaican" in the way that a proletarian segment of Puerto Ricans invented and assumed a Nuyorican aesthetic (notably, Josefina Báez does affirm a form of "Dominican-York" poetic expression in Spanglish). This in-between category of "Nuyorican" arises when and where it does, according to Márquez, as a response to a sense of colonial invisibility in the absence of a republic, and as an affirmation of a specific historical and cultural space that New York Puerto Ricans and Cubans re-created as their own, alongside African Americans, in El Barrio, or Spanish Harlem.

Nancy Raquel Mirabal, Jesse Hoffnung-Garskof, and Kevin Meehan generatively historicize the relations and intersections of African Americans and Hispanic Caribbeans in New York. In the interview, de la Campa similarly asks and Márquez responds by underscoring the effect of the Cuban Revolution on this question of Caribbean cross-island translation as part of a historical process of decolonization:

> Es en Cuba donde por primera vez un país caribeño como parte de una política cultural consciente produce una apertura que empieza

a traducir poetas, escritores, pensadores de otros países antillanos y difundirlos a todo el pueblo cubano y a través de Cuba al pueblo latinoamericano. O sea, que en el momento en que Cuba toma posesión de su destino, vincula ese destino con los pueblos envueltos inevitablemente en el mismo destino. (de la Campa, "Entrevista a Roberto Márquez" 45)

(For the first time in a Caribbean country, as part of its conscious cultural politics, Cuba launches a program through which to begin to translate poets, writers, thinkers of other Caribbean countries and to disseminate them throughout Cuba and through Cuba to Latin American countries. In other words, at the moment when Cuba takes possession of its destiny, it links this destiny with other countries inevitably involved in the same destiny.)

This interpretation of Cuba's role as a promoter of Caribbean translation as a means of thinking more deeply about African-diaspora and Hispanic Caribbean connections directly echoes Rodríguez de Tió's two-winged bird metaphor. This formulation reveals an ideal of regional identity invested in incompletely realized political principles of self-determination and decolonization. While it may not have come to fruition, Márquez's and others' translations and theory of translation are the product of a specific moment of social upheaval, and of interrelated Cuban and Puerto Rican contributions to decolonizing U.S., Caribbean, and Latin American cultures.

"What Is This 'Black' in Latinx Popular Culture?"

Like Márquez, another *Areíto* contributor, Juan Flores, participated in the decolonial theory we have been examining through the introduction of a "new turn" in Puerto Rican diaspora literature. Whereas Márquez addresses common themes of post-plantation and postcolonial legacies in the islands and the diaspora, Flores' contributions to *Areíto* single out the diaspora rather than the nation as a space of inquiry. Flores thus developed the practice of Latinx cultural studies in the 1970s, simultaneous with and influenced by Afro-Jamaican critic Stuart Hall's studies of postcolonial diaspora cultures in Britain during the same period. These readings of the Puerto Rican diaspora in *Areíto* contribute a mode of centering critical attention upon the seemingly unmentionable "Black" in Latinx culture, which resulted in part from the Cuban Republican leadership's interpretation of

Martí as demanding the "silencing" of race (Ferrer). As a remedy to that denial of entrenched antiblack racism, Flores, Márquez, and Casal catalyzed the shift in race-consciousness in Cuban, Puerto Rican, and Latinx studies.

Although Hall raised the issue of race and racism in public intellectual activist work in Britain throughout the 1970s and 1980s, he diverged from the raceless or invisibilized Whiteness of Marxist theory by attending to race, class, diaspora consciousness, and what Hall called "position" or "location"—as an adaptation of Antonio Gramsci's thought—in the 1980s (see Hall, *Essential Essays*). Hall's essays on cultural identity and diaspora, which appeared in anthologies on film and Black popular culture, combined poststructuralist theory with readings of Black popular culture and brought the methodologies of Birmingham's Centre for Contemporary Cultural Studies to bear upon discussions of African diaspora cultures, which his students, Paul Gilroy and Hazel Carby, brought to readings of Black Atlantic music and Black women's organizing in the United States. These theoretical interventions, which take as a point of departure the exhaustion of binary oppositions and substitutions for thinking about Black culture in the West, resonate with and inspired Flores' work on the Puerto Rican diaspora and the articulation of a "Black" and Latinx or Afro-Latinx culture in the United States.[20] Flores was incubating this concern with Black and diaspora Puerto Rican culture many decades earlier, in articles on Nuyorican diaspora writers, hip hop, breakdance, and Puerto Rican music in *Areíto*. These essays likely resonated with Afro-Cuban youth desperate to connect with hip hop culture, a process that began with solidarity from the Black August Hip Hop Collective in the 1970s and exploded into the Afro-Cuban hip hop boom in the 1990s.[21]

A 1977 essay by Flores exemplifies the intertwining of Cuban and Puerto Rican cultural self-definition and decolonization, even without the achievement of the nationalist sovereignty to which Márquez aspired for his Caribbean ("Nicholasa Mohr y Louis Reyes Rivera"). A founding figure in Puerto Rican studies, Flores's publications in *Areíto* reflected on the outsized creativity and survival strategies of working-class, Black-identified, New York-Puerto Rican barrios, which diverged from the magazine's previous treatments of political and economic discussions of Puerto Rican independence. Flores's emphasis on the creativity of the Nuyorican diaspora resonated with *Areíto*'s articulation of a different Cuban exile, different both from the Cuban government's characterization of them as deserters and *gusanos* (worms), or the Miami and New Jersey anticommunist portrait of exiles who sought to visit the island as traitors deserving of death. Flores's theorizing of "diaspora from below" followed Casal's and Grupo Areíto's conceptualizing of Cubans and other Latin Americans outside the region as having "deep and abiding roots," with a keen interest in "new" and "imaginative" approaches to Latin American homelands and articulating them from the empire's belly, a position that emphasized the Latinx diaspora's continuing connections rather than excision (Casal, "Recognizing" 40).

Cubanist Lillian Guerra has noted how open criticism of antiblackness by Black Cuban intellectuals on the island met with silence or de facto censorship by the revolutionary regime in the period between 1968 and the first decade of the twenty-first century, when Walterio Carbonell's work, for example, began to be republished and circulated in Cuba. This antiblack consciousness seems to have changed due to pressure and protests from Black Cubans, which took on a more public character in 2012 with Roberto Zurbano's letter to the *New York Times*, as part of the Cuban Black-consciousness movement's calls for historical recognition of José Antonio Aponte's uprising in 1812, as well as an acknowledgment of an ongoing antiblackness, which has remained in place since long before the 1912 race war, or massacre of several thousand Afro-Cubans.[22] This twenty-first century shift in revolutionary government policy in Cuba and among Cuban intellectuals arrives decades after Hall's writings on Black popular cultural resistance to conservative Britain, after the midcentury theories of racialized coloniality by Fanon, and after the emergence of Afro-Latin@ as a category in the United States in the work of Flores and Miriam Jiménez Román. In their coedited volume, *The Afro-Latin@ Reader*, Jiménez Román and Flores enunciate a critique of the specific variety of antiblack racism that informs the "triple consciousness" of Afro-Latinx subjects, who ever feel their "three-ness"—as Latinx, "*negro*," and U.S. American. A riff on W.E.B. Du Bois's "double consciousness," this articulation of the category "Afro-Latin@" insists on the persistent need to acknowledge and undermine antiblackness within Hispanic Caribbean diasporas and Latinx culture more broadly.

Flores's invaluable theorizing of Afro-Latinx cultural studies began in the pages of *Areíto*. Much as de la Campa felt captivated by *Areíto* when he came across its aesthetic resonance with Guillermo Cabrera Infante's *Tres tristes tigres*, Flores came to collaborate with *Areíto* after he had departed from Stanford University's German Department and was remaking himself as a scholar of the emerging transdisciplinary field of Puerto Rican studies.[23] The Centro de Estudios Puertorriqueños (founded in 1973 by scholar-activist Frank Bonilla and later directed by Flores) came into being through the pressures of Puerto Rican community and student movements that demanded access to cultural capital and representation in the form of admissions, faculty and administrative jobs, curriculum, and research.[24] This call for diversity in higher education began at public research universities and expressed local echoes of global movements against colonialism in the late 1960s. Flores' research and activism, through his publications in *Areíto*, connected the New York barrio to Cuban and Latin American movements for decolonization.

A decade after the Cuban revolutionary government claimed to have resolved the problem of antiblack racism as of 1961, *Areíto*'s Puerto Rican contributors called attention to the intersection of class with race oppression and African-diasporic cultural expression as a decolonial response. Flores's reading of Nicholasa Mohr and Louis Reyes Rivera commits to an intersectional reading of writers from "El Bronx" and to representations of "Loisaida" or the Lower East Side that emphasized the ongoing relevance and centrality of African-descended culture at home and in the diaspora (Flores, "Nicholasa Mohr y Louis Reyes Rivera"). This essay documents a "new turn" in New York-Puerto Rican literary expression, away from the stereotypical "street" and "prison" fiction popularized by Piri Thomas, and away from the nationalism of Bernardo Vega. Mohr's prose critically remonstrates against the New York public school system that invisibilized the history and culture of Puerto Rico. Mohr refuses assimilation to the dominant White and Anglo New York milieu by documenting quotidian Boricua culture in El Bronx and Loisaida. The second half of Flores' essay in *Areíto* describes the aesthetics of Reyes Rivera's poetic performance, in the character of a janitor reciting poetry in keeping with the rhythm of his mop moving across a public stage in Harlem at a poetry event entitled "Bloodflower." These writers introduce new subjectivities imagining the world from the Black and Latinx working-class perspective, while surviving and interpreting the world with the protection of Afro-Caribbean divinities, the *Orichas* or Orishas.

Flores's essay in *Areíto* anticipates the definition of an Afro-Latinx critical category and diaspora-focused research agenda that Flores and Jiménez Román would establish against the persistent denials of antiblack racism. Flores's other major contribution concerns the protagonism and insight he attaches to Nuyorican diaspora writers, including women, against the sometimes disparaging portrayals of darker-skinned, working-class, and feminist diaspora writings by academic elites on the island.[25]

Conclusions

This chapter has proposed a scholarly return to the archive of *Areíto* to excavate and compare examples of groundbreaking Puerto Rican and Cuban collaboration in the 1970s United States. The contributions of Puerto Ricans to a twentieth-century progressive Cuban exile-led magazine built upon the ideas and actions of the previous century, in which such collaboration launched revolutionary anticolonial projects that have persisted into the present. We may read these Puerto Rican and Cuban translations and cultural studies interventions in the 1970s as grounding several transnational and transdisciplinary fields. Transdisciplinary and interisland collaborations in *Areíto* paved the way for studies of Black popular Latinx culture—including the study of hip hop music and dance, and new narratives of El Barrio—and should figure in any genealogy of the field of cultural studies in the United States, as it developed in tandem with cultural studies founded by displaced West Indian intellectuals in the United Kingdom. The "new turn" toward gender, class, and critical race consciousness in the diaspora suggests a turning away from nationalist, patriarchal, and conservative Cuban exceptionalism. As the United States abandons a long history of giving Cuban exiles a privileged immigrant status through the scrapping of the "wet-foot, dry-foot" policy in 2017 during President Barack Obama's final days in office, Cuba's exceptionalism and Puerto Rico's ongoing coloniality have exposed the need for more cross-border collaborations and comparative cultural studies.[26] Perhaps Cuba, too, needs to acknowledge more fully its debts to Puerto Ricans for major contributions to Cuban nationalist projects for more than a century. Puerto Ricans involved in *Areíto* contributed to the rise of cultural studies that valorize translation and recognize the Latinx and Afro-Latinx diasporas in the United States as theorists of their respective island's cultures. Excavating the aesthetics and politics of Puerto Rican and Cuban contributions to *Areíto* offers a usable past on which to draw as the Americas reimagine new histories of cultural studies and translation.

Notes

1. The contributions by Jenna Leving Jacobson, Iraida López, Laura Lomas, and Yolanda Prieto to a dossier on Lourdes Casal in *Cuban Studies* suggest Casal's involvement in interdisciplinary and ethnic studies. I am suggesting here that other contributors to the magazine (such as Flores and Víctor Fernández Fragoso) had similar intellectual commitments to these new fields.

2. See de la Campa, "Revista *Areíto*" 138. De la Campa would go on to make contributions to *Areíto* through incisive interviews such as "Entrevista con el dramaturgo argentino Osvaldo Dragún" and "Entrevista a Roberto Márquez," which I examine more closely below.

3. See Jesse Hoffnung-Garskof's historical excavation of this cast of Black characters whose families emerged from generations of Hispanic Caribbean slavery to contribute to the Cuban and Puerto Rican independence movements (*Racial Migrations*). See also Lamas, *The Latino Continuum*; Lomas, "Migration and Decolonial Politics in Two Afro-Latino Poets," and Hoffnung-Garskof, "To Abolish the Law of Castes."

4. In "Juventud, búsqueda, reencuentro," *Areíto* explores the divergent trajectory of Cubans exiled in Puerto Rico from that of Cubans exiled in Miami or the Northeast of the United States. In Puerto Rico, exiled Cubans enjoy relatively more comfortable economic conditions as compared to the average Puerto Rican yet, because of cultural commonalities, many Cubans in Puerto Rico identified with Puerto Rican independence and decolonial projects more than Cuban exiles in the conservative Cuban-controlled Miami.

5. María de los Angeles Torres, for example, describes experiencing racism after she left Cuba as a Pedro Pan child and her Cuban exile family established themselves in Cleveland, Ohio. Casal encouraged her to pursue graduate study of the Cuban diaspora. She had to convince her advisors of the significance of the Cuban voting bloc, but found encouragement from the founder of Puerto Rican studies, Frank Bonilla, and others in the Inter-University Program on Latino Research. See Torres, *In the Land of Mirrors* 5.

6. See Nelson W. Canals' essay in *Areíto*, featuring photos of nationalists Lolita Lebrón, Lillian Caballero, Nelson Canals, Andrés Figueroa Cordero, and Rafael Cancel Miranda. Eduardo Lalo refers to "colony economy" to gloss Puerto Rico's economy controlled by the United States since 1898, in which abundant imported consumer goods inhibit local self-sufficiency (Lalo 35).

7. *Areíto* reports disconcerting threats from Abdala in Puerto Rico in 1978 ("Areíto: Informaciones y ataques"). See the special issue on Muñiz Varela's assassination in 1979 and "Testimonio."

8. Manuel Maldonado-Denis, "Imperialismo y dependencia: El caso de Puerto Rico." The Dominican Republic, Chile, Panama, Brazil, Bolivia, and Central America all receive attention in the magazine either through original essays or translations of previously published research into Spanish.

9. See similar language in the first "Editorial" of *Areíto*, cited above.

10. "Nuestroamericanismo" ("ouramericanism") derives from the title of José Martí's influential 1891 essay, "Nuestra América," published simultaneously in New York and Mexico City, and refers to the mutual affiliation of the countries of Latin America and the Caribbean as a region defined by cultural, historical, and political ties, with the potential to defend itself against outside aggression. The U.S. occupation and annexation of Puerto Rico—along with the Philippines—in 1898 severed Puerto Rico from the "United States of South America," toward which Martí aspired as a counterbalance to the increasingly expansionist United States.

11. Puerto Rican accounts of the "Great Migration" after Operation Bootstrap (1945–

65) similarly critique the racism and exclusion migrants from Puerto Rico faced in the United States. Guillermo Cotto-Thorner's *Trópico en Manhattan/Manhattan Tropics*, and Bernardo Vega's classic memoir, which Flores translated, document the racial and economic exclusion that Hispanic Caribbean migrants faced in New York, despite the creativity and industriousness of a pro-independence movement rooted in the 1880s and in Albizu's nationalist movement in the 1930s.

12. For example, Piri Thomas's father in *Down These Mean Streets* was an Afro-Cuban who married a Puerto Rican immigrant, then passed as Puerto Rican, and demonstrated preference for his lighter-skinned children, while unjustly afflicting his darkest son, Piri, with greater punishment and a lack of support for his interest in examining his family's connections to the African diaspora.

13. Through a federally funded and Catholic Church–administered program, Operation Pedro Pan airlifted fourteen thousand unaccompanied children from Cuba to foster homes, children's group homes, and orphanages in the United States. Cuban parents wanted to protect their children from what they perceived to be a threat that the Cuban revolutionary government posed to them, by removing their *patria potestad* (legal custody rights), and voluntarily sent their children into exile between 1960 and 1962. See Anita Casavantes Bradford's study of the centrality of children in both Cuban government and Miami exile Cuban political discourse, *The Revolution Is for the Children*.

14. See Félix Ojeda Reyes' study of exiled Puerto Rican patriots, including Francisco "Pachín" Marín, who perished in a Cuban swamp while fighting for Cuban independence.

15. See Kevin Meehan, César Salgado, and Jesse Hoffnung-Garskof on Schomburg. See Roberto Zurbano on the twenty-first century antiracist movement in revolutionary Cuba.

16. Márquez cites Rodríguez Furé and articulates this common theme of decolonization in the interview with de la Campa, 41–42.

17. I refer to Hegel's problematic claims in *The Philosophy of History* and James Anthony Froude's colonialist recycling of Hegelian ideas in his book, *The English in the West Indies* (1888), to which the Trinidadian critic, John Jacob Thomas, responded with the polemic, *Froudacity: West Indian Fables Explained* in 1889.

18. Vera Kutzinski's review of Fredric Jameson's edition of the University of Minnesota edition notes the problematic lack of acknowledgment of the historical context and history of translation of this text. She notes the Cuban political context of Heberto Padilla's imprisonment for its first writing, and notes Latin Americanist debates in which Fernández Retamar and Emir Rodríguez Monegal were engaged in the pages of *Diacritics*. These debates, however, miss they key point that Márquez and Casal would later make in the pages of *Areíto*: Calibán issued the call for decolonization through the transformation and repurposing of Prospero's language, from inside the Afro-Caribbean barrios of New York.

19. See Casal, "Relecturas: Calibán," and discussion of it in Lomas, "Translation and Transculturation in the New York-Caribbean Borderlands," 159–60.

20. Flores cites Hall in Jonathan Rutherford's anthology, in which Hall published a brilliant reading of diaspora musics. Hall, "New Ethnicities."

21. Sujatha Fernandes mentions the "Black August Hip Hop Collective," formed in

the 1970s California prison system and expressing solidarity with Afro-Cubans, in "Fear of a Black Planet" (580).

22. Antiracist discourse in Hispanic Caribbean contexts, articulated through the partnership of White leaders like Martí with his Afro-Latinx collaborators, Schomburg, Sotero Figueroa, Rafael Serra, Juan and Gerónimo Bonilla, became twisted into the violent repression of race-conscious criticism in both Cuba and Puerto Rico, one instance of which was the "Guerrita," or massacre of three to six thousand Blacks in 1912, as Ada Ferrer argues in "The Silence of Patriots." Lillian Guerra describes how a group of Black intellectuals—including Walterio Carbonell, Nancy Morejón, Nicolás Guillén Landrián, Sara Gómez, Rogelio Martínez Furé, and Eugenio Hernández, who prepared a statement in 1967 to submit to the 1968 World Culture Congress—suffered repercussions such as reduced access to publication opportunities upon being branded as "troublemakers" (273-74). Zurbano's article in a special 2012 issue of *Universidad de La Habana* articulates the need for a new discussion on antiblack racism and how to reopen the debate in Cuba. For a dossier of the "Caso Zurbano" that resulted after his *New York Times* editorial, see the special issue of *Afro-Hispanic Review* (2014).

23. See María Josefina Saldaño-Portillo's brief recounting of Flores' departure from Stanford University in her epilogue to the *Cambridge History of Latina/o American Literature*.

24. See Flores' interview with Juan Poblete (Flores, "Latino Studies").

25. I am thinking here of René Marqués' characterization of Puerto Rican Blacks, women, and migrants in *La carreta*, and in "El puertorriqueño dócil." See Flores, *From Bomba to Hip Hop*; "Thinking Diaspora from Below"; and Jiménez Román and Flores.

26. See Yarimar Bonilla's critique of the effects of coloniality which prevented the entry of emergency supplies to Puerto Rico during the environmental and economic crises related to hurricanes and earthquakes in 2017-19.

Works Cited

Afro-Hispanic Review. Special Issue on the Zurbano Affair. Vol. 33, no. 4, 2014.
Aparicio, Frances R., and Susana Chávez-Silverman, editors. *Tropicalizations: Transcultural Representations of* Latinidad. Dartmouth College P, 1997.
Areíto. "Areíto: Informaciones y ataques." *Areíto*, vol. 4, nos. 3-4, 1978, p. 81.
———. "Editorial." *Areíto*, vol. 1, no. 1, 1974, p. 1.
———. "Editorial." *Areíto*, vol. 1, no. 2, 1974, p. 52.
———. "Editorial." *Areíto*, vol. 5, nos. 19-20, 1979, p. 2.
———. "Entrevista con el licenciado Noel Colón Martínez: Conferencia de solidaridad con la independencia de Puerto Rico." *Areíto*, vol. 2, nos. 2-3, 1975, pp. 50-57.
———. "Juventud, búsqueda, reencuentro." *Areíto*, vol. 1, no. 4, 1975, pp. 16-21.
———. "La minoría cubana en EE.UU." *Areíto*, vol. 1, no. 1, 1974, pp. 7-9.
———. "Número extraordinario." *Areíto*, vol. 5, nos. 19-20, 1979.
———. "Reseña de Cayman Gallery." *Areíto* vol. 3 no. 1, 1976, pp. 46-47.
———. "Testimonio." *Areíto*, vol. 6, no. 21, 1979, pp. 34-38.

Belnap, Jeffrey, and Raúl Fernández, editors. *José Martí's Our America: From National to Hemispheric Cultural Studies*. Duke UP, 1998.
Bonilla, Yarimar. "The Coloniality of Disaster: Race, Empire, and the Temporal Logics of Emergency in Puerto Rico, USA." *Political Geography*, vol. 78, 2020, pp. 102–81. https://doi.org/10.1016/j.polgeo.2020.102181.
Bradford, Anita Casavantes. *The Revolution Is for the Children: The Politics of Childhood in Havana and Miami, 1959–1962*. U of North Carolina P, 2014.
Canals, Nelson W. "Libertad para los presos puertorriqueños." *Areíto*, vol. 3, no. 1, 1977, pp. 22–24.
Casal, Lourdes. "Memories of a Black Cuban Childhood." *Nuestro: The Magazine for Latinos*, vol. 2, no. 4, 1978, pp. 61–62.
———. "Recognizing Our Roots." *Nuestro: The Magazine for Latinos*, vol. 1, no. 1, 1977, pp. 39–40.
———. "Relecturas: Calibán." *Areíto*, vol. 6, no. 24, 1980, p. 44.
Cortázar, Julio. "Lucas, sus meditaciones ecológicas." *Areíto*, vol. 3, no. 1, 1976, p. 39.
Cotto-Thorner, Guillermo. *Manhattan Tropics/Trópico en Manhattan*. Translated by J. Bret Maney. Introduction by Cristina Pérez Jiménez. Arte Público P, 2019.
de la Campa, Román. *Cuba on My Mind: Journeys to a Severed Nation*. Verso, 2000.
———. "Entrevista a Roberto Márquez." *Areíto*, vol. 4, nos. 1–2, 1978, pp. 39–46.
———. "Entrevista con el dramaturgo argentino Osvaldo Dragún." *Areíto*, vol. 3, no. 4, 1977, pp. 46–49.
———. "Revista *Areíto*: Herejía de una nación improbable." *Encuentro de la Cultura Cubana*, no. 40, 2006, pp. 137–41.
Edwards, Brent Hayes. *The Practice of Diaspora: Literature, Translation, and the Rise of Black Internationalism*. Harvard UP, 2003.
Fernandes, Sujatha. "Fear of a Black Planet: Local Rappers, Transnational Crossings, and State Power in Contemporary Cuba." *Anthropological Quarterly*, vol. 76, no. 4, 2003, pp. 575–608.
Fernández Retamar, Roberto. *Caliban and Other Essays*. Translated by Edward Baker. U of Minnesota P, 1989.
Ferrer, Ada. "The Silence of Patriots: Racial Discourse and Cuban Nationalism, 1868–1898." *José Martí's Our America: From National to Hemispheric Cultural Studies*, edited by Jeffrey Belnap and Raúl Fernández. Duke UP, 1998, pp. 228–49.
Flores, Juan. *From Bomba to Hip Hop: Puerto Rican Culture and Latino Identity*. Columbia UP, 2000.
———. "Latino Studies: New Contexts, New Concepts." *Critical Latin American and Latino Studies*, edited by Juan Poblete. U of Minnesota P, 2003, pp. 191–205.
———. "Nicholasa Mohr y Louis Reyes Rivera: Un nuevo giro en la expresión literaria puertorriqueña en Nueva York." Translated by Ricardo Campos. *Areíto*, vol. 6, no. 22, 1980, pp. 47–50.
———. "Thinking Diaspora from Below." *The Diaspora Strikes Back: Caribeño Tales of Learning and Turning*. Routledge, 2008, pp. 15–32.
Franco, Jean. "¿Qué le ha pasado al coro? García Márquez y el Premio Nobel." *Areíto*, vol. 8, no. 32, 1983, pp. 18–22.
González Echevarría, Roberto. "Concierto barroco." *Areíto*, vol. 3, no. 1, 1976, pp. 48–50.

———. *Cuban Fiestas*. Yale UP, 2010.

———. "'En la más alta esfera' (cuento)." *Areíto*, vol. 2, no. 1, 1975, pp. 41–45.

Grupo Areíto. *Contra viento y marea*. Casa de las Américas, 1978.

Guerra, Lillian. *Visions of Power in Cuba: Revolution, Redemption, and Resistance, 1959–1971*. U of North Carolina P, 2014.

Hall, Stuart. *Essential Essays*, edited by David Morley. 2 vols. Duke UP, 2019.

———. "New Ethnicities." *Stuart Hall: Critical Dialogues in Cultural Studies*, edited by David Morley and Kuan-Hsing Chen. Routledge, 1996, pp. 442–51.

———. "What Is This 'Black' in Black Popular Culture?" *Stuart Hall: Critical Dialogues in Cultural Studies*, edited by David Morley and Kuan-Hsing Chen. Routledge, 1996, pp. 468–78.

Hoffnung-Garskof, Jesse. "The Migrations of Arturo Schomburg: On Being *Antillano, Negro*, and Puerto Rican in New York, 1891–1938." *Journal of American Ethnic History*, vol. 21, no. 1, 2001, pp. 3–49.

———. *Racial Migrations: New York City and the Revolutionary Politics of the Spanish Caribbean*. Princeton UP, 2019.

———. "To Abolish the Law of Castes: Merit, Manhood, and the Problem of Colour in the Puerto Rican Liberal Movement, 1873–1892." *Social History*, vol. 36, no. 3, 2011, pp. 312–42.

Jacobson, Jenna Leving. "Race and Reconciliation in the Work of Lourdes Casal." *Cuban Studies*, vol. 46, 2019, pp. 39–50.

Jiménez Román, Miriam, and Juan Flores, editors. *The Afro-Latin@ Reader: History and Culture in the United States*. Duke UP, 2010.

Kutzinski, Vera M. "Review of *Caliban and Other Essays*." *Modern Philology*, vol. 89, no. 2, 1991, pp. 307–10.

Lalo, Eduardo. *Simone: A Novel*. Translated by David Frye. U of Chicago P, 2015.

Lamas, Carmen. *The Latino Continuum and the Nineteenth-Century Americas: Literature, Translation, and Historiography*. Oxford UP, 2021.

Lee, Felicia R. "New Topic in Black Studies Debate: Latinos." *The New York Times*, 1 Feb. 2003, p. A1.

Lomas, Laura. "Migration and Decolonial Politics in Two Afro-Latino Poets: 'Pachín' Marín and 'Tato' Laviera." *Review: Literature and Arts of the Americas*, vol. 47, no. 2, 2014, pp. 155–63. https://doi.org/10.1080/08905762.2014.956519.

———. "'El negro es tan capaz como el blanco': José Martí and the Anti-Racist, Anti-Imperialist Politics of Late-Nineteenth Century *Latinidad*." *The Latino Nineteenth Century*, edited by Jesse Alemán and Rodrigo Lazo. New York UP, 2016, pp. 301–22.

———. "On the 'Shock' of Diaspora: Lourdes Casal's Critical Interdisciplinarity and Intersectional Feminism." *Cuban Studies*, vol. 46, 2018, pp. 10–38.

———. "Translation and Transculturation in the New York-Hispanic Caribbean Borderlands." *Small Axe*, no. 51, 2016, pp. 142–62.

López, Iraida H. "Entre el ideal de la nación mestiza y la discordia racial: 'Memories of a Black Cuban Childhood' y otros textos de Lourdes Casal." *Cuban Studies*, vol. 46, 2018, pp. 63–86.

———. *Impossible Returns: Narratives of the Cuban Diaspora*. UP of Florida, 2015.

Mahler, Anne Garland. *From the Tricontinental to the Global South: Race, Radicalism, and Transnational Solidarity*. Duke UP, 2018.

Maldonado-Denis, Manuel. "Imperialismo y dependencia: El caso de Puerto Rico." *Areíto*, vol. 2, no. 4, 1974, pp. 5–11.

Marqués, René. *La carreta: Drama en tres actos*. Cultural, 1983.

———. *El puertorriqueño dócil y otros ensayos 1953–1971*. Cultural, 1977.

Márquez, Roberto. *A World among These Islands: Essays on Literature, Race, and National Identity in Antillean America*. U of Massachusetts P, 2010.

Márquez, Roberto, editor. *Puerto Rican Poetry: An Anthology from Aboriginal to Contemporary Times*. U of Massachusetts P, 2007.

Meehan, Kevin. *People Get Ready: African-American and Caribbean Cultural Exchange*. UP of Mississippi, 2009.

Mirabal, Nancy Raquel. *Suspect Freedoms: The Racial and Sexual Politics of Cubanidad in New York, 1823–1957*. New York UP, 2017.

Noel, Urayoán. *In Visible Movement: Nuyorican Poetry from the Sixties to Slam*. U of Iowa P, 2014.

Ojeda Reyes, Félix. *Peregrinos de la libertad: Documentos y fotos de exiliados puertorriqueños del siglo XIX localizados*. Instituto de Estudios del Caribe, Editorial de la Universidad de Puerto Rico, 1992.

Prieto, Yolanda. "Lourdes Casal and Black Cubans in the United States: The 1970s and Beyond." *Cuban Studies*, vol. 46, 2018, pp. 51–62.

Prohías, Rafael J., and Lourdes Casal. *The Cuban Minority in the U.S.: Preliminary Report on Need Identification and Program Evaluation*. Arno P, 1980.

Saldaño-Portillo, María Josefina. "Epilogue: Latina/o Literature: The Borders Are Burning." *The Cambridge History of Latina/o American Literature*, edited by John Morán González and Laura Lomas. Cambridge UP, 2018, pp. 711–36.

Salgado, César A. "The Archive and Afro-Latina/o Field-Formation: Arturo Alfonso Schomburg at the Intersection of Puerto Rican and African-American Studies and Literatures." *The Cambridge History of Latina/o American Literature*, edited by John Morán González and Laura Lomas. Cambridge UP, 2018, pp. 371–93.

Thomas, Piri. *Down These Mean Streets*. 13th ed. Vintage, 1997.

Torres, María de los Angeles. *In the Land of Mirrors: Cuban Exile Politics in the United States*. U of Michigan P, 1999.

Vega, Bernardo. *Memoirs of Bernardo Vega: A Contribution to the History of the Puerto Rican Community in New York*. Edited by César Andreu Iglesias and translated by Juan Flores. Monthly Review P, 1984.

Zurbano, Roberto. "Cuba: Doce dificultades para enfrentar al (neo)racismo o doce razones para abrir el (otro) debate." *Universidad de La Habana*, no. 273, 2012, pp. 266–77.

8

Psychological and Physical Space in Puerto Rican and Cuban Twentieth-Century Theater

MAIDA WATSON

Theater is distinguished from other genres by the fact that the *mise-en-scène*, or staging of a play, changes the written text and that stage directions play a role unique to theater. The function of dramatic space,[1] not usually present in the novel, short story, or poem, though these genres can sometimes have aspects associated with theater, is counterbalanced in some twentieth-century plays with the role that psychological theatrical space plays. In sixteenth- and seventeenth-century Spain, plays were staged outdoors and many times in theatrical courtyards, which were specifically dedicated to theatrical performances. The lack of financial and technological resources during this period made it necessary for the actors to create through their words more complicated spaces (Regueiro). But it is above all during the twentieth century that the use of psychological spaces based on physical dramatic space, and which reflected the psychological reality of the characters, increased. As a result of the influence of Bertolt Brecht's epic theater, Antonin Artaud's Theatre of Cruelty, and the Theatre of the Absurd, many playwrights during the second half of the twentieth century rejected realistic theater and wrote plays where psychological space played an important part, as we can see in the three plays analyzed in this chapter.[2]

Psychological space, suggested by the words, gestures, or actions of the actors or by props, music, and lighting used in the physical staging, results from the effect that the imagination of the characters in the play has on the imagination of the audience. This space is an important part of the plot, especially when the psychological or imaginary space of the play is in opposition to the dramatic or physical space described in the play's stage directions.

Two Cuban plays, *La noche de los asesinos* (1958) by José Triana and *Lila, la mariposa* (1954) by Rolando Ferrer, and one Puerto Rican play, *Los soles truncos* (1958) by René Marqués, precisely present this conflict between the dramatic and the psychological space that takes place and serves as a key element in the structure of the dramas. In each of these plays, the psychological space imagined by the characters is based on elements of the dramatic space, such as props, lighting, music, and costumes. In addition, in all of these plays, the psychological space is a closed space[3] in which the characters are trapped and the closed or confined nature of this space also determines the ideology and characteristics of the psychological space. In *Los soles truncos*, the psychological space created by the words of the three sisters and the lighting, stage props, and music of the dramatic or physical space serves to re-create the glorious past of the three old ladies and contrasts it with the poor and rundown nature of the physical or dramatic space of their present, a dilapidated house. In *La noche de los asesinos*, the psychological space is created not only by the stage props and the dialogue of the characters but also by the gestures and repetitive actions of the three siblings, such as when they rub knives against each other to simulate the pretended murder of their parents.

This psychological space is so pervasive and strong that at times it replaces the physical or dramatic space completely. An example is found in *La noche de los asesinos* where the characters underline the replacement of this physical space by the psychological space when they say, "La sala no es la sala. La sala es la cocina. El cuarto no es el cuarto. El cuarto es el inodoro" ("The living room isn't the living room. The living room is the kitchen. The bedroom isn't the bedroom. The bedroom is the toilet") (Triana 167).[4] Their words reflect the replacement of the "real" world by the imaginary world created by the three actors through their use of stage props such as the knives, lighting, and their voices.

In *Los soles truncos*, the imaginary world created by the sisters' memories completely replaces the outer world of the brutal reality of the world portrayed through the broken-down furniture of the physical theatrical space. Finally, in *Lila, la mariposa*, the psychological space created by the mother Lila to make sure that her son never grows up invades the physical space of the boy's reality through the control of his mind by his mother, who pretends that he is three years younger. The protagonist, Lila, creates a closed psychological space in which to keep her son from growing older and thus leaving her.

The Political Function of Psychological Space in *Los soles truncos* and Marqués' Independentist Ideology

Psychological space can have a strong political symbolism. In *Los soles truncos*, Marqués presents the story of the three aged Burkhart sisters who were once members of a rich landowning Puerto Rican family, but who are now poverty-stricken. They are still living in the same house in which they had lived when they were opulent, but they now survive by selling their jewelry. The door to the house has an opening in which three setting suns, each of a different color, form the glass of the top part of the door. When the play opens, the sisters are about to lose their house because of not paying their bills. One of them has already died but they have no money to bury her. This is the moment that Marqués chooses to begin the play, during which the dramatic space is represented by the physical aspects of the house, located in the historic district of Old San Juan, Puerto Rico.

Marqués chooses to describe the physical aspects of the house through detailed stage directions. He says about the house:

> Sala amplia en antigua casa de la calle del Cristo; segundo piso. Al fondo, tres puertas persianas que dan al balcón. Las puertas están cerradas... La casa está casi en ruinas. La sala empapelada de verde y rosa, diseño floreado ya muy desvaído. En algunos lugares se ha roto el empapelado. La pared de la derecha, muestra una enorme mancha de agua cuyo diseño ha tomado la forma de un mapa: desde el techo hasta el piso, dos continentes unidos por un istmo... Ocupan la sala, precariamente, restos heterogéneos de mobiliario de una época que conoció la suntuosidad y el refinamiento. Un piano de palo de rosa, al fondo centro, un poco hacia la derecha, dejando amplio espacio para moverse a su alrededor. (Marqués 13–14)

> (A large living room in an old house on del Cristo street, second floor. In the back, three shutter doors lead to the balcony. The doors are closed... The house is almost in ruins. The living room wallpaper is green and pink with flowers and is very worn. In some places the wallpaper is broken. The wall to the right has a great water stain that

has taken the shape of a map which shows from the ceiling to the floor two continents joined by an isthmus . . . There are tottering pieces of furniture in the living room from a time when this room was the center of sumptuousness and refinement. A piano made of rosewood, in the middle of the back wall, a little to the right, allowing lots of space to move around it.)

Within this very real and tactile physical space, Inés and Emilia, the two remaining sisters, create a psychological space, based on the memories of the past about which each of the stage props reminds them. Through the use of words and gestures, the two old women re-create the ornate physical space of the living room that had been the scene for many turning points of their lives. They first appear on the stage surrounded by old and broken pieces of furniture, as specified clearly in the stage directions. Some of these pieces of furniture, especially the Louis XV chair and the Viennese rocking chair, serve a function beyond that of just being a symbol of a disappeared world and are essential not only for the creation of the psychological space but also for the development of the action of the play. As Margarita Vargas points out:

> Two seemingly trivial domestic incidences highlight the parents' differences and their territorial instincts. The first one entails a disagreement about the appropriate place for a piece of furniture. While *mamá* Eugenia has reserved the living room exclusively for her Louis XV pieces, *papá* Burkhart wants his favorite Viennese rocking chair in the same room. Every evening, out of respect for his lordship, the maid brings the chair into the living room before he gets home (42). The sisters follow the maid's example, and after *mamá* Eugenia dies, the rocker finds a permanent place in the living room. The reconciliation of the disparate pieces of furniture can only occur after the death of their owners, and alludes to the sisters' desire to construct a world of unity and peace, which evokes the unified imaginary community of nation builders, a community otherwise at odds. (48)

Another important element of the psychological space are the dream sequences created through the dialogue. They are short dream intervals during which the women appear at important moments in their lives. Hortensia is shown when she is 19 years old (Marqués 22–26), 30 years old (31–36), and 25 years old (47–48), as in the scene in which Inés wears Hortensia's wedding clothes (43–44). All of these dream scenes, along with the dialogue and the actors' gestures and movements, contribute to the building of the psychological space.

The music and colored lights, another aspect of the dramatic or physical space, also serve to create the psychological space in this play. The dream sequences are introduced each time through special music and colored lights. Iconic music such as a waltz by Frédéric Chopin, the Wedding March, a funeral dirge, and the "Ride of the Valkyries" in Richard Wagner's opera serve to symbolize both important people and recall special moments in the gilded past of the three protagonists (Marqués 21, 47). Marqués presents this mixture of music and lighting in his detailed stage directions when he writes:

> Breve intervalo. Empiezan a escucharse, muy débilmente, los acordes de la Marcha Nupcial. Sobre las escaleras cae una tenue luz purpurina. En lo alto aparece Emilia llevando en sus brazos el traje de novia, el velo de encajes y la corona de azahares. El vuelo enorme del traje oculta su bata raída, los encajes flotan a su alrededor. La Marcha Nupcial sube de volumen y va in crescendo a medida que Emilia desciende muy lentamente, disimulando en lo posible su cojera, erguida y transfigurada bajo la luz purpurina ... (Ya en la sala, Emilia se va aproximando a Inés. La luz purpurina en la escalera empieza a extinguirse, pero la Marcha Nupcial sube apoteótica, ensordecedora, a medida que Emilia avanza ...) (Marqués 34)

> (A short interval. The sounds of the Wedding March begin to be heard, though very weakly. A soft purple light falls on the stairs. At the top Emilia appears carrying in her arms a bridal gown, a lace veil, and a crown of orange blossoms. The fullness of her dress hides her worn robe, lace floats around her. The Wedding March increases in volume and stays at its peak while Emilia comes down the stairs very slowly, trying to hide her disability, standing tall and transfigured under the purple light ... (Once she is in the living room, Emilia comes close to Inés. The purple light in the stairs starts to fade, but the Wedding March goes up in volume, apotheotic, deafening, while Emilia comes down ...)

The classical music by Chopin and Wagner not only recalls the sisters' affluent past, but it serves as a symbol for both their mother and father's ethnic backgrounds. Wagner was Hitler's favorite composer and *The Valkyries* an opera that Hitler used to identify with his Nazi ideology. Chopin represented the refinement of their mother who was described as "una reina mora" ("a Moorish queen") by one of the sisters (20), but promptly corrected by the other who says that their mother had no Moorish blood but was instead of pure Spanish descent from Málaga, Spain. Chopin was associated with the Spanish island of Mallorca, where he spent his winters, as well as French refinement. The two sisters talk about how their father was good-looking like a Norse god, and how Hortensia was thus considered his Valkyrie, underlining the function that the music from this opera will have in the play. Talking about their father, they say:

> INES: Es hermoso como un dios nórdico.
> HORTENSIA: (*Riendo.*) Lo cual me convierte a mí en Walkiria. (20)
> (INES: He is beautiful like a Norse God.
> Hortensia: (*Laughing.*) That turns me into a Valkyrie.)

The classical music of Chopin and Wagner contrasts with the loud and unmusical voice of the man who passes in front of the sisters' house, selling his wares and announcing them in unharmonious tones and who forms part of the physical or dramatic space based on the "here and now." The contrast with this outside world, which the sisters are trying to keep out of their lives, is formed by not only the sounds of the play but also by the lighting. The outside light barely enters through the windows and the exterior world can only be seen through the opening in the door with the three setting suns that give the play its name. These setting suns represent the sisters who have hidden themselves in their world and shut out the outside lighting. Despite their living in the tropics, the sisters light the house with an artificial light. The symbolism of this sun is underlined by the words of one of the three sisters, who says that the outside sun is so strong that it makes it difficult for her to see herself and comb her hair.

The contrast between the physical or dramatic space described in the initial stage directions and the psychological space created by the sisters' memories is related to another relationship of opposites: the symbolism of the outside world as one inhabited by "the barbarians," and as one of the sisters says: "siempre son bárbaros los que cambian el mundo que más amamos" ("those who change the world that we love the most are always barbarians") (Marqués 27), and the interior of the house, where the sisters try to live without having any contact with the outside world to preserve their "aristocratic notions of lineage and skewed views of pure blood" (Vargas 42).

After Emilia tells Hortensia that her boyfriend has been unfaithful to her, Hortensia locks herself in her house and says that the light from outside will never enter. By having the three sisters fall in love with the same man, and by preventing Hortensia from marrying him, Marqués keeps the triad intact. Marriage would have further diluted the purity of their "blue blood," a blood already tarnished by the couple's racial mixture and the mother's "anemia perniciosa" ("pernicious anemia") that caused her death (33). Also, by not marrying the man who deceived her with a woman from a much lower class, Hortensia avoids rivalry with her sisters. And by deciding to go into seclusion, the three manage to guard, for over forty years, against the invasion of their hermetic world. Thus, they preserve the values and beliefs of an old patriarchal system, which ultimately was no less male-centered than the new one that threatened them (Vargas 48).

Dramatic Space and Psychological Space

The inside of the house is also the place where Inés and Emilia live out the psychological space created by their sense of guilt. It is the same place where their purification by fire will take place. As stated by Wenceslao Gil, inside the Burkhart home, instead of a physical way of escaping, their memories—presented through flashbacks—will have to serve as an escape route, a type of mental way out which they take without going outside or leaving the house (Gil 5). That Hortensia shuts herself into her house and does not allow any exterior light to enter has strong political symbolism. Critics have stated that the end of the family represents the end of Puerto Rico's special political status as a Free Associated State (Vargas 43). According to George McMurray, Marqués was "an outspoken advocate of independence, [who] abhorred the domination of his homeland by the United States, which has led to the industrialization of the island's agricultural economy and to the contamination of its Hispanic culture" (209). The physical or dramatic stage, that is the playwright's directions, again serves to highlight this relationship between the psychological stage and the physical one. Marqués' stage directions state that on the wall of the house the water leaking from the roof of the sisters' house should form a map of the American continent which clearly shows Puerto Rico but is overwhelmed in size by the United States. This map, created by the broken roof, not only underlines the poverty of the sisters who do not have the money to repair their house but also Marqués' worry about Puerto Rico's dependence on the United States.

Puerto Rico is a real place that appears on a real map, but it is transposed to the fictional space of the psychological stage. On the other hand, the map on the wall is an imagined place that becomes part of the real dramatic stage. Thus, one space builds on the other, just as other elements of the physical space, such as the scenery, music, and lighting serve to create an imaginary world. The protagonists of *Los soles truncos* find no other solution but to immolate themselves in a closed house, run down by the passing of time. The women are the symbols of a Puerto Rico invaded by the United States and the loss it felt by not being a part of Spain anymore (Rivera Méndez and del Vallé Vélez 57). The title of the play, *Los soles truncos*, refers to the cut out setting suns in the door of the old house, but the Spanish word *trunco* also means incomplete. The lives of the three sisters are incomplete, like the Puerto Rican society they represent, which can only survive like they do in a psychological, unreal, and imaginary space.

Psychological Space in Triana's *La noche de los asesinos* and the Dysfunctional Family as a Metaphor for the Cuban Nation

In *La noche de los asesinos*, three siblings (Cuca, Lalo, and Beba) play at killing their parents in a ritual ceremony. During the play they symbolically play act the murder of their parents, a game in which they take the parts of not only their parents but also their neighbors and the criminal justice system. The dysfunctional family portrayed in the play represents Cuban society and its authoritarian government, which does not allow the siblings to think for themselves and takes away their freedom in return for satisfying their basic needs. It is not clear whether the government represented by the family structure in the play is the Fulgencio Batista dictatorship or the current communist regime.

Erminio Neglia has indicated in his study of the play that it contains two spaces: a dramatic space in which the actual events of the play take place and a second imaginary space suggested by the three actors, which is not seen by the spectators who are forced to create a visual image of this space (141). Matías Montes Huidobro in his book *Cuba detrás del telón* has built on this idea by arguing that Lalo's character, the leader of the three children, not only wants to change the location of the objects in the dramatic space but also wants to change the physical dramatic space into another thing, as Lalo desires "la transformación de este en otra cosa" ("its transformation into something else") (115).

This something else is created with the use of a dialogue borrowed from the Theatre of the Absurd. This includes sentences that have no meaning, as when the three siblings play the part of friends of their parents who come to visit and ask each other absurd questions that replicate the falsity of their relationship:

> CUCA: ¿Funciona bien su vejiga?
> BEBA: ¿Todavía no se ha operado el esfínter?
> CUCA: ¿Y la hernia? (Triana 116)
> (CUCA: Is your bladder working well?
> BEBA: You still haven't had your operation of the sphincter?
> CUCA: And your hernia?)

With the addition of the sound produced by stage props such as the rubbing of two knives together, which form part of the repetition in the dialogue, the siblings create the psychological space that gradually replaces the dramatic space of the "here and now." Influenced by Artaud's dramatic theories about the use of gestures and sounds (Barranco), Triana indicates in the stage directions the importance of gestures and sounds to create the psychological space in which the siblings will free themselves mentally through the imaginary murder of their parents. The sounds the siblings make as they enact the imaginary ritual murder of their parents are indicated in the stage directions as well as the screams to which they refer in their dialogue, as when Beba says to Lalo: "Esos gritos de los mil demonios por cualquier bobería" ("Those deadly screams because of any silly thing we do") (Triana 123). The repetition of the chant "La sala no es la sala. La sala es la cocina. El cuarto no es el cuarto. El cuarto es el inodoro" ("The living room isn't the living room. The living room is the kitchen. The bedroom isn't the bedroom. The bedroom is the bathroom") (Triana 132) and the sound of the knives rubbing against each other underline Triana's stage directions: "Los elementos que se emplean en ella (la escena) son: los sonidos vocales, los golpes sobre la mesa y el taconeo acompasado" ("In this act the elements used are sounds of voices, blows on the table, and the rhythmic clicking of shoe heels") (Triana 140).

Another important aspect in the creation of the psychological space is the role of the physical house in the play. In his stage directions, Triana explains how the physical space should be laid out. It should be "Un sótano o el último cuarto-desván. Una mesa, tres sillas, alfombras raídas, cortinas sucias con grandes parches de telas floreadas, floreros, una campanilla, un cuchillo y algunos objetos ya en desuso, arrinconados" ("A basement or a utility room. A table, three chairs, old torn rugs, dirty curtains with great patches of flowered cloth, flower bases, a little bell, a knife, and some objects not in use anymore and forgotten in dirty corners") (Triana 110).

The dramatic work begins with the mention of the house by Cuca, one of the two sisters, when she says, "hay que arreglar esta casa. Este cuarto es un asco" ("we have to clean this house. This room is a dirty mess") (Triana 112). The need to tidy up the house seems to the three children more important for their parents than the existence of their own two daughters and son. Lalo states, "¿Qué importa esta casa, qué importan estos muebles, si nosotros no somos nada, si nosotros simplemente vamos y venimos por ella y entre ellos, igual que un cenicero, un florero o un cuchillo flotante?" ("What importance do this house and this furniture have if we are nothing, if we simply come and go through this house and among our parents, just like an ashtray, a flower vase, or a floating knife?") (119).

Throughout the play the house is described several times as a closed place where fear exists. A large part of the structure of the dramatic space as well as the psychological space is based on the theme of the house and its relationship to the three siblings. The house is a closed space within which the parents scold and punish the children for not cleaning. According to Birgitta Berglund, a house can serve at the same time as both a prison and a place of refuge. This double function of the house is evident when Lalo, through the use of the stage prop of the chair, changes the dramatic space of the "here and now" into the psychological space of the play.

> LALO: Tita, no te das cuenta que lo que yo propongo es simplemente la única solución que tenemos. (Coge la silla y la mueve en el aire.) Esta silla, yo quiero que esté aquí. (De golpe pone la silla en un sitio determinado.) Y no aquí. (De golpe coloca la misma silla en otro lugar determinado.) Porque aquí (Rápidamente vuelve a colocarla en el primer sitio.) me es más útil: puedo sentarme mejor y más rápido. Y aquí (Sitúa la silla en la segunda posición.) es sólo un capricho, una bobería y no funciona . . . (Coloca la silla en la primera posición.) Papá y mamá no consienten estas cosas. (Triana 149)

> (LALO: You don't realize that the only solution that we have is what I propose (Takes the chair and moves it in the air.) This chair, I want it here. (He abruptly puts the chair in a certain place.) And not here. (Abruptly, he takes the same chair and moves it to another predetermined place.) Because here (He rapidly moves the chair to its original

place) it is more useful for me; I can sit better and more quickly. And here (He moves the chair to the second place) this is just a whim, a foolish thing and it doesn't work... (Puts the chair back again in its first location). Father and mother don't agree to these things.)

Nevertheless, the siblings do not want to leave the house. The house in *La noche de los asesinos* serves one of the functions indicated by Berglund, as a place of refuge. The siblings are scared to leave the house, a place where they have always lived. At the level of political symbolism, the house represents an authoritarian government. This government could be the Cuban communist regime that provides its citizens with food, education, and basic medical assistance, but does not let them think for themselves.

Lalo explains this ambivalent feeling about the house when he says that he feels like a prisoner in his own home: "Quiero andar y hacer cosas que deseo o siento. Sin embargo, tengo las manos atadas. Tengo los pies atados. Tengo los ojos vendados. Esta casa es mi mundo" ("I want to do the things that I feel or want to do. Nevertheless, I have my hands tied. I have my feet tied. I have my eyes blindfolded. This house is my world"). He adds, referring to his family which by association represents the Cuban government: "Ellos me hicieron un inútil" ("They made me useless") (Triana 119). When Cuca asks him why he does not leave the house, he answers: "Siempre he tenido que regresar con el rabo entre las piernas" ("I've always had to return with my tail between my legs") (121).

Erminio Neglia has focused on the fact that the play takes place in a specific part of the house, the basement or utility room. Neglia argues that the choice of this room symbolizes that the three siblings have been forgotten by both their family and society in general (143). Nevertheless, the interesting aspect of this play is that the dramatic space and the psychological space feed upon each other to create an opposition between "lo real" ("the real") and "lo imaginario y lo imaginado" ("the imaginary and the imagined"). The author creates a dramatic space in which the psychological space grows. It is not as important that the physical or dramatic space be accepted as a concrete, realistic space, but instead that it be seen as a symbol of Cuba under the control of a dictator. The house becomes a microcosm that refers to the macrocosm of the country. What is important is that the subversive game that the sisters and brother play is the tool used to change the dramatic space into a psychological space that allows them to enjoy the freedom and liberation denied them by their family. Hence the words "La sala no es la sala. La sala es la cocina. El cuarto no es el cuarto. El cuarto es el inodoro" ("The living room isn't the living room. The living room is the kitchen. The bedroom isn't the bedroom. The bedroom is the bathroom") (Triana 167) take on a power and a meaning not usually associated with them. These are the words that express their characters' rebellion against the space controlled by their parents.

Psychological Space versus Dramatic Space in *Lila, la mariposa* by Ferrer

In Ferrer's play[5] the protagonist is a seamstress, Lila, who controls her son whom she wants to keep forever a child by creating a psychological reality in which her son never ages. According to Montes Huidobro, the symbolist playwright Maurice Maeterlinck and the psychological themes popular with the French dramatist Henri-René Lenormand influenced Ferrer's theater. The play takes place within the dramatic space of the protagonist's house in a poor neighborhood of Havana near the ocean, which becomes the main symbol in the play. As in *La noche de los asesinos* and *Los soles truncos*, the protagonist replaces the actual, physical space as represented by the stage directions with an alternative reality of her own creation.

The play uses elements of Santería, the Afro-Cuban religion, to create the psychological space of those who are dead. One of the characters, María, is the only one who can see things that others cannot see, such as the faces of the departed. She is a *Santera* and her world of traditional forms of knowledge based on elements of nature is very much related to the dead whom she calls upon, the glass of water she carries with her, the needles, and her use of witchcraft.

The author uses the symbol of the butterfly in Lila's name to create the psychological world of the two women in the play, Lila and Hortensia, which becomes more real than the actual, physical world that surrounds them. Lila hovers over her son "Dándole vueltas / como una mariposa / hasta que se queme" ("Hovering over him / like a butterfly / until she gets burned") (Ferrer 67), which anticipates her doom.

The theme of the enclosed space and its function in creating the psychological space as seen in *Los soles truncos* and in *La noche de los asesinos* also appear in this play. For Marino, Lila's son, his house has become a jail: "Y yo me siento como si me tuvieran amarrado. Los demás muchachos saltan, brincan . . . Las matas de mi tía crecen y rompen las macetas. Pero yo no puedo crecer. (Llora)" ("I feel as if I was tied up. The other boys jump, run . . . My aunt's plants grow and break the sides of their pots but I can't grow. [He cries]") (85). But just as in *La noche de los asesinos*, the psychological space becomes stronger than the physical space and the characters are unable to break loose and free themselves. Once Marino has the possibility of going to sea with his friend Capitán, he decides to stay and be a sailor on land. Just like Lalo in *La noche de los asesinos*, who says that each time he leaves home he has to return with his tail between his legs.

As in *Los soles truncos*, the characters in Ferrer's play portray different aspects of each other to create the psychological reality in which they live. They serve as opposing aspects of the same psychological reality. In *Los soles truncos*, the disabled daughter, Inés, is compared to the beautiful daughter and the disabled one ruins her sister's engagement in revenge. In *Lila, la mariposa*, the old maid aunt Hortensia is the other side of Lila, both aspects of the same lack of satisfaction. One of them depends on the other; the first is fragile and exquisite and suffers from nervous diseases. The other has taken upon herself the role of the victim and accepts this as her destiny. As Hortensia says,

> Yo quería ser como ella. Siempre viví a través de los otros; y como ella se reía tan bien, yo no me reí más; como yo no tengo hijo, tengo que querer al suyo. Como hablaba tan bonito, yo me callé y, poco a poco, me he ido convirtiendo en esto que soy ahora, una máquina, un mulo de carga, la tía, la flaca, la aguanta velas. Y mi gran miedo es que a Marino le pase lo mismo. (87)

> (I wanted to be like her. I always lived through others and since she laughed so well, I stopped laughing; since I didn't have a son, I had to love hers. Since she talked so well, I stopped talking and little by little I started to become what I am now, a machine, a mule for transportation, the aunt, the skinny one, the one who takes on all the responsibilities. And my great fear is that the same thing will happen to Marino.)

The idea that the outside world represents a danger to the psychological world created by the characters through their dialogue, gestures, and props is presented in *Los soles truncos* when the surviving sisters talk of the danger of the outside world, peopled by barbarians. The ocean serves the same function in *Lila, la mariposa* as the sunlight in *Los soles truncos*. Lila fears the ocean because it took Marino's father away con "ese rumor eterno, como si un gentío enorme hablara y hablara sin cesar" ("with that constant sound, as if a large crowd were talking and talking without stopping") (69).

It is at the same time a dream for Marino who sees it as the way of breaking the umbilical cord and running away from the maternal womb. At the end of the second act, Marino wants to go and find work and Lila tries desperately to stop him. She hides in her room, the audience suddenly hears a scream, and the next Act is in the funeral parlor, a reminder of the contrast between imagined or psychological space and physical space in the play.

Other important elements in creating the psychological space are the stage props used and the people associated with Lila's job as a seamstress. Physical space in the play is closely related to the world of women since it takes place in a small shop, called *La Mariposa* (The Butterfly), where clothes are made, and which is located very close to the entrance of the port of Havana. Ferrer's interest in the world of women, especially lower-middle class women in the Cuba of this period, is portrayed through the space of a seamstress's shop. All elements of the business of sewing, such as a sewing machine, thread, ribbons, and accessories, are seen and heard in the play and acquire various symbolic values. The job of seamstress was usually that of a poor woman and the physical elements of this work serve to create the psychological space inhabited by Lila and her sister-in-law. The women who work in the shop as seamstresses represent the three goddesses of fate of classical mythology, who weave and take apart Lila's fate while they tell riddles, talk in sayings and proverbs, and play on words. They are an interracial trio, composed of Black, *mulatta*, and White women: Lola, Clara, and Meche, the goddesses of fate who represent the main racial groups of twentieth-century Cuba. According to the author, they are "mágicas encarnaciones de las fuerzas naturales desencadenantes de la tragedia" ("magic incarnations of the natural forms set loose by tragedy") (Ferrer 61–62) in the physical space.

Conclusion

In the three plays examined in this chapter, the creation of an imaginary space that reflects the characters' ideas and mindset, called psychological space, plays a crucial role in the plot. In *Los soles truncos*, the theme of the destruction of the former patriarchal and landowning class by the new society, as a result of U.S. control over Puerto Rico, is presented through the contrast between the actual physical space of the house and the psychological space of the past re-created through the words and gestures of the three old ladies who live in the decrepit mansion. The dramatic space is portrayed through the use of the sun coming in the windows and the sounds of street vendors, while the psychological space is created not only through the sisters' dialogue but through elements of the dramatic space such as the lighting, sound, and function of some of the theatrical props such as the antique chairs. The sisters cannot allow the outside world of the dramatic space to conquer their interior psychological space and their only solution is to incinerate themselves and the house, thus purifying their past sins without coming to an acceptance of the modern world.

In *La noche de los asesinos*, the three actors who play the roles of the children, as well as the parents, the friends, and the members of the criminal justice system who try them for their imaginary murder, are able not only to replace the dramatic space of the play with that of the psychological space but also to create this psychological space with elements from the dramatic space. Using Artaud's techniques, they manage through the vehicles of sound, gesture, and screams to create a new psychological space that becomes the play's main theme. This psychological space causes us to reevaluate the reality of the dramatic space and stage props and to question the whole relationship of the two sisters and the brother with their family and by extension Cuban society.

In the three plays, stage props also play an important role in the creation of the psychological space. The Louis XV armchair and the Austrian rocking chair in the house of the Burkhart sisters in *Los soles truncos* and Lalo's chair in *La noche de los asesinos* are exterior symbols of the previous life of the Burkharts and the fight of the three siblings against their parents' authoritarian rule. The needles, cloth, and other items associated with the business of making clothes are exterior signs of the psychological reality that has taken the place of the physical reality in the mind of the main character, Lila.

In the three plays, the houses where the action takes place function not only as dramatic spaces but also as closed spaces that provide for the characters either a refuge, as in the case of *Los soles truncos*, or a prison from which the characters in the plays try to escape, as in the case of *La noche de los asesinos* and *Lila, la mariposa*. For this reason, doors in two of these plays, which are referred to often, play an important role. In *Los soles truncos*, on top of the main door of the sisters' decrepit mansion are three cut out semicircles that represent the setting suns referred to in the play's title. This door keeps the outside world, representing modernity, away from the psychological space, represented by the sisters' world, which exists only in their minds. The outside world contains the men, called barbarians by the sisters, who want to take over their house. It also contains the sun, kept by the sisters out of their house through the filter of the setting suns in the doorway, and which is not allowed by one of the sisters to shine in their house, lit by artificial lights. As Inés says: "Aquí estábamos las tres, llorando. Reunidas como siempre en la gran sala. Las tres puertas de dos hojas cerradas como siempre sobre el balcón. Los tres soles truncos oponiendo al sol sus colores: azul, amarillo, rojo" ("Here we were, all three of us crying. Gathered together as usual in the main living room. The three doors were closed over the balcony. The three setting suns with their blue, yellow, and red colors opposing the sun") (Marqués 47–48). In *La noche de los asesinos*, the door of the basement where the three children play act the murder of their parents separates the real world represented by the dramatic space of the actual stage from the psychological world, where the imagined murder takes place. An example of the function of the basement door in the creation of the psychological space is the much-quoted phrase "Cierra esa puerta" ("Close that door"), with which Lalo begins the play and which he repeats at the beginning of the second Act (Triana 133) and at the end of the play (156).

In all three plays, the playwrights clearly use the contrast between dramatic space and psychological space, not only to explore the individual tragedies and psychological realities of their characters but also to comment on the political or social realities of their surroundings.

Notes

1. For a definition of the different spaces in theater, such as the dramatic space that results from the instructions in the playwright's annotations, the scenic space with its stage decorations and props, and finally the space formed by the physical stage and the seats of the audience, see Balme (152) and Pavis (118–23).

2. See the discussion of psychological space in theater in Cazorla (185–93).

3. The closed spaces created by Marqués and Triana have much in common with the closed spaces imagined by the Spanish playwrights of this same period, as mentioned in Bauer-Funke, *Die Generación Realista*; "Espacios urbanos, ventanas y balcones"; "Espacios urbanos y sus funciones."

4. All translations are my own.

5. A new updated version of *Lila, la mariposa* was staged in 1987, in which the play was modernized and changed in a way that allowed for more social criticism and a greater didactic Brecht-influenced introspection. The play's chronological events were changed, beginning with Lila's wake instead of finishing with this event as in the original

version. The new second act repeats Lila's wake but this time it has become a cabaret show in which the conflicts presented in the play are condensed in the actions of Marino, the son who has fought to free himself from his overwhelming mother. Marino becomes a part of the audience of the cabaret and is replaced by another actor who takes his place on stage, thus allowing Marino to see himself acting (see Pianca).

Works Cited

Balme, Christoph. *Einführung in die Theaterwissenschaft*. Erich Schmidt, 2014.

Barranco, Jesús. "Artaud y *La noche de los asesinos*." *Encuentro de la Cultura Cubana*, nos. 4–5, 1997, pp. 46–52.

Bauer-Funke, Cerstin. *Die Generación Realista: Studien zur Poetik des Oppositionstheaters während der Franco-Diktatur*. Vittorio Klostermann (Analecta Romanica), 2007.

———. "Espacios urbanos, ventanas y balcones y su función dramática en algunas obras de Antonio Buero Vallejo." *Monteagudo: Revista de Literatura Española, Hispanoamericana y Teoría de la Literatura*, no. 21, 2016, pp. 49–74.

———. "Espacios urbanos y sus funciones en el teatro de la generación realista." *Espacios urbanos en el teatro español de los siglos XX y XXI*, edited by Cerstin Bauer-Funke. Olms, 2016, pp. 51–91.

Berglund, Birgitta. *Woman's Whole Existence: The House as an Image in the Novels of Ann Radcliffe, Mary Wollstonecraft, and Jane Austen*. Lund UP, 1993.

Cazorla, Hazel. "Cárceles de la conciencia y fugas pasionales: Espacios psíquicos en dos estrenos recientes de Antonio Buero Vallejo y Antonio Gala (*Las trampas del azar* y *Los bellos durmientes*)." *Entre actos: Diálogos sobre teatro español entre siglos*, edited by Martha T. Halsey. Estreno, 1999, pp. 185–93.

Ferrer, Rolando. *Lila, la mariposa. Teatro. Rolando Ferrer*. Selection, prologue, and notes by Nancy Morejón. 1954. Editorial Letras Cubanas, 1983, pp. 57–111.

Gil, Wenceslao. "La mujer en casa cerrada: Represión y opresión en *La casa de Bernarda Alba* de Federico García Lorca y *Los soles truncos* de René Marqués." *Hispanet Journal*, vol. 1, 2008, n.p., www.hispanetjournal.com/Volume1.html.

Marqués, René. *Los soles truncos*. *9 dramaturgos hispanoamericanos del siglo XX*, edited by Frank Dauster et al. Vol. 3. Girol Books, 1979, pp. 7–44.

McMurray, George R. *Spanish American Writing since 1941: A Critical Survey*. Ungar, 1987.

Montes Huidobro, Matías. *Cuba detrás del telón II: El teatro cubano entre la estética y el compromiso (1962–1969)*. Ediciones Universal, 2008.

Neglia, Erminio. "El asedio a la casa: Un estudio del decorado en *La noche de los asesinos*." *Revista Iberoamericana*, vol. 46, nos. 110–111, 1980, pp. 139–49.

Pavis, Patrice. *Dictionnaire du théâtre*. Revised and corrected edition. Dunod, 1996.

Pianca, Marina. "El teatro cubano en la década del ochenta: Nuevas propuestas, nuevas promociones." *Latin American Theatre Review*, vol. 1, no. 24, 1990, pp. 121–33.

Regueiro, José M. *Espacios dramáticos en el teatro español medieval, renacentista y barroco*. Reichenberger, 1996.

Rivera Méndez, Myrna, and Jesús del Vallé Vélez. "*Los soles truncos*: La obra, el autor, su visión, su representación y su travestismo." *Mitologías Hoy*, vol. 12, 2015, pp. 51–69.

Triana, José. *La noche de los asesinos*. *9 dramaturgos hispanoamericanos del siglo XX*, edited by Frank Dauster et al. Vol. 1. Girol Books, 1979, pp. 103–56.

Vargas, Margarita. "Dreaming the Nation: René Marqués's *Los soles truncos*." *Latin American Theatre Review*, vol. 37, no. 2, 2004, pp. 41–55.

9

Hechos and *desechos*
Environmental Degradation and Violence in Mayra Montero's *Tú, la oscuridad*

MARY ANN GOSSER ESQUILÍN

> Cuba y Puerto Rico son
> de un pájaro las dos alas,
> reciben flores o balas
> sobre el mismo corazón . . .
>
> (Cuba and Puerto Rico are
> two wings of a bird,
> they receive flowers or bullets
> into the same heart . . .)
>
> Lola Rodríguez de Tió
> ("Cuba and Puerto Rico: Two Wings of the Same Bird")

> It's more than climate change; it's also extraordinary burdens of toxic chemistry, mining, depletion of lakes and rivers under and above ground, ecosystem simplifications, vast genocides of people and other critters, etc [sic], etc [sic], in systematically linked patterns that threaten major system collapse after major system collapse, after major system collapse.
>
> Donna Haraway
> ("Anthropocene, Capitalocene, Plantationocene, Chthulucene: Making Kin")

Lola Rodríguez de Tió's assertion that "Cuba and Puerto Rico are / two wings of a bird," begs the following questions: where is the body of the bird and how is it doing a hundred years later? If we take off in a flight of fancy with the exiled poet and allow ourselves a bird's eye view over the geopolitical map, I posit that the synecdochic body of the bird is Hispaniola, nestled between the two Hispanic Greater Antilles, and that, environmentally, it is not doing well. The novelist and journalist Mayra Montero, who was born in Cuba, but has lived her adult life in Puerto Rico as an exile, has a heart—like the one described by Rodríguez de Tió—that beats lovingly for both islands. Through her writings she dispenses metaphorical flowers and bullets not just about her two homelands but also about the nations in between (Haiti and the Dominican Republic). Her pan-Caribbean interests and preoccupations have led her to write about Hispaniola, where she has set three of her novels. These highlight the interconnected reality of the "bird/body politic" of the region. Her concerns attain greater urgency in *Tú, la oscuridad* (1995; *In the Palm of Darkness*, 1997), which revolves around the disappearance of a frog in Haiti as that nation grapples with political unrest, economic duress, and ecological devastation. As the plot unravels, the readers learn that the losses encompass more than a frog.

This novel, according to Lizabeth Paravisini-Gebert, "is an avowedly environmentalist novel—the region's first" (192) and establishes historic and scientific *hechos* (facts) that underscore the ripple effects of the *desechos* (discards) that environmental degradation and violence in Haiti have on the entire planet. Montero's novel literally establishes a bridge between her native island and her adopted one by providing a lens through which readers are made aware of the global repercussions of the ecological and political situations on the island between them. Rodríguez de Tió, as an exile from one Spanish colony in another, as a consequence of her work toward the abolition of slavery as well as her commitment to independence for both Cuba and Puerto Rico, is aware that the Cuban economy is inextricably tied to sugar. She probably also knew that

> it was not until the drop in Haiti's production and the arrival of the Industrial Revolution that the dynamics of relationships with foreign markets, complemented by the triumph of economic liberalism, became powerful enough to devour rapidly the many resources sheltered by (Cuba's) forests. . . . It cannot be ignored that the way Cuba became the world's principal exporter of sugar inflicted great damage on the environment and became a permanent mortgage on the island's future, in not simply environmental but also economic, social, and political terms. (Funes Monzote 6)

Given Montero's interest in the environment, she has certainly taken notice of the impact of such an industry on her native Cuba. Therefore, in spite of the hundred years or so that separate the poem from the novel, both authors are keenly aware that the destinies of the three islands are closely entwined.

To the linguistic, political, and racial differences that separate these islands, especially after 1959, Montero adds the pressing ecological concerns to shine a distinctive and focused Caribbean light. Her writing is akin to the meticulous and dedicated search for specimens by a herpetologist.

In the introduction to their *Caribbean Literature and the Environment*, Elizabeth M. DeLoughrey, Renée K. Gosson, and George B. Handley explain that,

> although North American ecocritics often inscribe an idealized landscape that is devoid of human history and labor, the colonization and forced relocation of Caribbean subjects preclude that luxury and beg the question as to what might be considered a natural landscape... we argue that addressing the *historical and racial violence* of the Caribbean is integral to understanding literary representations of its geography... so that a gesture of destruction against land becomes an act of violence against a *collective memory*. (2; emphasis added)

Given the Caribbean's unique ecosystem, if that of one nation is destroyed and/or its human capital diminished, then the entire region suffers the consequences. If one does not pay attention to the correlation between all parts of the bird, and not just its wings, then the region's collective memory, ensconced in culture, would eventually be lost, perhaps become a *desecho* as well. According to Serenella Iovino and Serpil Oppermann, "every living creature, from humans to fungi, tells evolutionary stories of coexistence, interdependence, adaptation and hybridization, extinctions and survivals. Whether perceived or interpreted by the human mind or not, these stories shape trajectories that have been a formative, enactive power" (7). Thus, Montero's fictional work, an "enactive power," based on ecological *hechos* about the disappearance of species, sounds the alarm for Cuba, Puerto Rico, the rest of the Caribbean, and certainly the world. Hers is a cautionary tale about a place, Haiti, that many consider a *desecho*, because it is the poorest nation in the Western Hemisphere with a majority (95 percent) population of mostly African descent. Yet, Montero recognizes Haiti's historical and cultural significance especially when read against the resounding words of ecofeminist philosopher Donna Haraway quoted in the epigraph: "vast genocides of people and other critters... threaten major system collapse after major system collapse, after major system collapse" (159). The novel of this Cuban–Puerto Rican author warns that as Haiti's story of violence and ecological devastation progresses, it could shape the trajectories of the stories of other nations.

Why would Montero be so interested in the neighboring island and more specifically Haiti? In an interview, she shared that when working for a newspaper in San Juan, she came into contact with Haitian leaders, exiled in Puerto Rico and fleeing the Duvalier regime, and they told her stories about Haiti (qtd. in Boling 61). She would certainly relate to being an exile due to political reasons. We also know that she is an admirer of Alejo Carpentier and is certainly aware of what he declared in the 1949 prologue to his novel set in Saint-Domingue/Haiti, *El reino de este mundo* (*The Kingdom of This World*): "todo resulta maravilloso en una historia imposible de situar en Europa, y que es tan real, sin embargo, como cualquier suceso ejemplar de los consignados, para pedagógica edificación, en los manuales escolares. ¿Pero qué es la historia de América toda sino una crónica de lo real-maravilloso?" (12-13) ("everything seems marvelous in a story it would have been impossible to set in Europe and which is as real, in any case, as any exemplary event yet set down for the edification of students in school manuals. But what is the history of all the Americas but a chronicle of the real marvelous?") (31). For Montero, as a Cuban–Puerto Rican author writing in the 1990s, the events in the Caribbean should no longer be chronicles of the real marvelous, but of the ecological and the feminist: factual and frightening. Her fiction is built on *hechos* and the remaining *desechos* of those who have left their imprints on the Caribbean's ecosystem.

Montero is drawn to an island that has been stigmatized and marginalized by its own neighbors, yet has been at the epicenter of the history of the Americas since 1492 when Christopher Columbus, who will ironically establish there the first "settlement" (Fort Navidad) with the *desechos* of his shipwrecked *Santa María*, writes about certain *hechos* of his first voyage, thus incorporating the Caribbean into the vortex of Western history. However, this misfortune is not what he shares with Treasurer Lord Rafael Sánchez in the letter he sends on 15 February 1493. *Au contraire*, he extols the beauty and lush greenery of this newly found paradise on earth:

> La Spañola es maravilla: las sierras y las montañas y las vegas y las campiñas y las tierras tan hermosas y gruesas para plantar y sembrar, para criar ganados de todas suertes, para edificios de villas e lugares. Los puertos de la mar, aquí no habría crehencia sin vista, y de los ríos muchos y grandes y buenas aguas, las más de los cuales traen oro. En los árboles y frutos y yerbas ay grandes diferencias de aquellas de la Iuana (Cuba); en ésta ay muchas specierías y grandes minas de oro y de metals. (221)

(In that island also which I have before said we named Española, there are mountains of very great size and beauty, vast plains, groves, and very fruitful fields, admirably adapted for tillage, pasture, and habitation. The convenience and excellence of the harbours in this island, and the abundance of the rivers, so indispensable to the health of man, surpass anything that would be believed by one who had not seen it. The trees, herbage and fruits of Española are very different from those of Juana (Cuba), and moreover it abounds in various kinds of spices, gold, and other metals.) (5–6)

The strategy is to evoke the Eden-like qualities of the land and the Adamic ability to name and, in Columbus's case, to rename. Re-creating Genesis is a way of recycling the story for the consumption of European monarchs who need resources (which according to Columbus are plentiful). The description of the bounties of this seemingly "virgin" landscape, sets up the patterns of aggressive economic pursuits that signal the environmental devastations to come. The violence to the ecosystem (nonhuman Others—such as trees and rivers—and human Others—such as the "Indians" and their culture) is presented as an expected *hecho* by Columbus since he mentions that he has seized some of the "Indians" to help him with the local language. The intent is to propose a plan for exploitation with no concern for what exists *in situ*. He foresees the cultivation of plants (sugar will be brought during his second voyage); the raising of cattle (pigs, cows, and horses will also come in the second voyage) since he sees none around; the construction of buildings à la European; and the conversion of these human Others into Catholicism. His narrative suggests a landscape that, given the temperate weather, has not been exploited to its full potential. Should it come as a surprise then that soon thereafter, on this paradise, the system of *encomiendas* (lands and native workers granted to a conqueror) is imposed, sugarcane is planted, slaves from Africa are bought and sold, and plantation societies take hold? The *hechos* of the first Governor of the Antilles (1492–99) bequeathed destruction, discord, and divisiveness, which become ever more evident centuries later when Saint-Domingue becomes the richest colony of France, and the wingbeats of the ideals of the French Revolution together with the slaves' revolts fan the fires of the Haitian Revolution and the establishment of the sovereign state of Haiti on 1 January 1804, as the first independent nation in Latin America and the Caribbean, the second republic of the Americas, and the only nation in the world to be established after successful slave uprisings. These are the *hechos*; but what about the societal and environmental *desechos* that a plantation society generates in its aggressive path of production and consumption?

When Montero publishes her environmentally focused novel, it is not coincidental that the action of the novel occurs exactly five hundred years after the Columbus letter we quoted. The action in Haiti takes place between November 1992 and 16 February 1993. The narration takes us through desolate urban and desertic rural landscapes. It is an *hecho* that much of the desertification is due to the cutting of trees by Haitians themselves to make coal to meet their everyday needs. Montero's text not only examines the *desechos* wrought about not just by this aspect of the ecological crisis of the nation but also those of the human tragedies, the result of almost two centuries of political conflicts, foreign interventions and occupations, and drug trafficking. By the start of the novel, the military coup of 30 September 1991 has occurred. Jean-Bertrand Aristide, the first Haitian president to be elected in democratic elections, has been deposed. When Aristide is forced out of government, thousands of Haitians flee their country and head to the Dominican Republic (where, as a rule, they are not welcomed) and/or seek political asylum in the United States (the so-called boat people). Between 1991 and 1994, the paramilitary group Front Révolutionnaire Armé pour le Progrès d'Haiti, known by its acronym FRAPH—a play on words with *frapper* (to hit)—is responsible for over 4,000 political assassinations and rapes of women. Given the violent backdrop of Papa Doc Duvalier's *tonton macoutes*, the paramilitary, the drug traffickers, and everyone else caught in the middle, one begins to see the pan-Caribbean connections that Montero as a Cuban–Puerto Rican author seeks to establish through the story of the quest for the specimen of a coveted frog—a rather small amphibian. With her late twentieth-century sensibilities as a woman writer concerned with the broader issues of ecological devastation, Montero presents Haiti as a focal point of Caribbean environmental concerns.

Unfortunately, this violence of 1992/1993 in Haiti tragically repeats itself. The cyclical nature of the destruction of the ecosystem set against such violent backgrounds becomes evident through the voices in the novel: those of foreign explorers and catalogers of the Caribbean space, those of the Haitian people, and those of the biota. Their combined stories bridge different genders, sexualities, eras, locales, and the state of the biota throughout the world.

The novel is divided into twenty chapters told through two distinct voices: that of Victor Grigg, a U.S. herpetologist, who narrates the odd chapters in the first person; and that of Thierry Adrian Jr., the Haitian guide and devout practitioner of Voodoo, whose voice is heard in the even chapters, also in the first person (and eventually recorded by Victor). Between each odd and even chapter, a scientific vignette in the third person alludes to the disappearance of amphibians throughout the world, thus connecting the demise of Haitian frogs to those of other parts of the world. The one notable exception to this pattern occurs after what would be chapter 19. The last vignette appears after chapter 20 (the last chapter of the novel) and functions as an epilogue where readers are told, in the same objective and scientific tone of the other vignettes, about the disappearance of the last specimen of the frog (*Eleutherodactylus sanguineus* or *grenouille du sang*) together with the human protagonists who die when the *Neptune* sinks on 16 February 1993, exactly five hundred years plus one day after the letter written by Columbus. Curiously, the novel's first line is the prediction of Victor's death: "Un astrólogo tibetano le predijo a Martha [su esposa] que yo moriría en un incendio" (13). ("A Tibetan astrologer told Martha [his wife] I would die by fire") (1). The narrative arch starts with a death foretold and the means by which it should occur, yet it ends with the disappearance of three male beings, with no partners, no descendants, that is with no future, sterile, and in water. What has altered the prescribed plot? How has his time in Haiti changed Victor's path to death? Perhaps it is because he has begun to listen and pay attention to the political and violent situation. At the onset, he states that all he wants is to collect frogs and asks why would anyone care? His first-world arrogant status carries no weight in Haiti. He is not in contact with the reality he finds himself into in November of 1992. Before he starts to understand, Victor will be beaten and warned to stop searching for specimens in those mountains that serve to dispose of the mutilated bodies of everyday Haitians, victims of the reigning violence. It is important to note that it is not just frogs or Haitians, but also U.S. scientists who disappear. Not one entity is higher than another within the ecosystem; we are all interconnected and our biotic or abiotic destinies are intricately linked, especially when violence and environmental degradation play a part.

For Victor, this trip to "Haití . . . lugar peligroso para las expediciones" (19) ("Haiti . . . a dangerous place for field trips") (8), is above all a professional accomplishment because he has been asked to undertake it by an eminent Australian herpetologist, Vaughan Patterson. But it also provides the perfect excuse to be separated from his wife, Martha, who has grown more and more distant from him since she is in a lesbian relationship with a fellow scientist, Barbara. For Thierry, meeting with this foreign herpetologist allows him to tell his personal stories, which are intricately tied to the violence in his country and to the scientific investigations of another Australian herpetologist and mentor to Patterson, Jasper Wilbur (Papa Crapaud), for whom he had worked in Haiti in the 1950s. It allows him as well to leave Port-au-Prince and reconnect with the memory of his father (also a Voodoo practitioner and a *pwazon rat* hunter), of his family, and of his initiation into a male society ruled by the Law of Water. Through these stories, Victor learns how Thierry had seen the *grenouille du sang* as a young man in Casetaches Hill, near the town of Jérémie on the western end of the island and at the foot of the Massif de La Hotte. He had been asked to track a "mad" German woman who had run away from her husband. In short, he is very critical of this naked and bloody woman for not looking or behaving, in his view, like a woman should. He beats her and ties her up to deliver her to her husband, who will also beat her. Thierry is not fazed by this violence toward a woman and will suggest to Victor to do the same later in the novel. However, Thierry will poignantly recall his father, as well as the landscape of his youth and the tree-covered mountains before these were lost due to an "environmental collapse as the forests that were the frogs' habitat disappear . . . and the troubled landscape of Haiti . . . [which] has decayed precipitously due to political corruption, violence, institutional terror, murders, brutality, and religious turmoil" (Paravisini-Gebert 192–93) takes hold in the present-time of the narrative. Thierry notes that already in the 1950s, trees "empezaban a escasear" (77) ("were beginning to thin out") (53).

The tripartite structure of the text is a narrative strategy to eschew a hierarchy among the voices that recount the disappearances of life and culture, since biological, environmental, cultural, or spiritual losses, are not just regrettable but irreparable; there is no going back once the environment is degraded. The reader encounters the first-world voice of a male scientist associated with neo-imperialist and heteronormative views of the world; the voice of a religious and third-world heteronormative "subaltern Other" who belongs to a country subjected to economic exploitation since the colonial era; and lastly, the voices of human and nonhuman Others in an environment subjugated to anthropocentric and patriarchal views. Some of these "voices" appear in the vignettes documenting the disappearance of amphibians in Linnaean taxonomical terms as well as how they are popularly known in their respective countries. Most of these notes are updated up to the early 1990s (mostly 1992), signaling that these could be Victor's, who kept meticulous records on the disappearance of amphibians. Every vignette ends with a pessimistic note; for example: "todavía se ignoran las causas" (21) ("the causes are still unknown (9)); "los nativos le comunicaron que los sapos, simplemente, 'se habían ido'" (111) ("the natives reported that the toads had simply 'gone away'") (79). The voices of others, especially women, appear in the subplots and reveal the violence committed against them. In an eco-equalizer narrative gesture, Montero includes Sarah's voice, a U.S. botanist searching for the last female specimen of the *Pereskia quisqueyana* cactus in Casetaches. The name of the cactus alludes to the Dominican Republic (the other nation in Hispaniola), thus bringing in the third of the Hispanic Antilles into the novel. The narrative connects other endangered animals, other third-world Others, and other women who defy gender stereotypes throughout the planet. Montero's novel is representative of an "aesthetics of the earth" espoused by Martinican philosopher Édouard Glissant, who advocates for a postcolonial ecocriticism in order to "find a way to speak in ethical terms about the global and the local without reducing difference and without instituting old structural hierarchies" (qtd. in DeLoughrey and Handley 33).

Montero sets up these two male protagonists, who at first seem very dissimilar, to tell and to listen to stories, hence recognizing the significance and value of the Caribbean's oraliterature tradition.[1] Stories need to be told, but more importantly they need to be heard so they become part of the collective memory. At the onset, Victor dismisses Thierry's tales of the women in his past and the increase of violence in Haiti as *desechos* until he realizes that *hechos* about hearing the frog's song and the description of its habitat are part of the stories, and he starts to pay attention. As the plot progresses, readers begin to understand that the effects of both the environmental degradation and violence connect the foreign scientists, the Haitian guides, and the disappearing biota to us. The scientists do not always want to admit to it because they are obsessed with their scientific quests. The Haitians in the novel, especially the women besieged by violence and/or sexism in and outside the home, are themselves trying to survive and not disappear. So, even if they see the interconnectedness that links all of us to the ecosystem, what can they do to prevent its degradation?

Victor eventually begins to see the interconnectedness and despairs when he realizes that he may not be able to explain to Vaughn Patterson why the frog may never be found. In his stream of consciousness, constructed with rhetorical questions posed to himself as a way of constructing a narrative for the eminent Australian herpetologist, he will echo what Thierry had told him when they first met. Thierry tells Victor: "A veces pienso, pero no lo digo, que llegará el día en que venga un hombre como usted, alguien que atraviese el mar para buscar ranas, quien dice rana dice cualquier otro animal, y encuentre una gran loma de huesos en la orilla, una loma más alta que el pico Tête Boeuf. Entonces se dirá: 'Haití se terminó, gran Dios, esos huesos son todo lo que queda'" (26). ("At times I think, but keep to myself, I think that one day a man like you will come here, someone who crosses the ocean to look for a couple of frogs, and when I say frogs, I mean any creature, and he will find only a great hill of bones on the shore, a hill higher than the peak of Tête Boeuf. Then he will say to himself: 'Haiti is finished, God Almighty, those bones are all that remain'") (11). Patterson, a first-world scientist, will purportedly only understand *hechos*. But as Victor has discovered, plenty of so-called *desechos* are needed to complete the stories coming from Haiti where many are suffering because their habitats have been destroyed by political violence and drug trafficking:

> Los herpetólogos no entienden ciertas cosas . . . ¿ . . . cómo explicarle que Haití no era un lugar a secas, un nombre solo, una montaña con una rana sobreviviente? ¿Cómo contarle sobre Cito Francisque, el hombre que me había sacado a palos del Mont des Enfants Perdus? ¿Cómo hablarle de los animales que echaban todavía vivos a las hogueras, y del polvo y de las pestilencias, las abominables, impensables, desconocidas pestilencias? ¿Cómo describirle las calles, los albañales abiertos, la bosta humana en medio de la acera, los cadáveres del amanecer, la mujer sin sus manos, el hombre sin su rostro? ¿Cómo lograr que Patterson, muriendo de leucemia, su vida pendiente del hilo de la curiosidad, de rigor, de pasión científica que lo unía a esta rana, comprendiera que Luc, el guía de los botánicos, había sido enterrado sin sus pies, y que Paul, el hermano de Thierry, probablemente se estuviera pudriendo en una esquina, con un trozo de menos en su carne? ¿Cómo meterle en la cabeza que Haití, gran Dios, se estaba terminando, y que esa loma de huesos que iba creciendo frente a nuestros ojos, una loma más alta que el pico Tête Boeuf, era todo lo que iba a quedar? (226–27)

> (Herpetologists don't understand certain things . . . how would I explain that Haiti wasn't simply a place, a name, a mountain with a frog that had survived? How would I tell him about Cito Francisque, the man who had driven me off the Mont des Enfants Perdus? What would I say about the way they threw live animals onto their bonfires,

about the dust and the stink, that unbearable, unspeakable, unfathomable stench? How would I describe the streets, the open sewers, the human shit in the middle of the sidewalk, the corpses at dawn, the woman whose hands were missing, the man whose face was missing? How would I make Patterson—dying of leukemia, his life hanging by the thread of scientific curiosity, rigor, and passion that connected him to this frog—how would I make him understand that Luc, the botanists' guide, had been buried without his feet and that Paul, Thierry's brother, was probably rotting somewhere, missing a piece of his body? God Almighty, how would I make him see that Haiti was disappearing, that the great hill of bones growing before our very eyes, a mountain higher that the peak of Tête Boeuf, was all that would remain?) (170–71)

Victor also recalls that Thierry had not been able to tell him where the frogs had gone or for that matter where the fish, the wild pigs, the ducks, and even the iguanas had gone. Thierry asks Victor to look around: "Nada tiene que ver lo que queda de los hombres, mírelos con cuidado: los huesos se les asoman desde adentro, empujan por debajo de la piel como si quisieran escapar de allí, abandonar esa carniza floja donde son golpeados, ir a esconderse en otra parte" (26). ("Just take a look at what's left of humans, take a careful look: You can see the bones pushing out under their skins as if they wanted to escape, to leave behind that weak flesh where they are so battered, to go into hiding someplace else") (11). Thierry's allusion to the bones, wanting to separate from the flesh that contains them, signals how Haiti as a nation is not able to hold its skeleton together: too many intestine conflicts are breaking the body and its people are seeking to flee. So why should it come as a surprise that the frogs are also leaving? Dr. Emile Boukaka, a high member of the secret male society, will tell Victor that the great flight of the frogs (also emblematic of Haiti) is leaving; Damballah, the *lwa* (deity) creator of life, is calling the frogs. He too is speaking metaphorically; and, at that time, Victor still did not understand that the minuscule frog reflects the rest of the nation and that rampant violence is impacting the environment: "Ya empezó la gran huida ... Ustedes se inventan excusas: la lluvia ácida, los herbicidas, la deforestación. Pero las ranas desaparecen de lugares donde no ha habido nada de eso" (132). ("The great flight has begun ... You people invent excuses: acid rain, herbicides, deforestation. But the frogs are disappearing from places where none of that has happened") (96).

The novel presents scenes of beatings; finding buried, mutilated, and hung bodies; and reports of brutal killings of pregnant women as the country sinks in misery and lives in fear. This modern-day explorer is not seeing what Columbus saw five hundred years earlier. The land is no longer fertile; it is barren or unable to reproduce like that last specimen the herpetologist and the botanist seek to collect. What can anyone do if they are barely subsisting? This is particularly distressing in the Caribbean, as the Cuban Antonio Benítez Rojo theorizes the concept of a postmodern chaos amidst repeating islands. He seeks to understand the centrality of the archipelago within the history of the world because the area "can also be regarded as a cultural sea without boundaries, as a paradoxical fractal form extending infinitely through a finite world" (314). One can certainly affirm that Caribbean cultures are so diverse that they can expand through multiple iterations, almost infinitely, past their frontiers. However, from an ecological perspective, can the diversity of the biota extend infinitely? No, it cannot; and given the conditions, as documented by Victor, for example, the future of some species, even though they are very small beings, is not guaranteed. Such a paradoxical fractal moment occurs in that last vignette as Victor and Thierry are about to go down with the shipwreck of the *Neptune* (perhaps echoing Columbus's experience).

As mentioned earlier, Victor had been told about his death by fire. In Haiti, thanks to Thierry and Emile Boukaka, he has learned about Damballah and Agwé Taroyo, the *lwa* of the sea; about the Law of Water, and how "el agua apaga la candela" (102) ("water puts out the flame") (73). So, by the time Victor boards the ferry with the frog, he is listening to Thierry's advice. This last chapter is titled "*Neptune*" and once aboard the ferry, Thierry ties the loose ends of his stories and shares that he had killed a man when ordered by the Society. His story and how he conceives of telling it, echo Benítez Rojo's concepts of the paradoxical fractal and the polyrhythmic and syncretic nature of Caribbean culture. As they are on the *Neptune*, with specimen in hand, he wonders what type of a word is that to name a boat. Thierry may not know, but Victor and the readers do: he is the Roman god of the waters, the counterpart of the Haitian Agwé Taroyo. Ironically, addressing Victor, Thierry immediately adds:

> Un hombre repite sus caminos, los repite sin darse cuenta y se hace la ilusión de que son nuevos. Ya no tengo ilusiones, pero tengo que caminar mis propios pasos, los pocos que me queden, tengo que hacer los míos y usted los suyos, y la mujer que se quedó allá arriba

y que se morirá mañana, caminará otra vez lo que le toca. Hasta Cito Francisque, con ser tan poderoso, tiene que repetirlo todo, de loma en loma, de sangre en sangre. (238)

(A man repeats all his roads, he repeats them without realizing it, his illusion is that they're new. I have no more illusions, but I do have to walk my own steps, the few I have left, and you have to walk yours, and the woman who stayed up there and will be dead tomorrow, she will walk again on the path that is hers. Even Cito Francisque, as powerful as he is, has to repeat it all, from mountain to mountain, from blood to blood.) (181)

These words reflect the paradoxical iterations of syncretized elements that abound in the Caribbean and are key to understanding the situations, political or environmental, which may not seem evident at first. It is in the process of repeating and syncretizing elements that one gains insight or is enlightened. The repetitions or iterations add layer upon layer that a careful reader of Caribbean culture must learn to dissect since *hechos* and *desechos* become intermingled in stories as they extend infinitely in the collective memory.

So, how will the telling of this story with its inevitable repetitions throughout the paradoxical Caribbean, or the repetition of the loss of amphibians throughout the world illuminate the readers about the wings of the synecdochic bird: Cuba and Puerto Rico? The second question is much easier to answer since the sixth vignette is about the disappearances of three frogs in Puerto Rico and the news that two more are in danger of becoming extinct. They share the first part of their Linnaean name, *Eleutherodactylus*, with the frog that Victor seeks in Haiti, thus immediately establishing a recognizable connection. Their household names all refer to the *coquí* (*coquí dorado*, *coquí palmeado*, *coquí de Eneida*, *coquí duende*, and *coquí de Richmond*). The *coquí*, in popular culture, is the quintessential emblem of Puerto Rican people, and reputedly, if taken out of its natural habitat on the island, it will die. It is very significant that Montero includes this vignette with some that are extinct and the alarming news that two more could possibly disappear. Ecological devastation does not only occur in Haiti. And if we recall the statement by DeLoughrey, Gosson, and Handley "that a gesture of destruction against land becomes an act of violence against a *collective memory*" (2; emphasis added), Montero's vignette points to the danger of such violence on the collective memory. What would it mean to be Puerto Rican if there were no more *coquíes* to sing loudly and represent us?

But, what about Cuba? Where is it in the text? Where is it repeated? The signifier "Cuba" is absent, but fragments of the signified, much like Edgar Allan Poe's purloined letter, are hidden in plain sight and scattered throughout the novel. We just need to be like herpetologists: hear for the beginning of its sound much like the song of the frog; look for it in the dark and shine a light on it and try to take a look at it before it disappears again. Montero offers us a clue, also buried within one of Thierry's stories. He is telling Victor about the first time, as a child, he heard the call of the *grenouille du sang*; he caught a fever (probably malaria) and saw death coming for him. The next time, he heard it was when he had gone up Casetaches Hill on the hunt for the "mad" German woman. He wanted to catch the frog and bring it to Papa Crapaud, but in the end, he does not. What is significant is the process to catch an elusive frog/signifier that in turn reveals how one must approach the Montero novel: be ready to "listen" for it, but do not be confused if it is not where you expect to find it; try to shine a light on it, but let it reveal itself to you, and like Thierry, do not try to silence it even though you are afraid of its call:

> Papá Crapaud me había enseñado a no dejarme confundir, me había advertido que a veces cuando se oye el canto por un lado, quiere decir que la ranita anda por otro . . . aparté unas hojas y alumbré con la linterna el suelo y los huecos de los troncos. La rana se calló cuando sintió que la buscaban, desvié la luz para que volviera a cantar y entonces, en la oscuridad, vi aquellos ojos . . . Me acerqué un poco y le eché la luz encima para cegarla: tenía la mitad del cuerpo oculto debajo de una piedra, pero vi que era tan roja como una fruta, o como el corazón de un animal. (50–51)

> (Papa Crapaud had taught me not to become confused, he had warned me that sometimes when you hear the call in one place it means the frog is somewhere else . . . I moved some leaves aside and shined the light on the ground and into the hollows of trees. The frog stopped singing as soon as it knew it was being hunted; I turned off the light so it would start to sing again, and then in the darkness, I saw its eyes . . . I moved a little closer and shined the light right on it to blind it: It was hiding under a rock, but I could see that it was red as a fruit, as red as the heart of an animal.) (30)

With this advice, and following the narrative's logic and Thierry's strategy for capturing elusive beings in the ecosystem, if Puerto Rico is in a vignette, would the fragments of the "Cuban" signified be in the other vignettes? A closer reading reveals that indeed they can be found in the fastidious repetition of the letter "C" in the proper names of the geographic locations mentioned in the other vignettes: C-olorado, C-oncorde Ranges, C-osta Rica, C-olombia, C-alifornia, C-usco, and even C-astaches.

With this last wing revealed, the twentieth-century version of the ecological bird is complete and given the environmental focus of the novel against a backdrop of violence, what can we say about that bird today? One may say that the ecosystem has suffered and continues to suffer in all of the islands due to a combination of factors. But that knowledge and dissemination of information are crucial elements. Even Damballah, "una deidad callada, el único dios mudo del panteón" (132) ("the silent deity, the only mute god in the pantheon") (96) will borrow a toad's voice to let the frogs know when to begin the great flight. If we believe in interconnectedness, then *coquí*=Puerto Rican; *grenouille du sang*=Haitian; and frogs, in general, are stand-ins for people in the rest of the world. The novel shows how environmental degradation affects all entities in the ecosphere. Violence perpetrated on one species heralds the demise of others. According to Haraway, "No species, not even our own arrogant one pretending to be good individuals in so-called modern Western scripts, acts alone; assemblages of organic species and of abiotic actors make history, the evolutionary kind and the other kinds too" (159). Therefore, it should be frightening that in Haiti frogs, cacti, women, men, habitats, and culture are disappearing because it signals that the Caribbean bird *in toto* could disappear. What happens in Hispaniola should be of great import to us. We need to learn what the *hechos* are throughout all the islands, so that our bird is neither metaphorically nor literarily buried in *desechos* and suffocate.

Note

1. Carolyn Cooper coined the term "oraliterature" to describe the blend between oral and literary practices in Jamaican popular culture.

Works Cited

Benítez-Rojo, Antonio. *The Repeating Island: The Caribbean and the Postmodern Perspective*. Translated by James E. Maraniss. Duke UP, 1996.

Boling, Becky. "A Meditation on the Uses of Madness in Mayra Montero's *Tú, la oscuridad*." *La narrativa de Mayra Montero: Hacia una literatura transnacional caribeña*, edited by Kevin Sedeño Guillén and Madeline Cámara. Aduana Vieja, 2008, pp. 61-71.

Carpentier, Alejo. "Prólogo." *El reino de este mundo*. Edición Arca, 1966, pp. 7-13.

———. "Prologue to *The Kingdom of This World* (1949)." Translated by Alfred MacAdam. *Review: Latin American Literature and Arts*, vol. 26, no. 47, 1993, pp. 28-32.

Colón, Cristóbal. "Carta a Luis de Santángel." *Cristóbal Colón: Textos y documentos*, edited by Consuelo Varela. 3rd ed. Alianza Editorial, 1992, pp. 219-26.

Columbus, Christopher. "First Voyage of Columbus." *Four Voyages to the New World: Letters and Selected Documents*. Translated and edited by R. H. Major. Corinth Books, 1978, pp. 1-17.

Cooper, Carolyn. *Noises in the Blood—Orality, Gender, and the "Vulgar" Body of Jamaican Popular Culture*. Macmillan, 1993.

DeLoughrey, Elizabeth, and George B. Handley, editors. "Introduction." *Postcolonial Ecologies: Literatures of the Environment*. Oxford UP, 2011, pp. 14-41.

DeLoughrey, Elizabeth M. et al., editors. "Introduction." *Caribbean Literature and the Environment: Between Nature and Culture*. U of Virginia P, 2005, pp. 1-30.

Funes Monzote, Reinaldo. *From Rainforest to Cane Field in Cuba: An Environmental History since 1492*. Translated by Alex Martin. U of North Carolina P, 2008.

Haraway, Donna. "Anthropocene, Capitalocene, Plantationocene, Chthulucene: Making Kin." *Environmental Humanities*, vol. 6, no. 1, 2015, pp. 159-65. *ResearchGate*, doi: 10.1215/22011919-3615934.

Iovino, Serenella, and Serpil Oppermann. "Introduction." *Stories Come to Matter: Material Ecocriticism*, edited by Serenella Iovino and Serpil Oppermann. Indiana UP, 2014, pp. 1-17.

Montero, Mayra. *In the Palm of Darkness*. Translated by Edith Grossman. HarperCollins, 1997.

———. *Tú, la oscuridad*. Tusquets Editores, 1995.

Paravisini-Gebert, Lizabeth. "'He of the Trees': Nature, the Environment, and Creole Religiosities in Caribbean Literature." *Caribbean Literature and the Environment: Between Nature and Culture*, edited by Elizabeth M. DeLoughrey et al. U of Virginia P, 2005, pp. 182-96.

Rodríguez de Tió, Lola. "A Cuba." "Cuba and Puerto Rico: 'Two Wings of the Same Bird.'" *SHEC: Resources for Teachers*. herb.ashp.cuny.edu/items/show/2511. Accessed 19 Oct. 2020.

10

Caribbean Dialogues by María Zambrano

MADELINE CÁMARA

Encountering the critical and stimulating thought of Spanish philosopher María Zambrano (Málaga, 1908–Madrid, 1991) creates a debt of gratitude. To write about her is just a way of retribution, being myself a Cuban academic in exile. As is well known, Zambrano lived and wrote while in exile from Spain during Franco's regime spanning over forty years. My chapter focuses on her Caribbean *séjours* (stays) in Puerto Rico and Cuba, where she met and worked with prominent local writers, thinkers, and politicians. I claim these dialogues enriched both Zambrano and these groups of Caribbean intellectuals. What I will call "the Antillean period" in her life covers from 1940 to 1953. Zambrano lived between islands during the key years of modernization, when local writers and artists rethought the concept of national identity. I argue that Zambrano influenced the consolidation of that position in bringing to the conversation her original and strong philosophical critique of Rationalism, as well as her solid faith in Democracy and Humanism, influenced by Greco-Latin ideals and Gnostic-Christian traditions.

While on the islands, Zambrano established personal ties with prominent political and cultural figures, such as the Cubans Lydia Cabrera and José Lezama Lima and the Puerto Ricans Inés María Mendoza and Jaime Benítez. She cultivated a prolonged friendship with Puerto Rican Elsa Fano and Cuban Josefina Tarafa, two women who have yet to receive the attention they deserve from Caribbean cultural and gender studies. Indeed, feminist theory has neglected the role of patronage (*mecenazgo*). I am unable to develop it here due to space restrictions. For the same reason, I only make brief references to the Dutch Dominican priest Martin Berntsen, a key participant in these transatlantic dialogues.

I review interpersonal relationships, which I analyze using the terms *sororities*, when I refer to Cabrera and Mendoza, and *sicigia* when discussing Lezama Lima and Benítez.[1] Later, when I discuss "Los cabañistas," a group of intellectuals who met in Puerto Rico during the 1940s, I introduce Michel Foucault's term *société du discours*. I propose that Zambrano fosters fruitful dialogues with Lezama Lima and other members of the Orígenes group in Cuba and, also, with Jaime Benítez and other members of "Los cabañistas." These dialogues emerge from the legacy of contemporary European thought, from Heidegger to Ortega y Gasset, among others; as well as classic traditions, from Aristotle, Plotinus, Seneca, and others. As a debtor and representative of these philosophies, Zambrano finds a ground already paved by the knowledge circulating in these heterodox Caribbean discursive communities. Also, through my discussion, I hope to emphasize Zambrano's contribution to gender equality in her *primus inter pares*' relations with female and male creators of the Caribbean.

Cuba: A "Prenatal Homeland" with a Black Mother

In 1939, Zambrano arrived in Mexico, the first stop of her Latin American exile. She realized her husband, Alfonso Rodríguez Aldave, would not be able to become a member of a closed and tightly-knit Mexican academic community. She was also not happy with her teaching position at the Universidad Michoacana de San Nicolás de Hidalgo, in Morelia. Thus, she embraced the opportunity to depart for Cuba following an invitation from José María Chacón y Calvo, who she had befriended in Spain during the Civil War. Upon her arrival in Cuba, Zambrano was welcomed by her beloved Lezama Lima and her future *habanera* patrons: Lydia Cabrera, María Teresa de Rojas, and Josefina Tarafa. Zambrano's professional life in Cuba's capital was successful, as reflected in her collaborations with literary institutions and multiple publications in magazines and newspapers (Arcos XIII–LXXIV). However, she confessed her economic difficulties to her family in Paris and some friends. Cabrera came to her rescue in various ways. They started a relation of sorority, not exempted of contradictions and complaints, that extended to the 1980s, as revealed in their last correspondence, which I discussed back in 2014 in my text "Sororidades habaneras: María Zambrano y Lydia Cabrera." Cabrera was instrumental in Zambrano's arrival to Havana. She arranged for Zambrano and Aldave to stay in La Quinta de San José, the maternal home of María Teresa de Rojas, who became Cabrera's companion and remained so until her death while exiled in Miami. In Cuba, Rojas and Cabrera provided financial help to the Spanish couple and facilitated Zambrano's contacts with institutions, offering her paid lectures. Cabrera also used her influence when Zambrano faced problems due to her immigrant status in Cuba. Let us document some of these acts of sorority between Cabrera and Zambrano.

In 1940, Zambrano wrote to Waldo Frank, a prominent U.S. writer, for support. She shared with Frank the utopia of *panamericanismo*—the unity of all American countries to combat external influence—as indicated in a letter from Frank: "we must still hope our destiny will make it possible to bring about a common action, an effort guided by clearly defined principles, those that only love discovers and respects" (qtd. in Elizalde, "16 cartas . . ." 129).[2]

In response to Zambrano's request for support to publish her texts in the United States, Frank proposed that Zambrano translate his book, *Chart for Rough Water: Our Role in a New World* ("16 cartas . . ." 122–23). Zambrano did not know English and rejected the offer but later accepted: "I will tell you one thing, Oh, and do not be surprised by my versatility because I will explain: if you do not have a translator for your book yet, I dare accept the offer that made me bring it to you in Spanish. I study English and also have someone who advises me knowing a lot" ("16 cartas . . ." 128). In a later letter, Zambrano was more specific: "I am helped by an extraordinary friend, Lydia Cabrera, of whom you will be friends right away"("16 cartas . . ." 130).

Her letter dated 23 January 1941 continued to promise that she would finish the translation and conveyed her hardships: "The University goes through an extremely complicated situation; it has been closed for two months, the student strike has not yet given in; the situation of 'La Institución Hispano-Cubana de Cultura' is bad economically; now I am giving in it a course on Greek Philosophy in eight lessons, but it has been subsidized by some friends" ("16 cartas . . ." 139).

While Zambrano did not mention their names, my research points that the friends in Cuba were Cabrera and Rojas. Zambrano was not remiss to respond to Cabrera's solidarity by supporting the dissemination of her book *Por qué . . . Cuentos negros de Cuba*, which appeared in 1948. In 1950, in the journal *Orígenes*, Zambrano welcomed the publication of Cabrera's book with an enthusiastic review entitled "Lydia Cabrera: Poeta de la metamorfosis," and claimed:

Lydia Cabrera stands out among all Cuban poets for a form of poetry in which knowledge and fantasy are intertwined to the point of no longer being different things, until it is called poetic knowledge . . . It is the world of the slave race to the lintel of our day that she releases. For how will the slave attain his freedom, but be heard and even more so receiving the word that sometimes does not have the form that is still lacking or left in the path of servitude? (13)

Zambrano insisted on the redemptive and liberating mission of *la palabra* ("the word"), as she would say, within a historical-cultural and racial context. She underlined how Cabrera gave voice to Blacks by rescuing the genomic imprint of Africa in *lo cubano* (Cubanness). At the same time, a mutual enrichment was taking place: when Cabrera introduced Zambrano to the magic of the Black world, the Spaniard expanded her ideas about "poetic knowledge." It is important to emphasize that this concept is key in later developments of Zambrano's philosophy, when "poetic knowledge" would become a bridge to "poetic reason," her main contribution to the critique of Rationalism.[3] The philosopher believes that the existence of a type of knowledge is possible: "[p]oetic knowledge is in its roots, even when it is assisted by the strictest discipline, one of the most rigorous methods of investigation" (qtd. in Ortega Muñoz 73). As we have previously examined, Zambrano applies the concept to describe how Cabrera, building on ethnological data, is able to express poetically her conclusions about Cuba's hybrid identity.

In doing so, Cabrera goes beyond the work of Fernando Ortiz, a prominent figure of Afro-Cuban studies, who was still under the influence of positivist views. Ortiz, who also was Cabrera's brother-in-law, uses a paternalistic tone to recognize Cabrera's work in his presentation of *Cuentos negros* (1940),[4] where he writes: "This book is the first of a Havana woman, who years ago we initiated to taste Afro-Cuban folklore. Lydia Cabrera, out of simple curiosity, started to penetrate the forest of the black legends of Havana; later, for pure delight; finally, she transcribed and collected them . . ." (7).

Fortunately, the poet José Lezama Lima, aware of Cabrera's artistic sensibility, appreciated the significance of her work. A decade later, Lezama referred to Cabrera's new book, *Refranes de negros viejos* (1954), and claimed: "The name of Lydia Cabrera is attached for me to certain magical associations of the Enlightenment. To the French botanical commissions classifying in the Bogotan gardens. To the twelve from the cubic stone, on the seals of Cagliostro... The sayings of Lydia Cabrera have the essential nobility to clarify the questionnaire that must be placed in the introduction to our culture..." (118).

We must consider now how Lezama Lima and Zambrano coincided in praising Cabrera's work for including spirituality to reveal the Cuban "essence" and how this accord cemented their intellectual friendship. We have to remember that it was precisely in the journal *Orígenes*, created by Lezama, where Zambrano published her influential essay "La Cuba secreta" in 1948 and continued to develop the concept of islands as spaces for metamorphosis, previously announced in 1940 in her book *Puerto Rico: Nostalgia y esperanza de un mundo mejor*. In *Orígenes*, she also published her views about insularism in her review of Cabrera's book in 1950. An underlying dialogue takes place with Lezama Lima's concept of *sensibilidad insular*,[5] released in early 1937 following the celebration of the "Coloquio con Juan Ramón Jiménez" in Havana. (Zambrano may also have been familiar with Antonio Pedreira's *Insularismo*, originally published in Puerto Rico in 1934.) At the time, Lezama Lima was not yet the influential author he became after publishing his novel *Paradiso* in 1966. Yet Zambrano took the chance to support his ideas. Since 1939, when they first met, Zambrano and Lezama Lima established a relationship of equals, what I would like to call a *sicigia*. Their affinities encompassed literature, philosophy, and religion. Zambrano placed him at the highest level of her human scale and called him a "true man," when she wrote his obituary ("Hombre verdadero" 219), a term she adopts influenced by Sufi thinkers.

As demonstrated, in the effort to create a new model to read Cuban identity, Lydia Cabrera, José Lezama Lima, the Orígenes group, and Zambrano were champions in defending culture at a moment when Positivism's crude materialism, together with the corrupt political environment, were not auspicious for this type of reflection on the island.

While in Cuba, Zambrano wrote some of her most important books: *Delirio y destino* in 1950, but published in 1989, and *El hombre y lo divino*, which appeared in 1955. More and more she wanted to focus her energies on writing. Unfortunately, Zambrano's desire for a permanent position at the University of Havana did not materialize. She left Cuba for Rome in 1953 in search of another "Matria" (the feminine version of the homeland).

In Puerto Rico: The Memoranda from the Governor's Wife

Before she left for Europe, Zambrano tried her luck in Puerto Rico. Indeed, she moved back and forth between Cuba and Puerto Rico during the 1940s. She arrived in San Juan in April 1940 and received support from a revolutionary woman named Nilita Vientós Gastón; from Elsa Fano, a refined intellectual nicknamed *la condesa* (the countess); from Jaime Benítez, the future chancellor of the University of Puerto Rico in Río Piedras; and from Inés María Mendoza, who became the spouse of the first elected governor of Puerto Rico.

I would like to take a pause to comment more on this extraordinary woman (Mendoza), not yet well recognized outside of her country of birth.[6] She was born in 1908 and died in 1990. As a public-school teacher, Mendoza was a transgressive pedagogue. In 1937 she was removed from her position after publicly criticizing a mandate to conduct in English all public-school teaching in Puerto Rico. She joined the island's feminist movement and for a while she was a member of the Nationalist Party led by Pedro Albizu Campos. Later, Mendoza married future Governor Luis Muñoz Marín and served as a minister without portfolio from 1949 to 1964. During these years Mendoza was a strategic ally of Puerto Rico's modernization process, as could be appreciated in the quotes below where she advocates for a more humanistic approach in the accelerated process of urbanization that was taken place. Also, as Licia Fiol-Matta has critically examined (in *A Queer Mother* 209), Mendoza uses Gabriela Mistral's expertise in education to incorporate technology to the classrooms.

Mendoza and Zambrano also became bonded by a sorority. Their actions have relevant public and private consequences. Julio Quirós' research opens a window to learn what went on behind the stage regarding the publication of Zambrano's book, *Persona y democracia*, first published in Puerto Rico. Quirós refers to Mendoza's 1955 memorandum to Antonio J. Colorado, head of Puerto Rico's Department of Public Instruction Press. The memorandum mentions a book Zambrano was writing while living under precarious economic conditions in Italy: "Perhaps the PR publisher could publish the book that María is writing and give her peace for a year to write it" (XXII). Zambrano welcomed the opportunity provided and *Persona y democracia* was published in Puerto Rico in 1958.[7] In her book, the Andalusian provides her most important reflections on democracy.

Unfortunately, at this time, Mendoza lacked the time to organize her own essays, newspaper articles, and speeches on the same subject, democracy, in the form of an autonomous publication, as she was raising her daughters and keeping her home tidy, the Governor's residence, referred to as La Fortaleza. "Doña Inés," as Mendoza is still called on the island, was also editing her husband's speeches to prevent his government from being characterized as a "dictatorship," by steering the policies of the Estado Libre Asociado (as the Commonwealth of Puerto Rico is known) so as not to contradict the postulates of the Popular Democratic Party. In a letter to the Chilean poet Gabriela Mistral, Mendoza refers to the Popular Democratic Party founded by Muñoz Marín: "He and I and the people from the countryside did it. No one knows it, I know it, and I tell you—keep the secret" (qtd. in Sánchez 43).

Thus, many of the decisive actions of "doña Inés" remain unknown, a secret. I now dwell on fragments of her thoughts to conceptualize her ideas about democracy, ideas she was not shy to include in her memoranda to government officials. I propose that hers is a feminine discourse that assumes and subverts the traditional space, an action to occupy a personal and clear place in history. As an example, I quote her memo to the Chairman of the Puerto Rico Planning Board, addressing public housing:

> Once a person is not able to communicate, all possibility of intimate happiness and social happiness is closed ... Democracy develops a compulsive way of communicating with people, by sheer good intentions. It is often expressed in excessive planning ... thinking for others ... losing the habit of using the senses for people, seeing them, hearing them, feeling them ... We democrats, if we are not careful, with great love for justice in governments as facilitators of the common good, we slide towards becoming owners of other men ... (Inés María Mendoza to Ramón García Santiago, Memorándum, 3 Oct. 1963, ALMM)

In her passionate, and, in her own words, "confused" allegation, Mendoza uses strong images to criticize a development concept that imposes modernization to "store people horizontally or perpendicularly," deprives them of drinking "their cup of coffee ... on a comfortable bench to contemplate the infinite star and their own short time," an image of Zambranian affinity. But immediately, she picks up a familiar and intimate tone: "The truth is, my dear friend, is that ... they are not masses of men or masses of households but only to the extent that our resistance to delivering them en masse ... I resist to deliver to Puerto Ricans the darkness of expressive and crippling anonymity" (Mendoza, Memorándum).

In her memo, the dialogue between Mendoza's thought and that expressed by Zambrano in *Persona y democracia* comes alive: the continuity of the same idea about the indissoluble unity that must exist between the exercise of democracy, the cultivation of one's own freedoms, and the dignification of the people as a community of individuals. As Zambrano concludes in her book *Persona y democracia*, "If democracy were to be defined it could be done by saying it is a society where it is not only allowed, but demanded, to be a person" (121).

I hope that the texts I have quoted highlight the specific and deep concerns for practicing the concept of democracy in the interaction between government and people (specifically, the criticism of demagoguery as a possible degeneration of democracy), and a care to differentiate "people," from the pejorative concept of "mass." In the face of these dangers, both thinkers, Zambrano and Mendoza, propose an "antidote" by cultivating the status of a "person" in society.

The Rebel Disciple

How did Zambrano meet Benítez? I believe it happened at "La Cabaña," the liberal intellectual bastion mentioned earlier. How did they become collaborators and friends, and later distanced from each other? I will briefly discuss their complex interactions that fits a particular type of *sicigia* based on a discipleship.[8]

In April 1940, Zambrano arrived in Puerto Rico invited by the Association of Women Graduates from the University of Puerto Rico. Her first lecture, "Estoicismo" ("Stoicism"), began on April 17. Two days later she offered "El estoicismo en la vida española" ("Stoicism in Spanish Life"). Her last presentation, "Seneca y el estoicismo español" ("Seneca and Spanish Stoicism"), took place on April 22. In her lectures Zambrano pointed to our heritage of Western classical thought as indispensable to promote any country's culture.

Once in Puerto Rico, Zambrano regularly participated in the talks going on among "Los cabañistas," allowing her to approach Jaime Benítez and his sister Clotilde. Zambrano first approached Clotilde and then befriended the young Jaime who she considered to be her disciple. At first, Zambrano tried to influence Jaime through philosophical and religious ideas (both were admirers of the classical Greco-Latin heritage, Catholics, and devotees of the Virgin Mary). Below is an extended quote of a letter from Zambrano to Benítez:

> I have to talk to you seriously, dear Jaime, because I see that the latest events are printing a new twist on your life... I ask you first and foremost to be relentless with yourself: I will do it; it is the only thing I can offer you. Try to have two or three hours every day when you are alone with yourself, not only bodily but only in your consciousness, dedicate yourself to throwing masks... We must get to it [the truth] revealing. To discover what really is inside us especially when we prepare for *action* [original emphasis]... the worst is that, when intellectuals get involved in politics, they are not precise about their aspirations... Make yourself a program, inexorably meditate what your mission is. Your mission I see it this way: reform the university, give it effectiveness, life, and full intellectual dignity. And be the advisor on the general issues of education and think about democracy, think it relentlessly, *chastely* [original emphasis]... We have no right to turn it into a joy for ourselves, for our enjoyment, that which involves the life of our country, of thousands of beings who do not have our food our daily bread and the other's bread, of the spirit. No one should play with people's hunger... (letter dated 22 July 1940).⁹

Zambrano's letter illustrates that she considers herself to be a teacher, a guide, in the ethical-political field, to Benítez. In 1942, when Benítez was only thirty-three years old, he became Chancellor of the University of Puerto Rico in Río Piedras, where he proceeded to implement initiatives to create a multicultural academic environment that he called the *casa de estudios* (center of learning). He created the University Press that translated into Spanish numerous classics. He was the founder of a university museum that exhibited pieces of art from around the world. He promoted a program for students to visit Europe to learn firsthand "the origins of Western culture" he admired and proclaimed:

> by our will, choice, pride, and loyalty... we have chosen to be with Spain and with the United States. With pride and loyalty, we say: politically, we are American citizens, and in the depth of our soul, we are Spaniards. This Puerto Rican clamor takes place to defend our Spanish language and our American citizenship (*Desafíos 1942–1971*, 13–14).

It may well be that Benítez did not view Zambrano as essential as Juan Ramón Jiménez, the Spanish poet in exile who brought a Nobel Prize to the Río Piedras campus in 1956. But I propose that Benítez saw Zambrano as a binding feminine figure who helped build a cosmopolitan and erudite atmosphere in Puerto Rico. Benítez admired and followed Spanish philosopher José Ortega Gasset. As Ortega Gasset's disciple, Zambrano was aware she represented these values. In addition, Zambrano's presence in Río Piedras would be useful to Benítez's efforts to Westernize and modernize the island's classrooms.

I will not discuss here Zambrano's difficulties to obtain a work visa in Puerto Rico given the island's subordination to U.S. laws, which did not provide asylum to Spaniards claiming exile. I reviewed these difficulties in a previous work ("Panamericanism"). Ruiz and Avilés-Ortiz also cover this subject. Benítez, then Zambrano's ally, helped her navigate these difficulties. She did not hesitate to manipulate him when necessary since she knew how to play her cards within the fragile space she and her husband found themselves in. She prioritized her stays in Havana to participate in conferences or to teach courses and kept Puerto Rico as a secondary option. With support from the Chancellor, she returned to Puerto Rico several times. Her displacements, exhausting as they probably were, allowed her to receive the income needed to help her mother and sister in Paris. She even helped her husband who did not have a steady job. This was one of the reasons that caused their separation in 1948 and their divorce in 1953.

Earlier I indicated Zambrano's efforts to instill in Benítez, an ambitious and promising individual who combined political audacity and intellectual curiosity, the model Seneca provides for a public figure, one she wanted Benítez to imitate in his administrative career. However, in the correspondence between the two as well as between Zambrano and Clotilde Benítez, Jaime's sister, as well as with Lulú Benítez, Jaime's wife, we learn that Jaime did not always follow Zambrano's advice. I suggest then that Benitez's actions can be seen as a result of prejudice against a female figure of the intellectual stature of Zambrano, presenting a complex character arising out of the difficult circumstances she faced. In any event, Zambrano did not feel rewarded for her work as a guide she felt compelled to perform for Benítez. After Zambrano returned to Spain, where she now enjoyed support and recognition, she wrote to Nilita Vientós Gastón in 1986, apparently referring to the period when Benítez served as university chancellor: "As for not being able to receive Jaime Benítez, I would ask to remind you that owing me so much, during a period when he has so much power he did not show any interest in my situation, neither physical nor material, that is, economic" (Fundación María Zambrano, Serie Correspondencia Personal, Box No. 41).

Disappointed by Benítez, Zambrano distanced herself from her disciple. In turn, Benítez became closer to Rodríguez Aldave. Following the couple's separation in 1953, Rodríguez Aldave remarried and settled with his new wife, Françoise, in Mexico, where he started a business. The letters Rodríguez Aldave exchanged with Benítez over the following years reveal a strong affinity between the two, which appears to be fueled by their distancing from Zambrano. A letter dated 20 December 1989 from Rodríguez Aldave to Benítez reveals a male complicity when Aldave referred to Zambrano as "the so-called philosopher." Yet, following Zambrano's death in 1991, Benítez writes an emotionally laden obituary published in San Juan, on 3 September 1991 in *El Nuevo Día*. However, beyond the words are the facts and they display two lives devoted to the enhancement of public service: two great intellectuals engaged with their culture and the politics of their countries.

The Countess, the Dominican Friar, and Lunches in La Cabaña

On Elsa Fano's family property situated in Río Piedras, stood a rustic structure built out of wood and straw known as La Cabaña. Today no material vestige of that structure remains. Fortunately, we are able to imagine the atmosphere at La Cabaña thanks to the graphic testimony of Spanish painter José Vela Zanetti, exiled and living in the Dominican Republic, who visited Puerto Rico during the 1940s, and also thanks to the oral testimony of Sergio Marxuach, Fano's nephew. In the summer of 2010, I visited Puerto Rico and had the opportunity to visit Marxuach's house in the company of Julio Quirós. Marxuach showed us two paintings from Vela Zanetti depicting La Cabaña. Besides, Sergio shared with us stories about visiting this place as a teenager, thus bearing witness to events fundamental to the cultural history of Puerto Rico.

The gatherings at La Cabaña brought together intellectuals whose voices became decisive to the fate of the country. Among those voices were the ones from Jaime Benítez, Juan Antonio Corretjer, Margot Arce, Ricardo Alegría, Isabel Gutiérrez Arroyo, and Inés María Mendoza, together with a figure insufficiently known but of great importance: the Dutch Dominican priest Martin Berntsen (1886–1958), who was the spiritual and intellectual guide.[10] Elsa Fano and her sister Ester hosted these gatherings. The newspaper *El Piloto: Seminario Apologético*, directed by Berntsen, published many of the concerns raised during the gatherings.

As documented by testimonies, correspondence, and photos, Zambrano participated in some of these Sunday gatherings, where she found fertile ground to address her heterodox concerns both within Catholicism and philosophy. We can only imagine how excited she was to participate in such an elite group. However, if we read Zambrano's correspondence with her mother and sister, we learn about how this woman of such a high intellect, while exiled and in a precarious financial condition, felt about her experiences in Puerto Rico. In a colloquial tone, she writes: "Elsa asked me to write an essay about Freudian concepts—one of those North American diseases—and, after it was reviewed by a Dutch Dominican Father, very different than Spaniards, had it published by Altolaguirre's Press—I'll send you a copy—and became involved in selling it to everyone, sending me the money which was more than what was actually sold . . ." (Fundación María Zambrano, Sección Correspondencia personal. Havana, 1 Jan. 1946).

The letter reveals Zambrano's gratitude for the intellectual and financial help provided by Elsa Fano to publish in 1940 *El freudismo: Testimonio del hombre actual,* which was released by La Verónica press in Havana. The letter also reveals, in a tongue-in-cheek manner, Father Berntsen's editorial authority and leaves no doubt as to the interactions among Fano, Berntsen, and Zambrano during the writing of this book. How many times did they discuss Freud at the Río Piedras house?

I do not know of any research dedicated entirely to "Los cabañistas." Nevertheless, I will attempt to contribute to the study of this significant intellectual group. To further the cultural significance of the group's meetings at La Cabaña, I propose we consider it a *société du discours* as defined by Foucault in his book *L'ordre du discours*, which I quote from the original French version. Foucault defines several aspects enabling the control of discourse within what he calls *sociétés de discours* (41). One is the *ritual* (41); the other, *doctrines* (45). I consider the Sunday gatherings at La Cabaña to be *rituals*. They were meetings surrounded by a natural environment, always on Sundays after lunch, separated from the world of academia, sharing certain ideas only accessible to the group (the *initiated*); in the talks were lovers of Greek Humanism and, at the same time, several were fervent Catholics. This is what Foucault calls *appartenance* (belonging), one of the aspects defining the *nuclei* of the *sociétés de discours*. Foucault claims, "l'appartenance doctrinale met en cause à la fois l'énoncé et le sujet parlant, et l'un à travers l'autre" (44; "doctrinal belonging involves at the same time the statement and the speaking subject through each other"). Thus, *l'appartenance* functions as what we may refer to as a union among the members of the group and, at the same time, a separation from other discursive communities. As to *l'appartenance*, the ideas the group discusses are also distinctive and isolated. The latter contributes to the fact that the ideas discussed are poured into a particular written medium, the Catholic newspaper *El Piloto*.

El Piloto often published these ideas, without the author's name, in a column named "Ganduleando," derived from the Spanish verb *gandulear*, literally meaning "to lounge around" or not profitable. Even though the ideas published are consequential, the term attempts to trivialize the conceptual character of the discussions presented to the public. Knowing that Elsa Fano was considered the "secretary" of *El Piloto*, I do not doubt she could be the author of some of these columns. However, Father Berntsen himself may have penned some columns, who, as suspected by other Dominican priests, devoted much of his time to this publication. In any event, a subtitle of the column suggests a collective author, "By la Cabaña / Por la Cabaña." One must also consider that Father Berntsen appeared to focus on a column named "Buzón de Preguntas" ("Mailbox of Questions"), where he answered questions raised by the public and, with his usual rigor, reflected upon ethical, spiritual, and social issues. The Dominican priest, well versed in the art of argumentation, introduced dialogues to his readers about some of his deep conceptual concerns without disappointing those who simply sought spiritual help.

I claim here that the anonymous column "Ganduleando," as well as some of the readers' responses, could be interpreted as writing forms for *l'appartenance*. They are traditionally modalities of "minor" journalistic genres, not appropriate for philosophical debate, but *El Piloto* uses them to circulate heavily intellectual topics discussed at the gatherings taking place at La Cabaña. To support my hypothesis, I have a few examples of textual quotations from *El Piloto* gathered during my visit to the University of Puerto Rico in Río Piedras. While I was unable to make copies, I offer some incomplete bibliographic information in case another researcher may want to follow up topics included in the column "Ganduleando" during 1939. Here I just offer some leads: Issue 677, April 1939, discusses topics related to spiritualism and science; Issue 678, 6 May, discusses occultism; Issue 679, 13 May, mentions the theory of "perspectivism" from Ortega y Gasset and argues against skepticism; Issue 688, 15 July, criticizes Rationalism.

I must highlight that all these topics were of interest to Zambrano and, even though published in *El Piloto* in 1939, before her arrival to Puerto Rico in 1941, were ongoing conversations. Finally, another column was published in 1939 on mysticism, particularly about *quietismo*, a branch of Spanish mysticism found in Miguel de Molino's work. Zambrano was interested in Molino since her years in Mexico, but this author received special attention in Zambrano's later work. As happens with Freudism, conversations about the subject could have taken place in La Cabaña in those mutually enriching conversations on Sunday afternoons.

Toward an Incomplete Balance

My main goal in these pages was to map the relationships between María Zambrano and Caribbean intellectuals during the 1940s and 1950s, a time when important changes were taking place in the Americas. The archives still have much to offer. After Zambrano departed to Europe after years of exile in the Caribbean islands, she never ended her contacts with her friends there. She especially continued to correspond with Lezama Lima and Fano, thus confirming the finesse and fidelity of these relationships, which marked a way of life and explains Zambrano's ability to enjoy other types of disciples (men and women) upon her return to Spain. The 1980s were a time when a generation of Spanish intellectuals met Zambrano in her *pisito* (small loft) in Madrid, ready to hear and continue to explore her thoughts. To them, Zambrano offered *las palabras del regreso* ("the words of the return"). Meanwhile the Caribbean, and the extensive scope of its diaspora represented in this anthology, continues to listen.

Notes

1. I adopt the term "sorority" from Mexican feminist and academic Marcela Lagarde. It appears in her book *Los cautiverios de las mujeres* and more recently in the article "Pacto entre mujeres: Sororidad" (www.celem.org), whose title is already explanatory of the concept. The term *sicigia* comes from the Greek, meaning union. Gnosticism later adapted the term starting with the followers of Valentine, a thinker of the second century A.D. In the twentieth century, Carl Jung adopted it in psychology. Agustín Andreu, who has studied the influence of gnostic thought on Zambrano, in *Cartas de La Pièce* (41) offers a definition he says was followed by Zambrano: "Sicigía or partnership, typical of the kingdom that is not of this world and which far from being a carnal act, constitutes a true pure mystery, not subject to a licensed contest, but fulfilled only by the will and in full light" (Orbe 99). Zambrano also uses the term. In a letter to Andreu, she writes: "'*la syzyguía*' a small community about which we dream as utopically seen by Ara and me since we were little girls" (Andreu 123) (here Zambrano refers to her sister).

2. From now on quotes from Spanish are offered in English translation. I take the opportunity to thank my colleague and friend Dionel Cotanda for translating the essay.

3. The first mention of *razón poética* appears in Zambrano's 1937 article "Madre España," written in Chile. She continued to develop the term in "La guerra de Antonio Machado" in 1939. The same year, she went further by linking it to the concept of *conocimiento poético* in her book *Pensamiento y poesía en la vida española*. She expanded her idea in 1994 in a letter to Rafael Dieste written in Havana. I quote: "something that is poetic reason but also more encompassing, something that also slides internally, like a drop of oil that pacifies and smoothes, a drop of happiness. Poetic reason is what I am trying to find. And, she is not like the other, she has more forms, she will be the same in different genres" (102). The culmination of turning "poetic reason" into a philosophic method takes place in her book *Claros del bosque*, written during her exile in France in 1977.

4. The title of the text written by Fernando Ortiz to present the first Spanish edition of *Cuentos negros*, published in Havana by La Verónica in 1940, is not "Prologue" but rather "Prejuicio" ("Prejudgment"). The word was changed to "prologue" or "introduction" in later editions; I wonder whether this was Ortiz's method of indicating the negative reception to the Black heritage in Cuba back then. For those of us who disagree with Ortiz's prologue, the word "Prejudgment" functions as a metatext (as in Gerard Genette's theory) pointing to the limitations of Ortiz's positivist reading of *Cuentos negros*.

5. During a public dialogue, Lezama Lima took the opportunity to argue with Juan Ramón Jiménez, a well-known intellectual figure, about the existence of a peculiar Cuban "insular sensibility," one of its components being *la resaca* ("the undertow") (*Coloquio* 79–80), which, through a marine metaphor, suggests that the national must be enriched by the universal.

6. Mendoza required that her private records not to become public before 2008.

7. After publishing this book, thanks to Mendoza's solidarity, Zambrano continued to publish regularly in Puerto Rican magazines (*Semana*, *Escuela*, and *Educación*) during the 1960s, while she was living in Rome.

8. Discipleship, in a biblical sense, shows up among Jesus' first followers. The teacher's vision as a spiritual guide is a concept Zambrano amply develops in her book *Confesiones y guías*, edited by Pedro Chacón.

9. I accessed the original letter during my visit to Puerto Rico in 2010 but the archive had not been catalogued then. For that reason, I provide the following information listed by Ruiz on page 85 of his thesis: "Letter from Zambrano to JB, 22/02/1940, FJB. L11A C 27)," when he is referring to the same letter.

10. See Laura Albizu Meneses' "Padre Martín J. Berntsen, O.P., promotor y defensor de la nacionalidad puertorriqueña," and José Antonio Acevedo's "Padre Martín J. Berntsen, O.P., promotor y defensor de la nacionalidad puertorriqueña," included in the anthology *Los dominicos en Hispanoamérica y Filipinas a raíz de la guerra de 1898* (Barrado Barquilla and Rodríguez León). These authors study Berntsen and Albizu's friendship and present them as promoters of an anti-colonialist discourse. Luckily for those of us who did not know him, Berntsen's library is available at the Center for the Study of the Dominicans in the Caribbean (CEDOC), at the Central University of Bayamón, Puerto Rico, where one also finds editions of *El Piloto*.

Works Cited

Andreu, Agustín, editor. *Cartas de La Pièce: Correspondencia con Agustín Andreu*. Editorial Pre-Textos, 2002.

Arcos, Jorge Luis. "Estudio preliminar." *Islas*, by María Zambrano. Verbum, 2007, pp. XIII-LXXIV.

Avilés-Ortiz, Iliaris Alejandra. "María Zambrano en la isla de Puerto Rico: Crónica de una estancia particular." *Aurora*, no. 17, 2016, pp. 6-19.

Barrado Barquilla, José, and Mario A. Rodríguez León, editors. *Los dominicos en Hispanoamérica y Filipinas a raíz de la guerra de 1898: Retos y desafíos de la Orden de Predicadores durante la centuria del 1898 a 1899*. Editorial San Esteban and Instituto de Estudios Históricos Juan Alejo de Arizmendi.

Benítez, Jaime. *Archivo Jaime Benítez*. Universidad de Puerto Rico, Río Piedras.

———. *Desafíos (1940-1971)*. División de Impresos, n/d.

Cámara, Madeline. "Sororidades habaneras entre María Zambrano y Lydia Cabrera." *El Atlántico como frontera*, edited by Damaris Puñales-Alpizar. Verbum, 2014, pp. 152-66.

———. "María Zambrano: Hacia una relectura de su panamericanismo." *Transatlantic Studies Network*, no. 1, 2016, pp. 166-79.

Elizalde, María. "16 cartas inéditas de María Zambrano a Waldo Frank." *Revista de Hispanismo Filosófico*, no. 17, 2012, pp. 115-40.

Fiol-Matta, Licia. *A Queer Mother for the Nation: The State and Gabriela Mistral*. U of Minnesota P, 2002.

Foucault, Michel. *L'ordre du discours*. Gallimard, 1971.

Fundación María Zambrano. *Archivos*. Málaga, Spain.

Lagarde, Marcela. *Los cautiverios de las mujeres: Madresposas, monjas, putas, presas y locas*. Siglo XXI, 2016.

Lezama Lima, José. "Coloquio con Juan Ramón Jiménez." *Revista Cubana*, no. 11, 1938, pp. 73-95.

———. "El nombre de Lydia Cabrera." *Tratados en La Habana*. Universidad Central de Las Villas, Departamento de Relaciones Culturales, 1958, pp. 144-48.

Marxuach, Sergio. Personal interview. 7 May 2010.

Mendoza, Inés María. "Memorándum a Ramón García Santiago, Presidente de la Junta de Planificación, 3 de octubre de 1963." Sección XV, Serie 1, cartapacio 1127, documento 13. Archivo Luis Muñoz Marín (ALMM), Fundación Luis Muñoz Marín, San Juan.

Orbe, Antonio, editor. *La teología del Espíritu Santo: Estudios valentinianos*. Vol. 4. Libreria editrice dell'Università Gregoriana, 1966.

Ortega Muñoz, Juan Fernando. *Introducción al pensamiento de María Zambrano*. Fondo de Cultura Económica, 1994.

Pedreira, Antonio S. *Insularismo: Ensayos de interpretación puertorriqueña*. Tipografía Artística, 1934.

El Piloto. Biblioteca General. Sección de Revistas. Universidad de Puerto Rico, Río Piedras.

Quirós, Julio. "Notas sobre la publicación en Puerto Rico del libro *Persona y democracia* de María Zambrano." *Persona y democracia*. Fundación Luis Muñoz Marín, 2018, pp. IX–XXII.

Ruiz Sastre, Emilio F. *Una universidad posible en tiempos de Jaime Benítez (1942–1972): Los intelectuales españoles acogidos en la Universidad de Puerto Rico a raíz de la guerra civil española*. 2015. Universidad Nacional de Educación a Distancia. PhD dissertation, www.e-spacio.uned.es.

Sánchez, Daisy. *La que te llama vida: Inés M. Mendoza, su vida interior en sus diarios y cartas*. Grupo Editorial Norma, 2007.

Zambrano, María. "Carta a Rafael Dieste." *Boletín Gallego de Literatura*, no. 5, 1991, p. 102.

———. "La Cuba secreta." *Orígenes*, vol. 5, no. 20, 1948, pp. 3–9.

———. "Hombre verdadero: José Lezama Lima." *Islas*, edited by Jorge Luis Arcos. Verbum, 2007, pp. 219–23.

———. *Isla de Puerto Rico: Nostalgia y esperanza de un mundo mejor: Obras completas*. Vol. 2. Galaxia Gutenberg/Círculo de Lectores, 2016, pp. 31–51.

———. "Lydia Cabrera: Poeta de la metamorfosis." *Orígenes*, vol. 7, no. 25, 1950, pp. 11–15.

———. *Persona y democracia*. Fundación Luis Muñoz Marín/Fundación María Zambrano, 2018.

11

"The Two Ephemeral Wings of the Angel of Love"
Archipelagic Fantasies in the Narrative of Lourdes Casal and Manuel Ramos Otero

YOLANDA MARTÍNEZ-SAN MIGUEL

Cuba and Puerto Rico Are: Take One

The almost obligatory reference to think about the relationship between Puerto Rico and Cuba are the well-known verses of Lola Rodríguez de Tió (which some mistakenly attribute to José Martí), included in *Mi libro de Cuba* (*My Book of Cuba*), published in 1893.[1]

Cuba y Puerto Rico son
de un pájaro las dos alas,
reciben flores o balas
sobre el mismo corazón . . .
¡Qué mucho si en la ilusión
que mil tintes arrebola,
sueña la musa de Lola
con ferviente fantasía,
de esta tierra y de la mía
hacer una patria sola! (5)
(Cuba and Puerto Rico are
two wings of a bird,
they receive flowers or bullets
into the same heart . . .
How much if in the illusion
that a thousand dyes swirl,

Lola's muse dreams with fervent fantasy,
to make this land and mine
a single homeland!)

The central reference of the poem is the project of the Antillean Confederation, studied by Jossianna Arroyo, José Buscaglia-Salgado, Kahlila Chaar-Pérez, and Alaí (Irmary) Reyes-Santos, among others. However, in this chapter I have preferred to resist the temptation to a familiar reference and propose instead a Glissantian detour. I will take as the starting point of my reflection a rereading of Rodríguez de Tió's text, elaborated in "Poema 1," which opens the posthumous book *Invitación al polvo* (*Invitation to Dust*, 1991) by Manuel Ramos Otero:

Cuba y Puerto Rico son
las dos efímeras alas del ángel del amor.
Cuba y Puerto Rico son
dos hombres sudorosos exilados al sol.

(Cuba and Puerto Rico are
the two ephemeral wings of the angel of love.
Cuba and Puerto Rico are
two sweaty men exiled in the sun.)

Although Ramos Otero's poem has multiple historical and political intertexts, the leitmotif of the poem (and the book *Invitación al polvo*) is the homoerotic desire that complicates the nineteenth-century nationalist plot, most likely playing with the double meaning of *pájaro* ("bird") and *pato* ("duck") in the Cuban and Puerto Rican contexts (La Fountain-Stokes 19–20; Rosa). I will resist a biographical reading here to analyze the imaginaries about Cuba and Puerto Rico invoked in the poem. First, the two islands appear as two men engaged in an affective relationship, located in the tension of opposites and in the impermanence of love. The impossibility of that being "without being" is opposed by the imperiousness of a desire that enables the encounter of bodies and souls, of materiality and transcendence, of the "lustful taste of another orgasm" and "that passing angel." The second theme of the poem is the project of queering the nationalist and pro-independence political discourse (with echoes of the Antillean Confederation) on which Rodríguez de Tió's poem is based. Whereas in Rodríguez de Tió's text the identity and nationalist trope prevails, Ramos Otero's verses focus on the contradictory desires of the disenchanted Cuban and Puerto Rican present a century later.

And it is precisely from that perspective that I would like to propose a juxtaposed reading (recalling the methodology proposed by Juliet Hooker in her illuminating book *Theorizing Race*) of two tales produced by two writers, one Cuban and the other Puerto Rican, during the second half of the twentieth century, who project a queered imaginary of Cuban and Puerto Rican nationalities. I analyze two authors who could technically be considered part of the same generation, although they were born ten years apart (Lourdes Casal, 1938–91; Manuel Ramos Otero, 1948–90). Casal and Ramos Otero explored in their literary works the boundaries between history and fiction. Therefore, these two narrators work very closely on the issue of national imaginaries in the Caribbean in the 1970s and 1980s.

Let me briefly summarize the two stories I analyze here. Casal's "Los fundadores: Alfonso" ("The Founders: Alfonso," 1972) recounts the life of a Chinese immigrant who arrived in Cuba in 1874, as part of the influx of indentured workers to the island.[2] Alfonso López (the Hispanic name he was given in Cuba) first pairs up with a woman who has his daughter Eugenia and later dies of smallpox. With another woman from the Canary Islands, he has his daughter Leonor. Then, a little against his will, he marries the mulatto freedwoman Amalia, and they have a daughter and two sons: Carmen, Alejandro, and Sebastián. Each of the daughters represents different aspects of the foundations of Cuban identity, which exceed the authority of the patriarch of the family, and which set aside the stories of the two brothers, Alejandro and Sebastián. Eugenia falls in love with Colonel Isidro, a Black revolutionary who dies in one of the Cuban wars of independence. Leonor escapes the webs of heteronormativity and becomes a lieutenant of the revolution against Spain (Martínez-San Miguel, "Fantasy as Identity"). Carmen marries and from her probably descends the narrator of the story, Alfonso's great-granddaughter. This tale was supposedly part of a broader project of Casal, who planned to dedicate stories to different subjects representing the pillars of *cubanía* ("Cubanness") (Burunat 109). The story is divided into vignettes (entitled Great-granddaughter 1–3, Alfonso 1–6, History 1–4) depicting the plot from the perspective of various aspects of *cubanía*, and the entire narration is framed from the perspective of Alfonso's great-granddaughter, who reconstructs the past of her great-grandfather from the stories her grandmother (one of Alfonso's daughters) told her.[3]

The detective thriller genre inspires Ramos Otero's "Página en blanco y staccato" ("Page in White and Staccato," originally published in 1987). Critical work by Arnaldo Cruz-Malavé, Lawrence La Fountain-Stokes, Jossianna Arroyo, Daniel Torres, and Jason Cortés has informed my reading of this short story. It is a tale with a circular plot with two main characters. On the one hand is Samuel Fat Candelas, son of Ting Yao, a Chinese immigrant to the United States who moves from California to New York with plans to travel to Cuba; and on the other is Milagros Candelas, a Puerto Rican woman who lives in New York, but descends from a female lineage of daughters of Yemayá (the Yoruba deity) who was brought by a Dutch slave ship, first to Curaçao and from there to Puerto Rico in the nineteenth century. One of Sam Fat's ancestors had been burned at the stake by Bishop Nicolás Ramos de los Santos,[4] on Mondongo Street in San Juan, Puerto Rico. Because Sam's father dies before the child is born, Milagros raises his son as a Puerto Rican and a *santero* (a practitioner of the Afro-Cuban religion, Santería), and instills in him the story of revenge against the descendant of the bishop who murdered one of his ancestors, a writer named Ramos. Fat becomes a private investigator and places an ad in the newspaper to find his victim. The other character is the writer, a figure with several biographical references to Ramos Otero, who is already sick with AIDS, and seeks a double of the writer (a reference to another author of the 1970s Generation, Juan Antonio Ramos). The encounter between both characters triggers a series of parallel plots, suggesting that Fat has planned the encounter with the writer to kill him in revenge for his ancestor's grievance, and that the writer has planned the encounter with Fat for him to kill the writer, closing with a truncated love story between the two.

In this essay I propose, therefore, to read Casal's "Los fundadores: Alfonso" side by side with "Página en blanco y staccato" by Ramos Otero, from three analytical axes that interrupt the Creolist and Hispanophile definitions of Cuban and Puerto Rican identities: Blackness and *mulataje* ("mulattoness"); the Asian and queer conjunction of the Hispanic Caribbean; and the archipelagic and diasporic dimension of the insular Hispanic Caribbean. These two stories give title to the anthologies in which they were published, and both propose a critical view of the prevailing discourses on identity and nationalism in the Caribbean of the 1970 and 1980s in the context of translocation, postcoloniality, Creolization, and diaspora.

Densities of Blackness and *Mulataje*

The two stories were written before diasporic studies focusing on Asian immigrations to the Hispanic Caribbean reached their current maturity (García Triana, Hu-De Hart, Lee Borges, López, Yun).[5] Therefore, both Casal and Ramos Otero were working in a project of artistic speculation that confronted the gaps in historiography and national archives on the Afro-Asian dimensions of the Hispanic Caribbean. The most recent historical research has explored a similar issue through what Marisa Fuentes has called "constructive speculation" (50) with archives: to create coherent accounts based on inconsistent and fragmentary references to certain subjects and voices in the archive. In these cases, literature and history share a similar strategy: they take as a starting point the existence of a Black body of diasporic origins to explore the blind spots of the historical archive and national literature. Fiction is the poetic license that Casal and Ramos Otero use to speculate about the other dimensions of *cubanía* (Cubanness), *puertorriqueñidad* (Puerto Ricanness), the Caribbean, and its multiple diasporas.

Both stories engage in several forms of Afro-Caribbean representation. My reading of the work of Jossianna Arroyo, Lorgia García-Peña, and María Elizabeth Rodríguez Beltrán has informed my thinking on the various dimensions and definitions of Blackness in the Caribbean and the Americas. In Casal's tale, Blackness and *mulataje* appear mainly through two characters. The first is Amalia, the woman Alfonso marries, to establish the heteronormative nucleus of the national Cuban family. Amalia represents a series of key ruptures with the traditional representation of the "tragic mulatta" (Bost):

> El despalillo [del tabaco] era cosa de mujeres. Era allí que trabajaba Amalia, mujer ciertamente diferente, mulata zoqueta y montaraz, hija de negra de nación liberada por su amo-padre-blanco. Amalia, despalilladora en la fábrica más grande de entonces, en Güira de Melena (un chinchal, dirías hoy), Amalia que te puso los puntos sobre las íes cuando trataste de llevártela al monte: "Papelito-jabla-lengua" dijo burlándose con fingida media lengua. Y te explicó cómo su madre le había enseñado que con los hombres había que ser firmes y por eso ella no abría las piernas. "Primero a casarnos." Diste una vuelta en redondo y te marchaste sin decir nada. ¿Qué se creía esa mulatica del diablo? Ya tú habías tenido dos hijas—y nadie te había hecho firmar papelito todavía." [...] Vuelta en redondo. Le tiraste una piedra a la ventana. Se asomó. "Nos casamos." "¿Cuándo?," te preguntó. "Cuando tú quieras," le dijiste sonriendo tú también. "¿Un adelanto?," suplicaste medio en broma, medio en serio. La carcajada la oíste ya tras la ventana cerrada. (Casal, "Los fundadores" 24–25)

> (Stripping the [tobacco] leaves was women's work. That was what Amalia did. Amalia was certainly different; she was a mulatta, none too bright, it's true, but fierce as they come, the daughter of a black female slave freed by her White master-father. Amalia, a worker in what was then Cuba's biggest factory (a corner shop by today's standards) in Güira de Melena, spelled it out to you when you tried to lure her up into the hills: "Bit of paper, then talk," she said, mocking you, imitating your pidgin Spanish. And then she explained to you how her mother had taught her that you have to be firm with men, which was why she wasn't going to open her legs just yet. "Not until we're married." You turned on your heel and marched off without saying a word. Who did that little mulatta think she was! You had two daughters already and no one had ever made you sign a bit of paper before. [. . .] You turned around. You threw a stone up at her window. She looked out. "All right, we'll get married." She smiled at you. "When?" she asked. "Whenever you want," you said, smiling back. "Any chance of an advance?" you asked, half-joking, half-serious. (Casal, "The Founders" 184–85)

On the one hand, Amalia is a mulatto freedwoman, who at the same time is the half-sister of Salvador's wife, the man who offers Alfonso work after his contract expires and thus enables his stay and future life in Cuba. On the other hand, unlike the well-known fictional character Cecilia Valdés, Amalia demands marriage from Alfonso and mocks the liminal place that the man of Chinese descent has in the Cuban context. Finally, the Chinese-mulatto relationship illustrates a Cuban cultural root seldom explored by historiography and cultural studies, before the boom in Caribbean studies focused on the Asian presence in the Caribbean and the Americas. This relationship reminds us of the Cuban novel that is not as well-known as Cirilo Villaverde's opus, *Carmela* (1887) by Ramón Meza, which explores the avatar of the mulatta who marries a Chinese in the Cuban context and which Gema Guevara and Lisa Yun among others have studied in more detail.[6]

The second character is Colonel Isidro, described as "un negro gigantesco" (Casal, "Los fundadores" 25) ("a huge negro"; Casal, "The Founders" 186), with whom Eugenia, Alfonso's eldest daughter, falls in love. When the story presents this detail, the narrator deceives the reader by making her believe that Alfonso opposes marriage due to racism:

[Eugenia] Te miró a los ojos y te viste reflejado en unos ojos idénticos a los tuyos. "¿Qué es lo que está pasando?" Te sostenía la mirada, tan fiera como la tuya. "Que tengo novio, padre; él quería venir a hablar con usted y yo se lo dije a Amalia para que le pidiera permiso. Pero ella se puso furiosa." Dabas golpecitos con los pies desnudos en el piso que tus botas llenaron de barro. "¿Es el coronel Isidro?" preguntaste, y Eugenia asintió con la cabeza. Te zafaste el cinturón y lo dejaste caer en el piso, machete y todo. "No te quiero viuda antes que casada." [. . .] "Nadie va a matar a Isidro. No ha nacido el hombre que sea suficientemente hombre para eso. Nos casaremos en cuanto termine la guerra y ya eso será pronto. Lo único que quiero es que usted lo sepa y apruebe. No debe de saberlo nadie fuera de la casa." (Casal, "Los fundadores" 27)

(She looked at you straight in the eye and you saw yourself reflected in eyes identical to yours. "What exactly is going on?" She held your gaze, as proud as yours. "I'm engaged, Papa. My fiancé wanted to come and talk to you and I told Amalia so that she could ask your permission, but she just flew into a rage." You were drumming your bare feet on the floor that your boots had left covered in mud. "Is it Colonel Isidro?" you asked and Eugenia nodded. You took off your belt and dropped it on the floor, machete and all. "I don't want you to be a widow before you're even married." [. . .] "No one's going to kill Isidro. The man hasn't been born who could do that. We'll get married when the war is over, and that will be any day now. I just wanted you to know and to give us your blessing. No one else outside this house must know anything about it." (Casal, "The Founders" 187–88)

By the time this scene occurs, we know that Isidro has died in the war, as the news is revealed at one of the times when Alfonso recalls with disappointment the invisibility of his ancestors in the history of Cuba's war of independence: "La gente ni sabe que hubo chinos que pelearon. [. . .] El marido de una de tus hijas llegó a coronel en la guerra del 95 y ¿qué ganó? Que lo balearan a traición, negro guapo que era, el coronel Isidro . . ." (Casal, "Los fundadores" 23). ("People do not even know that any Chinese fought in the war. [. . .] The husband of one of your daughters reached the rank of colonel in the 1895 war and what did he get for it? They shot that handsome black, Colonel Isidro, in the back") (Casal, "The Founders"

182–83). In this way Casal establishes a solidarity link between Chinese and Blacks in their invisibility in the prevailing discourse on *cubanía*, a topic also hinted by Esteban Montejo in *Biografía de un cimarrón* (Barnet and Montejo).

In Ramos Otero's story, Blackness occupies a simultaneously foundational and invisible place. Black subjectivity enters the narrative through two characters: Sam Fat and his mother Milagros Candelas. Milagros' Blackness is *ancestral* and is traced through a female *lineage*:

> La madre de Milagros se llamaba Madama Candelas y su nombre acusaba sin tapujos la furia de un remoto agravio. La abuela de Milagros, había sido Madama Candelas Humphreys Johannes, quien fue hija de Yemayá, como lo había sido su madre y la madre de su madre hasta la primera mujer cuya cabeza había sido iniciada en el Valle de Ifé, antes de que un barco negrero holandés las desarraigara hasta el Caribe y a ella le tocara un nacimiento en la isla de Curaçao y luego, en el siglo 19 puertorriqueño, terminara siendo esclava en el ingenio cañero de Vieques y con alegría y pañuelos blancos deshilachados en el viento, hubiera dicho adiós a los españoles que se fueron con el rabo entre las patas en 1898, para que luego recibiera con los mismos pañuelos y la misma alegría a los norteamericanos que llegaron a Vieques ese mismo año. (Ramos Otero, "Página en blanco y staccato" 77)

> (Milagros's mother was called Madame Candelas and her name straight off revealed the fury of a remote grievance. Milagros's grandmother had been Madame Candelas Humphreys Johannes, who was Yemayá's daughter, as had her mother and the mother of her mother until the first woman whose head had been initiated in the Ifé Valley, before a Dutch slave ship uprooted them to the Caribbean and she was born on the island of Curaçao and then, in nineteenth-century Puerto Rico, ended up being enslaved in the Vieques sugar mill and with joy and white handkerchiefs frayed in the wind, she would have said goodbye to the Spaniards who left with their tails between their legs in 1898, and then received with the same handkerchiefs and the same joy the Americans who arrived in Vieques that same year.)

Milagros relocates from Puerto Rico to New York during the "Great Migration" of the 1940s and there she meets Sam Fat's father.

Sam's Black identity is, however, contextual, not biological or genetic: the son of Chinese and Puerto Rican migrants to New York, the child grows up as an ectopic Puerto Rican:

> Desde el momento en el que vio al recién nacido, supo que el niño sufriría la agonía del rechazo. Sam Fat había heredado de su madre la negrura de su piel; había salido a su padre en el pelo de aguja, las facciones mongólicas y el ensimismamiento. Los chinos nunca lo aceptaron como uno de ellos (no sólo porque su madre no lo era, sino porque nadie supo enseñarle ni la lengua ni las tradiciones chinas); los puertorriqueños trataron de ser más tolerantes, pero en el apodo que le pusieron al niño antes de que aprendiera a hablar, Chino, se advertía un tono abusivo de rechazo. (Ramos Otero, "Página en blanco y staccato" 76)

> (From the moment she saw the newborn, she knew that the child would suffer the agony of rejection. Sam Fat had inherited from his mother the blackness of his skin; he had taken after his father in his needle hair, Mongolian features, and self-absorption. The Chinese never accepted him as one of them (not only because his mother was not, but because no one could teach him Chinese language or traditions); Puerto Ricans tried to be more tolerant, but in the nickname they gave the child before he learned to speak, Chino, an abusive tone of rejection was evident.)

Milagros initiates her son in Santería, as the son of Orunla (also Orunmila or Orula, the orisha of wisdom, knowledge, and divination, the supreme oracle of human destiny), and tells him tales about the island. When the mother becomes ill and the end of her life looms, Sam takes care of her and returns with her to Puerto Rico, "preparado para volver a un lugar que nunca había habitado nada más *que en cuento*" ("prepared to return to a place that he had never inhabited in anything but a *story*" (Ramos Otero, "Página en blanco y staccato" 83; my emphasis) and there he inherits the narrative of revenge of his ancestors that is completely alien to him, because it is a "return" to a place of origin where he has never been before:

> Otra tarde, el crepúsculo los sorprendió en una playa con acantilados de rocas negras; allí se sentaron en la arena y sobre una alfombra de paja Milagros echó sus 16 caracoles y se los leyó a Sam Fat. Hijo de

Orunla, le leyó, maestro del pasado, presente y futuro; ése es tu compromiso, si lo quieres. Sam Fat percibió en las palabras de su madre la fuerza de la venganza. Pero ese mundo de orishas no era su mundo como tampoco lo eran aquelllas ruinas tropicales ni las crónicas de los mandarines chinos. (Ramos Otero, "Página en blanco y staccato" 83–84)

(Another afternoon, twilight surprised them on a beach with black rock cliffs; there they sat in the sand and on a straw carpet Milagros threw out her 16 snails and read them to Sam Fat. Son of Orunla, she read to him, teacher of the past, present, and future; that's your obligation, if you want it. Sam Fat perceived in his mother's words the force of vengeance. But that world of orishas was not his world, nor were those tropical ruins or the chronicles of Chinese mandarins.)

In both stories by Ramos Otero and Casal, diasporic accidents represent the mulatto and Black foundation of the Hispanic Caribbean, and the translocal subjectivities undermine the telluric narratives of national identity. Isidro, Amalia, Milagros, and Sam signal the complexity of Cuban and Puerto Rican identities, but they cannot become the complete answer, nor can they offer the comfort of indigenous continuity with the island territories.[7] In both cases, two additional coordinates complicate the national narrative and make its fabric denser in the context of the forced diasporas and extended colonialism of the insular Hispanic Caribbean.

Queer Orientalism

The alliance between queer and Asian (and the Orientalist motif) depicted by Casal or Ramos Otero is not a new literary topic. Calvert Casey, Severo Sarduy, and many other Latin American writers resorted to the Orientalist motif to invoke the marginalized or invisible spaces of the nation, as Laura Torres-Rodríguez has studied in the Mexican case, in her recent book *Orientaciones transpacíficas: La modernidad mexicana y el espectro de Asia*, as well as Ignacio López-Calvo for the Cuban case in *Imaging the Chinese in Cuban Literature and Culture*. However, what seems unique to me in Casal's and Ramos Otero's cases is the elaboration of the Asian and queer as ways of intervening in the Creolist, Hispanophile, heteronormative, masculine, and patriarchal accounts of Cuban and Puerto Rican nationalist discourse

(Gelpí, Fowler). Both stories advance alternative imaginaries that go beyond feminist or *negrista* projects in the Caribbean.

I am interested in exploring the Alfonso-Leonor conjunction in Casal's text. On the one hand, Alfonso represents an imaginary Chinese character who arrived in Cuba at the end of the first mass migration of Chinese, lands in the midst of the Ten Years' War (1868–78), and witnesses the third war of independence on the island (1895–98). Alfonso's story could very well coincide with that of some of the cases Kathleen López has found in the archives, especially because Chinese indentured workers, once emancipated, became an intermediate sector between the White Creole elite and the large enslaved and freed Black population on the island. As López ("Afro-Asian Alliances") documents, it was common for a mulatto or Black woman to marry a Chinese man to improve her position within the Cuban racial structure.

What makes Alfonso an interesting character, however, is his displaced or dislocated position, if you will, vis-à-vis the Cuban patriarchal and virile discourse. In the beginning of the narration, Alfonso appears as a patriarch obsessed by domestic order and peace:

> Contaba mi abuela que su padre, ya ciego, a los setenta años y a los cincuenta de su llegada a Cuba, se enfurecía espumosamente si movían cualquier mueble de su sitio. Recorría la casa como guardián infalible del orden del mundo, cuadrando las sillas, constatando que las mesas estaban en sus lugares precisos. Enhiesto, con los bigotes canos chorreándoles [*sic*] sobre la barba lampiña y las manos nudosas viendo el mundo y reconstruyéndolo. (Casal, "Los fundadores" 19)

> (My grandmother used to tell me that when her father was seventy years old and blind—this was fifty years after his arrival in Cuba—he would fly into a seething rage if he found so much as one piece of furniture out of place. He would roam the house like some infallible guardian of order in the world, setting chairs straight and checking that tables were in the proper position. Very erect, with his grey moustache cascading down over his hairless chin, he used his gnarled hands to see the world and to reconstruct it.) (Casal, "The Founders" 178)

The text constantly subverts the figure of the macho father, no doubt alluding to the stereotype of the Oriental man as weak and effeminate (Chou,

Eng, Park). Maintaining the order of the house replaces Alfonso's possible intervention in the dynastic war of the Great Peace in China, or in Cuban political affairs.[8] Alfonso's story is the account of women's questioning of his plan to form a heteronormative and patriarchal family. Amalia forces him to marry her before consenting to his sexual demands; Eugenia challenges the father when she partners with Isidro; and Leonor questions Alfonso's manhood through a gender expression that defies the categories of the feminine and the masculine in the life of war and in social discourse:

> Ya bastantes problemas tenías con tu hija segunda—Leonor—la que tuviste con aquella canaria de Colón y que te había salido marimacho y rebelde. Leonor, que se parecía mucho a Wu Liau y un poco a ti, se escapó una noche a caballo y por poco revienta al animal, tratando de llegar a Oriente. (Casal, "Los fundadores" 26)

> Leonor se sentó en un sillón al lado tuyo y se echó contigo—mano a mano—una botella de ron peleón. En eso llegó el coronel Isidro y le dijo: "usted es de verdad una generala" (que así le decían a Leonor desde la guerra, aunque en realidad sólo había llegado a teniente). Y se sentó a beber con Leonor y contigo y se tomaron (ahora a pico de botella) una de aguardiente cada uno. Y cuando Leonor dijo: "Me los echo a los dos," Isidro y tú le aceptaron el reto y apostaron lechón asado para toda la familia, a pagar por el que se cayera primero, y dos galones de ron, a pagar por el que se cayera segundo. Y cuando llegó la hora de contar, Isidro y tú estaban por el suelo y Leonor dijo: "Que no es con los cojones que se bebe" y fue a levantarse y se cayó redondita y hubo que dejarlos dormir en el patio a los tres, tal era la peste a aguardiente que tenían. (Casal, "Los fundadores" 29)

> (You had had quite enough problems with your second daughter—Leonor—the one you had with that woman from the Canary Islands who lived in Colón. Leonor turned out to be a rebellious tomboy, very much like Wu Liau [Alfonso's father] and a little bit like you. She disappeared one night on horseback and nearly rode the poor animal into the ground trying to reach Oriente. (Casal, "The Founders" 186) Leonor sat down in an armchair beside you and matched you drink for drink—a whole bottle of cheap rum. At that point, Colonel Isidro arrived and said to her: "You certainly live up to your rank as general" (that's how they always addressed Leonor after the war, although

in fact, she only ever made lieutenant). He joined you and Leonor and you each took a swig of brandy, straight from the bottle. And when Leonor said: "I could drink you both under the table," you and Isidro accepted the challenge and bet a whole roast suckling pig for the whole family, to be paid by the first to pass out, and two gallons of rum, to be paid by the second. When the hour of reckoning came, you and Isidro were both sprawled on the floor and Leonor said: "You see, you don't need balls to drink," but when she went to get up, she keeled right over and they left the three of you out in the courtyard because you all stank to high heaven of brandy.) (Casal, "The Founders" 189–90)

In the imaginary proposed in Casal's story, Orientalism and queer identity are combined to question the virile, patriarchal, and Creole dimensions of *cubanía*, central coordinates in the discourse elaborated by Martí (Martí, Fowler, Quiroga).

In Ramos Otero's tale, the Orientalist and queer conjunction is embodied in the character of Sam Fat, who descends from a Chinese man who arrives in New York and connects with Puerto Rican history through his contact with the Puerto Rican diaspora in the United States. Sam Fat's presence as a Black and Puerto Rican Chinese opens the door to the presence of Chinese in Puerto Rico, which José Lee Borges has studied in his book *Los chinos en Puerto Rico*.[9] I would argue, however, that Fat's importance in the text is that his homoerotic relationship with the writer provides a glimpse at the unexplored difference in the coordinates of *puertorriqueñidad*, processed through the imbrication of Blackness, Chinese identity, and the queer element, which is constitutive of the tension between literature and national history on which Ramos Otero's narrative is put together:

> Los ojos de Sam Fat se quedaron abiertos, viendo caer la capa de la lluvia del hombre, anticipando que cuando su cuerpo se despojara de todo, que cuando el hombre estuviera tan cerca, su aliento no dejaría que sintiera escalofríos y entonces su carne, tan húmeda como el casco de un juey, lo arroparía. Por primera vez Sam Fat probó el sabor del mar y supo lo que era ser una isla. Estaba saliendo el sol por los cristales del techo cuando el hombre le dijo: *Yo cuento cuentos y hace mucho tiempo que estuve esperando a Sam Fat para inventarlo. Pase lo que pase yo contaré tu cuento.* (Ramos Otero, "Página en blanco y staccato" 82–83; my emphasis)

(Sam Fat's eyes were left open, seeing the cloak of the man's raincoat, anticipating that when his body was stripped of everything, that when the man was so close, his breath would not let him feel chills and then his flesh, as wet as a crab helmet, would tuck him in. For the first time Sam Fat tasted the taste of the sea and knew what it was like to be an island. The sun was coming out through the glass of the ceiling when the man said to him, *I tell stories and I've been waiting a long time for Sam Fat to invent him. Whatever happens, I'll tell your story.*)

The homoerotic encounter, although apparently legitimating for both characters, does not fit the genre of the story of a return to an organic national identity, nor does it reside comfortably within the script of the love story. Nor can it be understood as that key moment that Audre Lorde explores of in her essay "Uses of the Erotic: The Erotic as Power," in which eroticism and sensuality reduce the threat of difference. The encounter between the protagonist and the antagonist is actually an exercise in fiction, in which a "vínculo milenario" ("millennial bond," Ramos Otero, "Página en blanco y staccato" 71) or an "anacronismo étnico" ("ethnic anachronism," Ramos Otero, "Página en blanco y staccato" 88) closes a cycle of mutual revenge against the violence imposed by the Puerto Rican nationalist discourse (both literary and historical) against Black, Chinese, and homosexual subjectivities. In other words, what interests Ramos Otero is using the imagination to infringe upon the blind spots, silences, and omissions on which the presumed homogeneity of Hispanophile, Creole, and nationalist discourse in Puerto Rico is based. This narration precisely occupies the uncomfortable territory among autobiography, history, and fiction. Several simultaneous stories take place in that territory. The master narrative of *puertorriqueñidad* does not win the game here. The plot of the writer who contradicts the metanarratives of national history and literature, and who refuses to reify his autobiography, prevails in the end. Ramos Otero's success is using the detective novel and the double unfolding of the action elaborated in Jorge Luis Borges' "La muerte y la brújula" ("Death and the Compass") to interrogate the theme of national fraternity—proposed by Benedict Anderson in his renowned book *Imagined Communities*—and to highlight, through mutual murder, a place in the history of fiction that has been denied in the fiction of history.

The Archipelagic and Diasporic Caribbean

The two tales by Casal and Ramos Otero contain stories of diaspora and family reproduction, which invoke colonial displacement in an archipelagic context. In Casal's "Los fundadores," the archipelago appears indirectly, through the origin of Wu Lau and his possible displacement to Manila or Cuba; Chinese mass migration, which reaches the Americas through the Philippines, the Caribbean, or California; and the history of Alfonso's mating partners, originally from the Canary Islands (Leonor's mother) or the Caribbean. The "family" reconstructed in the text is an affective network established and maintained through a constellation of ports and cities articulated through the logic of colonialism and the indentured labor of the nineteenth and twentieth centuries. The archipelagic then functions as a spatial system that surpasses the national narrative but resignifies the family bond. In Casal's account, the act of founding is multiple, multifocal, and multilocal. The numerous vignettes (Alfonso, history, great-granddaughter) reconstruct the history of the Cuban foundation by imbricating instants, sequences of moments of the Chinese migration to Cuba; the particular inflection of Alfonso's fictional history; and the meticulous reconstruction of the great-granddaughter, who closes the narration in the cyclical temporality of the Chinese year: "Pero el dragón, más allá del desfile, más acá del sueño; el dragón desfilando ya, el dragón—en realidad termina mordiéndose la cola—" (Casal, "Los fundadores" 30). ("But the dragon, after the parade, after the dreams, the dragon, deflated now, the dragon . . . always ends up biting his own tail" (Casal, "The Founders" 191).

In Ramos Otero's text, the archipelagic theme appears through the story of the writer's ancestors and Sam Fat, who intersect and separate cyclically. The meeting between the first Ramos (the inquisitor bishop) and the first Candelas (the heretic victim) begins the journey from Spain, Africa, and China, to Curaçao-Vieques-New York in the case of Milagros, and in California-New York-Cuba, in the case of Ting Yao. Here New York serves as a crossroads and meeting point, where the archipelagic network is articulated:

> Y entonces, está también New York, un punto esencial del continente, corazón de un imperio que no se le parece, adonde predomina la plaza común del desarraigo, de mujeres y hombres transplantados por la fuga, desde países lejanos que los periódicos locales no mencionan,

de mujeres y hombres que todavía creen que vivir en New York es un tiempo prestado (un pacto con el diablo) para luego volver al puerto inicial de un recuerdo colectivo: Puerto Rico, Jamaica, Guyana, Granada, Santo Domingo, Colombia, Panamá, St. Thomas, Haití, el Sur. (Ramos Otero, "Página en blanco y staccato" 74)

(And then there is also New York, an essential point of the continent, the heart of an empire that does not resemble it, where the common square of uprooting predominates, of women and men transplanted by escaping from distant countries that local newspapers do not mention, of women and men who still believe that living in New York is a borrowed time (a pact with the devil) and then return to the initial port of a collective memory: Puerto Rico, Jamaica, Guyana, Grenada, Santo Domingo, Colombia, Panama, St. Thomas, Haiti, the South.)

In Casal's account, the archipelago articulates the structure of the story: the narrative mounts a network of senses that flow within the vignettes on the same subject, and which is activated in the episodic imbrication of different ways of telling the story. History, individual parental experience, and female memory function as a system of simultaneous voices in which each tell their story but together participate in a choir that complicates the imaginary of *cubanía*.

Ramos Otero's text uses another strategy. Two characters, summoned and articulated through their ancestors and lineages, intersect in a common narration over time, but in the process invert their roles and places, thereby complicating the Creolist and Hispanophile Puerto Rican imaginary. Similarly, history and fiction compete, intersect, and appear in tension as two ways of recounting the memory of multiple Puerto Rican colonialities, to implode the idea of the foundation as a localizable act in a subject, a voice, a perspective, or a place. The origin or foundation arises from the creative tension between the detective's characters and the storyteller, the inquisitor and his victim, the lover and the beloved, who on the brink of death confront the "tragedia basada en un anacronismo étnico" ("tragedy based on an ethnic anachronism," Ramos Otero, "Página en blanco y staccato" 88).

Cuba and Puerto Rico: Take Two

I want to refer again to Ramos Otero's "Poema 1" from *Invitación al polvo*, with which I opened this reflection, and which allows me to engage the relationship between Cuba and Puerto Rico from a racial, spatial, and geographical perspective. Ramos Otero's poem serves as a subtext for me to think about the queer, fragmentary, and episodic relationship of the imaginaries proposed by Casal and Ramos Otero in their tales. Both stories bet not on Otherness as a motif by itself, but on less visible aspects of *cubanía* and *puertorriqueñidad*, which may not be part of the archives or official history, but which inhabit the bodies of the characters that run through the imaginaries of both authors. In Ramos Otero's poem, the subtext is two desiring queer bodies, which produce a contextual and incomplete plot: two subjects "who lived / nightmares embraced to doubt / of love that doesn't last / and the happiness that ends / of the body that softens / with the eternity of the sea, / and just as the sea wanders / from one island to another island / like the one who wants to fly . . ." (9). Ephemeral loves and happiness, bodies that are touched by the immensity of the sea . . . that is the affective motif that replaces the narrative of the Antillean Confederation on which Lola Rodríguez de Tió's poem was founded. The nation gives way to lust, to the infinite, to the passing angel. No political teleology culminates in the nation-state or confederate archipelago.

I propose that the stories of Casal and Ramos Otero suggest something similar. The mulatto, Black, Chinese, and queer elements are not invoked in a diasporic tale to articulate a unified nation or an Antillean confederation. The different conjunctions put together in these texts point to the gaps of the Cuban, Puerto Rican, and Caribbean historical archive to find points of tension that complicate traditional definitions (Hispanophile, patriarchal, Eurocentric, and Creolist) of Hispanic Caribbean identity. In Casal's and Ramos Otero's accounts, the Hispanic Caribbean resembles more closely the English and French Caribbean through ethnic and racial coordinates, in the coloniality of diaspora, and in the perversity of a polymorphous desire that exceeds familiar narratives. In this context, both storytellers implode the national discourse to privilege the centripetal forces and tensions of the diaspora and the archipelago as a geographical accident that subverts the continuing myth of continental and Eurocentric imaginaries. Both narratives identify various aspects of communities defined in tension with their differences and from the reality of bodies that interrogate the voids or silences of the archives (Arroyo, "Manuel Ramos Otero"). It is in this context that Cuba and Puerto Rico are rearticulated as "the two ephemeral wings of love," always fragile and perverse, always passing through, wings of a bird or an angel that no longer looks back (like Walter Benjamin's angel of history) but only passes and leaves behind a trail, a wake.

Notes

1. I wrote the first version of this chapter in dialogue with the work of my colleague Jorge Duany. Encouraged by his research on the recent mass migration of Puerto Ricans to Florida in the aftermath of Hurricane Maria (Duany, "The Puerto Rican Exodus to Florida"; "The Puerto Rican Exodus to Florida before and after Hurricane María"), I discuss the multiple contacts and relationalities between these two Caribbean countries, which at the same time share "the cursed circumstance of water everywhere"—to recall the verse with which Virgilio Piñera opens his terrible and beautiful poem "La isla en peso" ("The Whole Island") and the comings and goings of memories, people, and financial, affective, and cultural remittances. This essay integrates and revises sections of previous publications about Lourdes Casal and Manuel Ramos Otero included in Martínez-San Miguel, *80Grados* and *Caribe Two Ways*; "Releyendo a Lourdes Casal"; "Fantasy as Identity"; "'Cuba y Puerto Rico son . . .'"; "'La puerta del mar'"; as well as Negrón Muntaner and Martínez-San Miguel. The comparative reading of Casal's and Ramos Otero's narratives to propose an alternative imaginary for the Caribbean is the original contribution of this essay. Translated by Jorge Duany.

2. Antonio Chufatt Latour's work is an early study of Chinese in Cuba. According to López, a total of 141,515 Chinese departed to Cuba between 1847 and 1874, and a total of 124,793 were sold in Havana (23).

3. Elsewhere I have written about the woman-centered perspective from which Casal rewrites the history of Cuba. See Martínez-San Miguel, "Fantasy as Identity."

4. This is a reference to Puerto Rico's third Catholic bishop, Nicolás Ramos de los Santos (Cheney).

5. José Buscaglia-Salgado uses *mulataje* as the Caribbean counterpoint to the Latin American paradigm of *mestizaje*. In the Hispanic Caribbean, miscegenation is mostly imagined as taking place between European Whites and African Blacks, while in Mexico this same process usually refers to the offspring produced from interracial relationships between European Whites and indigenous subjects. Buscaglia-Salgado conceptualizes *mulataje* as a legacy of the Iberian contact zone from before 1492 (79). The first use of *mulataje* that I know of is Gabriela Mistral's in her 1932 essay entitled "El tipo del indio americano" (Fiol-Matta 18, 25, 24–28), where she differentiates the Mexican and Brazilian racial imaginaries.

6. In many respects, "Los fundadores: Alfonso" replicates and corrects the failed foundational narrative of Chinese-mulatto integration contained in *Carmela*, since in Casal's story Amalia and Alfonso produce a family and legacy that are still impossible to imagine in Meza's novel. For a comparative reading of *Carmela* and *Cecilia Valdés*, see Guevara.

7. On the continuities and discontinuities between indigeneity and Blackness in the Caribbean, see Wynter and Newton.

8. The Taiping Rebellion (1850–64) was one of the main reasons behind Chinese internal and overseas migration. The oppositional movement was called the "Heavenly Kingdom of Great Peace," referenced in the story as the "Great Peace."

9. Although much smaller than in Cuba's case, José Lee Borges has identified some

350 Chinese immigrants who arrived in Puerto Rico between 1865 and 1880. In the twentieth century, in the wake of the triumph of the Cuban Revolution, Puerto Rico received another significant Chinese-Cuban immigration that remains an underexplored aspect of Puerto Ricanness.

Works Cited

Anderson, Benedict. *Imagined Communities: Reflections on the Origin and Spread of Nationalism.* Rev. ed. Verso, 1993.
Arroyo, Jossianna. "Historias de familia: Migraciones y escritura homosexual en la literatura puertorriqueña." *Revista Canadiense de Estudios Hispánicos*, vol. 26, no. 3, 2002, pp. 361–78.
———. "Itinerarios de viaje: Las otras islas de Manuel Ramos Otero." *Revista de Estudios Iberoamericanos*, vol. 71, no. 212, 2005, pp. 865–85.
———. "Manuel Ramos Otero: Las narrativas del cuerpo más allá de *Insularismo*." *Revista de Estudios Hispánicos*, vol. 21, no. 1, 2005, pp. 303–24.
———. "Revolution in the Caribbean: Betances, Haiti, and the Antillean Confederation." *La Habana Elegante* (second series), no. 49, 2011, www.habanaelegante.com/Spring_Summer_2011/Invitation_Arroyo.html. Accessed 16 Dec. 2020.
———. *Writing Secrecy in Caribbean Freemansonry.* Palgrave Macmillan, 2013.
Baltar Rodríguez, José. *Los chinos de Cuba: Apuntes etnográficos.* Fundación Fernando Ortiz, 1997.
Barnet, Miguel, and Esteban Montejo. *Biografía de un cimarrón.* Instituto de Etnología y Folklore, 1966.
Benjamin, Walter. *Illuminations.* Schocken, 1969.
Bost, Suzanne. "Fluidity without Postmodernism: Michelle Cliff and the 'Tragic Mulatta' Tradition." *African American Review*, vol. 32, no. 4, 1998, pp. 673–89.
Borges, Jorge Luis. "La muerte y la brújula." *Revista Sur*, no. 92, 1942.
Burunat, Silvia. "El arte literario de Lourdes Casal (1938–1981)." *Confluencia: Revista Hispánica de Cultura y Literatura*, vol. 1, no. 1, 1985, pp. 107–11.
Buscaglia-Salgado, José F. *Undoing Empire: Race and Nation in the Mulatto Caribbean.* U of Minnesota P, 2003.
Casal, Lourdes. "Los fundadores: Alfonso." *Exilio*, vol. 6, no. 1, 1972, pp. 109–17.
———. *Los fundadores: Alfonso y otros cuentos.* Ediciones Universal, 1973.
———. "The Founders: Alfonso." *The Voice of the Turtle: An Anthology of Cuban Stories*, edited by Peter Bush. Translated by Margaret Jull Costa, Grove Press, 1997, pp. 178–91.
Chaar-Pérez, Kahlila. "'A Revolution of Love': Ramón Emeterio Betances, Anténor Firmin, and Affective Communities in the Caribbean." *Global South*, vol. 7, no. 2, 2013, pp. 11–36.
Chang-Rodríguez, Raquel. "Crítica: Nota sobre *Los fundadores: Alfonso y otros cuentos*." *Areíto*, vol. 5, nos. 19–20, 1979, pp. 63–64.
Cheney, David M. "Archbishop Nicolás Ramos y Santos." *The Hierarchy of the Catholic Church*, http://www.catholic-hierarchy.org/bishop/bramosn.html. Accessed 16 Dec. 2020.

Chou, Rosalind S. *Asian American Sexual Politics: The Construction of Race, Gender, and Sexuality*. Rowman & Littlefield, 2012.

Chuffat Latour, Antonio. *Apuntes históricos de los chinos en Cuba*. Molina y Cía, 1927.

Cortés, Jason. "Buscando al otro: Ética y alteridad en 'Página en blanco y staccato' de Manuel Ramos Otero." *Revista Iberoamericana*, vol. 68, no. 198, 2002, pp. 165–75.

Cruz-Malavé, Arnaldo. "Para virar el macho: La autobiografía como subversión en la cuentística de Manuel Ramos Otero." *Revista Iberoamericana*, vol. 59, nos. 162–63, 1993, pp. 239–63.

DeCosta-Willis, Miriam. "Lourdes Casal: Identity and the Politics of (Dis)location in Lourdes Casal's Narratives of Place." *Daughters of the Diaspora: Afra-Hispanic Writers*, edited by Miriam DeCosta-Willis. Ian Randle Publishers, 2003, pp. 194–201.

Duany, Jorge. "The Puerto Rican Exodus to Florida: A Demographic, Socioeconomic, and Cultural Portrait." Pietrantoni Méndez & Alvarez LLC, 9 Dec. 2015, San Juan, PR. Report.

———. "The Puerto Rican Exodus to Florida before and after Hurricane María." Hispanic Economic Growth Summit, Hispanic Chamber of Commerce of Metro Orlando, 2 Nov. 2018, Orlando, FL. Keynote address.

Eng, David. *Racial Castration: Managing Masculinity in Asian America*. Duke UP, 2001.

Fiol-Matta, Licia. *A Queer Mother for the Nation: The State and Gabriela Mistral*. U of Minnesota P, 2002.

Fowler, Víctor. "Homoerotismo y construcción de la nación." *La Gaceta de Cuba*, vol. 36, no. 1, 1998, pp. 2–6.

Fuentes, Marisa. *Dispossessed Lives: Enslaved Women, Violence, and the Archive*. U of Pennsylvania P, 2018.

García-Peña, Lorgia. *The Borders of Dominicanidad: Race, Nation, and Archives of Contradiction*. Duke UP, 2016.

García Triana, Mauro. *Los chinos en Cuba y los nexos entre las dos naciones*. Sociedad Cubana de Investigaciones Filosóficas, 2003.

Gelpí, Juan. *Literatura y paternalismo en Puerto Rico*. Editorial de la Universidad de Puerto Rico, 2005.

Glissant, Édouard. *Caribbean Discourse: Selected Essays*. Translated by J. Michael Dash. UP of Virginia, 1999.

Guevara, Gema R. "Inexacting Whiteness: *Blanqueamiento* as a Gender-Specific Trope in the Nineteenth Century." *Cuban Studies*, vol. 36, 2005, pp. 105–28.

Hooker, Juliet. *Theorizing Race in the Americas: Douglass, Sarmiento, Du Bois, and Vasconcelos*. Oxford UP, 2017.

Hu-De Hart, Evelyn. *Across the Pacific: Asian Americans and Globalization*. Asia Society, 1999.

Hu-De Hart, Evelyn, and Kathleen López. "Asian Diasporas in Latin America and the Caribbean: A Historical Overview." *Afro-Hispanic Review*, vol. 27, no. 1, 2008, pp. 9–21.

La Fountain-Stokes, Lawrence. "1898 and the History of a Queer Puerto Rican Century: Gay Lives, Island Debates, and the Diasporic Experience." *Centro Journal*, vol. 11, no. 1, 1999, pp. 91–109.

———. *Queer Ricans: Cultures and Sexualities in the Diaspora*. U of Minnesota P, 2009.

Lee Borges, José. *Los chinos en Puerto Rico*. 2nd ed. Ediciones Callejón, 2015.
———. "El gran dilema: La introducción de trabajadores chinos a Puerto Rico." *80 Grados*, 24 Sept. 2016, https://www.80grados.net/el-gran-dilema-la-introduccion-de-trabajadores-chinos-a-puerto-rico/#_ftnref7. Accessed 16 Dec. 2020.
López, Kathleen. "Afro-Asian Alliances: Marriage, Godparentage, and Social Status in Late-Nineteenth-Century Cuba." *Afro-Hispanic Review*, vol. 27, no. 1, 2008, pp. 59–72.
———. *Chinese Cubans: A Transnational History*. U of North Carolina P, 2013.
———. "'One Brings Another': The Formation of Early-Twentieth-Century Chinese Migrant Communities in Cuba." *The Chinese in the Caribbean*, edited by Andrew R. Wilson. Marcus Wiener, 2004, pp. 93–127.
López-Calvo, Ignacio. *Imaging the Chinese in Cuban Literature and Culture*. U of Florida P, 2008.
Lorde, Audre. "Uses of the Erotic: The Erotic as Power." *Sister Outsider: Essays and Speeches*. The Crossing Press, 1984, pp. 53–59.
Martínez-San Miguel, Yolanda. *Caribe Two Ways: Cultura de la migración en el Caribe insular hispánico*. Ediciones Callejón, 2003.
———. "'Cuba y Puerto Rico son . . .': Lola Rodríguez de Tió y Manuel Ramos Otero." *80 Grados*, 3 May 2019, https://www.80grados.net/cuba-y-puerto-rico-son-lola-rodriguez-de-tio-y-manuel-ramos-otero/. Accessed 16 Dec. 2020.
———. "Fantasy as Identity: Beyond Foundational Narratives in Lourdes Casal." *Cuban Studies*, vol. 45, 2017, pp. 91–114.
———. "'La puerta del mar': Ficción, historia y memoria en el imaginario decimonónico de Manuel Ramos Otero." *Cruce: Crítica Socio-Cultural Contemporánea*, 17 May 2021, pp. 98–121. https://issuu.com/revistacruce/docs/cruce_-_homenaje_a_manuel_ramos_otero_-_17_de_mayo. Accessed 11 May 2022.
———. "Releyendo a Lourdes Casal desde su escritura en queer." *80 Grados*, 16 Oct. 2015, http://www.80grados.net/releyendo-a-lourdes-casal-desde-su-escritura-en-queer/. Accessed 16 Dec. 2020.
Martínez-San Miguel, Yolanda, and Frances Negrón-Muntaner. "En busca de la 'Ana Veldford' de Lourdes Casal: Exilio, sexualidad y cubanía." *Debate Feminista* (Mexico), vol. 17, no. 33, 2006, pp. 166–97.
Martí, José. "Nuestra América." *Prosa y poesía*. Kapelusz, 1968, pp. 122–33.
Meza y Suárez Inclán, Ramón. *Carmela*. Editorial Arte y Literatura, 1978.
Negrón-Muntaner, Frances, and Yolanda Martínez-San Miguel. "In Search of Lourdes Casal's 'Ana Veldford.'" *Social Text*, vol. 25, no. 3, 2007, pp. 57–84.
Newton, Melanie. "Returns to a Native Land: Indigeneity and Decolonization in the Anglophone Caribbean." *Small Axe*, vol. 17, no. 2, 2013, pp. 108–22.
Park, Michael. "Asian American Masculinity Eclipsed: A Legal and Historical Perspective of Emasculation through U.S. Immigration Practices." *The Modern American*, vol. 8, no. 1 2013, pp. 5–17.
Piñera, Virgilio. *La isla en peso/The Whole Island*. Translated by Mark Weiss. Shearsman Books Ltd, 2010.
Quiroga, José. "Unpacking My Files: My Life as a Queer *Brigadista*." *Social Text*, vol. 32, no. 4, 2014, pp. 149–59.
Ramos Otero, Manuel. *Invitación al polvo*. Editorial Plaza Mayor, 1994.

———. *Página en blanco y staccato*. 2nd ed. Editorial Playor, 1998.
Reyes-Santos, Irmary. "On Pan-Antillean Politics: Ramón Emeterio Betances and Gregorio Luperón Speak to the Present." *Callaloo*, vol. 36, no. 1, 2013, pp. 142–57.
Rodríguez Beltrán, María Elizabeth. "Under the Surface of *Negrura*: A Literary Analysis of Blackness and Communality in Caribbean and Brazilian Texts." In progress. Rutgers University, Ph.D. dissertation.
Rodríguez de Tió, Lola. *Mi libro de Cuba*. Imprenta La Moderna, 1893.
Rosa, Luis Othoniel. "Grave Melodies: Literature and Afterlife in Manuel Ramos Otero." *Revista Hispánica Moderna*, vol. 64, no. 2, 2011, 167–79.
Torres, Daniel. "An AIDS Narrative." *Centro de Estudios Puertorriqueños Bulletin*, vol. 6, nos. 1–2, 1994, 178–79.
Torres-Rodríguez, Laura J. *Orientaciones transpacíficas: La modernidad mexicana y el espectro de Asia*. U of North Carolina P, 2019.
Villaverde, Cirilo. *Cecilia Valdés*. Biblioteca Ayacucho, 1981.
Wynter, Silvia. "Jonkonnu in Jamaica: Towards an Interpretation of Folk Dance as a Cultural Process." *Jamaica Journal*, vol. 4, no. 2, 1970, pp. 34–48.
Yun, Lisa. *The Coolie Speaks: Chinese Indentured Laborers and African Slaves in Cuba*. Temple UP, 2008.

III

Manifestations of Cuban and Puerto Rican Culture

12

Listening to Our New Possessions
Music and Imperial Writings on Puerto Rico and Cuba, 1898–1920s

HUGO R. VIERA-VARGAS

The orchestra music was excellent, and the instrument quite similar to those of the theater orchestra in the United States.
Albert James Norton (*Norton's Complete Hand-Book of Havana and Cuba*)

Much that passes under the name of music could more properly be called noise, but where Porto Ricans have had opportunity for study and development, they have proved that musical ability is not wanting among them.
George Milton Fowles (*Down in Porto Rico*)

The imperial gaze that followed the United States invasion of Puerto Rico and Cuba after 1898 produced a literary corpus that both speculated about the islands' economic possibilities and revealed an exotic fascination about its inhabitants' customs and lives. The gaze was far-reaching, incisive, and heterogeneous—but somewhat contradictory. Along with the U.S. troops arrived government officials, correspondents, journalists, speculators, and adventurers. Employing a range of writing devices and media, many of these visitors sought to capture the new colonial enterprise's features for a U.S. public eager to consume the foreign. The construction of colonial subjects through these means was an extension of the U.S. effort to benefit from acquiring lands for agricultural production, new markets for its products, and the fruits of the native population's labor. The colonial project also arrogated responsibility for guiding both islands to achieve self-rule, improving the inhabitants' morals, and providing better educational infrastructure to justify its colonial project. As such, the imperial discourse implied a hierarchical order in which the United States held a superior position politically, economically, socially, and morally, concurrently suggesting the absence of civilized societies on both islands.

This discourse was strengthened by enlisting Western aesthetic ideals to assess the culture, music, and sounds of both Caribbean islands. In books, magazines, and newspapers, colonial agents listened to and decoded the sounds of children's cries, the shouts of a bread or fruit vendor, the strum of the Cuban *tres* (a small string instrument) or the crisp sound of the Puerto Rican *güiro* (a hollow gourd used as a percussion instrument). Such interpreting transpired in the translation between what the visitors heard and what they wrote; indeed, this was an ideological process that hierarchized sounds and music through what Jennifer Lynn Stoever calls the "listening ear." This racializing form of listening "represents a historical aggregate of normative American listening practices and gives a name to listening's epistemological function as a modality of racial discernment. An aural complement to and interlocutor of the gaze [is] . . . a socially constructed ideological system producing but also regulating cultural ideas about sound" (Stoever 43). Filtering the sounds and music through the listening ear was essential to what I refer to as the sonic colonial discourse—a term indebted to Stoever's concept of the sonic color line. Like the sonic color line—which "enables the listener to construct and discern racial identities based on voices, sound, and particular soundscapes" (Stoever 27)—the sonic colonial discourse, for the purpose of my work, is the knowledge that derives from the characterization of colonial agents about the sounds and music of their colonized territories. Further, it is part of a broader discourse that typically cast colonized territories as ambiguously backward and in need of colonial tutelage.

However, the aural perceptions were marginal in many of these colonial agents' narratives. Their interests fluctuated from providing practical information on agricultural and commercial possibilities to assessing the character and capacity of Cubans and Puerto Ricans to govern themselves (Matos-Rodríguez 38). Nevertheless, their writings conveyed their ideas on music, sounds, and noises of the lands and people subject to their gaze. This chapter argues that the sonic discourse—a dimension of the emerging U.S. colonial discourse toward the Caribbean—was racially and politically suitable to fit the United States' political and economic agendas about Puerto Rico and Cuba. Therefore, the transformation of these two Caribbean islands' sonorous worlds into texts was not an innocuous description of culture but also a subtle subterfuge to extend new ways of domination.

Several scholars have examined both islands' representation at this precise historical juncture (Thompson, "'Estudiarlos, juzgarlos y gobernarlos,'" *Imperial Archipelago*; Duany, "Cómo representar a los nuevos colonizados," *The Puerto Rican Nation on the Move*; Matos-Rodríguez; García; Santiago-Valle; Anazagasty and Cancel; Anazagasty; Louis Pérez; Evered; Charnon-Deutsch; Domínguez). This literature has prioritized textual and visual analysis, allowing researchers to analyze the same sources that colonial agents saw. However, my work has highlighted the aural, an ephemeral phenomenon captured by the observer's pen. Therefore, the sonic descriptions of the colonial agents must be understood as the result of a cognitive and ideological process that sought to understand the societies of these newly acquired territories, to exercise control and establish the optimal conditions to further the complex and diverse agenda of the colonial State.

The pages that follow offer an overview of what the colonial agents heard, decoded, and penned about Cuba and Puerto Rico during the first decades of the twentieth century. By no means was this a monolithic process. Authors consumed and represented Puerto Rico's and Cuba's natural resources and people through all of their senses and multiple ways. Listening was not done in isolation but rather in conjunction with all the human senses. These writers saw people, huts, roads, bays, houses, beaches, and mountains. Moreover, they experienced the aroma of oil and garlic, coffee, the smell of saltpeter, and the humid scent of the morning's dew. And they tried to comprehend what they saw, smelled, and heard by combining their preconceived assumptions of sound, music, race, gender, and class. In a sense, these pages are a partial endeavor, for I have prioritized the aural interpretation over other sensory experiences to understand the past.

This chapter sheds light on how the colonial sonic discourse justified U.S. policies by portraying and representing colonial subjects as socially and culturally backward and, therefore, unfit for self-rule and in need of tutelage. The idea of constructing a colonial subject in Cuba and Puerto Rico was differentiated by how the two islands were visually and sonorously represented. It is not my intention to evoke romantic similarities between Puerto Rico and Cuba or to create victims in need of redemption. It was clear that, albeit Puerto Rico and Cuba shared Spanish colonial political and social institutions, their historical and economic developments differed substantially. With its wide bay in Havana, Cuba became one of the most critical shipyards of the Spanish fleet up till the eighteenth century. Its fertile lands and access to capital and technological resources allowed Cuba to become one of the most lucrative sugar producers of the nineteenth century. On the contrary, although Puerto Rico experienced a boom in sugar and coffee production during the nineteenth century, it was primordially a military outpost whose prime worth was its strategic location in the Caribbean Sea.

The first section of this chapter analyzes books, magazines, newspaper articles, and government publications about Puerto Rico and Cuba between 1898 and the 1920s to shed light on the differential representations of the islands by colonial agents. This section proposes that such distinctions were crucial in nurturing a colonial discourse that managed the new possessions according to U.S. economic and geopolitical interests in the region. The second section examines the sonic descriptions in this literary corpus to underline how listening was a powerful medium to construct colonial subjectivities. This part underscores how these colonial subjectivities followed and nurtured the differential logic discussed in the first section.

The Differentiated Construction of the Colonial Discourse on Puerto Rico and Cuba

The construction of the colonial subject was wed to the usurpation of the natural wealth and a self-assigned responsibility of guiding the inhabitants of the newly acquired territories in the art of governing, regenerating their morals, and ordering their education. In 1899, Frederick A. Ober affirmed this duality by stating that "the acquisition of these islands ... will enable us eventually to supply all our wants ... and [they] will look to us for all their machinery, flour, cotton, and wooden goods—in fact, for everything necessary to civilized communities" (2). Under this new political paradigm, not only would the United States benefit, but Puerto Rico and Cuba would also obtain what they needed to civilize. This narrative implied a favorable position for the United States and assumed, in turn, the need to civilize Puerto Rican and Cuban societies. Colonization was justified, then, as Lanny Thompson points out, "to civilize the primitive, to cultivate paradise, to educate the child, and to conquer the woman" ("'Estudiarlos, juzgarlos y gobernarlos'" 688). To carry out this enterprise, it was necessary to create an Other that could be malleable and predisposed to social and political regeneration through contact with the democratic institutions brought by the United States. However, this process required nuances that could explain the particularities and contradictions of the colonial discourse toward Cuba and Puerto Rico. Although both islands were of geopolitical and economic interest to the United States, they were not represented identically in the discourse of domination (Duany, *The Puerto Rican Nation on the Move*; Thompson, *Imperial Archipelago*). The underlying premise was the contrast between the civilized United States and an ambiguously primitive Cuba and Puerto Rico.

According to this framework, the newly acquired territories showed economic potential but lacked the experiences of democratic life. Moreover, each island differed in its prior experiences with democratic and representative government. Therefore, a clear classification scheme was an indispensable tool for balancing U.S. economic and political interests and addressing the new possessions' social, economic, and political circumstances. According to David Spurr, it was a crucial ideological rhetorical recourse that "serves to demonstrate the fundamental justice of the colonial enterprise by ranking native peoples according to their relative degree of technical and political sophistication as seen from the European point of view. On a practical level, these distinctions were made to show that each category of native requires its own administrative tactic" (Spurr 69).

In the eyes of William Dinwiddie, for example, Puerto Ricans lived in a "primitive simplicity in which the human needs are few and readily met with a minimum amount of labor, but as existence for the civilized man, it is a horrible fantasy" (Dinwiddie 156). Thus, the material and existential poverty exhibited by Puerto Ricans was natural but unsustainable for civilized men. William D. Boyce, a Chicago-based journalist, expressed himself in a similar tone when he affirmed that "the jíbaro [peasant] leads an extremely simple life. It is difficult for Americans to understand him since they belong to different civilizations. He is extremely poor, but he is extremely proud" (Boyce 97). Simplicity meant unsophistication, a lack of progress, and affinity with modernity. The dichotomy between civilization and barbarism was much more explicit in Puerto Rican descriptions than in Cuban representations—as we will elaborate later in this chapter. Arthur D. Hall was certain "that in the end, Porto Rico will become one of the most important of our possessions. Superstition and tyranny will be driven from this most fertile island and hope and peace, under the Stars and Stripes, will be brought to the thousands so long underfoot" (171). Puerto Rico was still in a primordial state in which despotism, delusion, and vagrancy prevented achieving a sophisticated level of understanding for democratic life. Americans, with their Puerto Rican collaborators, occupied the island to do the job. Geologist Robert Hill pointed out that Puerto Ricans "swing themselves to and fro in their hammocks all day long smoking their cigar and scraping the guitar... they are not disposed to continuous work" (168). Reverend Henry Carroll, in his voluminous report on Puerto Rico, noted that "few of the laboring classes are robust" (Carroll 50). That was certainly the idea that librarian Rudolph Adams Van Middeldyk had of the *jíbaros*, whom he described as intellectually and physically poor. He added: "his illiteracy is complete; his speech is notoriously incorrect" (Van Middeldyk 199). The passage of time did not change some of the ideas that were common to colonial discourse; in a 1929 letter in response to an editorial of *The New Republic* ("Cubans vs. Puerto Ricans"), W.Z.W. wrote that Puerto Ricans continued to be a "supine, stodgy, [and] spiritless race. They have not even as yet developed a spirit of nationalism at a time in world history when among cultured people nationalism has started on the way to join the family, the clan and the city fetishes in the realm of the dodo" (230). His disdain went even further when he pointed out that "had the Porto Ricans existed two thousand years ago they would inevitably have been the slaves of whatever virile people wanted them, if any" (W.Z.W. 230).

These authors accentuated a dichotomy between the United States and the Puerto Rican people. However, such differences must be read as part of a larger discourse that set up distinctions between the United States and its overseas possessions. This process led to an indirect, hierarchical comparison between territories, prompting a judgment about their population's attributes, experiences, and qualifications (Thompson, *Imperial Archipelago*). Yet, beside the harsh depictions was the hope that the United States could instill in Puerto Ricans a better appreciation and adherence to democratic principles and civility.

The evidence presented above provides a glimpse of how Puerto Ricans were contrasted with Cubans. While the Cubans were a familiar Other, Americans had an unclear idea of who were the Puerto Ricans. Despite differences in character, customs, and language, Cuban and Americans shared some core values. The Cubans, noted Hill, were a laboring people who "under the influence of their surroundings they have developed into a gentle, industrious, and normally peaceful race. They have strong traits of civilized character, including honesty, family attachment, hospitality, politeness and a respect for the golden rule" (100). These shared values made the Cuban a distant relative, capable, if the conditions permitted, of emulating the North American Republic's great achievements. Arthur D. Hall seems to agree with Hill, when he rhetorically asked, "Can the Cubans, if they obtain freedom, govern themselves, or will not a free Cuba become a second Hayti with all the horrors of that island?" His reply was forceful: "Cuba will be able to govern itself" (Hall 175). He based his affirmative response on Cubans' efforts to organize, fight, and establish a provisional government against Spanish rule during the war years.

Americans clearly had conflicting views on the ability of Cubans to govern themselves. Senator Oliver Platt recognized their devoted ideas toward liberty but imperfection in the practical duties or responsibilities of a free government (Platt 152). Thompson argues that U.S. colonial agents represented Cubans, particularly Whites, with the caliber to achieve self-government. However, these self-government qualities were in an embryonic stage and needed guidance (*Imperial Archipelago*). In sum, uncertainty and lack of trust best describe colonial agents' analysis of Cuba's possibilities for independence. On the other hand, Puerto Ricans were not recognized as demonstrating the same level of political acumen and courage as Cubans.

The differences in the colonial discourse were supported by readings of the political, economic, and social developments in each territory and by the economic and geopolitical interests that each territory represented for the United States in the present and the future. To fully understand Cuba and Puerto Rico's different representations in the United States, it is crucial to contextualize them in light of their prior history with the United States. The United States had a closer economic and social relationship with Cuba than Puerto Rico prior to 1898 (Hoffnung-Garskof; Lisandro Pérez; Poyo; Greenbaum). My point has not been to exhaust the representations of Cuba and Puerto Rico as other scholars have researched them, but to highlight the differences in the colonial discourse, as Thompson has proposed.

Music and Sound of the New Possessions

The island sounds inevitably reached the ears of the colonial agents and motivated a tepid interest. The noise of the market, the cry of a seller of bread, eggs, or other agricultural products, or the screech of the wheels of a rusty cart tore the silence. Knowlton Mixer described this swarm of sounds in Puerto Rico as a noise produced by "the overcrowding of the Island and the constant pressure of humankind ... Street noises, however, while constant, are not always unpleasant. The musical lit of the vegetable peddler as he pushes his cart toward town and the song of the egg man add a harmonious touch to the confusion" (Mixer 108). The street sounds, although unruly, had a certain musicality, a "musical lit." The cadenced proclamation of a humble vegetable seller or *pregonero* provided a harmonious "touch" to the daily cacophony. Oscar Phelps Austin, a U.S. statistician quoted by

Ober, commented on this same quasi-musical quality when he underlined how the "street sellers ... announce their wares in strange and not unmusical cries" (267). The shouting of street sellers must have been quite a spectacle and clearly caught the attention of Americans on the islands (*New York Times*). The *pregón*, an old tradition in Cuba and Puerto Rico where street sellers created songs to sell their products, was perceived among the cities' cacophony and described ambiguously between noise and music.

The raucousness also included the loud human voices emerging from San Juan and Havana's streets, cafes, restaurants, and homes. These sounds caught the attention of a U.S. observer in Havana, who noted that it "is one of the noisiest of cities. Night and day an uproar of loud talk arises from cafes and restaurants, and there is a ceaseless bustle in the streets" (Clark 151). These urban sounds transgressed the sound space of the colonial agents who attempted to understand the cultural and aural setting in which they were imbued. However, understanding and classifying these "noises" implied an act of power over the bodies of those who emitted the sounds. According to these observers, San Juan and Havana were rowdy places, where a bustling city mingled with human voice and sounds. We can suppose that the human voices were judged as loud and boisterous, as descriptions of non-human sounds were minimal. Noise was a significant metaphor to write about cities and people, for noise is untamed sound, disorder, disturbance: "to make noise is to interrupt a transmission" (Attali 26). On the other hand, sounds, but particularly music, are vehicles to appease the unruly and to manifest order. The U.S. audience that consumed this sonic literary corpus read and imagined the people described with exoticism and confirmed or rebutted preconceived ideas about the Other. These ideas inevitably helped to nourish political action on how the newly acquired territories should be governed. The connection is not easy to establish since subjectivity dominates the world of music and sound listening. Yet, the texts about the aural were inscribed in a larger context, one in which the U.S. public and politicians shaped their ideas through what others wrote about the new territories.

If Puerto Rico's and Cuba's sounds were perceived and decoded in a similar vein, the sociomusical spaces' narratives marked a distinction between the islands. José Anazagasty has argued that these sonic descriptions of Puerto Rico exhibited a textual economy that assigned a differential value to the island's music as opposed to U.S. and European music. Not surprisingly, music was described as "primitive," "barbaric," or unsuitable for U.S. ears. However, was the music that was heard transposed into the text as unbearable noise? Did these descriptions reflect the aural reality, or did they produce a sonic archive that created an alternative representation? What do the silences tell us about the colonial agenda?

The sonic archive that emerged from imperial listening inscribed a deficiency among musicians and music-making in Puerto Rico. For George Fowles, Puerto Rican "ideas of music are most primitive" (50). He observed that "the instruments are chiefly of inferior make, and owing to the climatic conditions, the wires become rusty, and the tones produced are decidedly 'tin-panny.' These are played with but little expression, the idea seemingly being to make as loud a sound as possible" (50). Fowles, notwithstanding, recognized signs of musicality among the elite that played the piano and in brass bands that performed in the plazas. However, he advised readers that the piano rarely "arouses the enthusiasm of a musician" and the bands, although some "produce fairly good music . . . [some] of them are simply nerve-racking" (50). Like those of many other colonial agents, Fowles' descriptions were ambivalent in the way they conceived local musical practices. Writing ambivalently about Puerto Rico's music and sounds required presenting the inhabitants of the conquered territories as subtly different, perhaps in degree, but with the capacity to improve their cultural level according to the colonial power's ideas.

This inconsistency can also be seen in U.S. policies toward Puerto Rico developed and implemented during this period.[1] It is not surprising that Fowles granted certain musicality and the possibility that if Puerto Ricans underwent good musical training and studies, they could become excellent musicians. But, as long as this did not happen, "much that passes under the name of music could more properly be called noise" (Fowles 50). Far from these dull descriptions, the first commercial recordings attest to the musical quality and confirm the popularity of various Western musical genres in Puerto Rico. In 1910, Columbia Records made its first recordings in Puerto Rico. In an improvised studio, their agents recorded several Puerto Rican orchestras, including Domingo "Cocolía" Cruz's Orchestra, Manuel Tizol's Orchestra, the Banda del Regimiento de Infantería de Puerto Rico, Andino's Orchestra, the singer Teresina Moreno Calderón, and Dr. Arturo Ygaravídez. Given the number of pieces that it recorded during these sections, Cocolía's Orchestra seems to have been one of the most popular on the island at the time. They recorded fifty-four pieces, of which fifty-one were Puerto Rican danzas, two waltzes, and the famous seis de Andino. The Banda del Regimiento de Puerto Rico recorded only six pieces, of which two were danzas, two pasodobles, and two polkas. All of Teresina Moreno

Calderón's recordings were danzas from Juan Morel Campos, Ríos Ovalle, and Félix Astol. Dr. Ygarivídez's repertoire was, to some extent, more popular; he recorded "Canción del ciego," with cuatro and güiro, "Aguinaldo de Noche Buena," "Aguinaldo," and Declaración de amor de dos campesinos de Puerto Rico." Except for Ygarivídez, most of the pieces were danzas by famous island composers. Some pieces where from the European dance repertoire adapted to the instrumental format of the bands. The recording agent sought to record the most palatable and Westernized version of Puerto Rican music that could appeal "across social, educational, and cultural differences, no matter how deep and abiding those divisions might be" (Kenney 68). In this regard, the danza was still considered Puerto Rico's most exquisite musical form, at least among the best-trained musicians and potential Puerto Rican consumers.[2]

Yet, for a U.S. visitor, the musicians of the town band created a sort of cacophony where each musician "played whatever piece of music he happens to like, in his own pitch, time, and style. Horns, flutes, violins, cellos, drums and cymbals, all go at once, each one is happy to disregard anybody else" (Blythe 78). The image of the orchestra Verdadera Juventud gives us an iconographic idea of the instruments used in dance bands during these years that are all within the Western musical tradition (see Figure 12.1). In his work *De las bandas al Trío Borinquen*, Pedro Malavet Vega quotes an ad published in *Puerto Rico Ilustrado* on 6 March 1910, from Casa Euterpe, the musical store of José Laza, which reveals the type of instrumentation common for the big bands at the turn of the century. Among the instruments were "Piccolos, Flutes . . . Flageolets, Requinto, Clarinets, Oboes, Saxophones, Bassoons, Figles, Bugles, Violins, Mandolins, and Basses" (Malavet Vega 87).[3]

The colonial agents seemed to be hesitant to confer a familiar sonority to Puerto Rican music in an attempt to exalt aural differences. This could suggest the attempt to balance the representation in these writings of the undesirable Other and the reformable colonial subject. Demarking a sonorous difference therefore required portraying a gulf between U.S. and Puerto Rican musical traditions. This was not an easy task to achieve, as musical practices were, for the most part, embedded in Western musical traditions. In Puerto Rico, musicians developed their musical abilities and tastes in relation to their global, local, and family experiences. Through these experiences, they were exposed to the myriad of genres and musical styles that ranged from the Western classical repertoire to seises, décimas, plenas, or Cuban sones, boleros, or U.S. fox-trots. They experienced and

Figure 12.1. Orchestra Verdadera Juventud, conducted by Juan Madera. *Puerto Rico Ilustrado*, no. 484, 7 June 1919. Photo courtesy of Noel Allende Goitía.

lived these genres within a complex set of interactions among race, gender, family, and class: factors that mediated their understanding of music, musical tastes, and their investment in the musician's craft. The creation of this gulf required the erasure of a long tradition of music-making on the island and the selection of musical practices that could demonstrate the dissimilarities without being unsurmountable for their social, economic, and political regeneration.

The hollow gourd called güiro was the native instrument that metaphorically demarcated sonic and cultural differences for many of these writers. It was a versatile and adaptable instrument to various musical formats and genres, whether native or new to popular taste. Its percussive role made it an object of elite criticism in the history of popular music in the nineteenth century, particularly its use in the danza. Dinwiddie witnessed the adaptability of the güiro when he listened to the famous waltz *After the Ball* (1891) by Charles K. Harris.[4] He was impressed when he heard that "a new sound strikes the ear; in quality, it is between the rattle of a snake and the pit-a-patting of a clever shuffle-dancer on a sanded floor. The instrument is called a 'guida' (weé-da)" (Dinwiddie 162). The author's familiarity with the popular waltz struck with the strange sandy-clicking of an instrument

Figure 12.2. "A group of 'jíbaros' who formed Orquesta Brava of Aguadilla, which took part in the evening of the Ateneo discussed in this chronicle." *Puerto Rico Ilustrado*, No. 319, 8 Apr. 1916. The *güiro* is the third instrument pictured from right to left. Photo courtesy of Noel Allende-Goitía.

unknown to the Western musical paradigm, the güiro. The adaptation of the güiro to a Western musical ensemble, like that of the orchestra of *música brava* (peasant music) depicted in Figure 12.2, demonstrates the pervasiveness and popularity of the instrument, so much so that a U.S. observer mentioned that it was "used in balls in society, as an accompaniment to the piano and other modern instruments. It is even adopted by the Spanish military bands when they play the country dances" (Forbes 89–90).

Some years later, Marian George, possibly building on Dinwiddie's observations, made her own aural descriptions of the güiro and posited that, albeit Puerto Ricans seemed to like its sound, "we should not call it music at all. No orchestra is complete without it, and one can hear the scratching of this instrument almost at any time, in any home in Puerto Rico" (George 35–36). The güiro's characteristic sound, which was defined at times as noise, was similarly noted for its association with Blackness and the popular classes. This characterization is not fortuitous. The ear-piercing sound of the güiro, its primitive design, its inability to adjust to a Western tempered scale, its rhythmic patterns (some of them associated with Afro-Caribbean rhythmic traditions), and, most of all, who was playing it, produced in the eyes of colonial agents, a questionable sonorous metaphor for Puerto Rico.

Figure 12.3. "Music of the Poor." *Boletín Mercantil*, 1903. Postcard Collection, Puerto Rican Collection of the University of Puerto Rico Library System, Río Piedras Campus.

Figures 12.3 and 12.4 serve as the backdrop for Henry Northrop's perception of the association of the güiro and the hand-organ (presumably an accordion that was popular for the emerging plena) with the Black population and laboring classes. After describing a "nicer" scene in the Plaza de Armas in San Juan, he pointed out that "the whole lower strata will be found in the narrow, badly lighted streets, or in the plaza Cristobal Colon and the small places of the densely populated city. Here hands organs and dirty wandering minstrels, who perform semi-barbaric music upon cracked guitars and raspy mandolins, accompanied by the güero" (Northrop viii). What is not explicit in Northrop's text, but observable in the pictures, is that these street musicians are overwhelmingly Black. Northrop and other writers rhetorically silenced Blackness through textual description to appease the uncomfortable sounds of "crude" musical instruments. Indeed, Hill finds a very quiet moment in Puerto Rico "when one does not hear the scratching of this instrument" (Hill 164). As others cited above, Hill did not hide the annoyance that the sound of the güiro had on him and that he referred to it

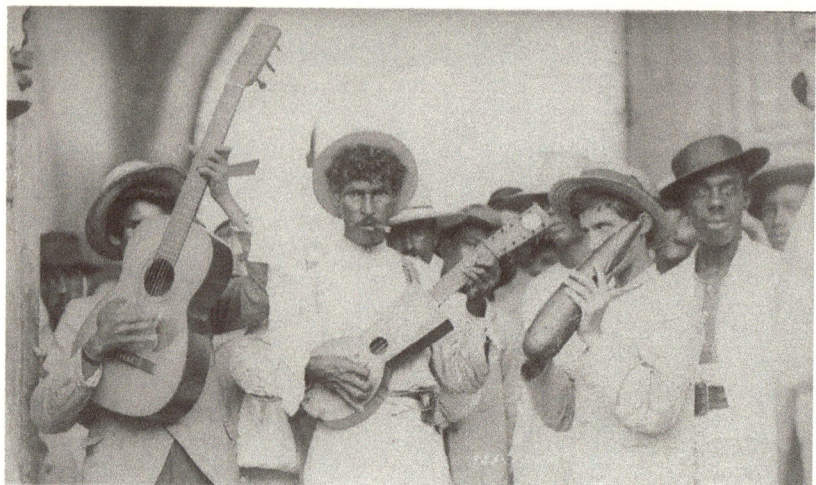

Figure 12.4. "Native Musicians, Porto Rico," circa 1898. Unknown source. The *cuatro* player in the middle is identified as Eusebio González.

as noise. These descriptions cannot erase other, more sympathetic observers who saw the musical qualities of the güiro. On 28 November 1898, in a Connecticut newspaper, *The Waterbury Evening Democrat*, a U.S. correspondent noted the instrument's importance in Puerto Rican music: "in the hands of a native," the observer remarked, "the sound of the güiro becomes music." Other commentators did not miss the opportunity to refer to the güiro as one of the most popular instruments among musicians in Puerto Rico. Its versatility was captured in the words of a *New York Times* reporter, who noted that it was always used in orchestra music and in all "music of the streets" ("Native Puerto Ricans"). However, its use in dance orchestras and its musical ubiquity made it difficult to classify according to Western musical organology.

A superficial reading of these accounts could point out that it is a question of taste and that the music and instruments played by Puerto Ricans were not to the colonial agents' liking. However, these stories informed and represented the new territories and their people to a U.S. audience that took these narratives to inform themselves about the inhabitants of these lands. This literature comes at a crucial time when the future of the relationship between the new territories and the United States is still being discussed. Although seemingly irrelevant to political or economic issues, this information helped define who the people were over whom colonial policies would be applied and the nature of future relations with these people.

The music heard was not described as music; it was a selective listening, an act of sonorous misreading. These sonic representations intersected with racial and gender preconceptions that helped underpin Puerto Rican music's devaluation (Anazagasty). Some Spanish-speaking observers even concluded that songs, if not of a silly, meaningless character, were often obscene; sometimes, they betrayed the existence of a poetic sentiment (Van Middeldyk 199).

In comparison, the colonial "listening ear" was sympathetic to Cuba's musical scene. As we will see in the next few pages, Cuba's sounds were portrayed as much closer to the United States' sociomusical experiences. This approach contributed to the silencing of Afro-Cuban musical spaces that had no place in like-minded ears. This does not mean that there were no descriptions of Afro-Cuban musical traditions, but that the sonic descriptions that I have seen centered primarily on what was considered Whiter musical scenes.[5] However, the effects were comparable to the observations in Puerto Rico; the altering of the soundscape suited an imperial discourse to conform to U.S. interests in these territories.

The description of Cuba's soundscapes detailed a more sophisticated society than Puerto Rico. For instance, U.S. journalist Trumbull White recounted a sociomusical event in Havana's Paseo del Prado with lovely music and a genial atmosphere full of elegance and grace. "Here, you will listen to the dreamy melody of these latitudes, Spanish love songs, and Cuban Waltzes so softly pretty that you wonder why all the world does not sing and play them" (White 557). Judging from White's notes, Cuba displayed a musical sound—dreamy, as he described it—palatable to a U.S. ear and taste. He was not alone in his appreciation. Albert James Norton also remarked on an agreeable moment in a Havana theater: "there were eighteen musicians in the orchestra. Among them were several coal-black negroes who mingled freely with the other members. The orchestra music was excellent, and the instruments quite similar to those of theater orchestras in the United States" (Norton 62). Although Norton does not explicitly remark about Black and White musicians working together in the orchestra, he was taken aback by the music's quality and instrumental familiarity. This was certainly the case when traveler Reau Campbell observed that mixed-race theater orchestras were "satisfactory" and often played "as good or better music than in the best American theatres" (11). It can be argued that Havana, Cuba was a more sophisticated city compared to San Juan, Puerto Rico. Havana actually had many more and larger theaters—such as the Teatro Tacón—where this type of orchestra performed (Sublette 128–29).

However, Fernando Callejo argued in his book *Música y músicos puertorriqueños* (1915) that Puerto Rico had a strong musical history associated with the Western classical repertoire.

Nevertheless, White, Norton, and Campbell established a musical connection with a sound familiar to U.S. "ears." Unlike the examples discussed about Puerto Rico's music and sounds, Cuba was portrayed as sonorously familiar for a U.S. audience that might expect it. The following examples reveal a Cuban soundscape that allowed the reader to have an appreciation—although ambiguous—closer to representing a life grounded in order and modernity.

It was common to describe Cubans, like Puerto Ricans, as music lovers. The former, however, were described more favorably. For instance, in his travelogue Thomas Terry claimed that music was "a highly developed Cuban character, and is loved by all classes" (51). He documented prominent musical institutions in Cuba since colonial times, like the Filarmónica, the Santa Cecilia, El Liceo, and others (Terry 55). The mention of these musical institutions gave a historical character to the development of music in Cuba. Contrary to the classification of Puerto Rican music as primitive, this historical reference allowed the U.S. reader to locate Cuban music as part of a shared musical tradition and history. Terry also mentioned the scroll of famous musicians that students of music in Cuba should be familiar with, followed by the statement that Cubans are extraordinarily skillful musicians.

The descriptions of the popular *retretas* or public square feasts were common in the literature about Cuba. These were concerts attended by a cross-class audience gathered around the main public squares to enjoy themselves, usually in the evening. The *retretas* were racially and socially stratified sound spaces where people of higher socioeconomic positions tended to occupy the squares' central areas, while the popular classes spread around the margins. However, they were one of the few public places where these two sectors socialized in the presence of music. The *retreta* was the place to see and be seen. Some visitors to Cuba were mesmerized by the air of graciousness of the *retretas*. Hill, who also visited and wrote about Puerto Rico, witnessed one in the Plaza de Armas in Havana. There he saw "well-dressed citizens" promenade while listening to music, which, for him, gave an "air of gaiety" to the evening (Hill 111). This social and musical spectacle was not unique to Havana society. In "Cienfuegos one may still see ... many señoras and señoritas wearing graceful mantillas ... parade[d] about the plaza while the band plays dreamy Spanish music beneath the rustling palms" (Hyatt 157). Examples of these joyful evenings in plazas abound in depictions of Cuban towns and cities. They must have been a colorful scene of delightful music in a tropical paradise to the U.S. reader. Cuba was also an important destination for internationally renowned artists, given the assumed well-versed audience in music that could appreciate artists of the stature of the opera singer Adelina Patti, for example. Likewise, these images gave the U.S. reader a sense of a cosmopolitan city filled with lovely walks and great theaters, like those of U.S. major cities (Boyce 51–52).

Some of these authors enjoyed walks around Havana. Unfortunately, it is impossible to tell who accompanied them, for the authors left no information about this detail. They described, however, an urban landscape within which they included people, sounds, and music. The strolls through the city allowed some U.S. travelers to appreciate the afternoons of leisure among the houses of the city's wealthier sectors. Charles Morris, for example, found family gatherings cheerful and attractive, "peals of gay laughter floating across from house to house, songs, or the sound of instruments making the air musical, and from afar the music of the military band now and then swelling into audible strains" (99). This was the same impression that William Bryan had of Havana when he mentioned that he came across numerous clubhouses where "is almost constantly the scene of some brilliant gathering, in the nature of a ball, musicale or other fetes." (11). The descriptions' spirit points to an interest in situating Cuba's lifestyle and music within a cosmopolitan and urban style. The shared notion of musicality and mores presented in these writings helps account for the U.S.'s ambiguous and contradictory intervention on the island.

However, the silences in the descriptions are more significant to understand the intentions of these authors. Why did these authors emphasize so much on a sophisticated sound and a Westernized musical tradition? What musical scenes could they have witnessed but did not write about, and why? We will never know, and I do not have a conclusive answer. However, these silences may respond to an attempt to parallel Cuban and American musical experiences to foster a discourse that sought to create the impression that Cubans were ripe for political regeneration as long as they allowed the United States to guide them in the proper path.

Conclusion

This chapter might seem odd to the reader familiar with the historiography of Cuba's and Puerto Rico's representation to a U.S. audience after 1898. In the preceding pages I have underscored how the colonial agents' "listening ear" chose to hear selectively what it would represent from both islands' music. The aural descriptions of Cuba, for example, offer alternative readings of Cuba's representation in cartoons and photographs, analyzed by other scholars (Evered; Louis Pérez; Thompson, *Imperial Archipelago*; Charnon-Deutsch). In effect, the sonic interpretations that I have presented here undermine the iconographical analysis that this same literature engenders. Though embedded in broader narratives about Cuba's representation, such sonic narratives do not entirely fit into easy dichotomies of the civilized and the uncivilized. Cuba's sociomusical spaces were described with a greater degree of inclination toward Western musical traditions in an effort to characterize Cuba as a closer and more civilized Other. If, on the one hand, other analyses have emphasized the idea of the Cuban population's devaluation, musical descriptions point to the exaltation of music values shared with the U.S. public. The United States, from its initial intervention in the War of 1898, was reluctantly willing to grant Cuba independence once hostilities ceased (although it imposed the Platt Amendment to the Cuban Constitution, justifying future U.S. interventions on the island). The process was longer and more biased than many imagined. Still, some authors thought necessary to represent these new Cuban subjects as capable of self-government, although in need of support and tutelage. Louis Pérez captures this familiarity clearly: "Cuba revealed itself as a figment of the imagination, the Island inscribed itself deeply into the very certainties by which American arrived at a sense of themselves as a nationality and as a nation" (2). In sum, these descriptions destabilize the dichotomous narratives about the representation of Cubans in the United States and point to a more nuanced and ambiguous but closer relation that Cubans and Americans had developed over more than half a century before the War of 1898.

If the idea of a familiar Other is implicit in the aural descriptions made by colonial agents in Cuba, Puerto Rico, paradoxically, was depicted as sonorously alien. The variations between the descriptions were not the product of substantial differences in the two islands' music. The close musical relationships between Cuba and Puerto Rico's music since the nineteenth century are well documented (Manuel; Viera-Vargas; Allende-Goitía; Ruiz-Vega). The difference lies in who listened, how they interpreted what they heard, and how they wrote about it. U.S. colonial agents selected what to represent about Puerto Rican music to establish an Other, sufficiently different but willing to regenerate. That is to say, while the representations of Cuba built a familiar Other, capable of governing themselves but without the experience to do so, the musical representations of Puerto Ricans created a different, backward Other, willing to be guided in the arts of self-government. In both cases, however, an emerging imperial discourse justified the presence of the United States in the islands.

Notes

1. After two years of military rule, the U.S. Congress enacted the Foraker Act that established the island's first U.S. colonial administration structure in 1900. The Foraker Act stipulated an Executive Council composed of eleven members nominated by the President and ratified by the United States Senate. Of the eleven members, five were Puerto Ricans while the others were Americans. The act also created a House of Delegates and the post of Resident Commissioner. The Puerto Rican commissioner, nonetheless, did not have a vote on the U.S. House of Representatives. Seventeen years later, the U.S. Congress enacted the Jones Act that made Puerto Ricans U.S. citizens. However, granting U.S. citizenship did not mean a substantial change in the colonial relationship between the United States and Puerto Rico.

2. In December 1916, Thomas Terry of the Victor Recording Company was in charge of the second recording session on the island. On 10 January 1917, Manuel Tizol's Orquesta Azul recorded ten danzas, two pasodobles, and two danzones. During those days, Terry also recorded the Banda de Regimiento de Puerto Rico, the Rafael Hernández Orchestra (three danzones), the tenor Francisco "El Paisa" Quiñones, Arguinzoni's Orchestra, the San Juan Municipal Band, Germán Hernández's Trio, and a women's chorus performing Virgilio Dávila's school songs. Puerto Rican danzas, Cuban danzones, and other Westernized art musical forms tended to dominate the music production in these early recording sessions. The repertoire choices corresponded to the attitude of deference held toward Western forms of art shared by both trained musicians and the recording industry's initial commercial interest. Rafael Duchesne in an interview with Gustavo Batista recalls how Tizol's Orchestra enlightened the musical taste of Puerto Ricans with great classical music: "I will tell you I learned to love good music with Tizol because Tizol played Beethoven's Fifth Symphony . . . I tell you that it seemed like a theater, people with a tremendous fervor listening to that band" (Duchesne). This repertoire was also standard in the programs announced in *La Democracia* for their weekly retretas in the plaza Baldorioty in San Juan. For example, in November 1915, the Banda Municipal announced for the upcoming concert the following program: "Pasodoble Andalúz, Fantasia of the Operetta, La Mascotte, rigaudon of the operetta, Donna Juanita, One-step, Hezekiah by Don Richardson, and the Cuban Danzón, Bombín de Barreto" ("Concierto Banda Municipal").

3. These typical ensembles, like the Verdadera Juventud or Municipal Bands, required lavish budgets, not always in line with the fiscal priorities of most mayors. This was evident in 1911, for example, when the Attorney General of Puerto Rico prohibited public funds to support municipal bands (Malavet Vega 87). It was a mortal blow for the traditional bands supported by the State during the Spanish regime. However, they did not entirely disappear and continued to perform, although in a limited form, in Sunday retretas at the principal plazas.

4. Words and music by Charles K. Harris, arranged by Joseph Clauder, published in 1891 by Chas. K. Harris, New York City.

5. In opposition to a musical scene considered White, the descriptions of Black musical spaces included drums associated with the Afro-descendant population, antiphonal choirs, and a specific description of performers and participants as Black. Here is an example: "A negro band began suddenly to play, and in the music alone I immediately found the potent actuality of danger. I was without the knowledge necessary to the disentangling of its elements: there were fiddles and horns and unnatural kettle drums, and an instrument made from a long gourd, with a parallel scoring for the scrape of a stick. The music was first a shock, then an exasperation hardly to be borne, but finally it assumed a rhythm maddening beyond measure. It was Africa and something else" (Hergesheimer 213).

Works Cited

Allende-Goitía, Noel. "La Habana Artística": Cuba como plaza de trabajo y lanzamiento artístico para los músicos puertorriqueños, 1890–1940." *Revista Cruce*, 16 Feb. 2020, pp. 34–43.

Anazagasty, José. "'The Music Is Weird': American Texts and the Devaluation of Puerto Rican Music 1898–1926." *Americana: E-Journal of American Studies in Hungary*, vol. 6, no. 1, 2010, americanaejournal.hu/vol6no1/anazagasty.

Anazagasty Rodríguez, José, and Mario R. Cancel. *Porto Rico: Hecho en Estados Unidos*. Editora Educación Emergente, 2011.

Attali, Jacques. *Noise*. U of Minnesota P, 1985.

Blythe, Marion. *An American Bride in Porto Rico*. Fleming H. Revell Company, 1911. *EBSCOhost*, search.ebscohost.com/login.aspx?direct=true&db=edshtl&AN=edshtl.MIU01.102786545&site=eds-live.

Boyce, W. D. *The Hawaiian Islands and Porto Rico, Illustrated*. Rand, McNally, & Company, 1914. Retrieved from the Library of Congress, lccn.loc.gov/15000174.

———. *United States Dependencies; Cuba, Dominican Republic, Haiti, Panama Republic, Illustrated*. Rand, McNally & Company, 1914. Retrieved from the Library of Congress, lccn.loc.gov/15002095.

Bryan, William S., editor. *Our Islands and Their People, as Seen with Camera and Pencil*. Thompson Publishing, 1899.

Callejo Ferrer, Fernando. *Música y músicos puertorriqueños*. Editorial Coquí, 1971.

Campbell, Reau. *Around the Corner to Cuba*. C. G. Crawford, 1889.

Charnon-Deutsch, Lou. "Cartoons and the Politics of Masculinity in the Spanish and

American Press during the War of 1898." *Revista Prisma Social*, no. 13, Dec. 2014, pp. 109–48. *EBSCOhost*, search.ebscohost.com/login.aspx?direct=true&db=edb&AN=100464769&site=eds-live.

Carroll, Henry K. *Report on the Island of Puerto Rico: Its Population, Civil Government, Commerce, Industries, Production, Roads, Tariff, and Currency, with Recommendations*. Government Printing Office, 1899.

"Concierto banda municipal." *La Democracia*, 15 Nov. 1915, p. 8.

"Cubans vs. Porto Ricans." *New Republic*, vol. 58, no. 749, Apr. 1929, p. 230. EBSCOhost, search.ebscohost.com/login.aspx?direct=true&db=eue&AN=15278655&site=eds-live.

Dinwiddie, William. *Puerto Rico: Its Conditions and Possibilities*. 1899. Fundación Puertorriqueña de las Humanidades, 2005.

Domínguez, Virginia R. "When the Enemy Is Unclear: US Censuses and Photographs of Cuba, Puerto Rico, and the Philippines from the Beginning of the 20th Century." *Comparative American Studies*, vol. 5, no. 2, 2007, pp. 173–203. doi: 10.1179/147757007x204448.

Duany, Jorge. "Cómo representar a los nuevos sujetos colonizados." *La Torre: Revista de la Universidad de Puerto Rico* (third series), vol. 14, nos. 53–54, 2009, pp. 1–22.

———. *The Puerto Rican Nation on the Move: Identities on the Island and in the United States*. U of North Carolina P, 2002.

Duchesne, Rafael. Interview by Gustavo Batista. April 1980.

Evered, Kyle T. "Fostering Puerto Rico: Representations of Empire and Orphaned Territories during the Spanish-American War." *Historical Geography*, vol. 34, 2006, pp. 109–36. *EBSCOhost*, search.ebscohost.com/login.aspx?direct=true&db=hus&AN=509841881&site=eds-live.

Fogg, E. Review of *Industrial Cuba* and *Commercial Cuba*. *Journal of Political Economy*, vol. 7, no. 4, 1899, pp. 571–74. *EBSCOhost*, search.ebscohost.com/login.aspx?direct=true&db=edo&AN=ejs38995498&site=eds-live.

Forbes-Lindsay, Charles Harcourt Ainslie. *America's Insular Possessions*. The J. C. Winston Co., 1906.

Fowles, George Milton. *Down in Porto Rico*. Revised ed. Eaton & Mains, 1910.

García, Gervasio Luis. "I Am the Other: Puerto Rico in the Eyes of North Americans, 1898." *The Journal of American History*, vol. 87, no. 1, 2000, pp. 39–64. *JSTOR*, www.jstor.org/stable/2567915. Accessed 5 Nov 2020.

George, Marian Minnie. *A Little Journey to Puerto Rico: For Intermediate and Upper Grades*. A. Flanagan Company, 1900.

Greenbaum, Susan D. *More Than Black: Afro-Cubans in Tampa*. UP of Florida, 2002.

Hall, Arthur D. *Porto Rico: Its History, Products and Possibilities*. Street & Smith, Inc., 1898.

Hergesheimer, Joseph. *San Cristóbal de La Habana*. Knopf, 1927.

Hill, Robert T. *Cuba and Porto Rico, with the Other Islands of the West Indies: Their Topography, Climate, Flora, Products, Industries, Cities, People, Political Conditions, Etc.* The Century Co., 1898.

Hoffnung-Garskof, Jesse. *Racial Migrations: New York City and the Revolutionary Politics of the Spanish Caribbean, 1850–1902*. Princeton UP, 2019.

Kenney, William H. *Recorded Music in American Life: The Phonograph and Popular Memory, 1890–1945.* Oxford UP, 2003.

Malavet Vega, Pedro. *De las bandas al Trío Borinquen (1900–1927).* Ediciones Lorena, 2002.

Manuel, Peter L. "Puerto Rican Music and Cultural Identity: Creative Appropriation of Cuban Sources from Danza to Salsa." *Ethnomusicology*, vol. 38, no. 2, 1994, pp. 249–80.

Matos-Rodríguez, Félix. "Their Islands and Our People: U.S. Writing about Puerto Rico, 1898–1920." *CENTRO: Centro de Estudios Puertorriqueños*, vol. 11, no. 1, 1999, pp. 32–49.

Mixer, Knowlton. *Porto Rico: History and Conditions Social, Economic, and Political.* Macmillan, 1926.

Morris, Charles. *Our Island Empire: A Hand-book of Cuba, Porto Rico, Hawaii, and the Philippine Islands.* J. B. Lippincott Company, 1899.

The New York Times. "Light-Hearted Porto Rico; Simple Pleasures that Amuse the Natives at San Juan." 20 May 1900, p. 12, www.nytimes.com/1900/05/20/archives/light-hearted-porto-rico-simple-pleasures-that-amuse-the-natives-at.html.

———. "Puerto Rico's Autonomy." 5 Jan. 1897, www.nytimes.com/1897/01/05/archives/puerto-ricos-autonomy.html.

Northrop, Henry Davenport. *The New Century History of Our Country and Island Possessions from the Discovery of the American Continent to the Present Time.* National Pub. Co, 1900. Retrieved from the Library of Congress, lccn.loc.gov/00004761.

Norton, Albert James. *Norton's Complete Hand-Book of Havana and Cuba: Containing Full Information for the Tourist, Settler, and Investor; Also, an Account of the American Military Occupation, With . . . Illustrations and a Map of Havana.* Rand, McNally & Co., 1900.

Ober, Frederick A. *Puerto Rico and Its Resources.* Appleton and Co., 1899. Retrieved from the Library of Congress, lccn.loc.gov/99000077.

Pérez, Lisandro. *Sugar, Cigars, and Revolution: The Making of Cuban New York.* NYU P, 2018.

Pérez, Louis A. Jr. *Cuba in the American Imagination: Metaphor and the Imperial Ethos.* U of North Carolina P, 2008. JSTOR, www.jstor.org/stable/10.5149/9780807886946_perez. Accessed 5 Nov. 2020.

Platt, Orville H. "Our Relation to the People of Cuba and Porto Rico." *The ANNALS of the American Academy of Political and Social Science*, vol. 18, no. 1, 1901, pp. 145–159, doi:10.1177/000271620101800108.

Poyo, Gerald E. *Exile and Revolution: José D. Poyo, Key West, and Cuban Independence.* UP of Florida, 2014.

Ruiz-Vega, Omar. "New York, Puerto Rico and Cuba's Latin Music Scenes and the Emergence of Salsa Music: A Comparative Analysis." *CENTRO: Journal of the Center for Puerto Rican Studies*, vol. 32, no. 2, 2020, pp. 4–52.

Santiago-Valles, Kelvin A. *"Subject People" and Colonial Discourses: Economic Transformation and Social Disorder in Puerto Rico, 1898–1947.* State U of New York P, 1994.

Spurr, David. *The Rhetoric of Empire: Colonial Discourse in Journalism, Travel Writing, and Imperial Administration.* Post-Contemporary Interventions. Duke UP, 1993.

Stoever, Jennifer Lynn. *The Sonic Color Line: Race and the Cultural Politics of Listening.* Postmillennial Pop, 17. Reprint. NYU P, 2016.

Sublette, Ned. *Cuba and Its Music.* Chicago Review Press, 2004.

Terry, Thomas Philip. *Terry's Guide to Mexico: The New Standard Guidebook to the Mexican Republic, with Chapters on Cuba, the Bahama Islands, and the Ocean Routes to Mexico; with 2 Maps and 27 Plans.* Revised ed. Houghton, Mifflin Company [etc.], 1923.

Thompson, Lanny. "'Estudiarlos, juzgarlos y gobernarlos': Conocimiento y poder en el archipiélago imperial estadounidense." *La nación soñada: Cuba, Puerto Rico y Filipinas ante el 98*, edited by Consuelo Naranjo et al. Ediciones Doce Calles, 1995, pp. 685–93.

———. *Imperial Archipelago: Representation and Rule in the Insular Territories under U.S. Dominion after 1898.* U of Hawai'i P, 2010.

Van Middeldyk, R. A., and Martin Grove Brumbaugh. *The History of Puerto Rico, from the Spanish Discovery to the American Occupation.* D. Appleton and Co., 1903. Retrieved from the Library of Congress, www.loc.gov/item/03008353/.

Viera-Vargas, Hugo R. "A son de clave: La dimensión afrodiaspórica de la puertorriqueñidad en la música popular, 1929–1940." *Latin American Music Review*, vol. 38, no. 1, 2017, pp. 57–82.

Waterbury Evening Democrat. "Puerto Rican Music." 28 Nov. 1898, chroniclingamerica.loc.gov/lccn/2016270503/1898-11-28/ed-1/seq-1.

White, Trumbull. *Our New Possessions: A Graphic Account, Descriptive and Historical, of the Tropic Islands of the Sea Which Have Fallen under Our Sway* . . . National Educational Union, 1898.

13

The Musical Impact of the Mariel Boatlift on the Latin Music Scene of New York City and Interethnic Collaboration among Puerto Ricans and Cubans

BENJAMIN LAPIDUS

Cubans and Puerto Ricans have been collaborating musically throughout history, yet their collaborations were greatly impacted in new ways by the Mariel boatlift of 1980. Among the roughly 125,000 people who made the perilous journey from the port of Mariel in Cuba to Key West in the United States between April and September 1980, was an important cohort of musicians and dancers whose musical contributions and legacy, both in New York City and the United States, have been mostly omitted from narratives concerning Cuban music or the development of Latin music in New York City. Existing scholarship on Cuban and Latin music in the United States has mostly been limited to the period before and immediately after 1959 and has overlooked several important musicians who brought the newest Cuban musical information to the United States in the late twentieth century. This chapter discusses the immediate musical impact of the Mariel boatlift by examining some of the dancers and musicians who arrived in New York City at that time, such as Orlando "Puntilla" Ríos, Felipe García Villamil, Manuel Martínez Olivera (*El llanero solitario*, "the Lone Ranger"), Roberto Borrell, Rita Macías, and Xiomara Rodríguez. The musical activities of these and other musicians would have long-term effects on the folkloric and Latin popular dance music scenes in New York and the greater United States, not only as performers but in many cases also as teachers for subsequent generations of Cuban and non-Cuban musicians. These musicians worked with and taught many Puerto Rican musicians based in New York City; their collaborations contributed greatly to a thriving and dynamic music scene dedicated to both secular and religious folkloric music as well as popular styles. These collaborations also produced organic hybrid forms of both Cuban and Puerto Rican genres. This group of Cuban artists who arrived in 1980 would also serve as important points of connection for Cuban musicians and dancers who would arrive after them in the early 1990s, in the era of the *balseros* (rafters), and who would fit into established networks of Cuban and Puerto Rican musicians. Through ethnography, recordings, and video examples, this study provides an analysis of an overlooked chapter of musical history.[1]

Afro-Cuban Music in Postrevolutionary Cuba and the U.S. Reception

The so-called *Marielitos* were caught between two competing narratives. The Cuban government shaped a narrative that the exodus from Mariel purged Cuba of criminals, homosexuals, and other "undesirables," including a surreptitious dumping of the institutionalized population. At the same time, the U.S. media and earlier Cuban arrivals stigmatized the *Marielitos* for their "Blackness," their criminality, and the belief that they had willingly lived in Cuba through the Revolution, making them communists. Ramón Grosfoguel and Chloé S. Georas described the phenomenon of Cuban Mariel arrivals being "Puerto Ricanized in New York City and 'African Americanized' in Miami ... [they faced] racial discrimination and suffered marginalization in the labor market ... they became part of the colonial immigrants living a social process similar to the colonial/racial subjects of the U.S. empire" (Grosfoguel and Georas 97). Nancy Mirabal wrote that the arrival of Mariel Cubans, and subsequent waves such as the *balseros*, "reconfigured a language of race, sexuality, culture, and gender that was not always understood or employed community making among Cuban exiles" (Mirabal 203). But the musicians and practitioners of Afro-Cuban music and cultural traditions had additional reasons for leaving during the Mariel boatlift that were tied to the complexity of identity as well as freedom of religious and cultural expression.

In the early years of the Cuban Revolution, Afro-Cuban religions were seen as primitive, sick, and anti-Marxist; the State prohibited artists who sang songs with religious references from performing them (Moore 213). Nevertheless, numerous folkloric ensembles were founded and, by the late

1970s, Afro-Cuban folklore was worked into the musical educational system through university ensembles such as the *Conjunto Folclórico Universitario* (Díaz 2019). The music was also seen and heard in weekly television and radio programs, albeit in a limited capacity on television shows such as *Arte y folclor* and Radio Cadena Habana's radio show dedicated to rumba (Díaz 2019). There was also a shift toward documenting these traditions on record and film, despite the ambivalence of their affiliation with religious practices and their being viewed negatively by the Cuban government at that moment in time. Román Orozco and Natalia Bolívar explore the complicated history of the relationship between the Cuban State and Afro-Cuban religion in their book, *Cubasanta: Comunistas, santeros y cristianos en la isla de Fidel Castro*, and convey the difficulties that some practitioners of Afro-Cuban religions faced in the postrevolutionary period prior to the Mariel boatlift (Orozco and Bolívar 350–92). This would change significantly in the period following Mariel, particularly in the early 1990s, when religious practices of all kinds were given new official protection from discrimination by the State.

Folklore and Religious Knowledge in New York

Katherine Dunham documented how the immediate effect of the Cuban exodus in 1959 strengthened the orisha-based religious community in New York City and exposed many people to the tradition (Moreno Vega 607). The same effect happened on a larger scale as a direct result of the Mariel arrivals, which steered the tradition of Afro-Cuban musical folklore and ritual music in New York City and beyond. Two important contributors to this phenomenon were Felipe García Villamil and Orlando "Puntilla" Ríos. These two musicians represented different traditions and lineages, one being from Matanzas and the other Havana, respectively. Both were active performers in Cuba before reestablishing their careers in New York as performers, educators, and ritual drummers.

García Villamil was born in Matanzas in 1931; he is a *batá* drummer, drum maker, *babalawo* (priest), *abakuá*, and *palero* (both terms referring to Afro-Cuban religions) who had organized his own group in 1970, called Emikeké (small group) (Vélez 79). Once established in New York City in 1983, he got his *aña* (sacred drum talisman) to New York and was thus able to play his own consecrated drums (Vélez 112). Through various ups and downs, García Villamil eventually started teaching and formed his own group, once again calling it Emikeké. He was the only Cuban in the group;

the others were North Americans and Puerto Ricans (Vélez 114–15). García Villamil's career also shows how the arrival of *Marielitos* in New York City impacted other Afro-Cuban and Afro-Caribbean religious practices in New York, such as *palo* and *espiritismo*, practiced largely by Puerto Ricans, through exchanges of information and rituals (Vélez 136). However, because García Villamil was from Matanzas, he experienced being a "minority within the *Santería* community" in the United States, since the majority of "the *Santería* practices that have developed in the United States among Cubans mainly follow the Havana tradition" (Vélez 109). His contemporary, fellow ritual drummer and *Marielito*, Orlando "Puntilla" Ríos, was much more successful and impactful among Puerto Rican musicians.

Ríos (1947–2008) was a supremely talented drummer and a gifted singer who had been active in Cuba as an *abakuá*, a *rumbero*, and as a *batalero*. He was a student of the famed drummer Jesús Pérez and had also learned with Pancho Quinto (Francisco Hernández Mora). "Puntilla" was a percussion teacher with the title of *auxiliar técnico docente* (assistant instructor) at the National School for the Arts (ENA, for its Spanish acronym) from 1971–78 and performed in the best venues in Havana, including the Tropicana Club and the Hotel Riviera (*Cubaencuentro*). As discussed in the film *Rumba Clave: Blen, Blen Blen*, he was also the musical director of the *comparsa* group, *Los Dandys de Belén*. Possessing deep knowledge of *arará* (Cuban Dahomey-based) musical and religious traditions, he single-handedly transformed the Yoruba-based orisha ritual music scene in New York City and the United States through his playing and teaching. Prior to Puntilla's arrival, the *ocha* (Santería) drumming tradition was largely secret and elder players such as Julito Collazo, Francisco Aguabella, and Carlos "Patato" Valdés guarded their knowledge, only teaching a select few musicians in New York City. They took issue with "Puntilla" teaching *batá*. Prior to these drummers, Chano Pozo is acknowledged as the first to have played, sung, taught, and recorded rumba as it really was in 1947, as heard on the seminal SMC recordings made in New York City. In many ways, Ríos would parallel Pozo in his time in New York City, but he would largely surpass him.

Word of Puntilla's arrival in New York City spread quickly. In 1980, a young Nuyorican drummer named Felix Sanabria went to what he remembered as a brief incarnation of the New Rican Village at East 116th Street and Second Avenue, where he first saw Puntilla at a gig with Eugenio "Totico" Arango (1934–2011). Prior to this, Sanabria recalled his upstairs neighbor Danny Santos running up to his apartment one day after seeing a Coke-bottle glasses-wearing Puntilla singing and playing at the Central

Park rumba. At the New Rican Village, an important venue for Puerto Rican theatre, music, and politics, Sanabria recalled seeing Totico sing his rumbas and when Puntilla got on the *quinto* (a small conga drum) and also sang for *Eleguá*, Totico was pacing up and down behind him completely stunned, with a facial expression that was wondering where this guy came from (Sanabria 2014). Totico represented the old guard of Afro-Cuban music, having come to the United States in 1959 and recording in the jazz and Latin realms. However, he was best known in New York and abroad for one seminal rumba recording called *Patato and Totico*. This record had been the gold standard of rumba for New York musicians since its release in 1967 and is a classic. The other participants on this recording included Israel "Cachao" López (bass), Arsenio Rodríguez (*tres*), Mario "Papaito" Muñoz (percussion), Carlos "Patato" Valdés (percussion), Juan "Curva" Dreke, Hector and Mario Cadavieco, Francisco "Panchín" Valdez, Tony Mayarí, and Virgilio Martí. Many of these Cuban musicians collaborated with Puerto Rican musicians who were their contemporaries and mentored younger Puerto Rican musicians. Patato was an important drummer in Cuba who had worked with Conjunto Casino and carried his fame with him to New York City when he arrived in the early 1950s. He can even be seen teaching Brigitte Bardot how to dance mambo in the 1956 film *And God Created Woman*. Totico's reaction to Puntilla that fabled evening was telling of the musical changes that were ahead as well as being a portent of collaboration among subsequent arrivals of Cuban musicians with those established in New York and the United States.

Cuba y Puerto Rico son ...

While older established Afro-Cuban and non-Cuban musicians might have felt competition from the newcomers from Cuba, the younger Puerto Rican musicians sought them out for lessons. One of Puntilla's best students and an excellent musician who performed and recorded with Mongo Santamaría was Eddy Rodríguez (1954–2019), who is purported to have sold his blood to pay for classes with Puntilla. Felix Sanabria received his aña ritual on 21 September 1985 and around the same time he won a $2,500–3,000 grant to study with Puntilla. For young Nuyorican drummers like Sanabria, Abraham Rodríguez Jr., Eddie Bobè, Alberto Serrano (1964–2018), Bobby Sanabria, and others who did not go to Cuba until much later in life, the arrival of the Mariel Cubans "was their way of going to Cuba" (Sanabria

7 Feb. 2018). With these young Puerto Ricans and other students, Puntilla recorded several important folkloric recordings in New York City that would supplant the classic *Patato y Totico* rumba album. These recordings included *From La Habana to New York* (1983) as well as various other collaborations. Many of Puntilla's Puerto Rican students would go on to lead their own groups and document their unique musical vision, combining their experiences as New Yorkers steeped in Cuban tradition but also reflecting their own personalities. These include Sanabria's *Los Afortunados*, Bobè's *Central Park Rumba*, Abraham Rodríguez Jr.'s *Los Inolvidables*, and Emilio Barreto's *Santisimo*. As Kenneth Schweitzer writes in "The Cuban Aña Fraternity: Strategies for Cohesion," "Puntilla began to send U.S. American drummers to Cuba to learn how to play with Pancho and to be sworn to aña with Pancho and Enrique" (Schweitzer 175–76).

The 1981 album, *Totico y sus Rumberos*, pays tribute to *Patato y Totico*, but it marks the first recording with the old and new generation of New York City *rumberos*, indicating the passing of the drumming torch. Beyond Puntilla's sublime singing and drumming, the participation of Totico, and several young Puerto Rican New Yorkers such as Andy (1951–2020) and Jerry González (1949–2018), and Abraham Rodríguez Jr., mark a new course that included Afro-Cuban ritual music as well as doo-wop. Abraham Rodríguez Jr. is a Nuyorican vocalist and musician who grew up singing jazz, soul, doo-wop, and both Cuban and Puerto Rican music. The result of his combination with the Cuban drumming tradition is a unique New York doo-wop rumba masterpiece arrangement of the 1962 Don and Juan song "What's Your Name?" that highlights the best of these traditions and Latin music in New York unlike any previous recording. *Totico y sus Rumberos* features many important Puerto Rican and non-Cuban drummers whose contributions to the scene are preserved for all of history. These Puerto Rican and non-Cuban drummers would go on to share their drumming and vocal talents with many musical groups and recordings, as well as tour internationally as acknowledged masters of the Afro-Cuban ritual and folkloric traditions.

The *Marielitos* as Teachers

Some of the new musical information from Cuba began making it through the folkloric community at formal performances and rehearsals, but also at regularly occurring informal gatherings. For Sanabria, Mariel arrivals, such as the choreographer, vocalist, visual artist, and actor Alberto Morgan (1939–2020), danced for the orisha Babalú Ayé better than anyone he had ever seen (Sanabria 2014). Morgan can be seen in the role of Ángel in the 1964 film *Soy Cuba/I Am Cuba* and since arriving in New York in 1980 he worked as an actor and visual artist (Sánchez 2020). Morgan is listed as a performer on Daniel Ponce's seminal recording *New York Now*, alongside other Mariel *rumberos* such as Francisco Rigores. For Sanabria, Enrique "Kike" Dreke was another Mariel arrival who spent a lot of time mentoring him and other young New York drummers. Dreke came during the Mariel boatlift and joined his brother Juan "Curva," who can be heard singing on the *Patato y Totico* record (1967). Kike Dreke was extremely acrobatic and can be seen dancing a *rumba columbia* expertly from 3:36 to 4:38 in the 1960 Mario Gallo-directed film *Al compás de Cuba*. I met Dreke around 2000 and he was still in good shape. Sanabria also remembered another great Cuban folklore dancer who arrived during Mariel, named Narciso.

While Sanabria studied the orisha tradition formally with Puntilla, he and his peers also learned the deeper intricacies of rumba with Manuel Martínez Olivera a.k.a. *El llanero solitario*. Prior to his arrival in New York, Martínez is acknowledged as being responsible for coining the term *guarapachangueo* upon listening to the rumba group, *Los Chinitos*, and qualifying their unique style. Martínez was born in Marianao in Havana on 1 January 1932, and his repertoire of rumbas stretched back to songs he had learned as a child as well as some of his own compositions. He spent much of his youth in Matanzas learning the local traditions. Martínez was also a first cousin of Carlos "Patato" Valdés. I was lucky to perform with Martínez regularly from 1997 to 1999 and later from 2000 to 2003 as part of Sanabria's folkloric group *Los Afortunados* and always enjoyed his singing and musicianship immensely. *El llanero solitario* can be seen singing with a version of *Los Afortunados* made up of Skip Burney, Gene Golden, Felix Sanabria, Alberto Serrano, Paula Ballan (1945–2020), Ernest "Chico" Álvarez, and others in many YouTube videos (Video 1 *Los Afortunados* 2). Martínez Olivera died on 29 January 2010, yet his legacy in the New York City rumba community remains.

This group of Nuyorican musicians also spent time under the tutelage of master dancer choreographer, Roberto Borrell. Prior to his arrival in the United States, Borrell had been a dancer in the *Conjunto Folklórico Nacional de Cuba* (1968–70) and led his own folkloric music and dance ensemble called Kubatá (Borrell 2018). Once he arrived in the United States in 1980,

Borrell became active in the Cuban folkloric music scene and formed another version of his group Kubatá, which included Sanabria and his future wife Susan Richardson, Abraham Rodríguez Jr., and other New Yorkers in Cuban religious and folkloric music.

In a 1982 video of Borrell's group rehearsing, one can see the celebrated Nuyorican drummers and educators Frankie Malabe and Louis Bauzó ("Ensayos Groupo Kubata 1982 Part 1"). In another YouTube video from a 1980s performance by *Los Afortunados*, Borrell can be seen dancing the Abakuá *ireme* (masked dancer), however, without the traditional costume ("Los Afortunados–Abakua"). While in New York, one important group that Borrell recorded with was *Los Soneros*, which featured the flamboyant vocalist Fernando Lavoy, another Mariel arrival, also known as *La nariz que canta* ("the singing nose") for his large nose. After recording and performing popular music with several important New York City–based Latin music groups, Borrell eventually settled in California and has continued teaching Cuban music and dance. For a Nuyorican like Sanabria, the Cubans who came in the Mariel exodus mixed very well with the Puerto Ricans, African Americans, and Americans in general. And they opened the doors for Cuban musicians who would come for the next thirty years.

It was not a one-way street in terms of musical exchanges. Other musicians who came in the Mariel boatlift and who were later associated with the Grammy™-nominated Afro-Cuban folklore group *Raíces Habaneras* included percussionist Vicente Sánchez as well as dancers Xiomara Rodríguez and Rita Macías. These two women went on to teach many students to dance for the orishas, but they have also danced with Afro-Puerto Rican folklore groups. As Rodríguez explained in the documentary *Rumba Clave: Blen, Blen Blen*:

> Estoy muy agradecida de mi profesión. He visto frutos de todas las personas que yo he enseñado a bailar. Que yo sé que hay muchas que han aprendido sobre todo los bailes de los orishas ... Yo vine en el 80 por el Mariel ... Yo bailo bomba, olvídate al estilo cubano, pero lo bailo, porque lo siento. La bomba para mí es como la colombia. Te estoy hablando de cosas que nadie sabe. ¿Es o no es?

> (I am very grateful for my profession. I have seen the blossoming of all my students. Many women have learned to dance to the orishas ... I came in 1980 through Mariel ... I dance the [Puerto Rican]

bomba in a Cuban style, but I dance it because I feel it. *Bomba* for me is like Columbia [a fast style of Cuban rumba]. I'm talking to you about things that no one knows. Am I right, or am I right?)

Another fixture for informal musical exchanges between *Marielitos* and Cubans in general with Puerto Ricans and other musicians has been the Central Park Rumba. Filmmaker Arístedes Falcón Paradí has documented some of these exchanges in his film *Rumba Clave: Blen, Blen Blen*, and scholars such as Berta Jottar and Lisa Maya Knauer have also explored these themes in their work on the history of the Central Park rumba and, more generally, the Afro-Cuban drumming community in New York City (Jottar, "Central Park Rumba" and "Zero Tolerance"; Knauer).

Conclusion

In my recent book *New York and the International Sound of Latin Music, 1940–1990*, I discuss other aspects of the impact of the *Marielitos* in popular music, including performance spaces, the SAR/Guajiro record label, and its numerous LPs that featured Mariel musicians such as Fernando Lavoy, Gerardo "Taboada" Fernández, Juan González, and others alongside Puerto Ricans and Cuban musicians who arrived even before the Revolution, such as Cándido Camero, Alfredo Valdés Jr. and Sr., and Alfredo "Chocolate" Armenteros. I also show how some of the *Marielitos* such as Gabriel Machado, Ignacio Berroa, and Daniel Ponce worked in jazz bands led by Lionel Hampton, Dizzy Gillespie, Herbie Hancock, and other jazz and pop luminaries, as well as numerous groups that fit under the umbrella of salsa and merengue. Starting in musical groups organized in refugee camps at Fort Chafee and Fort McCoy, many Mariel arrivals entertained their fellow arrivals and later became important teachers of Cuban folkloric music and dance who influenced a generation of Puerto Rican and non-Cuban performers. These musicians and dancers also provided Cuban and non-Cuban practitioners of Afro-Cuban religions, particularly Puerto Ricans, with complete and up-to-date information on ritual and musical performance practice, whereas earlier Cuban arrivals would have shared this information with only a select few in the non-Cuban Latino community.

Note

1. Another version of portions of this chapter appears in my book *New York and the International Sound of Latin Music, 1940–1990*.

Works Cited

Cubaencuentro. "Fallece el conocido percusionista Orlando 'Puntilla' Ríos." 14 Aug. 2008, accessed 21 Feb. 2018, https://www.cubaencuentro.com/cultura/noticias/fallece-el-conocido-percusionista-orlando-puntilla-rios-103846.

Díaz, Román. Personal Interview. 20 June 2019.

Grosfoguel, Ramón, and Chloé S. Georas. "Latino Caribbean Diasporas in New York." *Mambo Montage: The Latinization of New York City*, edited by Agustín Laó-Montes and Arlene Dávila. Columbia UP, 2001, pp. 97–118.

Jottar, Berta. "Central Park Rumba: Nuyorican Identity and the Return to African Roots." *Centro Journal*, vol. 23, no. 1, 2011, pp. 5–29.

———. "From Central Park, Rumba with Love!" *Voices: Journal of New York Folklore*, vol. 37, 2011. http://www.nyfolklore.org/pubs/voic37-1-2/rumba.html.

———. "Zero Tolerance and Central Park Rumba Cabildo Politics." *Liminalities: A Journal of Performance Studies*, vol. 5, no. 4, 2009, pp. 1–24.

Knauer, Lisa Maya. "Audiovisual Remittances and Transnational Subjectivities." *Cuba in the Special Period: Culture and Ideology in the 1990s*, edited by Ariana Hernández-Reguant. Palgrave Macmillan, 2009, pp. 159–77.

Lapidus, Benjamin. *New York and The International Sound of Latin Music, 1940–1990*. UP of Mississippi, 2021.

Mirabal, Nancy Raquel. "Scripting Race, Finding Place: African-Americans, Afro-Cubans, and the Diasporic Imaginary in the United States." *Neither Enemies nor Friends: Latinos, Blacks, Afro-Latinos*, edited by Anani Dzidzienyo and Suzanne Oboler. Palgrave Macmillan, 2005, pp. 189–207.

Moore, Robin D. *Music and Revolution: Cultural Change in Socialist Cuba*. U of California P, 2006.

Moreno Vega, Marta. "The Yoruba Tradition Comes to New York City." *Kaiso! Writings by and about Katherine Dunham*, edited by VèVè A. Clark and Sara E. Johnson. U of Wisconsin P, 2005, pp. 603–11.

Sanabria, Felix. Personal Interview. 2 May 2014.

———. Personal Interview. 7 Feb. 2018.

Schweitzer, Kenneth. "The Cuban Aña Fraternity: Strategies for Cohesion." *The Yoruba God of Drumming: Transatlantic Perspectives on the Wood That Talks*, edited by Amanda Villepastour. UP of Mississippi, 2015, pp. 171–91.

Vélez, María Teresa. *Drumming for The Gods: The Life and Times of Felipe García Villamil, Santero, Palero, and Abakuá*. Temple UP, 2000.

Discography

Emilio Barreto. *Santisimo*, Luz Production, 1996.
Eddie Bobè. *Central Park Rumba*, Piranha, 1999.
Fernando Lavoy y Los Soneros. *Fernando Lavoy y Los Soneros*, SAR, 1982.
Patato and Totico. *Patato and Totico*, Verve, 1967.
Ponce, Daniel. *New York Now*, Celluloid, 1983.
Puntilla. *From La Habana to New York*, Puntilla Folkloric Records, Co., 1983.
Raíces Habaneras. *Raíces Habaneras*, Latin Jazz, 2010.
Ríos, Orlando Puntilla. *From La Habana to New York*, Puntilla Folkloric, 1983.
Rodríguez, Jr., Abraham. *Cachimba Inolvidable: Son Borin Cubano*, Relief, 2008.
Rosewoman, Michele, and New Yor-Uba. *Hallowed*, 2019.
———. *30 Years: A Musical Celebration of Cuba in America*, Advance Dance Disques, 2013.
Totico y sus Rumberos. *Totico y sus Rumberos*, Montuno, 1981.

Film

Al compás de Cuba. Directed by Mario Gallo, 1960. https://youtu.be/QuI_aiDacRo. Accessed 8 Feb. 2018.
Rumba Clave: Blen, Blen Blen. Directed by Arístides Falcón Paradí. Paradí Productions, 2013.
Soy Cuba/I Am Cuba. Directed by Mikhail Kalatozov. Mosfilm/ICAIC, 1964.

Internet

"Los Afortunados—Abakua." *YouTube*, Accessed 20 Feb. 2018, https://youtu.be/ECZcdrmgdOo.
"Los Afortunados." Unreleased Rumba Gems, 1985, accessed 27 Oct. 2020, https://www.mixcloud.com/JR_Alvarez/unreleased-rumba-gems/.
"Ensayos Groupo Kubata 1982 Part 1." *YouTube*, accessed 20 Feb. 2018, https://www.youtube.com/watch?v=4eZFqyOoYM.
Sánchez, Gretchen. "Muere en Nueva Jersey el artista y religioso cubano Alberto Morgan." *Cibercuba*, 1 Oct. 2020, accessed 27 Oct. 2020, https://www.cibercuba.com/noticias/2020-01-10-u199370-e199370-s27315-muere-miami-alberto-morgan-artista-religioso-recordado.
Vadim, Roger, director. *And God Created Woman*. Cocinor, 195, accessed 7 Mar. 2018, https://www.youtube.com/watch?v=gaFTmZ4zQCU.
"Video 1 Los Afortunados 2." *YouTube*, accessed 20 Feb. 2018, http://www.robertoborrell.com/bio.html.

14

Allora and Calzadilla
Noise and the Politics of Sonic Decoloniality

ALAN WEST-DURÁN

Jacques Attali reminds us that the understanding of our world has been overwhelmingly visual, and he argues that beyond ocular legibility we also need audible comprehension, a poetics of listening. "Our science has always desired to monitor, measure, abstract, and castrate meaning, forgetting that life is full of noise and that death alone is silent: work noise, noise of man, and noise of beast. Noise bought, sold, or prohibited. Nothing essential happens in the absence of noise" (Attali 3). The term noise is rarely used in a positive sense. Opposed to both music and natural sound, noise is both unwanted and seen as a form of pollution. We often disparage music we do not like as noise, but any music played loud enough becomes noise. However, natural sounds can be unpleasant, whether the shriek of a bird, the roar of a volcano, even some people's voices. And with industrialization and technical innovation we have a panoply of sounds (and noises) that did not exist in the nineteenth century: jet and car engines, jackhammers, automatic weapons, atom bombs, and more benignly the beeping, buzzing, and humming of computers, laptops, and cellphones.

Noise is viewed as accidental, as resisting interpretation. In the work of Jennifer Allora and Guillermo Calzadilla (A & C), a collaborative duo of a U.S.-born and a Cuban-born visual artist who live in Puerto Rico, noise is often not entirely accidental and not only resisting interpretation but also interrupting it, shuffling it around, refashioning it.[1] Although their work has an undeniable visual power, it invites us to reconsider visual *and* aural forms of perception and knowing. As Salomé Voegelin observes, "Vision, by its nature, assumes a distance from the object . . ." and implies a "meta-position" that "enables an objectivity that presents itself as truth. Seeing is believing" (Voegelin xi, xii). Sound, in contrast, is both ephemeral and invisible. "Hearing is full of doubt: phenomenological doubt of the listener and himself hearing it. Hearing does not offer a meta-position; there is no place where I am not simultaneous with the heard. However far its source, the sound sits in my ear" (Voegelin xii). This implies an intersubjectivity between subject and work that is "generated concomitantly and [is] as transitory as each other" (Voegelin xii). Vision, with its ocularcentric bias, tends to theories, ideas, ideology, and truth, whereas hearing as enquiry produces affect, experience, and experimentation.

With these distinctions in mind, I would like to discuss A & C's Vieques videos (2003–10). (Vieques is an island municipality off the east coast of Puerto Rico.) Prior to these videos, the artists began with a series of installations—performances titled "Landmark" (1999, 2003, 2006), which were informed by the following question put forth by them: "How is land differentiated from other land by the way it is marked? Who decides what is worth preserving and what should be destroyed? What are strategies for reclaiming marked land? How does one articulate an ethics and politics of land use?" (qtd. in McGee, *Vieques Videos*, n.p.).

The "Landmark" used footprints in the sand; the soles making the imprint had messages, some of a political nature (*Ni una bomba más*; "Not a single more bomb"), others not. During this period A & C also made three videos, *Returning a Sound* (2004; 5:45 min), *Under Discussion* (2005; 6:25 min), and *Half Mast/Full Mast* (2010; 21:11 min). My focus will be on the first of the three. *Returning a Sound* was made after four years of protest (1999–2003) and civil disobedience finally removed the U.S. Navy's military presence from the eastern part of the island of Vieques, with some of the land being returned to the civilian population.

The resistance was sparked by the accidental killing of David Sanes, in April 1999, and many sectors of Puerto Rican society (churches, political parties, environmental activists) and the international community came together to end the militarization of the island, which the U.S. Navy had used for maneuvers and as a bomb site since 1941. The demilitarization was to be followed by decontamination (the land was strewn with lead, cadmium, depleted uranium, arsenic, and napalm), a costly and slow process so far, and future economic development, much of it to be centered on tourism.

To a degree, the video was celebrating the success of a grassroots effort that dislodged a powerful adversary, but the artists seem keenly aware that it was a precarious victory, with no assurance that the island's future would be unproblematic. Still, the video has a quiet, upbeat vibe to it. In the piece we follow Homar, an activist in the demilitarization struggle, who would be familiar to most Vieques residents, riding a moped throughout the island. The moped has a trumpet welded to the muffler. As the camera follows Homar's trajectory, all the jolts, bumps, revving, or spurts produce a unique sound that has been described as "the siren of an ambulance, Luigi Russolo's Futurist Intonarumori or experimental jazz" (McGee, *Vieques Videos*, n.p.).[2]

But more significantly, the sounds of the trumpet, which are almost weirdly mellow, are a counterpoint to a sound that Vieques endured for decades: bombs and explosions. The artists (A & C), in speaking about the piece, said they wanted to create a counter-anthem. When they investigated the etymological origins of that word they saw it also meant "returning a sound," hence the name of the piece. Instead of adopting the usual triumphal—and often militaristic—sound of conventional anthems, they opted for an anthem with little fanfare.

More broadly, *Returning a Sound* can be read as "noise," as a political statement that interrupts normal political discourses, especially those that are conventionally patriotic, and certainly counters the noise of militarization (helicopters, bombs, missiles, and amphibious landings). Visually, there are few reminders of the militarization or the opposition to it. We see a slogan, *Bieke o Muerte* ("Vieques or Death," Taíno spelling), early in the video, a sign by the U.S. military that warns people to stay away ("No Trespassing/Authorized Personnel Only/Danger Explosives"), and the magazine warehouses that stored ammunition for the war games conducted by the Navy. Aside from these moments, the lush countryside and tranquil roads of the island contribute to the serene rhythm of the film.

Anthems have religious roots, as they were part of the Christian mass where the congregation did not sing. Not surprisingly, in England anthems became associated with the monarchy, revealing in compositions such as "God Save the King!" the theological underpinnings of political sovereignty. (In Spanish, *himno nacional* captures this interrelationship perfectly.) And indeed, anthems are a way to uphold a civic religion, expressing national unity (as do flags); they are meant for the ritual of group settings. Nothing binds a crowd—small, medium, or huge—more than singing in unison to express its patriotic fervor.

For Jean-Jacques Rousseau, music's great power is its ability to move us. "Music, viewed as the language of emotions is both the symbol and the instrument of a utopian order in which the subjective emotion assists in the establishment of a collectivity" (Buch 26). Anthems are—with exceptions, like Puerto Rico's—music in which the text often exalts physical courage, sacrifice, and a willingness to take up arms for the national cause; witness "La Marseillaise," "The Star-Spangled Banner," and Cuba's "La Bayamesa" ("¡Al combate corred, bayameses! . . . Que morir por la patria es vivir." "People of Bayamo rush to battle! . . . To die for the homeland is to live"). In short, these are battle hymns.

The anthem in *Returning a Sound* has nothing epic or even remotely belligerent. Nothing is heroic about Homar on his moped, perhaps exemplifying the "ordinary heroism" we see in the characters (especially the women) in films by Ousmane Sembene. Moreover, no words are spoken, just the warbly trumpet sounds powered by the engine of the moped, and Homar is the only person seen. His solitary presence on the moped, along with the uneven sound of the trumpet, is a humble response, modestly celebratory, but without a hint of boastfulness or fanfare. It is an anthem without any intimation of violence, even as it commemorates overcoming the violence of an imperial power, all without firing a shot.

Might the video and its anthem be an allusion to Pierre Boulez's "Anthèmes I" (1992)?[3] The piece by the French composer is for a solo instrument, the violin, and begins with a seven-note figure, which is repeated several times; it also uses a repeated note over a glissando. Because of its title, some critics label the piece—over eight and a half minutes—solemn. I disagree. It is not solemn but intense and requires great virtuosity on the part of the violinist. Its repetitions, interruptions, and abrupt turns alternate with more balanced passages; in the score some measures have indications like *calme* and *regulier*. That calm and regularity echo the continuous sound on the trumpet by A & C's Vieques video. On the other hand, the differences between them are unmistakable: "Anthèmes I" is performed by a musician not a moped, so the changes and turns in the piece are much more dramatic (and deliberate) than the sounds in the video. A & C's work inhabits a sonorous plane between music and noise, questioning the boundaries between them, whereas Boulez's work leaves no doubt that this is a musical composition through and through, with a written score as well. When listening to the video, and specifically to the trumpet played (powered) by the moped, one is aware of a certain regularity in the sound of the instrument, even as it fluctuates. For John Cage, the trumpet would be voicing a musical composition, though it would be hard to argue that what we hear constitutes a melody, with a developing theme or even discernible notes.

Cage also said—I paraphrase—that when we are more attentive to the noise around us, we become more attentive to music. For Cage, what we normally consider noise can always become music (Novak and Sakakeeny 112, 125). On his part, Pierre Schaeffer (1910–95), pioneer of concrete music and author of *Treatise on Musical Objects*, argues for separating noise from its source in order to achieve a more concentrated form of listening, which he termed acousmatic (Schaeffer 15). A & C seem closer to Cage than Schaeffer, but their video does not use natural sound. It is the forward motion of the moped that "produces" the sound of the trumpet; what seems to be non-diegetic sound becomes diegetic to the maximum. Furthermore, the sound of the trumpet is not "background music"; it occupies a place almost more significant than the image. The trumpet is simultaneously noise, hymn, and soundtrack pushed to center stage, a wordless voice, an alarm, a celebration; in effect, a complex sign that invites multiple interpretations.

In trying to answer A & C's question about land and how it is marked, their Vieques videos deal crucially with the issue of sovereignty, be it at the real, symbolic, political, or spatial level. Beginning with political sovereignty, this clearly underlines Puerto Rico's colonial relationship with the United States, one that dates back to 1898. The video alludes to this history with the images of the naval presence, but also affirms one of the paradoxes of sovereignty: that it is "both a name for absolute power, and a name for political freedom" (Brown 53). The former is seen by the history of the Navy's dominion from 1941 to 2003, in almost strict Hobbesian sense. The latter would be represented by Homar and the trumpet as a political symbol moving through areas previously off limits as they were bombing ranges littered with ordinance (some still unexploded). The trumpet is the sound of autonomy. In her insightful book *Walled States, Waning Sovereignty*, Wendy Brown discusses the origins of sovereignty (both State and individual) and how the genesis of the social contract is related to the enclosure of land (or "marking" to use A & C's term). Carl Schmitt, referring to John Locke, writes, "the essence of political power is its jurisdiction over land" (qtd. in Brown 44). Schmitt uses Locke's comment to build his own concept of *Nomos*, which is "the production of political order through spatial orientation ... it is through the walling off of space from the common that sovereignty is born" (Brown 45).

Returning a Sound can be seen as a return to the common, and a return to the sovereign (in terms of popular sovereignty, not absolute power), underlined visually by the journey on moped, and aurally by the sound of the trumpet. It is tempting to label the trumpet a voice (of the people?) but the artists' gesture suggests otherwise. Like a voice, the trumpet is the sound of self- or collective assertion, but one that is suspicious of power and authority. It speaks, but not with univocal meaning. The trumpet resists interpretation; it becomes a sign without a fixed referent (or signified), or perhaps a sign with mobile, elusive, and multiple referents.

Douglas Kahn highlights this mutability of noise:

> Noise is the forest of everything. The existence of noise implies a mutable world through an unruly intrusion of another that attracts difference, heterogeneity, and productive confusion; moreover, it implies a genesis of mutability itself. Noise is a world where anything can happen, including and especially itself. In a predictable world noise promises something out of the ordinary, and in a world of frantic pursuit of the extraordinary noise can promise the banal and the quotidian. In a predictable world it can generate possibility and then obligingly self-destruct. (Kahn 22)

A & C seem to embrace this mutability as part of the uncertain future of Vieques, harboring the hope "that noise is a world where anything can happen." (After all, who would have imagined at the beginning of 1999 that the U.S. Navy would cease its overt military actions by 2003?) This "productive confusion" of noise is consistent with their use of music, sound, and noise in many of their pieces, including "Clamor" (2006), where they try to disrupt the militarization of music. In another work for the Venice Biennale of 2011 ("Track and Field"), the artists invited the public to walk over the right track of an overturned tank as if it were a treadmill. They skillfully used an emblem of war and transformed it into something ordinary (and nonviolent), visually analogous to the Vieques trumpet; Mexican artist Pedro Reyes did something similar when he took pistols and rifles and made them into musical instruments.

To conclude with Vieques and its future, there are also a mutability and productive confusion that concern the issue of sovereignty, even though some land has returned to the civilian population. It is represented by Capital, which has become an emerging global sovereign, "perpetual and absolute, increasingly unaccountable and primordial, the source of all commands, yet beyond the reach of the *nomos*. Capital produces life absent provisions of protection and ties of membership, turning populations around the world into *homo sacer*" (Brown 64). Vieques' biopolitical future is tied to the global sovereign of capital, under the guise of eco-friendly tourism and gentrification, a delicate balancing act, given that the cleanup of toxic materials and ordinance is supposed to be accomplished by 2024, but these predictions may need revising (some predict it will drag on into the 2030s). At the most elemental biopolitical level, it is worth remembering that the population of Vieques, by its long exposure to contaminants, has a cancer rate that is 35 percent higher than the rest of Puerto Rico's population.

A & C's political exploration of sound, music, and noise is strikingly illustrated by their performance piece "Stop, Repair, Prepare: Variations on Ode to Joy for Prepared Piano" (2008; heretofore Ode). The artists take on an iconic piece of the classical canon, Beethoven's Ninth Symphony (1824). The focus is on the fourth movement, which features the vocal segment based on Friedrich Schiller's poem "Ode to Joy." The performance lasts about fifteen minutes, with a pianist and prepared piano (no vocals). By prepared piano I mean a hole cut into the piano that eliminates two octaves. The pianist goes underneath the piano, emerges from the hole standing, and then leans over to play the keyboard. The piece allows room for improvisation, and, at different junctures, the pianist moves the piano around the performance space, while still playing the "Ode to Joy." It gives new meaning to the expression "running performance" or "music that moves you." Spatially, it creates a counter-nomos, the sound of inclusion.

The notion of a prepared piano clearly evokes Cage's compositions for prepared piano, but the sound and purpose are quite different, aiming to deconstruct a classic, again using noise. With no vocal part, A & C interrupt or introduce disorder into the piece, but not entirely since the melody is recognizable. First, the piece is on piano (not full orchestra), which reduces the scale and power of the piece. In the performance that I witnessed, the pianist plucked the strings inside the piano, producing a striking flattening effect.[4] Second, with two octaves missing, the rendition had something "off" and dissonant, further reducing its aura. Third, the pianist had to learn how to play the piece "backward" since the left hand was playing the higher notes and the right the lower ones. Could this playing backward be a conscious or unwitting attempt to de-Eurocentrize the piece? Fourth, the physical movement of the piano was both refreshing and unnerving, like a large black vehicle moving about but making sound (and music). Pianos are probably the last instrument we imagine as moving about on stage. So aside from the skills to play backward, the pianists had to have the physical strength and exertion to move the instrument (on wheels, thankfully). In a subtle but chilling historical reminder, the piano used for the performance was a Bechstein, favored by German Jews up through the Third Reich.

The German publication about the performance (with English translation), including an essay by Slavoj Žižek, displayed many photos meant to ponder the political history and uses (or abuses) of the Ninth. Among them are shots of Pope Benedict XVI, Ian Smith, Wilhelm Furtwängler, Abimael Guzmán, Mao Zedong, Leonard Bernstein, Ottoman emissaries, and even an image from *Neon Genesis Evangelion*, the Japanese anime. Žižek's essay foregrounds these political uses (and abuses), trying to comprehend how they could be appropriated by a racist regime (Rhodesia), Hitler and the Nazis, communists of various stripes (Stalin, Mao, Guzmán, and Sendero Luminoso), the head of the Catholic Church, the post–World War II German Olympic teams, the European Union (without the words), and the Austrians to commemorate the victims of the Mauthausen concentration camp, to name only a few. This without naming its endless uses in films, the best-known and alarming being Stanley Kubrick's *A Clockwork Orange*.

In his essay, but also in the film *The Pervert's Guide to Ideology* (2012), Žižek discusses the power and perversions of the Ninth. He refers to ideology's flexibility by noting that it can be an empty container where anything can be put in as content (the Ninth being that kind of empty container). Hence, the Ninth can be used to exalt an enlightened monarch of the nineteenth century and promote a fascist dictator of the twentieth (Hitler), not to mention communist tyrants as well (Stalin). Why this appeal and fungibility of the Ninth? Schiller's poem evokes "the brotherhood of man," something that could resonate with communist ideology. For Catholics, this brotherhood seems like the precept of "love thy neighbor," not to mention the benevolence of the Creator, also praised in the Schiller poem. And the fact that the poem is not overtly nationalistic and exudes a universalizing (if pan-European) sentiment, would make it appealing as an anthem for the European Union.

Žižek is apparently saying that if the Ninth is an empty receptacle, then the content does not matter. That would be absurd. He insinuates but does not openly state that the content is not a particular ideology but promotes the idea of community, of belonging. What the Ninth conjures is that community, be it a body of believers (religions), a fraternity of revolutionaries (communism), a phalange of followers (fascism), a civic union of citizens (nationalism), or a society of consumers (capitalism). Secondly, this community is not an abstract idea but a performative condition that renews itself through group activities, including rituals, songs, speeches, preaching, marches, and hymns. To hear or sing the Ninth Symphony is to renew that sense of belonging as Rousseau defined it: "a symbol and instrument of a utopian order . . . that helps to establish a collectivity."

But Žižek warns that Schiller's and Beethoven's community of brotherhood has blind spots. The essay, titled "Beethoven's Turkish March," referring to a *marcia alla turca* from the score, reveals that the formation of a community, which highlights inclusion, also, by definition, means exclusion. And using the Turkish march he draws attention to Turkey's exclusion from the European Union. For Žižek this means critically asking, "What is Europe?" or more pointedly "What does it mean to be European?"

Kubrick's handling of inclusion/exclusion is seen in *A Clockwork Orange* through the plight of Alex, a brutal thug who is a menace to society. (Žižek deals with Kubrick in *The Pervert's Guide*, not in this essay). Alex fantasizes with images of violence—sexual and otherwise—to Beethoven's music, particularly the Ninth. Kubrick's use of Beethoven and violence seemed scandalous at the time of the film's release (1971), but as Peter Höyng has suggested, Beethoven's Ninth contains subtle—or even suppressed—references to violence. Schiller's original poem (1785) referenced the bloody overthrow of a tyrant as the condition for joy. In the version Beethoven used (1803), those words were removed. Höyng alludes to a primordial violence at the core of the formation of communities, a founding violence to establish a new order. The original version of the Schiller poem, while seemingly emphasizing unity, might also ask us to ponder, "Unity at what cost?"

Is this creation of a "brotherhood of man" sought by Schiller and Beethoven built on exclusion and violence? Höyng admirably summarizes the dilemma, as well as the ambiguity of violence:

> If we agree on the premise then when traced back to its origin, every society is based on some acts of violence (which Beethoven accepts but Schiller seeks to repress), that its law and order emerge from power structures based on this original violence, and that the new society is inherently linked to the dialectics of inclusion and exclusion, sooner or later one begins to differentiate between good and bad violence or at least contemplate the good and bad power structures that secure established law. In other words, violence is inherently ambiguous since our interpretation of it depends where one is positioned in the community or society. (Höyng 169)

In his film, Kubrick exploits those ambiguities in dizzying fashion, creating a kind of fairy tale of retribution, where the violence unleashed by Alex (and his *droogs*) in the first half is visited on him during the latter part of the film (the bad vs. the good violence; individual vs. State violence). The authorities apprehend him after murdering a woman, and give him a fourteen-year sentence, but after two years he agrees to undergo the Ludovico treatment, a mind control technique where he is given drugs and made to watch films of criminal, political, and sexual violence, including the atrocities of the Third Reich. The drugs are meant to induce nausea and retching, and the treatment, apparently, is successful, except that the music played while Alex is undergoing the "treatment" is Beethoven's Ninth. Alex develops a visceral aversion to Beethoven, to the point where later in the film he is locked into a room where the Ninth is played full blast, causing him to jump out of a window to kill himself (miraculously, he survives).

Kubrick unblinkingly looks at both good and bad violence. For society, Alex is a sadist thug who must be controlled, and so his imprisonment and acquiescence to the Ludovico Technique are therapeutic and their "success" signifies he is "healed." The community is strengthened, made safer. But his treatment, at the same time, is a form of torture and has made Alex a being devoid of free will. The novel and film remind us that the brotherhood of man, under the guise of the Kingdom of God, the purity of race, the new socialist man, the good society, or other forms of societal "purification," can lead to horrific crimes for those who are Other (politically, racially, sexually, religiously).

Kubrick's film comes to mind when considering the concert by the Vienna Philharmonic Orchestra at Mauthausen, Austria, in 2000, where the Ninth was played in an event that commemorated those who perished there, some 100,000 souls.[5] Leon Zelman, a camp survivor, conceived the idea of the concert. Despite widespread support, many survivors were highly critical of the endeavor. Complicating the matter was Jörg Haider's high-ranking presence in the Austrian government, a hard-right wing anti-immigration politician known for his anti-Semitic views. He was not invited. For some, the commemoration and concert were to be an atonement for Austria's dark past, including the fact that between a third and half of the Vienna Philharmonic had been members of the National Socialist Party.

Perhaps one can view the Mauthausen event as a collective Ludovico treatment meant to expiate for Austria's sins during the war, while at the same time trying to absolve Beethoven of the manipulation he had been subjected to under the Third Reich. Critics were harsh, saying, what does the "Ode to Joy" have to do with those slaughtered in an extermination camp? What brotherhood of man, under the gentle gaze of the Creator as people were gassed? Marta Halpert, a Viennese journalist, said: "This is the worst of event culture, like taking the Three Tenors to the Baths of Caracalla. You can hear the screams in the quarry. You should not make any other sounds. Mauthausen should be what it is: a place of death and a place for reflection and learning" (Halpert qtd. in Kettle). Halpert's remark contextualizes how music and sound's perception can be reversed under certain circumstances: music, even Beethoven's Ninth, is seen as obscene (noise), while the screams of those killed is the more appropriate sound for the circumstance.

To be fair to the Austrians, before the Ninth was played, the chief rabbi of Vienna recited the Kaddish, as was "El Maleh Rachamim," a prayer for the soul of the departed. The audience, which numbered some 11,000, was told not to clap, since the performance was not considered a concert. They remained silent, all holding candles.

The Mauthausen event urges us to critically reconsider attempts to use the Ninth as therapy or healing, and not only because of unintended consequences, as happened to Alex in *A Clockwork Orange*. The words of Hannah Arendt are a sober reminder that the Shoah is "a wound that will not heal" (West-Durán 56). Anthony Burgess, the author of the novel *A Clockwork Orange*, in pondering the issues of evil and art, recalls the story of a commandant from a camp who had no qualms about killing thousands of Jews, but burst into tears of joy upon hearing his daughter playing a Schubert sonata. He asks, "How is this possible? How could a being so dedicated to evil move without difficulty into a world so divinely good? The answer is that the good of music has nothing to do with ethics. Art does not elevate us into beneficence. It is morally neutral, like the taste of an apple" (Burgess 157). I do not entirely agree with Burgess in that one can separate aesthetic good and ethical good so harshly, but I do take it as a warning about not expecting art to do what it is not capable of doing.

The dilemma of aesthetic and ethical good is at the heart of Allora and Calzadilla's "Ode to Joy" and how to perform Beethoven in the twenty-first century as a non-Eurocentric, decolonizing practice, as well as a warning about the possibilities of sublating violence. This decolonial gesture is manifested through sound and performance; as Voegelin reminds us, hearing offers no metaposition, it upholds a sovereignty (and an aesthetic autonomy) that is not imposed. Like Capital, Beethoven has become a global sovereign, a cultural symbol almost beyond reproach. The classical music world tends to be haunted by "textual authenticity" and maintaining a tradition (be it the instruments or performance) and would see changes to the Ninth—and certainly those enacted by A & C—as unacceptable, if not outrageous. Richard Tarushkin reminds us that "reification and sacralization of musical texts . . . promulgates an overly narrow vision, one that overrides the alteration of offensive pages or disavows music's power" (qtd. in Clark 803–4). Allora and Calzadilla's "Ode to Joy" directly confronts that "reification and sacralization" with its "productive confusion," always intimating a world where anything can happen. Hitting the keys where the strings have been removed is a haunting reminder of those no longer with us. It is the hole in the piano that reminds of Beethoven's dream of making us whole. But that is not up to Beethoven, that is up to us.

Notes

1. Jennifer Allora was born in Philadelphia in 1974. She studied at the University of Richmond (Virginia) and the Massachusetts Institute of Technology, where she earned a Master's in science (2003). She had a fellowship-residency from the Whitney Museum in 1998–99. She and her colleague Guillermo Calzadilla have received many awards and fellowships and have exhibited in world-class museums. They both live in Puerto Rico. Calzadilla was born in Havana in 1974, but at a young age moved to Puerto Rico and studied at the Escuela de Artes Plásticas de San Juan (1996) and earned an M.F.A. in Art from Bard College (2001). The artists met in Florence (1995) and have since worked as a team. Hereafter, I will refer to them as A & C.

2. A full version of *Returning a Sound* is available on YouTube, but the movement is a little jerky. https://www.youtube.com/watch?v=i-fGxVNa2OQ&t=2s.

3. The French word *anthème* is a neologism from the English anthem. For Boulez it is also an aural play-on-words since *en thème* (on theme) is a homonym, alluding to one of Boulez's key concerns about thematic and non-thematic music. In the case of A & C, the sound is non-thematic (yet still has meaning), but not the video, since it deals with an historic struggle and the problematics of sovereignty, to be discussed further on.

4. "Ode to Joy" was part of an exhibition at the Fundació Antoni Tapies in Barcelona that ran from 6 February 2018 to 20 May 2018. It included videos, installations, and performances from 2005–18. The "Ode to Joy" I witnessed was on 19 May 2018. YouTube has different versions of the piece.

5. Some sources allege that the camp claimed 300,000 lives (1938–45). Mauthausen was built for the most implacable foes of the Third Reich, so the treatment there was harsher than in other camps. It was the last camp to be liberated by the Allied Forces, on 5 May 1945.

Works Cited

Allora and Calzadilla. *Stop, Repair, Prepare.* Texts by Julienne Lorz and Slavoj Žižek. Haus der Kunst, 2008.
Attali, Jacques. *Noise: The Political Economy of Music.* U of Minnesota P, 1985.
Brown, Wendy. *Walled States, Waning Sovereignty.* MIT P, 2010.
Buch, Esteban. *Beethoven's Ninth: A Political History.* U of Chicago P, 2003.
Burgess, Anthony. "Human Perfectibility, Dystopias, and Violence." *A Clockwork Orange.* W. W. Norton, 2011, pp. 157–64.
Clark, Caryl. "Forging Identity: Beethoven's Ode as European Anthem." *Critical Inquiry*, vol. 23, no. 4, 1997, pp. 789–807.
Höyng, Peter. "Ambiguities of Violence in Beethoven's Ninth through the Eyes of Stanley Kubrick's *A Clockwork Orange.*" *German Quarterly*, vol. 84, no. 2, 2011, pp. 159–76.
Kahn, Douglas. *Noise, Water, Meat: A History of Sounds in the Arts.* MIT P, 1999.
Kettle, Martin. "Ode to Joy in Mauthausen." *The Guardian*, 28 Apr. 2000.
McKee, Yates. *Vieques Videos 2003–2010.* Lisson Gallery Informational Sheet, 2011.
———. "Wake, Vestige, Survival: Sustainability and Trace in Allora and Calzadilla's 'Land Mark.'" *October*, no. 133, 2010, pp. 20–48.
Novak, David, and Matt Sakakeeny, editors. *Keywords in Sounds.* Duke UP, 2015.
Schaeffer, Pierre. *Treatise on Musical Objects: An Essay across Disciplines.* Translated by Christine North and John Dark. U of California P, 2017.
Voegelin, Salomé. *Listening to Noise and Silence.* Continuum, 2010.
West-Durán, Alan. "Hannah Arendt: How to Think about a 'Wound That Will Not Heal.'" *Socialism and Democracy*, vol. 29, no. 2, 2015, pp. 56–69.

Videos and Films

A Clockwork Orange. Directed by Stanley Kubrick. Warner Bros., 1971.
Half Mast/Full Mast. Directed by Alora and Calzadilla. Video, 2010.
The Pervert's Guide to Ideology: Slavoj Žižek. Directed by Sophie Fiennes. Zeitgeist Films, 2012.
Returning a Sound. Directed by Allora and Calzadilla. Video, 2004.
Stop, Repair, Prepare. Directed by Allora and Calzadilla. Video, 2008.
Stop, Repair, Prepare. Taped by Alan West-Durán, 19 May 2018 at Tapies Foundation, Barcelona.
Under Discussion. Directed by Allora and Calzadilla. Video, 2005.

15

The Narratives and Life Projects of *Orientales* from Cuba in Puerto Rico and Florida
An Initial Comparative Study

BLANCA ORTIZ-TORRES AND MARIO A. RODRÍGUEZ-CANCEL

Five main waves of Cuban migration to the United States since the Cuban Revolution have been described: that of the historical exiles (1959–62), the so-called Freedom Flights (1965–73), the Mariel exodus (1980), the rafter crisis (1994), and the post-Soviet wave (1995–) (Castro 3; Duany, "Cuban Migration"). Several factors influencing this migration have been discussed, among them: internal processes of Cuban society (political and economic transformations and social class contradictions); migratory chains that have been established; development of social networks; and labor mobility (Aja Díaz, "Emigración de Cuba" 9). Some authors point out that Cuban migration since the 1990s has been mostly made up of younger people who emigrate mainly for economic reasons (Aja Díaz, "Emigración de Cuba" 15; Ortiz-Torres and Rodríguez-Cancel, "Primera mirada migración" 127) and the scarcity of opportunities for professional development in Cuba (Duany, "Migración cubana" 164). According to Antonio Aja Díaz, the migration shift toward younger people partially responds to the economic crisis ("Emigración de Cuba" 15). He argues that some sectors of the population, mostly young people, felt a lack of motivation, disinterest, and a general distrust in how the Cuban social process could contribute to materialize their projects (Aja Díaz, "Migración desde Cuba" 10). Thus, according to many analysts, current Cuban migration is less motivated by ideological factors and more by economic and family-related factors.

By 1940, 307 Cubans were living in Puerto Rico (Duany, "Caribbean Migration" 48). According to the 2019 American Community Survey estimates, 11,753 persons of Cuban origin now live in Puerto Rico. This figure represents a considerable decrease of this group in Puerto Rico when compared to the 17,860 registered in 2010 (U.S. Census Bureau). Although some arrive in transit to the United States, currently, Cubans in Puerto Rico comprise approximately 0.4 percent of its 3.2 million inhabitants. According to the 2019 American Community Survey, 1,589,455 Cubans were living in Florida, comprising 7.4 percent of the state's total population. At the policy level, Cubans are probably the immigrant group with most political power in Florida (Eckstein 7).

In addition to differences stemming from the specific migration wave to which they belong, Cubans differ based on the region where they were born or identify with before migrating. Those differences are linked to historical, economic, racial, cultural, and linguistic factors between various Cuban provinces (Bodenheimer 211–13, 215–17; Fuster and Ortiz-López 142). Nadja Fuster and Luis Ortiz-López have examined linguistic differences between Cubans from Oriente (the eastern region of Cuba) and those born and living in other regions. According to them, *habaneros/as* (persons from Havana) usually have more prestige in Cuba than *orientales* (persons from the eastern provinces), among other reasons because the latter are perceived as less White and less educated than the former. Fuster and Ortiz-López consider that language, phenotype, political ideology, and socioeconomic status play an important role when evaluating the acceptance and prestige of other Cubans, where *lo oriental* has a traditionally negative connotation (25, 125). Extant research suggests that, in Cuba, White individuals are still perceived as superior to Blacks (Colás 254).

The presence of a higher number of Black people in Oriente can be tracked to the late eighteenth and nineteenth centuries. According to Louis Pérez (89), by 1862 "the combined number of free people of color and slaves still made up 52 percent of the total eastern population," while in the west Whites were already a majority of the population.

In the past two decades, Havana has received a significant migration from other provinces, particularly from Oriente, mostly by people looking for better job opportunities (Bodenheimer 215). The internal migration from the eastern part of Cuba has been seen as a "Black assault" on the capital (de la Fuente 327).

Since 2017, we have been conducting research on the transformations in the narratives and life projects of Cuban migrants from Oriente who have lived in Puerto Rico for the past twenty years. The results of the first two phases of this study are presented in two previously published articles

(Ortiz-Torres and Rodríguez-Cancel, "Primera mirada migración"; "Transformación de las narrativas").

The first phase of our research showed that many participants experienced exclusion and discrimination while living in or visiting Havana (Ortiz-Torres and Rodríguez-Cancel, "Primera mirada migración"). Ramón Colás asserts that government policies as well as other structural factors perpetuate racism in Cuban institutions. Political, cultural, economic, and social institutions sustain discrimination by distinguishing people based on phenotypic traits (253).

Fuster and Ortiz-López have stated that an *oriental* accent is sometimes a source of ridicule and discrimination in Havana (9). Bodenheimer argues that

> despite the revolutionary government's official rhetoric, which stresses national unity and celebrates the population's total and ongoing dedication to socialist ideals of egalitarianism and cooperation, many Cubans cling tightly to their regional identities. This means not only a fierce loyalty to one's province of birth, but often an explicit antagonism toward people from other provinces, particularly between *Habaneros* (people from Havana) and *Orientales* (people from the eastern provinces). (211)

These findings are consistent with ours from previous research. We found that some *orientales* feel they are considered less smart than *habaneros/as* in Cuba. They also report feeling like second-class citizens, or immigrants in their own land (Rodríguez-Cancel and Ortiz-Torres, "Microagresiones" 39–48), as reflected in the popular derogatory term *palestino/as* (literally, Palestinians). Many report frequent racist slurs against them. Participants in the first phase of our research were predominantly White, professional, and highly successful; however, they were convinced that *habaneros/as* would cast doubt on their achievements and would question their presence in Havana (Rodríguez-Cancel and Ortiz-Torres, "Microagresiones" 40–41).

We focus on narratives as a way of deconstructing oppressive ideologies because minorities' narratives are rarely heard. The exploration and description of these narratives can generate counter-narratives to challenge the hegemonic narratives (Sonn, "Engaging with the Apartheid" 432–33).

We learned from our previous research that *orientales* in Puerto Rico perceive that those who migrate to the state of Florida develop narratives and life projects different from those who stay in Puerto Rico. Motivated by these findings, we decided to move to a third phase to begin a comparative study between the two groups.

Method

The present chapter represents the second and third phases of a qualitative study in which we conducted nine semi-structured interviews in Puerto Rico and two focus groups (n=6): one in Miami and one in Tampa, Florida. Findings from the first phase were described by Ortiz-Torres and Rodríguez-Cancel elsewhere ("Transformación de las narrativas"). The interview guide for the second phase was developed based on the findings of the first phase.

Interviewed participants were recruited after being nominated by participants in the first phase. Once authorized by those nominated, we contacted them by telephone, to explain the nature and objectives of the study. If they agreed, we conducted the interview at a private location. Consent was procured from participants after reading a form authorized by the Institutional Review Board at the University of Puerto Rico. Participants were between 27–59 years old at the time of the interview.

In Florida, we recruited participants through contacts the principal investigator (Ortiz-Torres) had in Miami and Tampa. We asked permission to contact the participants, before we made contact by phone. As stated before, we explained to potential participants the nature and objectives of the study, and, if they agreed, they were given the date and location of the focus groups. One focus group was conducted at each city with a total of six participants. The Miami group was conducted at Carlos Albizu University; the Tampa session was conducted at a medical clinic, owned by a Cuban collaborator. The ages of the participants fluctuated between 32 and 72 years.

Interviews and discussion groups were conducted in Spanish and transcribed to facilitate the analysis process. For the purpose of this chapter, the authors translated participants' verbalizations into English. A content analysis was performed to systematically identify emerging topics in the text. Content analysis allows investigating the content of "communications" by classifying into "categories" elements or manifest contents of said communication or message (Aigeneren 4).

Results

According to participants interviewed in Puerto Rico, the migration route often begins by moving from Oriente to Havana, seeking individual and economic growth opportunities. Many of them identified better opportunities for the education of their children, as well as access to health services. Also, they were convinced that migration out of Cuba was easier from the capital. Some of those who did not move to Havana before leaving the country expressed that they did not do so because they did not have the opportunity.

Orientales and *Habaneros/as* Are Different

Participants both in Puerto Rico and Florida perceive important differences between *habaneros/as* and *orientales*. According to them, *habaneros/as* are more open, extroverted, superficial, have spark (*con chispa*), and are constantly hustling for a living. They are, according to the participants, more interested in what they wear than in what they eat, and dislike hard work. The following verbalizations illustrate this perception: "Yes, *habaneros* are not used to breakfast, lunch, and dinner like *orientales*. The *oriental* has a diet, he likes to eat. Not *habaneros*; they're more of junk food. They eat bread for lunch." This notion of *habaneros/as*' eating habits was consistent throughout all the research phases. Other participants believed that Havana transforms the people who move there; one participant shared the following observation: "I think that Havana itself changes people because many times you see people who have been there for five or ten years and... they have become *habaneros* from head to toe... I think it's Havana that makes people like that." One participant characterized *habaneros/as* as "pragmatic, they live day by day... family life is crazy for them. When an *oriental* arrives in Havana, he [or she] keeps a close relationship with his family members."

These differences contribute to the participants' common feeling that moving to Havana is like migrating to a different country. This perception is strengthened by *habaneros/as*' reactions toward *orientales*: "In Cuba, they call us *palestinos* because there is the notion that all *orientales* want to emigrate to Havana and when one gets to Havana, they always have the fear that you will stay, as if it was a separate country where 'you are going to usurp my rights and my possibilities.'..." Participants also identify differences related to their accent, aspirations, and everyday living. According to one participant, *habaneros/as* "give you these looks... Then, to avoid being looked at that way, you can't talk with our accent." A consistent finding among participants was that to avoid discrimination, they would imitate *habaneros/as*' accent, or what they refer to as *pasar como habanero* (pretending to be an *habaneros/a*).

Participants report that *habaneros/as* seem to be afraid that *orientales* will overpopulate Havana more than what it already is. One participant shared the following comment: "Yes, ummm... when an *oriental* arrives in Havana... *habaneros* think 'they are going to flood us.' Also, there is this thing that as soon as *orientales* get there, because of their idiosyncrasy, they get to own a house and many *habaneros* live in rented houses." Both in the focus groups and in the interviews several participants raised the apparent irony that Fidel and his brother Raúl Castro were *orientales* and apparently did not face the exclusion and discrimination our participants describe. René González Rego cites two of Fidel Castro's speeches, in which Fidel stated that "it is true that our problems are aggravated with migration" (1989), and that "the provinces have filled up Havana which complicates the housing, water and electricity situation... thousands of homes have been built, the problem is alleviated, and the illegals come in again" (González Rego).

Exclusion and Discrimination

Both in Puerto Rico and Florida, participants report feeling discriminated in Havana. This is particularly the case when they are called *guajiros/as* (peasants) or *palestinos/as* (Palestinians) and are questioned about their reasons to be in Havana. A Miami participant said that he and his wife had the same experience in Miami, where most Cubans are *habaneros/as*. He shared the following experience:

> [In Havana] at the university they made fun of us; they say that *orientales* speak as if they were singing, that we mispronounce words... So I, in a certain way, revived it... arriving in Florida. I immigrated from Cuba to Canada. Eight years later I moved from Canada to here, where, as I already said, the population is mostly western [from the western region of Cuba]. So, when I entered a work center where I was the only *oriental*, it was a joke; at the same time, it was mockery. I felt that again; I felt... that they criticized the way I spoke, the way I approached others, I was like a strange entity. They even saw me as

a person with a different value system. I am going to give a particular example . . . , eh, at my workplace there was a person who was a lesbian, and she was going to get married, the only person she did not invite to the wedding was me, why? Because she said she was ashamed to invite me and because she thought that I was not going to accept that kind of relationship.

A participant from Tampa shared an experience about her younger cousin. "They currently live in Havana and . . . he, at school, suffered a lot when they called him *guajiro*, 'you are a *palestino*.' And what happened? That about three years after in his Havana school, an *oriental* boy was admitted, and what was he doing? [he started telling the boy] 'you are a *palestino*, you are a *guajiro*.' The same thing they did to him, he passed it on to that boy, because that's what he experienced at school too."

Reasons to Migrate

Reasons to migrate were similar among *orientales* in Puerto Rico and Florida. They report leaving their country to study, to improve financially and professionally, and to reunite with their family. Several participants in Puerto Rico migrated to join their relatives. One participant shared the following experience: "I left Cuba because of my father . . . I was a student, and . . . as a student, there are things that are not in one's control . . . I had to wait for immigration authorization and then organize my life."

In both samples, age at migration seems to influence participants' expectations and aspirations. In Florida, those older than fifty years expect to receive government subsidies when "they get old," and those under fifty are determined to develop their professional lives and to guarantee a house for their family as their most important life projects. A participant over fifty said: "I wish I could have arrived here earlier . . . to start here when I was younger and to be able to . . . Now I have had to adapt myself; I get some governmental aid. I am pleased with what they give me, because I have not worked in this country, I am very grateful." A younger participant who resides in Tampa expressed that he wants "to procreate children, to keep moving my business . . . never be a conformist . . . To keep always going forward. I already have my house, my car, the toys that I always wanted, a boat. Now I have to focus on raising a family, my wife, children, and business."

Context Changes Narratives

When exploring which factors may have facilitated their adaptation to Puerto Rico or Florida, participants mentioned family, willingness to work, and a sense of independence. A participant in Miami said: "In my particular case, my family is here, I don't feel that lonely. My sister is here. I have been able to move forward by myself, not depending on others. That has helped me a lot." Another participant attributed his success in adapting to the context to innate qualities; he feels that Cubans are nonconformists, they are always trying to do something new, and "they are always on the move." The role of the family has been central in our participants' narratives; one of them offered the following narrative:

> In my case . . . eh . . . the family. When I got here from Canada, I did not have a job, I did not have enough money to rent an apartment; hadn't it been for my family that welcomed me and offered a sofa to sleep, it would have been very difficult. Also, I believe that what helped me the most is the experience of having lived in a different country, because it has been easier for me to get into the job market because of the language. . . .

Most of our participants interviewed in Puerto Rico stated that having their family there helped immensely in their adaptation, but they also stressed that Puerto Ricans were fundamental in that process. In alluding to factors that contributed to her adaptation, one of the participants said: "The idiosyncrasy, the language, the similarity of the people, the kindness of the vast majority of Puerto Ricans . . ." Participants also identified obstacles they have faced in their adaptation process in Florida and in Puerto Rico. In Miami and Tampa, some of these barriers are related to the host culture and others to the nature of interactions with other Cubans.

> Well, I have him [talking about her husband], but initially you leave everything behind, your family, your things, in Cuba. You come here to start from scratch, to struggle with another reality that is full of Cubans, but there also people born here that look at you in a different way. You must adapt yourself to overcome the fact that everything is different—from riding a bus to go to work to learning to cross the street. You have to start from zero. Even the TV, people tell you "don't watch TV in Spanish, watch TV in English to learn the language." You have to make an effort to change everything.

One participant in Miami described his perception of Cubans in that city: "other Cubans regard you as competition; that is why it is difficult to make friends. It is unbelievable, but here you never get to make friends; I don't know if with time . . . you can reunite with old friends like in Cuba, but here it is very complicated." According to that participant, the social networking that was possible in Cuba becomes very difficult in Florida, for an array of reasons. In contrast, the sample from Puerto Rico consistently pointed out that Puerto Ricans did not impede their adaptation process. It should be noted that what our participants describe as the "*oriental* accent" is very similar to the dialect of Spanish spoken in Puerto Rico, which may facilitate their adaptation to the island.

One of the participants expressed the following when describing obstacles to his adaptation: "Perhaps systemic barriers that you are not prepared to face because you come from a different system. Of course, the Cuban system does not prepare you to live in a capitalist society; therefore, you must adapt to those things that shocked you, that could slow you down a bit in development. But I have never, of course, had problems . . . with [Puerto Ricans]." Another identified obstacle in their adaptation process was the absence of family members (especially parents). One of the participants expressed the following: "Well, the distance from the family, the family of origin, that is, uh, the most . . . I think that the most difficult . . . thing that has affected me is not having them here, especially after I gave birth."

Transformations in Life Projects

Participants in Florida and Puerto Rico describe transformations in their life projects, some of which are related to the reasons for migrating mentioned earlier. Some participants stated that they barely had life projects in Cuba because life there is about survival. In most cases, life projects revolve around improving the family's financial situation; said a Miami participant: "Well, in my case, life projects keep coming up and becoming real. I migrated with the aspiration of providing another life level to my family; I have accomplished that. I also wanted to get training in my specialty in a different country, and I got it. I just got it; after a traumatic divorce, I wanted to start a new family, and we are accomplishing that." When asked about the changes in her life projects, one of the Puerto Rico participants said that her current life projects are to "graduate as a psychologist and start working." Another participant from Miami described her new life projects as follows:

I would like to get a master's degree; go back to school, to be in a better position. That is part of a long-term life project because at least my husband has been able to position himself as a therapist. We are still missing things, and then, I could probably go to the university. For me it is more complicated, that is why my life project is a long-term one—a little more than five years, or something like that.

One of the participants in Tampa stated the following when asked about his life projects in Cuba:

Basically, what you think is to see how you can economically ... Yes, have money to have a house, to furnish it, to go out to places. It is what the Cuban thinks. To eat well. If you can travel, let's see how you can travel somewhere, even if you don't know it, even if you don't even know where it is located. Because we don't know anything else. Now with the Internet things are changing a little.

Another participant from the Miami focus group shared the following, when asked about his life projects in Cuba: "I think I was born wanting to leave Cuba ... So, my project was to migrate ... it is the goal of almost all Cubans to migrate here. The option I had was to go to Canada and that is where I went, but that was a big life project; to migrate ... with the dream of one day being able to expand my knowledge in another culture." The responses were consistent: most of the participants wanted to leave Cuba in search of a better future, both professionally and economically.

When describing their life projects in Cuba, *orientales* residing in Puerto Rico stressed that their only aspirations in Cuba were to work and survive. As one participant shared, "In Cuba, I didn't set many goals for myself; the first thing was to work, bring food home, and I never thought of developing myself anymore; that was for me, I never thought of studying or picking up another pencil..." (This participant went back to school in Puerto Rico and got a degree in an area completely different to his previous career.)

Many of our participants said that their lives in Cuba were "simple" and "straightforward," as stated by one of the participants: "Well, my life project, you know, was to go to work. I was the accountant for the municipality, so the whole day was going to work, leaving work, picking up the boys, and cooking. Bathe the boys, go to bed, and come back the next day to get up to the same thing. There was nothing else to do." When comparing those narratives with those from Florida, it is relevant to highlight that only one of the participants from the sample in Puerto Rico said that his life projects involved migrating to another country. When compared to *orientales* living in Puerto Rico, those who live in Miami and Tampa report a less favorable opinion about Cuba and are not interested in returning to their country when they eventually retire.

The narratives of the participants were consistent: hard work gets you to what was impossible in Cuba. According to them, the main difference with what they had in Cuba is that they see possibilities for a better life after migration. A participant in Puerto Rico said: "Of course, here everyone who arrives wants to get settled, to have a house of their own, have the family reunited. It is difficult, it takes time, you have to work a lot, to be able to help those who stayed there [Cuba] even if it just for them to eat." A participant in Tampa explained that she was tired of working and was looking forward to retirement: "Well, I want to retire when I turn sixty-five because I have my mother who already needs help. To be able to help her more because I work eleven hours a day . . . So, I don't want to work another day when I turn sixty-five."

Age plays a role in the development/transformation of life projects; younger participants talked more about laying a solid foundation, raising a family, reuniting with family members, and getting a degree. Older participants talked mostly about retirement while acknowledging that hard work was necessary to have a good retirement. While some participants in Puerto Rico considered retiring in Cuba, those in Florida did not see this as a possibility. Their perception of Cuba is less positive when compared to those living in Puerto Rico. This is illustrated by a Tampa participant's narrative: "My life project was to come to this country. I will never go to Cuba if I do not go with the American passport." *Orientales* in our Puerto Rican sample maintain constant communication with family and friends in Cuba and travel to that island at least once a year.

Perception of the Host Country

We asked participants, what was their perception of the United States prior to migrating from Cuba? Some shared that they already had family in the United States; therefore, what they knew about that country was mediated by what their relatives told them. One of the participants from Miami shared the following statement: "My family has been here for fifty years . . . and they visited Cuba very often; what they would tell us about U.S. What caught my attention was that they spoke like *habanero*[s] . . . and then my reflection was 'it must be because there are many *habaneros* in Miami and . . . that is why they speak like this . . ." In contrast, most of the participants from Tampa stated that they dreamed of moving to the United States, that they now feel more American than Cuban, and prefer to socialize and work with Americans. Participants in the Puerto Rico sample seemed to know less about Puerto Rico than about the United States before migrating. They were divided in their expectations regarding Puerto Rico prior to their arrival. Some believed it was "a paradise with better economic conditions than any other country in Latin America, where you would make a living in dollars." Some were concerned about violence and criminality.

We also explored whether perceptions of the host society have changed over the years. Most of the participants from the focus group in Tampa had a favorable view of Florida. One of the participants said this: "Florida is not what people think that people come just to retire, a city of older people. It's not like that, it's not like that. One hundred and forty-nine people immigrate daily from all over the country, I love it." Only one participant in that group did not share this view about Tampa and said that she did not like how they treat the elderly and that people tend to be cold. In contrast, what we found in Miami differed significantly from the Tampa group. One of the participants shared that he felt like he was in Cuba: "I had the opportunity to visit once before emigrating here and I felt that I was in Cuba and that is why I did not like it; it is the same idiosyncrasy, the same culture of the people, the same way of treating you in the street and then . . . no, I did not feel well, I still do not feel well." Over the years, *orientales* in Puerto Rico have discovered that Puerto Rico is, in their words, "more culturally compatible" with them and a "great country to grow." "Puerto Ricans give us advice, help us discard a lot of lies and false illusions, which allow us to work and grow."

Conclusions

The narratives presented in this chapter seem to respond, at least partially, to some of the questions raised by John Berry: "If culture is such a powerful shaper of behavior, do individuals continue to act in the new setting as they did in the previous one, do they change their behavioral repertoire to be more appropriate in the new setting, or is there some complex pattern of continuity and change in how people go about their lives in the new society?" (Berry 5).

Our findings support the notion that contextual factors, as well as their own personal histories, partially account for the differences between *orientales* residing in Puerto Rico and in Florida. For those who live in Puerto Rico, the adaptation process has been friendlier, particularly because they have not felt the exclusion and discrimination they experienced in their own country. For *orientales* living in Florida, the proximity to a majority of *habaneros/as* expose them to experiences similar to what they faced in Havana. The two samples share similarities in their new life projects. Participants in Puerto Rico have a more positive image of Cuba, than those living in the United States, who tended to show more critical views toward the Cuban government.

Dina Birman and Emily Bray have alluded to an ecological perspective on immigration that attends to the contexts that shape behavior. They underline the need to consider how immigrants might be "influenced by more than one microsystem" as well as by multiple cultures (313). The context of *orientales* migrating into Florida is quite different from the context in which they interact in Puerto Rico. María Cristina García has detailed how the Cuban American community in Florida, particularly in Miami, has developed an environment that accentuates *cubanidad* (Cubanness). She asserts that "in the process they forged a hybrid society, a uniquely Cuban-American culture. Miami has become Havana USA: the border town between Cuba and the United States" (118). This hybrid society is "one of the foremost examples anywhere of a true ethnic enclave" (Lisandro Pérez 251). This is different in Puerto Rico, where Cubans are a relatively small group that tends to blend with Puerto Ricans, having less visibility than their compatriots in Florida. In Florida they find a culture similar to Havana; in Puerto Rico, they feel at home in a context similar to Oriente.

Migration, whether voluntary or involuntary, entails complex processes, such as the rupture of community ties, social networks, and family connections. For immigrants, the process of displacement signifies the loss of what they know and what has been part of their everyday lives and histories (Sonn, "Immigrant Adaptation" 205). Immigration is also a process that eventually might bring opportunities and gains. Developing a sense of community within the receiving culture is central to the processes of transculturation (Sonn, "Immigrant Adaptation"). Both groups of *orientales* in Florida and in Puerto Rico seem successful in their efforts to belong to their diverse contexts.

Works Cited

Aigeneren, Miguel. "Análisis de contenido: Una introducción." *La Sociología en sus Escenarios*, 2009, pp. 1–52.
Aja Díaz, Antonio. "La emigración de Cuba en los años noventa." *Cuban Studies*, vol. 30, 1999, pp. 1–25.
———. "La migración desde Cuba." *Aldea Mundo*, vol. 11, no. 22, 2007, pp. 7–16.
Berry, John W. "Immigration, Acculturation, and Adaptation." *Applied Psychology: An International Review*, vol. 46, no. 1, 1997, pp. 5–68.
Birman, Dina, and Emily Bray. "Immigration, Migration and Community Psychology." *APA Handbook of Community Psychology: Methods for Community Research and Action for Diverse Groups and Issues*, edited by Meg A. Bond et al. Vol. 2. American Psychological Association, 2017, pp. 313–26.
Bodenheimer, Rebecca. "'La Habana no aguanta más': Regionalism in Contemporary Cuban Society and Dance Music." *The Musical Quarterly*, vol. 92, nos. 3–4, 2009, pp. 210–41.
Castro, Max J. "The New Cuban Immigration in Context." *A North-South Agenda Paper—North-South Center, University of Miami*, vol. 58, 2002, pp. 3–12.
Colás, Ramón Humberto. "Racismo estructural en Cuba y disidencia política: Breves antecedentes." *Cuba in Transition*, edited by the Association for the Study of the Cuban Economy. Vol. 20, 2010, pp. 253–57.
de la Fuente, Alejandro. *A Nation for All: Race, Inequality, and Politics in Twentieth-Century Cuba*. U of North Carolina P, 2001.
Duany, Jorge. "Caribbean Migration to Puerto Rico: A Comparison of Cubans and Dominicans." *International Migration Review*, vol. 26, no. 1, 1992, pp. 46–66.
———. "Cuban Migration: A Postrevolution Exodus Ebbs and Flows." *Migrationpolicy.org*, Migration Policy Institute, 6 July 2017, www.migrationpolicy.org/article/cuban-migration-postrevolution-exodus-ebbs-and-flows.
———. "La migración cubana: Tendencias actuales y proyecciones." *Encuentro de la Cultura Cubana*, no. 36, 2005, pp. 164–79.
Eckstein, Susan. "How Cubans Transformed Florida Politics and Gained National Influence." *La Florida: Five Hundred Years of Hispanic Presence*, edited by Viviana Díaz Balsera and Rachel A. May. UP of Florida, 2014, pp. 263–84.
Fuster, Nadja, and Luis Ortiz-López. "Variación geolectal y percepciones lingüísticas en Cuba." 2012. University of Puerto Rico, Río Piedras, M.A. thesis.
García, María Cristina. *Havana USA: Cuban Exiles and Cuban Americans in South Florida, 1959–1994*. U of California P, 1996.
González Rego, René A. "Migraciones hacia La Habana: Efectos en la conformación de su ambiente social." *Scripta Nova*, vol. 64, no. 94, 2001, www.ub.edu/geocrit/sn-94-64.htm.
Ortiz-López, Luis. "La variante hispánica haitianizada en Cuba: Otro rostro del contacto lingüístico en el Caribe." *Estudios de lingüística hispánica: Homenaje a María Vaquero*, edited by Amparo Morales et al. Editorial Universidad de Puerto Rico, 1999, pp. 428–56.

Ortiz-Torres, Blanca, and Mario A. Rodríguez-Cancel. "Una primera mirada a la migración de cubanos del Oriente de Cuba a Puerto Rico." *Caribbean Studies*, vol. 47, no. 1, 2019, pp. 125–44.

———. "La transformación de las narrativas y proyectos de vida de cubanos/as del Oriente de Cuba en Puerto Rico." *Interamerican Journal of Psychology*, vol. 53, no. 2, 2019, pp. 128–39, doi:10.30849/rip/ijp.v53i2.1065.

Pérez, Lisandro. "The Émigré Community and Cuba's Future." *Looking Forward: Comparative Perspectives on Cuba's Transition*, edited by Marifeli Pérez-Stable. U of Notre Dame P, 2007, pp. 240–61.

Pérez, Louis A. Jr. *Cuba: Between Reform and Revolution*. Oxford UP, 1995.

Rodríguez-Cancel, Mario A., and Blanca Ortiz-Torres. "Micro-agresiones: Estudio sobre las experiencias de orientales cubanos/as viviendo en Puerto Rico." 2012. University of Puerto Rico, Río Piedras, M.A. thesis.

Sonn, Christopher C. "Engaging with the Apartheid Archive Project: Voices from the South African Diaspora in Australia." *South African Journal of Psychology*, vol. 40, no. 4, 2010, pp. 432–42.

———. "Immigrant Adaptation: Understanding the Process through Sense of Community." *Psychological Sense of Community Research, Applications, and Implications*, edited by Adrian T. Fisher et al. Kluwer Academic/Plenum Publishers, 2002, pp. 205–22.

U.S. Census Bureau. *Explore Census Data: 2019 American Community Survey*, https://data.census.gov/cedsci/.

16

Becoming Cuba-Rican
A Personal Testimony

JORGE DUANY

Writing this essay has proven more challenging than other essays.[1] As someone trained primarily in the social sciences, I learned to write in the third person and erase most personal references from the text to appear more "objective" in my analyses. Moreover, the first person is problematic for me when referring to Cubans and Puerto Ricans, because I often feel caught between the two groups, as I will elaborate below. Composing an autobiographical narrative on my subjective positioning as a "diasporic Cuban" has forced me to find a different voice from most of my previous publications on the intertwined topics of identity, migration, and transnationalism. In this chapter, I will reflect upon how my experiences as a Cuban-born immigrant in Puerto Rico shaped my scholarly work and will adopt a personal rather than a sociological tone, a daunting task for someone not used to writing from this perspective.[2]

I hope this autobiographical disclosure will show more clearly the connections between my life history and those of many others who have left their countries of origin. As the sociologist C. Wright Mills put it so well, capturing the myriad intersections between biography and history is one of the hallmarks of the sociological imagination. As an anthropologist, I am primarily interested in exploring whether my self-revelations might resonate with other people who blur borders in their daily lives.

Writing in the First Person

Much of my academic work has centered on the socioeconomic and cultural adaptation of immigrants from the Hispanic Caribbean, namely, Cuba, Puerto Rico, and the Dominican Republic (see Duany, *Blurred*

Borders; The Puerto Rican Nation on the Move). My own diasporic condition (insofar as I belong to a displaced population that retains strong links to its homeland) has led me to inquire into how uprooted people settle down in a new environment and how they cultivate emotional, family, and cultural ties to their places of origin and settlement.[3]

I was born in Havana in January 1957, two years before the triumph of the Cuban Revolution. Thus, practically my entire biography is a historical byproduct of the Revolution and the continuous exodus it generated. I left Cuba with my mother and older brother in December 1960 for Panama, where my father had relocated months before. My parents' momentous decision to leave the island has always intrigued me, and I still do not understand it fully. In late 1958, my father, a television director and producer, had moved to Panama, where he helped establish the first TV station in that country, RPC.[4] After 1 January 1959, I imagine that my father was disturbed by the increasing politization and imminent nationalization of Cuba's TV stations, especially CMQ and CMBF, where he had worked before. My mother, who then sympathized with the Revolution like most of her family, remained on the island until she followed my father, together with my maternal grandmother, who returned to Havana after three months. My young mother must have been torn by the choice of keeping her marriage together or staying in her home country with her relatives.

Initially, we settled in Panama but moved on to Puerto Rico in 1966. I remember looking at a map of the Caribbean and wondering why on earth we were going there; I felt completely Panamanian by then. My growing family (I had two more siblings now) relocated in San Juan, where my father found a job directing and producing telenovelas (soap operas) and game shows. Also, my *padrinos* (godparents) were living there, as well as two of my parents' cousins on both sides of the family. I spent the rest of my childhood and adolescence in the San Juan metropolitan area. After graduating from high school, I pursued my university studies in the United States, first in New York, then in Chicago, and lastly at Berkeley. Upon earning my doctorate, I returned to Puerto Rico, married, started a full-time teaching career, and had two children. I later worked for a year at the University of Florida in Gainesville. Between 1988 and 2012, I lived mostly in Puerto Rico, with a few short stays in the United States. I wrote the original version of this chapter as a visiting professor in Gainesville during the spring of 2007. My professional and personal situation took a new turn in 2012, when I accepted an offer to direct the Cuban Research Institute at Florida International University in Miami. This is where I revised and updated the present essay.

Since I was very young, I was troubled by the constant question, "Where are you from?" I usually answered, "I was born in Cuba, but I grew up in Puerto Rico." Yet that answer never settled which country I felt most attached to, an issue that became periodically urgent, as when Puerto Rico's national team faced Cuba's in international sports competitions. If Cuba played against Puerto Rico, I would root for the Puerto Rican team. But when Cuba faced the United States, I usually sided with the Cuban team. I still have to think twice when I see the flags of the two islands, with their identical layout and inverted colors, before deciding which is which. Somebody once told me that the Cuban flag has the star within the triangle that is red like a heart, and that is how I usually solve my confusion.

One way I tried to assemble the puzzle of my divided loyalties was by visiting Cuba. Going back to the island was initially a way to—excuse the cliché—"search for my roots," to reconnect with a large part of my extended family that remained in Havana, and to experience the daily life of a society that was radically transformed after 1959. Since 1981, I have returned more than a dozen times (I have lost track of the exact count) to Havana and twice to Santiago de Cuba, the city of my father's birth. Santiago is where my father's ancestors lived for centuries and where many people know how to spell my strange surname with a y at the end. The founder of the Duany clan in Santiago, John Duany Lynch, was an Irish engineer who arrived in 1665 to help fortify the city's San Pedro de la Roca Castle. Meanwhile, my mother's side of the family, most of which lived in Havana, was of relatively recent Spanish origin, mainly from the Canary Islands and Galicia. Oral traditions, as well as online genealogical research, have preserved such family history details.

Every time I have been back to Cuba I have felt differently. At first, I felt very much at home, like a prodigal son, thanks to the warm welcome of my relatives on the island, especially on my mother's side. I was touched that they still remembered me as "Yoyi," as they used to call me as a child. Reconstructing a past shared by my parents with their siblings, nephews, nieces, and cousins; comparing the letters, pictures, recordings, belongings, and relics they kept of those of us who had left; and photographing (from outside) the house in the Havana neighborhood of La Sierra, where we lived until 1960, helped me reconcile my family's memories, splintered by several decades and many miles. My relatives on the island made sure that I knew where the old Spanish club (Casino Español) in Havana was located; the multiple houses where my maternal grandmother lived with her children; the Corpus Christi Church in Miramar, where my parents married; and the School of Education at the University of Havana, where my mother and her sisters studied, and my maternal grandfather taught before the Revolution. I was thrilled to see all these places, as if I could retrace my parents' footsteps during their childhood and youth. Unfortunately, I could not find my grandparents' graves either in the Colón cemetery in Havana or the Santa Ifigenia cemetery in Santiago.

I have grown more distant from Cuba over time, and felt increasingly attached to Puerto Rico, where I spent most of my life and where I raised my own family. I now prefer to say that "I grew up in Puerto Rico, but my parents came from Cuba." Half in jest, I often declare that I am Cuba-Rican, rather than Cuban American, because I had never lived continuously for an extended period in the United States until 2012, though I became a U.S. citizen in 1985.[5]

Studying Cuban Exiles, Knowing Myself

My diasporic condition has undoubtedly influenced my research agenda, centered on transnational migration from the Hispanic Caribbean. I began to study Cuban exiles in San Juan for my doctoral dissertation in 1983 (Duany, *The Cubans of Puerto Rico*). My first postdoctoral research project in 1987 focused on Dominican migration (much of it undocumented) to Santurce, Puerto Rico. I conducted a field study of Dominican transnationalism in New York City in 1993 (see Duany, *Los dominicanos en Puerto Rico*; *Quisqueya on the Hudson*). Over the past two decades, much of my intellectual efforts has dwelt on the Puerto Rican diaspora in the United States (see Duany, *The Puerto Rican Nation on the Move*). Despite the shifting terminology and objects of study, I have been largely concerned with how population displacements impact personal and collective identities.

I completed my doctoral dissertation in 1985, after a year and a half of fieldwork with Cubans in Puerto Rico. At the time, I thought of my work as an autoethnography, in the sense that I went back "home" to study "my people," not an exotic Other. It was clearly an autobiographical intellectual project, as I struggled to understand the community in which I had grown up but to which I no longer belonged. I felt estranged from older exiles who seemed fixed on recuperating *la Cuba del ayer* ("the Cuba of yesterday"), as they often referred to prerevolutionary society. Because I was too young to remember anything about my childhood in Havana, I had no emotional investments in that period, except through my parents' memories. Still, I had many Cuban friends and relatives in Puerto Rico and the United States.

As I approached this sensitive issue, I sought to avoid the popular myth of the Golden Exiles[6]—the almost instantaneous economic success of Cubans in San Juan as well as in Miami—and to explain their mode of incorporation, cultural adaptation, and ambivalent relationship with Puerto Rican society. Writing my dissertation, it was difficult to assume a "neutral" tone in describing the Cuban community in San Juan, a tone that was neither celebratory nor condemnatory. It was even more difficult to insert myself in a storyline dominated by a social scientific perspective in the third person.

To interpret the situation of Cubans in Puerto Rico, I resorted to the theoretical framework of "middleman minorities" (or trading minorities, to use a gender-neutral expression).[7] I elaborated this model in my dissertation as well as several articles and a book coauthored with the Cuban American sociologist José Cobas (see Duany, *The Cubans of Puerto Rico*; "The Cuban Community in Puerto Rico"; "Ethnic Identity and Socioeconomic Adaptation"; "Caribbean Migration to Puerto Rico"; "Two Wings of the Same Bird?" Cobas and Duany). A trading minority is a culturally distinctive group that specializes in the distribution of goods and services within the host economy. Examples of this type of socioeconomic adaptation include Jews in Western Europe, Chinese in Southeast Asia, Asian Indians in East Africa, Pakistanis in London, and Koreans in Los Angeles and New York City. Unlike most immigrants, who cluster in the lower rungs of the receiving society, trading minorities occupy an intermediate position between the local elite and working classes. Such a position largely derives from the group's socioeconomic traits, such as its class background, educational credentials, and transnational business connections. One of the attractions of the "middleman minority" model was that it illuminated significant angles of my family's and my own experiences.[8]

To begin, Cubans in Puerto Rico fit the occupational profile of trading minorities. Most are employed in commerce and services, especially retail trade and professional and business services. Many are business owners or work on their own. They have established numerous firms, including grocery stores, supermarkets, jewelry stores, clothing retail shops, car dealerships, restaurants, and cafeterias. Cuban exiles in San Juan have excelled in "the art of buying and selling," particularly as managers, administrators, sales, and office workers.[9] They were also well represented in the mass media (radio, newspapers, and television) as well as the professions (mainly medicine and engineering). My mother worked as a cosmetics salesclerk in several department stores, an itinerant clothing seller, a beautician, and an insurance agent (although she had been a schoolteacher in Cuba, she never practiced her profession in Puerto Rico). My father became programming director at one of Puerto Rico's leading television stations, WAPA-TV, until he lost his job after the company changed owners and he had to start again in Ecuador, where he died years later. My parents' occupations mirrored the concentration of Cuban exiles in the middle and upper levels of trade, communication, and other service sectors of the Puerto Rican economy, such as finance, insurance, and real estate.

Secondly, trading minorities everywhere tend to arouse hostility and suspicion from ample segments of the host society. Such minorities are usually stereotyped as stingy, unscrupulous, clannish, and materialistic in their ruthless pursuit and accumulation of wealth. Cuban exiles have often been dubbed "the Jews of the Caribbean" because of their business acumen and their reputation of maintaining social ties within their group. Puerto Rican folk humor typically portrays the exiles as pushy, ambitious, and sly entrepreneurs (see Duany, "The Cuban Community in Puerto Rico"; "Ethnic Identity and Socioeconomic Adaptation"). For instance, a Puerto Rican once told me the following riddle: "What do humble Cubans and Superman have in common? That they don't exist." Many Puerto Ricans associate the exiles with the *blanquitos* (literally, "little Whites") and *riquitos* (the "little rich people"), the White elite of San Juan. Although I am often called a *blanquito* in Puerto Rico, I resent the implication that I feel superior to members of the lower class.

Moreover, trading minorities often generate antagonism as well as sympathy from different sectors of the native population. The pro-independence movement and some nationalistic elements of the middle classes in Puerto Rico have tended to reject Cuban exiles because of their predominantly conservative ideology, while the pro-statehood movement has welcomed them as political allies. Many Puerto Ricans still perceive the exiles as unwanted outsiders who should not meddle in the island's internal affairs. In turn, many exiles continue to harbor deep-seated racial and ethnic prejudice against Puerto Ricans. A slur commonly used by Cubans to refer to Puerto Ricans is *boniato* (literally, sweet potato), a colloquial term for country bumpkin. To recycle Lola Rodríguez de Tió's famous metaphor, Cuba and Puerto Rico may well be like "two wings of a bird," but they are still far apart from each other (see Duany, "Two Wings of the Same Bird?").

I did not suffer direct discrimination as a Cuban growing up in Puerto Rico. Perhaps my middle-class status and light skin color shielded me from outright exclusion based on national origin. Nonetheless, I did experience more covert forms of prejudice. Being Cuban in San Juan—especially a *cubanazo*, a loutish Cuban—was the object of mockery more than scorn. For instance, if you drew too much attention to yourself, appeared conceited, or spoke Spanish with a strong Cuban accent, some Puerto Ricans would disapprovingly exclaim, ¡tenía que ser cubano! ("you had to be Cuban!"). Cubanness remains a stigma for many immigrants in Puerto Rico.

Finally, trading minorities are characterized by a high degree of ethnic solidarity that Cubans in Puerto Rico have displayed over the years, as well as a persistent cultural identity that has waned in the second generation, due among other reasons to a high outmarriage rate. On this last point, Cubans in Puerto Rico deviate from the typical experience of trading minorities, such as Jews or Chinese in other countries, who often remained endogamous for a long time. Linguistic, cultural, and religious affinities have encouraged intermarriage between Cubans and Puerto Ricans, at least among persons of similar class and racial backgrounds. In my sample of marriage licenses in San Juan, nearly 56 percent of Cubans had Puerto Rican spouses by 1983 (Duany, *The Cubans of Puerto Rico* 89). I myself represent a minority trend because I married a Cuban-born resident of Puerto Rico.

Cubans in San Juan had more than thirty-five voluntary associations in the mid-1980s, which helped them maintain strong symbolic bonds with their homeland. The most active of these organizations were Casa Cuba, a private social club where I spent much of my teenage years, and the Unión de Cubanos en el Exilio, a Catholic charity I have studied in some detail (Cobas and Duany ch. 6–7). Both institutions exemplified a strong trend toward ethnic encapsulation among first-generation immigrants. But most members of the second and third generations did not follow that pattern. As an adult, I did not join any Cuban associations in Puerto Rico, because of my growing detachment from the dominant institutions of the exile community. Before I moved to Miami, most of my social life revolved around Puerto Rican rather than Cuban friends.

For years, I was comfortable with the idea of belonging to the 1.5 generation of Cuban immigrants. I first learned about this in-between status reading the work of the Cuban American literary critic and poet Gustavo Pérez Firmat, who in turn borrowed a category coined by the Cuban American sociologist Rubén Rumbaut. Following this scheme, I found myself straddling the first generation, born and raised in Cuba (like my parents), and the second generation, born and raised abroad (like my children, who identify as Puerto Rican). However, I later met Rumbaut and he told me emphatically that I was not part of the 1.5 generation, but rather the 1.75 generation. According to the sociologist, this term refers to people who were born in one country but moved to another before they were five years old and entered school.[10]

In many ways, my experience is closer to the second generation of Cuban immigrants than to the first. I do not have a single memory of my early childhood in Havana; I learned to read and write outside the island; and I acquired a stronger Puerto Rican than a Cuban accent when speaking Spanish, after losing my Panamanian accent. I am unsure about fractioning an immigrant's cultural identity into so many decimal points (1.25, 1.5, 1.75, 2.5, and so on), but I am aware that my "Cubanness" differs from those who were brought up on the island and emigrated as adolescents or adults. I also know that the question of cultural identity has fascinated me and perhaps obsessed me for a long time.

In my view, Cuban and Puerto Rican cultures do not differ markedly. Both islands share a tropical climate, a prolonged Spanish colonial history, an Afro-Caribbean heritage, and a profound U.S. influence, although the latter is stronger in Puerto Rico. Regarding language, music, food, or religion, the two countries are indeed as closely linked as "two wings of a bird." Such cultural affinity is one of the reasons why many Cubans resettled in San Juan in the first place and their integration into Puerto Rican society has generally been swifter than in South Florida's enclave, where many Cuban practices and values remain virtually intact and relatively insulated from other cultures. Cuban Americans and Cuba-Ricans like me have developed distinctive identities, based on where we grew up and how we blended into the receiving countries. Several scholars have shown that the multiple meanings of the Cuban diaspora depend on when, how, why, and where one settled outside of Cuba (see, for instance, Behar and Suárez; Berg; Herrera; Pedraza). I believe it has been easier for Cubans to "assimilate" into Puerto Rican culture than into mainstream U.S. culture. Still, you must lose your Cuban "accent" to "pass" as Puerto Rican, as I often do, unless I am asked about my birthplace. In some quarters, I will never be fully accepted as part of the Puerto Rican nation because of my foreign birth. At best, I can aspire to become *un cubano buena gente* ("a nice Cuban"). Passing has its limits.[11]

A continuing source of friction with many Puerto Ricans is the exiles' prevalent political ideology. Although many, perhaps most, Cuban exiles favor Puerto Rico's annexation as a state of the American union, not all do. Nor can most exiles be caricatured as reactionary *batistianos* (supporters of Fulgencio Batista's dictatorship) who long to re-create "the Cuba of yesterday." I certainly would not describe my parents' ideological preferences that way, although my father was more conservative than my mother, partly because of their class and age differences. Many exiles in San Juan belong to the politically "moderate" sectors of the Cuban population abroad, who felt betrayed by the Revolution when it was radicalized in the early 1960s.[12] My analysis of various Cuban organizations and publications in Puerto Rico revealed a broad spectrum of opinion, ranging from the extreme right to the extreme left (Duany, *The Cubans of Puerto Rico* ch. 7–10). Nonetheless, most Cubans in Puerto Rico are staunch advocates of the island's permanent association with the United States.

An apparent paradox is the exiles' combination of a strong diasporic nationalism (vis-à-vis Cuba) and pragmatic annexationism (vis-à-vis Puerto Rico). My mother often pointed out that contradiction to her Cuban friends and acquaintances, which put her at odds with some of them. In addition, the dominant anti-Castro discourse insisted that exiles cut off all ties with their relatives on the island. I remember how my mother was ostracized when she decided to visit her family in Havana in December 1978, in the very first trip by émigré community members from Puerto Rico to Cuba.[13] At the time, many exiles considered traveling to Cuba blasphemous, a concession to peaceful coexistence with the Castro regime. According to a 2020 poll conducted by Florida International University, however, most Cuban Americans in Miami have traveled to Cuba and almost half send money to their relatives on the island (Steven J. Green School of International and Public Affairs).

Unless a massive migrant wave from Cuba to Puerto Rico arises in the near future—an unlikely event, given Puerto Rico's prolonged economic recession since 2006—Puerto Rican society will completely absorb its Cuban community within a generation, that of my children born on the island.[14] If you ask them what they are, most will quickly respond "Puerto Rican," even though their parents were born in Cuba. Unlike me, my children have no qualms about their national identity. As a member of the 1.75 generation of immigrants (following Rumbaut's classification), my position is more precarious than theirs.

Placing Myself in the Narrative

Writing about Puerto Rican national identity, I am often painfully aware that I am not one of the island's native sons. My Cuban birth, coupled with longtime residence in Puerto Rico, gives me an odd status somewhere in between stranger and near-native. I have often felt uneasy straddling this outsider/insider dichotomy, as when I am called a "Puerto Rican sociologist" (who is neither Puerto Rican nor a sociologist, but rather an anthropologist). But being labeled a "Cuban-born anthropologist" does not entirely resolve the problem either. This issue emerged sharply in a February 2004 interview with a Puerto Rican graduate student, Verónica Toro Ruiz, who translated several chapters of my book, *The Puerto Rican Nation on the Move*, into Spanish. Toward the end of our long and intense conversation, Toro Ruiz asked me about the use of the first person in my writing. Here is a passage from my response (translated from the Spanish original):

> I've realized, in the course of writing this book, among other things, that although I generally use the third person, when I'm going to introduce myself as part of the text, as part of the environment I'm observing, then I use the first person and I make the distinction, and that has to do partly with my own biography. To give you an example, a political science professor, Ángel Israel Rivera, told me one day in the hallway: "I'm glad that you're now saying, 'we Puerto Ricans.'" And it's difficult for me to say that because I don't totally feel Puerto Rican, since I was born in Cuba, although I grew up here. Nor do I feel very comfortable saying "we Cubans." Therefore, given that duality, that ambiguity, I normally don't say one thing or another. I resort to the third person: Cubans do this and say that, as well as Puerto Ricans. Every now and then, I use "we" when I feel part of what I'm writing. Perhaps that appears more explicitly when you're translating, the way in which sometimes I'd rather remain on the margins and don't place myself there.

Let me add a personal comment on language and identity. Someone once asked me when I first "became" bilingual. I answered that my parents had sent me to an all-English missionary school in the Panama Canal Zone during my third grade. Initially, I could not understand most of what was taught, except for Spanish class. But that year forced me to learn English quickly to survive academically. Moreover, I was often taken for an

American because of my pale skin, blue eyes, and light hair color, and many of my classmates were children of U.S. military personnel stationed in Panama. I would try to darken my hair by dampening it with water, combing it constantly, and repeating in front of the mirror, "I don't want to be a gringo." Anti-Americanism was entrenched in Panama City during my childhood years.

After moving to Puerto Rico, I was again placed in an all-English seventh-grade group called "Continental"—referring to the children of U.S. businesspeople on the island—because I did well in the English entrance exam. I did not enjoy that experience, as I felt isolated from the Spanish-speaking students in other classrooms. Again, many thought I was American because of my physical appearance, and I was commonly associated with the gringos. Even today, people routinely mistake me for an American, especially in public places with many U.S. tourists, such as airports, hotels, and restaurants. "But you don't look Puerto Rican," I am frequently told, and when I respond that I was born in Cuba, I may hear the rebuttal, "You don't look Cuban either." To which I may reply rhetorically, "What does a Puerto Rican (or a Cuban) look like?" I have often pondered on the irony of "looking American" while living in three of the countries where that attribution is most problematic (Cuba, Panama, and Puerto Rico), because of the long history of U.S. interventionism in the Caribbean region.

A decade of study in U.S. universities gave me the opportunity to develop fluency in the English language, to the point that I feel almost (though not quite) as comfortable writing in English as in Spanish. But language is a minefield for cultural politics because of Puerto Rico's colonial relation with the United States, and the unequal status of Spanish and English. As I noted in my interview with Toro Ruiz (cited above),

> This is the first question I'm always asked: "Why did you write this book in English?" One always feels under attack, and I always think, setting aside the differences, of the case of [the noted Puerto Rican writer] Rosario Ferré, who decided to write a book in Spanish and rewrite it in English, and she's still criticized for it. When my book is published in Spanish, I think the audience will be different [from the original one]; we'll see how the translation affects the socioeconomic and educational composition of the audience. I think that it'll be more self-reflexive; for example, some things in the English version are explained thoroughly, which won't be necessary in Spanish [because most of my readers will be Puerto Rican].

One result of my diasporic experiences has been shuttling between Spanish and English throughout my life. Although Spanish has always been the "native" language I speak at home, I now read and write in English every day. Spanish is the primary medium for my most intimate thoughts and feelings, while English is a more academic and professional mode of expression for me. I suppose this linguistic split is part of many migrants' lives, as well as a sign of increasing cultural hybridity. In my current daily routine in Miami, I continue to speak more Spanish than English, both at home and at work, and the two languages often overlap in that blend labeled "Spanglish."

Conclusion

Exiles, undocumented migrants, transnationals, and diasporas: these have been focal points of my research and writing for nearly four decades. The terms are all various ways, each with its own inflection, of naming the massive population displacements that have reshaped Caribbean societies. Whether they migrate primarily for political reasons (as exiles) or economic ones (as undocumented migrants), Caribbean people are constantly moving, circulating, and thereby creating transnational communities. The diaspora has become a defining feature of daily life, for those who live abroad (mainly in the United States), those who remain back home (in the Caribbean), and those who travel back and forth between the two places. But locating and identifying with the "homeland" are ever more difficult for many migrants, including myself. I was born in Cuba, grew up in Puerto Rico, live in Miami, and do not plan to return to live in Cuba. To use the terms I have often applied to others, I am the descendant of a trading minority that migrated to a colonial country, itself engaged in a massive diaspora and increasingly a transnational nation. In short, I became a Cuba-Rican.

Being the son of immigrants (I am not sure if my parents considered themselves "refugees" in the technical sense of having a well-founded fear of political persecution in their home country) has inexorably led me to probe the dilemma of identity, especially when the sources of that identity are fragmented. Returning to Cuba, if only infrequently and for brief visits, has helped me regain my sense of wholeness and connectedness to my native country, early childhood, and dispersed family. I now have close relatives in eight countries: the United States, Cuba, Puerto Rico, Panama, Chile, Spain, Switzerland, and Russia. This far-flung family map reflects some of the convoluted trajectories of the contemporary Cuban diaspora.

However, it has always been challenging to keep in touch with such a scattered kinship network.

My ailing mother's last letter to her older brother in Cuba is dated 31 December 1994, more than thirty-four years after we left Havana. I still keep a copy of that letter in my laptop computer. Because she could not write easily anymore, my mother dictated the following sentence to me (in Spanish): "Thank God, Jorge was able to travel to Cuba, which was a great dream of his, and that way we'll have the opportunity to see each other through him." When my mother passed away less than four months later, on 11 April 1995, I felt I had become the main liaison between my relatives in Cuba and abroad—that they somehow had "to see each other" through me, that it was now my turn to repair the family ties that were ruptured as a consequence of the Cuban Revolution. I felt a great burden upon inheriting my mother's role as a safekeeper of those fragile links that must be continually renewed across generations, long distances, and political discrepancies.

Like many transnational migrants I have met throughout my research, I find it indispensable to maintain emotional, family, and cultural connections with my country of birth. Returning to Havana every so often is a way of not burning the bridges back "home." Even though I might never go back to live there again, I would like to claim, with the exiled poet Heberto Padilla, that I have always lived in Cuba, if only in my mind.[15] Instead, I am now living in Miami, so close and yet so far from my native Havana, like many compatriots who have chosen to remake their family and professional lives here. I feel fortunate to have transplanted my Cuban roots in this crossroads of nomads, where most people come from somewhere else and everyone can develop a new sense of belonging.

Notes

1. The original version of this chapter was prepared for a volume edited by Ruth Behar and Lucía Suárez (Duany, "Becoming Cuba-Rican"). The text is loosely based on an earlier article (Duany, "Exiliados, indocumentados y diásporas"). I was proud of its publication by Casa del Caribe in Santiago de Cuba, located in Vista Alegre, the neighborhood where my father was born and grew up. A later version of the essay was published as "From Cuba-Rican to Cuban American." I appreciate the useful comments and suggestions by Ruth Behar, Lucía Suárez, Yolanda Martínez-San Miguel, Silvio Torres-Saillant, Eliana Rivero, Yeidy Rivero, and Carmen Haydée Rivera.

2. Behar has eloquently argued for a more intimate narrative style that acknowledges the anthropologist's vulnerable position vis-à-vis her ethnographic informants. See Behar, *The Vulnerable Observer*.

3. I have found it useful to apply a transnational approach in my work on Hispanic Caribbean migration. See Basch et al.; Schiller et al., "From Immigrant to Transmigrant"; *Towards a Transnational Perspective on Migration*.

4. Based on extensive archival research in Havana, Yeidy Rivero notes that Cuban television had entered a period of crisis since 1954, leading many TV directors, producers, actors, scriptwriters, and other technical staff to leave the island, mostly to Colombia, Venezuela, and Puerto Rico. See Rivero, "Havana as a 1940s–1950s Latin American Media Capital"; *Broadcasting Modernity*.

5. Here I use "Cuba-Rican" to designate someone born in Cuba and raised in Puerto Rico. Other scholars have employed the term to refer to the extensive cultural exchanges between Cuba and Puerto Rico since the nineteenth century, especially in popular music, theater, creative literature, and the mass media. See Rivero, "Caribbean *Negritos*"; Salgado. Martínez-San Miguel has aptly analyzed "the constitution of a diasporic Cuban-Rican imaginary" in the scant literature written by Cubans in Puerto Rico. See her essay, "Puerto Rican Cubanness," and her book *Caribe Two Ways*.

6. To my knowledge, Alejandro Portes was the first to use the expression *Golden Exile* in an academic article. The term has become synonymous with the first migrant wave (1959–62) after the Cuban Revolution, which drew mostly on the middle and upper classes. See also my essay, "Neither Golden Exile nor Dirty Worm."

7. The classic statement of this perspective remains Edna Bonacich's essay, "A Theory of Middleman Minorities."

8. The Cuban Revolution unleashed a massive number of refugees, primarily to the United States and secondarily to Puerto Rico. Between 1959 and 2019, the U.S. government admitted 36,052 Cubans in Puerto Rico (U.S. Department of Justice, *Annual Report*; *Statistical Yearbook*; U.S. Department of Homeland Security). The vast majority resettled in the San Juan metropolitan area.

9. Cuban migration to Puerto Rico since 1959 was more selective of the upper and middle classes than to other areas of the United States, producing a higher concentration of executives, entrepreneurs, professionals, and salespeople in San Juan than in Miami (Duany, *The Cubans of Puerto Rico* 41). According to 2019 census estimates, 58.4 percent of all employed Cubans in Puerto Rico were managers and professionals, while 21.4 percent were sales and office workers. Only 20.1 percent were blue-collar and service workers (Ruggles et al.).

10. Rumbaut first used the term "1.5 generation" to refer to the children of Indochinese refugees (from Vietnam, Laos, and Cambodia) who arrived in Southern California after reaching school age but before puberty. Pérez Firmat later developed the concept in a Cuban American setting, arguing that persons born in Cuba but raised in the United States are neither fully Cuban nor fully American. They straddle the linguistic and cultural boundaries between the first and second generations of Cuban immigrants. Isabel Alvarez Borland (7) refers to authors who were born in Cuba and came at an early age to the United States as "Cuban-American ethnic writers."

11. This exclusion is also true, to some extent, of persons of Puerto Rican ancestry born in the United States. The boundaries of "Puerto Ricanness" are highly contested and constantly confronted, especially in literary works by U.S.-based Puerto Rican au-

thors such as Tato Laviera and María Teresa "Mariposa" Fernández, who insist on more inclusive definitions of Puerto Rican national identity (see Torres-Padilla and Rivera).

12. Himilce Esteve (47) has highlighted that many "liberal" Cuban exiles settled in Puerto Rico after 1959—among them Roberto Agramonte, José Miró Cardona, Manuel Ray, Jorge Mañach, Leví Marrero, Carlos Alberto Montaner, and Anita Arroyo. Nonetheless, a small group of Cuban exiles engaged in politically motivated violence against the independence movement in Puerto Rico, especially during the 1970s (see Atiles-Osoria).

13. For a chilling account of "the Cuban exile wars" in Puerto Rico triggered by the émigré community's visits to Cuba, see Quiroga.

14. The Cuban population in Puerto Rico has decreased considerably since 1971, when it reached a high of 30,410, to 2019, when the census estimated only 11,753 persons of Cuban origin living in Puerto Rico (Duany, *The Cubans of Puerto Rico* 42; U.S. Census Bureau).

15. Padilla included the poem "Siempre he vivido en Cuba" ("I Have Always Lived in Cuba") in his controversial collection *Fuera del juego*. Lourdes Casal, who returned to Cuba after living almost twenty years abroad, wrote a poem with a similar line, featured in her posthumous anthology, *Palabras juntan revolución*. Thanks to Eliana Rivero for reminding me of Casal's poem. See also Román de la Campa's memoirs, *Cuba on My Mind*.

Works Cited

Alvarez Borland, Isabel. *Cuban-American Literature of Exile: From Person to Persona.* UP of Virginia, 1998.

Atiles-Osoria, José M. "The U.S. Response against Cuban and Puerto Rican Right-Wing Terrorism in the Pre and Post 9/11 Era." *Post 9/11 and the State of Permanent Legal Emergency: Security and Human Rights in Countering Terrorism*, edited by Aniceto Masferrer. Springer, 2012, pp. 259–84.

Basch, Linda, et al. *Nations Unbound: Transnational Projects, Postcolonial Predicaments, and Deterritorialized Nation-States.* Gordon and Breach, 1994.

Behar, Ruth. *The Vulnerable Observer: Anthropology That Breaks Your Heart.* Beacon, 1996.

Behar, Ruth, and Lucía M. Suárez, editors. *The Portable Island: Cubans at Home in the World.* Palgrave Macmillan, 2008.

Berg, Mette Louise. *Diasporic Generations: Memory, Politics, and Nation among Cubans in Spain.* Berghahn Books, 2011.

Bonacich, Edna. "A Theory of Middleman Minorities." *American Sociological Review*, vol. 38, no. 5, 1973, pp. 583–94.

Casal, Lourdes. *Palabras juntan revolución.* Casa de las Américas, 1981.

Cobas, José A., and Jorge Duany. *Cubans in Puerto Rico: Ethnic Economy and Cultural Identity.* UP of Florida, 1997.

de la Campa, Román. *Cuba on My Mind: Journeys to a Severed Nation.* Verso, 2000.

Duany, Jorge. "Becoming Cuba-Rican." *The Portable Island: Cubans at Home in the World*, edited by Ruth Behar and Lucía M. Suárez. Palgrave Macmillan, 2008, pp. 197–208.

———. *Blurred Borders: Transnational Migration between the Hispanic Caribbean and the United States*. U of North Carolina P, 2011.

———. "Caribbean Migration to Puerto Rico: A Comparison of Cubans and Dominicans." *International Migration Review*, vol. 26, no. 1, 1992, pp. 46–66.

———. "The Cuban Community in Puerto Rico: A Comparative Caribbean Perspective." *Ethnic and Racial Studies*, vol. 12, no. 1, 1989, pp. 36–46.

———. "Ethnic Identity and Socioeconomic Adaptation: The Case of Cubans in Puerto Rico." *The Journal of Ethnic Studies*, vol. 17, no. 1, 1989, pp. 109–27.

———. "Exiliados, indocumentados y diásporas: Las migraciones contemporáneas en Puerto Rico." *Del Caribe*, vol. 31, 2000, pp. 13–20.

———. "From Cuba-Rican to Cuban American." *Bridges to/from Cuba*, edited by Ruth Behar and Richard Blanco, 7 Aug. 2017, https://bridgestocuba.com/2017/08/from-cuba-rican-to-cuban-american/.

———. "Neither Golden Exile nor Dirty Worm: Ethnic Identity in Recent Cuban-American Novels." *Cuban Studies*, vol. 23, 1993, pp. 167–83.

———. *The Puerto Rican Nation on the Move: Identities on the Island and in the United States*. U of North Carolina P, 2002.

———. *Quisqueya on the Hudson: The Transnational Identity of Dominicans in Washington Heights*. 2nd ed. Dominican Studies Institute, CUNY, 2008.

———. "Two Wings of the Same Bird? Contemporary Puerto Rican Attitudes toward Cuban Immigrants." *Cuban Studies*, vol. 30, 2000, pp. 26–51.

Duany, Jorge, editor. *Los dominicanos en Puerto Rico: Migración en la semi-periferia*. Huracán, 1990.

Duany, Jorge Luis. *The Cubans of Puerto Rico: Socioeconomic Adaptation in a Caribbean City*. 1985. U of California, Berkeley, PhD dissertation.

Esteve, Himilce. *El exilio cubano en Puerto Rico: Su impacto político-social, 1959–83*. Raíces, 1984.

Herrera, Andrea O'Reilly, editor. *ReMembering Cuba: Legacy of a Diaspora*. U of Texas P, 2001.

Martínez-San Miguel, Yolanda. *Caribe Two Ways: Cultura de la migración en el Caribe insular hispánico*. Callejón, 2003.

———. "Puerto Rican Cubanness: Reconfiguring Caribbean Imaginaries." *Cuba: Idea of a Nation Displaced*, edited by Andrea O'Reilly Herrera. State U of New York P, 2007, pp. 47–76.

Mills, C. Wright. *The Sociological Imagination*. 40th anniversary ed. Oxford UP, 2000.

Padilla, Heberto. *Fuera del juego*. Unión de Escritores y Artistas de Cuba, 1968.

Pedraza, Silvia. *Political Disaffection in Cuba's Revolution and Exodus*. Cambridge UP, 2007.

Pérez Firmat, Gustavo. *Life on the Hyphen: The Cuban-American Way*. 2nd ed. U of Texas P, 2012.

Portes, Alejandro. "Dilemmas of a Golden Exile: Integration of Cuban Refugee Families in Milwaukee." *American Sociological Review*, vol. 34, no. 4, 1969, pp. 505–15.

Quiroga, José. "The Cuban Exile Wars: 1976–1981." *American Quarterly*, vol. 66, no. 3, 2014, pp. 819–33.

Rivero, Yeidy M. *Broadcasting Modernity: Cuban Commercial Television, 1950–1960*. Duke UP, 2015.

———. "Caribbean *Negritos*: Ramón Rivero, Blackface, and 'Black' Voice in Puerto Rico." *Television & New Media*, vol. 5, no. 4, 2004, pp. 315–37.

———. "Havana as a 1940s–1950s Latin American Media Capital." *Critical Studies in Media Communication*, vol. 26, no. 3, 2009, pp. 275–93.

Ruggles, Steven, et al. *IPUMS USA: Version 10.0 (Dataset)*. IPUMS, 2020, https://usa.ipums.org/usa/sda/.

Rumbaut, Rubén G. "Ages, Life Stages, and Generational Cohorts: Decomposing the Immigrant First and Second Generations in the United States." *International Migration Review*, vol. 38, no. 3, 2004, pp. 1160–1205.

Salgado, César A. "CubaRícan: Efectos de la capilaridad colonial." *La Habana Elegante* (second series), no. 46, 2009, http://www.habanaelegante.com/Fall_Winter_2009/Invitation_Salgado.html.

Schiller, Nina Glick, et al. "From Immigrant to Transmigrant: Theorizing Transnational Migration." *Anthropological Quarterly*, vol. 68, no. 1, 1995, pp. 48–63.

Schiller, Nina Glick, et al., editors. *Towards a Transnational Perspective on Migration: Race, Class, Ethnicity, and Nationalism Reconsidered*. New York Academy of Sciences, 1992.

Steven J. Green School of International and Public Affairs, Florida International University. *2020 FIU Cuba Poll: How Cubans Americans in Miami View U.S. Policies toward Cuba*. Steven J. Green School of International and Public Affairs, Florida International University, 2020, https://www.cri.fiu.edu/research/cuba-poll/2020-fiu-cuba-poll.pdf.

Toro Ruiz, Verónica. *La cultura puertorriqueña en movimiento: Identidades nacionales en la Isla y en los EEUU*. 2005. U of Puerto Rico, Río Piedras, MA thesis.

Torres-Padilla José L., and Carmen Haydée Rivera, editors. *Writing Off the Hyphen: New Critical Perspectives on the Literature of the Puerto Rican Diaspora*. U of Washington P, 2008.

U.S. Census Bureau. *Explore Census Data: ACS Demographic and Housing Estimates. Puerto Rico*. 2019, https://data.census.gov/cedsci.

U.S. Department of Homeland Security. *Yearbook of Immigration Statistics*. 2002–19, https://www.dhs.gov/immigration-statistics.

U.S. Department of Justice. *Annual Report of the Immigration and Naturalization Service*. U.S. Government Printing Office, 1959–77.

———. *Statistical Yearbook of the Immigration and Naturalization Service*. U.S. Government Printing Office, 1978–2001.

Contributors

Silvia Álvarez Curbelo is a retired professor in the School of Communication at the University of Puerto Rico in Río Piedras. She is currently affiliated with the Luis Muñoz Marín Foundation in San Juan. Her most recent publications include *Tiempos binarios: La Guerra Fría desde Puerto Rico y el Caribe* and *Los imprescindibles: Temas para entender el Puerto Rico de hoy.*

Madeline Cámara is professor of Latin American literature at the University of South Florida. She has published two anthologies: *María Zambrano: Between the Caribbean and the Mediterranean* and *María Zambrano: Palabras para el mundo.* Other publications include *Cuban Women Writers: Imagining a Matria* and *Cuba, the Elusive Nation: Interpretations of a National Identity.*

Jorge Duany is director of the Cuban Research Institute and professor of anthropology at Florida International University in Miami. He previously served as acting dean of the College of Social Sciences and professor of anthropology at the University of Puerto Rico in Río Piedras. He has published twenty-two books, including *Picturing Cuba: Art, Culture, and Identity on the Island and in the Diaspora* and *Puerto Rico: What Everyone Needs to Know.*

Jorge L. Giovannetti-Torres is professor in the Department of Sociology and Anthropology at the University of Puerto Rico in Río Piedras. His publications include *Black British Migrants in Cuba: Race, Labor, and Empire in the Twentieth-Century Caribbean, 1898–1948* and *Sonidos de condena: Sociabilidad, historia y política en la música reggae de Jamaica.*

Mary Ann Gosser Esquilín is professor of Spanish and comparative literature and the University Honors director at Florida Atlantic University. Her scholarly work has appeared in *Sargasso, CLA Journal, New Mango Season, Confluencia, CENTRO: Journal of the Center for Puerto Rican Studies, CU-ALLI,* and *Monographic Review,* among others.

Lillian Guerra is professor of history at the University of Florida in Gainesville. She is the author of many scholarly articles and essays as well as five books of history, including *Heroes, Martyrs, and Political Messiahs in Revolutionary Cuba, 1946–1958* and *Popular Expression and National Identity in Puerto Rico.*

Jesse Hoffnung-Garskof is associate professor of history and American culture at the University of Michigan, Ann Arbor. He is the author of *Racial Migrations: New York City and the Revolutionary Politics of the Spanish Caribbean* and *A Tale of Two Cities: Santo Domingo and New York after 1950.*

Benjamin Lapidus is professor of music at the John Jay College of Criminal Justice at the City University of New York. He is the author of *New York and the International Sound of Latin Music, 1940–1980* and *Origins of Cuban Music and Dance: Changüí.*

Laura Lomas is associate professor of English at Rutgers University-Newark. She is the author of *Translating Empire: José Martí, Migrant Latino Subjects, and American Modernities* and coeditor of the *Cambridge History of Latina/o American Literature.*

Yolanda Martínez-San Miguel is the Martha S. Weeks Chair in Latin American Studies and chair of the Department of Modern Languages at the University of Miami. She is the author of four books, including *Coloniality of Diasporas: Rethinking Intra-Colonial Migrations in a Pan-Caribbean Context,* and coeditor of several anthologies, most recently *The Routledge Hispanic Studies Companion to Colonial Latin America and the Caribbean, 1492–1898.*

Blanca Ortiz-Torres is professor of psychology at the University of Puerto Rico in Río Piedras. Some of her recent publications appear in *Revista Interamericana de Psicología, Psicología, Conocimiento y Sociedad,* and *Caribbean Studies.*

Carmen Haydée Rivera is professor in the Department of English at the University of Puerto Rico, Río Piedras. She previously served as dean of academic affairs and interim chancellor for the UPR-Río Piedras Campus. Her publications include a coedited collection of essays, *Writing Off the Hyphen: New Perspectives on the Literature of the Puerto Rican Diaspora*, and a critical biography titled *Border Crossings and Beyond: The Life and Works of Sandra Cisneros*.

Mario A. Rodríguez-Cancel is a Ph.D. candidate in psychology at the University of Puerto Rico in Río Piedras. He completed his master's thesis on the experiences of migrants from the eastern region of Cuba who now live in Puerto Rico.

Francisco A. Scarano is emeritus professor of history at the University of Wisconsin-Madison. He has written, edited, or coedited six books, three dozen articles or chapters, and many reviews in academic journals. His most recent books include *Puerto Rico: Cinco siglos de historia* and *The Caribbean: A History of the Region and Its Peoples*.

Monica Simal is associate professor in the Department of Foreign Language Studies at Providence College in Rhode Island. Her articles have appeared in U.S. and European journals such as *Latin American Research Review*; *Transmodernity: Journal of Peripheral Cultural Production of the Luso-Hispanic World*; *The Latin Americanist*; and *Letral: Revista Electrónica de Estudios Transatlánticos de Literatura*.

Hugo R. Viera-Vargas is assistant professor of Caribbean and Latin American studies and music at the New College of Florida. He is the coauthor of *Exploradores de la historia: Historia de Puerto Rico*. His articles have appeared in journals such as *CENTRO: Journal of the Center for Puerto Rican Studies, Latin American Music Review*, and *Caribbean Studies*.

Maida Watson is professor of Spanish at Florida International University in Miami. She has authored, edited, or coedited eight books and over forty-five articles and book chapters. Her work has appeared in scholarly journals such as *Revista Casa Museo Ricardo Palma, Antípodas, Revista Cayey*, and *Revista Iberoamericana*.

Alan West-Durán is associate professor in the Department of Modern Languages at Northeastern University. He is the author of *Cuba: A Cultural History* and *Tropics of Discourse: Cuba Imagined*, as well as editor-in-chief of *Cuba: People, Culture, History*. His essays have appeared in journals such as CENTRO: *Journal of the Center for Puerto Rican Studies, Encuentro de la Cultura Cubana*, and *Callaloo*.

Index

"A Cuba" (Rodríguez de Tió), 5, 107, 176, 209–10, 225
Abdala, 138, 152n7
Aboriginal populations of the Caribbean, 1, 63–64, 180. *See also* Taínos
Acosta-Belén, Edna, 10
Acosta Ithier, Geño, 62, 74, 75
African slavery, 1, 23n4, 33, 52n3, 128, 142, 144, 180; abolition of, 177; in Casal's "Los fundadores: Alfonso," 214, 219; in Cuba, 6, 65, 152n3, 281; depicted by Cabrera, 195; and fight for empowerment, 33; in the Hispanic Caribbean, 152n3; as key institution in Caribbean societies, 62, 142, 144; in Puerto Rico, 6, 65; in Ramos Otero's "Página en blanco y staccato," 212; and runaway slaves, 64; slave revolts during Haitian Revolution, 180; slave women, 128
Afro-Asian voices, 18, 213, 214
Afro-Caribbean: adaptations of Shakespeare, 145; Arroyo Pizarro's identity as, 122; divinities, 150; heritage, 302; intellectuals, 143; neighborhoods in New York City, 153n18; religious practices, 259; representations, 213; rhythmic traditions, 244. *See also* Afro-descendants
Afro-Cuban folklore, 195, 258, 262, 263
Afro-Cuban music, 71, 263, 264; in New York City, 258, 260; as perceived by U.S. travelers, 247; in postrevolutionary Cuba, 257
Afro-Cuban rebellion of 1912, 3. *See also* Race War of 1912
Afro-Cuban religions, 169, 212, 257, 258, 263, 264. *See also* Santería
Afro-descendants: in Cuba, 16, 35, 102, 144–49, 154n21, 252n5; from Cuba and Puerto Rico in the United States, 17, 115, 137, 141, 153, 154; in New York City, 101–8, 110, 138, 142
Afro-Latin@ Reader, The (Jiménez Román and Flores), 149

Afro-Latinx: collaborators with Martí, 154n22; as critical category, 150; culture, 148; cultural studies, 149; diasporas, 151; in New York City, 138, 143; migrants, 110; subjects, 149; working-class youth, 142
Afro-Puerto Rican, 71, 130, 153, 263
Aja Díaz, Antonio, 280
Albizu Campos, Pedro, 36, 38, 139, 153n11, 197, 206n10
Algarín, Miguel, 10, 11, 146
Alliance for Progress, 55, 56, 58
Allora, Jennifer, 21, 267–78
Alvarez Borland, Isabel, 11–13, 24n9, 24n11, 24n12, 318n10
Alvarez Curbelo, Silvia, 14
Anazagasti, José, 240
Anderson, Benedict, 222
Annexationism (Puerto Rico), 7, 8, 300, 303
Anónimo Consejo, 75
Anthems, 6, 55, 269–70, 274, 278n33
Antiblack racism, 35, 75, 143, 148, 149, 150, 154n22
Anticolonialism, 46, 138, 151. *See also* Decolonization
Anticommunism, 7, 13, 58, 148
Antillean Confederation, 64, 210, 225
Antiracism, 35, 138, 141, 143, 153n15, 154n22
Antonio Maceo Brigade, 138
Aparicio, Frances R., 142
Appadurai, Arjun, 19, 24n13
Arana Soto, Salvador, 23n4, 65, 66
Archipelagic perspectives, 4, 18, 22, 62–63, 126, 133, 187, 212; in Arroyo Pizarro's *Los documentados*, 125, 127; in Casal's "Los fundadores: Alfonso," 223; in Chan's painting, 132; in Ramos Otero's "Página en blanco y staccato," 223; in Rodríguez Iglesias' *Mi novia preferida fue un bulldog francés*, 132
Areíto (magazine), 17–18, 136–52
Arenas, Reinaldo, 12, 24n10

Aristide, Jean-Bertrand, 181
Arroyo-Martínez, Jossianna, 210, 211, 213
Arroyo Pizarro, Yolanda, 17, 121–34
Artaud, Antonin, 18, 158, 166, 172
Aruca, Francisco, 138
Asian migrations, to the Hispanic Caribbean, 18, 212–13, 218
Attali, Jacques, 267
Austin, Oscar Phelps, 239–40
Autonomism (Puerto Rico), 4, 6, 7, 33, 103
Avilés-Ortiz, Iliaris Alejandra, 201

Balseros (rafters), 21, 257, 280
Barrio Jauca (Santa Isabel, Puerto Rico), 79, 80, 81, 86, 89, 92
Batista, Fulgencio: coup d'état by, 3; created conditions for revolutionary movement in Cuba, 81; elected president of Cuba, 3; neocolonial regime of, 36; and President Kennedy, 52; regime represented in Triana's *La noche de los asesinos*, 165; rise and fall of, 15; rules Cuba indirectly, 3; supporters of, 303
Batista, Gustavo, 251n2
Bay of Pigs invasion, 34, 54, 55
Behar, Ruth, 307n2
Benech, Augusto, 100, 101, 103, 107
Benítez, Jaime, 192, 193, 197, 199–202
Benítez Rojo, Antonio: as exiled writer, 12, 24n10; as proponent of "repeating island," 62, 63, 66, 121, 187
Benoist, Jean, 76
Bergad, Laird, 65
Berglund, Birgitta, 167, 168
Berntsen, Martin, 193, 202, 203, 204, 206n10
Berry, John, 291
Betances, Ramón Emeterio, 9, 23n7, 100, 139
Betancourt, Rómulo, 14, 57
Biografía de un cimarrón (Barnet), 97n1, 216
Birman, Dina, 292
Black popular culture, 147–51
Blackness: in the Caribbean, 213, 226n7; in Cuba, 36, 212, 213; in Puerto Rico, 212, 216, 217, 221, 244, 245; of Mariel Cubans, 257
Bodenheimer, Rebecca, 282
Bolívar, Natalia, 258
Bomba (Puerto Rico), 263–64
Bonilla, Frank, 150, 152n5
Bonilla, Yarimar, 154n26
Boricuas, 143, 150
Borinquen, 64, 143

Borrell, Roberto, 262–63
Bosch, Juan, 57, 58
Boulez, Pierre, 270, 278n3
Boyce, William D., 237
Bradford, Anita Casavantes, 153n13
Braudel, Fernand, 66, 68
Bray, Emily, 292
Brecht, Bertolt, 18, 158, 173n5
Bryan, William, 249
Burchardt, Hans-Jürgen, 23n4
Burunat, Silvia, 24n11
Buscaglia-Salgado, José, 210, 226n5

Cabrera, Lydia, 20, 192, 193–96
Cabrera Infante, Guillermo, 12, 149
Cage, John, 270, 271, 273
Calderón, Tego, 75
Caliban: A Journal of New World Thought and Writing, 144, 145
"Caliban: Notes Towards a Discussion of Culture in Our America" (Fernández Retamar), 144–45
Callejo, Fernando, 248
Calzadilla, Guillermo, 21, 267–78
Cámara, Madeline, 20
Campbell, Reau, 247, 248
Carbonell, Walterio, 149, 154n22
"Carib Indians," 64. *See also* Aboriginal populations of the Caribbean
Caribbean anthropology, 62, 79, 80, 81
Caribbeanness, 121, 122
Carpentier, Alejo, 179
Carroll, Henry, 238
Casal, Lourdes: articulates study of "Cuban minority," 140, 141; as author of "Los fundadores: Alfonso," 18, 210–26, 236; as author of *Palabras juntan revolución*, 309n15; broad conception of *Latinidad* in, 140; catalyzes race-consciousness in Cuban studies, 148; as coauthor of *Contra viento y marea*, 190; criticizes Fernández Retamar, 145–46; dossier on her work in *Cuban Studies*, 151n1; encourages study of Cuban diaspora, 152n5; establishes solidarity between Chinese and Blacks, 216; founds *Areíto* magazine, 17, 36, 137; interested in migrants' roots in their homelands, 149; remembered by González Echevarría, 141; returns to Havana, 138, 309n15; rewriting of Cuban history from woman-centered perspective, 236n3; on translation and decolonization, 153n18

Casals, Pablo, 55
Castro, Fidel: born in Oriente, Cuba, 285; criticism of rule by, 40; criticized by Muñoz Marín, 54–55, 56; criticizes Democratic Left, 14; declares Cuba socialist, 3, 6; end of era of, 96; exiles' anger toward, 12, 13, 24n10, 303; launches guerrilla movement, 3; leads Cuban Revolution, 6, 12, 23n9; obsession by many Americans with, 56; on Puerto Rico's Free Associated State, 67; and one-party rule, 34; peaceful coexistence with, 303; speaks at Harvard University, 43–44; speeches of, 285; support for, 39, 40
Castro, Raúl: Black mobilization efforts in Cuba under, 36; born in Oriente, Cuba, 285; criticism of rule by, 40
Catholic Church: administers Operation Pedro Pan, 153n13; admired by Zambrano, 199, 203; among members of La Cabaña, 203; and *El Piloto* newspaper, 204; first bishop of Puerto Rico, 226n4; imposed on Spanish colonies, 1, 180; opposed to Muñoz Marín, 49; Taso's religious conversion from, 94; and Unión de Cubanos en el Exilio, 39
Centro de Estudios Puertorriqueños (Hunter College), 149–50
Chaar-Pérez, Kahlila, 210
Chan, Kathryn, 132, 133
Chávez-Silverman, Susana, 142
Chinese migration, 223, 226; and indentured service, 211, 219, 223; to Puerto Rico, 221, 226–27n9; and trading minorities, 299, 301; to Cuba, 211, 214, 215–16, 219, 223, 226n2; to the United States, 212, 217, 221, 223
Chufatt Latour, Antonio, 226n2
Ciboneys, 64. *See also* Aboriginal populations of the Caribbean
Cigarmakers, 35, 100, 101, 108, 113, 138
Club Borinquen (New York City), 104
Club Guerrilla de Maceo (New York City), 101, 105, 113
Club José Maceo (New York City), 105, 108, 109, 114
Club Las Dos Antillas (New York City), 15, 100–16
Cobas, José A., 299
Coffee industry in Puerto Rico, 65, 236
Colás, Ramón, 282
Cold War, 7, 34, 47, 66, 67, 75; binary spheres of influence under, 45; in the Caribbean, 63, 70, 71; economic growth under, 69; end in 1989, 72; influence on Muñoz Marín, 44, 53, 58; in Latin America, 40; Non-Aligned Movement as response to, 139; political ideology of, 67; proscription of contacts between the United States and Cuba under, 142
Colón, Jesús, 9, 10, 115
Colón Martínez, Noel, 138–39
Colonial discourse, 233–50; sonic, 19, 234, 235, 244, 246, 250
Colonialism: criticized by Arroyo Pizarro, 128; and diaspora, 235; in the insular Hispanic Caribbean, 1, 37, 218; global movements against, 150; and language, 122, 128, 144; and Muñoz Marín, 44, 45, 49, 50, 55, 60; in the nineteenth and twentieth centuries, 223; as part of Benítez Rojo's "repeating island," 62; in Puerto Rico, 36–45, 63–72, 146, 154n26, 271, 302, 305, 306; Spanish, 1, 2, 3, 6, 8, 81, 177; U.S., 36, 144, 234, 239, 251
Columbus, Christopher, 179, 180, 181, 182, 187
Commonwealth of Puerto Rico. *See* Estado Libre Asociado
Communism, 6, 44, 45, 142, 165; as bureaucratic socialism, 68; in Eastern Europe, 45; economic redefinition of, 73; as fraternity of revolutionaries, 274; led by Fidel Castro, 40; in Muñoz Marín's thought, 14, 51, 52, 53, 56; radical reexamination of, 72; repressed by "Gag Law" in Puerto Rico, 37, 38; repression of dissent under, 40; in Russia, 44, 50; as totalizing discourse, 40; under the Cold War, 70; in the world today, 3
Communist Party of Cuba, 39, 40. *See also* Cuban communism
Contra viento y marea (Grupo Areíto), 140
Cooper, Carolyn, 190n1
Coquí (frog), 19, 188, 189, 190
Cortés, Jason, 211
Cotto-Ojeda, Ramón, 23n4
Cotto-Thorner, Guillermo, 142, 153n11
Cruz-Malavé, Arnaldo, 211
Cuban Adjustment Act, 130
Cuban American ethnic writers, 12, 13, 308n10
Cuban and Cuban American studies, 22, 137, 139, 142, 148, 195
Cuban communism, 3, 14, 41, 67, 72, 168, 257
Cuban Constitution of 1901, 2, 6, 34, 250
Cuban exiles, 16, 24n9, 103, 136, 137, 141, 148, 151, 152n4; impact of Mariel exodus on, 12, 257; in Puerto Rico, 8, 138, 152n4, 280–92, 296–309. *See also* Cuban exodus to the United States

Cuban exodus to the United States, 3, 34, 76n1, 130, 141, 258, 281, 292, 302. *See also* Migration: from Cuba
Cuban-American Literature of Exile (Alvarez Borland), 11–13
Cuban Missile Crisis, 57, 58, 59n6
Cuban Research Institute (Florida International University), 22, 296–97
Cuban Revolution, 14, 34, 65, 96; Caribbean cross-island translation in, 146–47; connected to concerns of Puerto Rican literary critics, 145; criticized by Muñoz Marín, 53, 55; exodus through Mariel, 257; impact in Puerto Rico, 7–8, 50; provokes exodus, 3, 307, 308n6, 308n8; support for, 39, 138; triumph in 1959, 7–8, 43, 227n9, 296; views of Afro-Cuban religions in, 257–58; widening gap with Puerto Rico under, 68
Cuban Revolutionary Party, 15, 100, 103, 107
Cubanía (Cubanness): in Casal's "Los fundadores: Alfonso," 211, 213, 216, 224, 225; generational differences in, 302; as represented by Cabrera, 195; as represented by Martí, 221; as stigma in Puerto Rico, 301
Cubanidad. See *Cubanía*
"Cuba-Rican," 21, 298, 302, 308n5
Cultural studies, 136–51, 157–61, 192, 214, 224
Curanderismo, 93–94

Danza (Puerto Rico), 241, 242, 243, 251n2
de la Campa, Román: as coauthor of *Contra viento y marea*, 140; on Cuban studies, 142; interview with Márquez, 142, 143, 145, 146, 149, 152n2, 153n16; on *Areíto*, 136, 137, 139
de la Luz, Caridad "La Bruja," 11
de Quesada, Gonzalo, 105
Decolonization: as articulated by Márquez, 145, 153n16, 153n18; in Cuba and Latin America, 150; endorsed by *Areíto*, 17, 136, 139, 150; in Puerto Rico, 66, 152n4, 277; and translation, 142–44, 146, 147, 148
DeLoughrey, Elizabeth M., 178, 188
Democratic Left, 14, 52, 53, 55, 56
Diasporas. See Cuban exiles; Cuban exodus to the United States; Dominican migration to Puerto Rico; Migration; Puerto Rican exodus to the United States
Díaz Quiñones, Arcadio, 23n4
Dietz, James, 39
Dinwiddie, William, 237, 243
Doctrina de Martí (newspaper), 102, 105, 110
Dominican migration to Puerto Rico, 123, 124, 125, 126, 298

Downes v. Bidwell (1901), 3
Dreke, Enrique "Kike," 262
Du Bois, W.E.B., 159
Duany, Jorge, 21–22
Duchesne, Rafael, 251
Dunham, Katherine, 258
Duvalier, François (Papa Doc), 179, 181

East Harlem (El Barrio), 103, 111, 141, 142, 146; members of Club Las Dos Antillas in, 16, 101, 102, 110, 114
Edwards, Brent Hayes, 143
Eisenhower, Dwight D., 45, 54
El Barrio. *See* East Harlem
El Piloto (magazine), 202, 204–5, 206n10
Environmental degradation, 18–19, 177, 180, 182–84, 190
Environmentalist novel, 19, 177, 181
Epic theater (Brecht), 18, 158
Espada, Martín, 23n8
Estado Libre Asociado (Commonwealth of Puerto Rico), 14, 46, 49, 65, 66; as autonomous formula, 14; contested legitimacy of, 41; created in 1952, 4, 7; denial of greater autonomy, 43; limitations of, 58; Mendoza's influence on, 198; as model of democratic development, 51; as model of liberation for colonial peoples, 46; popular demands in, 40–41; ratified by U.S. Congress, 45; recognized by United Nations, 45; reduced value after Cold War, 72; referendum on, 27; represented in Marqués' *Los soles truncos*, 164; as semiautonomous limbo, 37
Esteve, Himilce, 309n12
Ethnoscapes (Appadurai), 19, 24n13
Ezratty, Barbara Tasch, 98n11

Falcón Paradí, Arístides, 264
Fano, Elsa, 20, 192, 202, 203, 204, 205
Fanon, Frantz, 143, 149
Feminism: afrofeminism, 122, 128; among Puerto Rican diaspora, 150; and Arroyo Pizarro, 128; in the Caribbean, 219; and Casal, 226n3; concept of sorority in, 205n1; ecofeminism, 178, 179; Mendoza joins movement, 197; role of patronage in, 192; and Zambrano, 198
Fernandes, Sujatha, 153–54n21
Fernández, María Teresa "Mariposa," 11, 309n11
Fernández Fragoso, Víctor, 131, 151n1
Fernández Retamar, Roberto, 144, 145, 153n18
Ferrer, Ada, 154n22
Ferrer, Rolando, 18, 159, 169, 170, 171

Figueres, José, 14
Figueroa, Sotero: as collaborator of Martí, 154n22; insists on racially mixed character of La Liga, 105; as mentor of Club Las Dos Antillas, 102, 103, 104; as model of interisland collaboration, 138; as part of "Pilgrims of Freedom," 9, 23n7
Fiol-Matta, Licia, 197
Flags of Cuba and Puerto Rico, 1, 44, 67, 297
Flores, Juan, 9, 143, 147–51, 151n1, 153n111, 153n20
Foraker Act, 251n1
Foucault, Michel, 193, 203
Fowles, George, 241
Frank, Waldo, 194
Free people of color: in Cuba, 211, 214, 219, 281; in Puerto Rico, 6
"Freedom Flights," 12, 280
Freire, Joaquín, 23n4
Friedrich, Carl, 46
Fuentes, Marisa, 213
Fukuyama, Francis, 74
Fusté, José, 102
Fuster, Melissa, 23n3
Fuster, Nadja, 281, 282

Gaddis, John Lewis, 43, 53
"Gag Law," 37, 38
García, María Cristina, 292
García, Ofelia, 24n11
García Canclini, Néstor, 125
García Passalacqua, Juan Manuel, 48
García-Peña, Lorgia, 213
García Villamil, Felipe, 254, 258–59
Gender relations, 83–84, 94, 104–5, 123, 127, 201, 202; in Arroyo Pizarro's and Rodríguez Iglesias' novels, 17, 122, 127, 134; in Casal's "Los fundadores: Alfonso," 220; gender-neutral expressions, 299; and imperial relations, 31; interconnected with other social categories, 4, 27, 31, 122, 123; and Mariel exodus, 257; in Montero's *Tú, la oscuridad*, 184; in Puerto Rican writing, 10; in rural society, 15, 84, 86, 181; in sonic representations, 247
Gender studies, 151, 192, 193
Georas, Chloé S., 257
George, Marian, 244
Gil, Wenceslao, 164
Gil Ayala, Carlos, 44
Glissant, Édouard, 121, 184, 210
Godkin Lectures, 43, 44, 48
"Golden Exiles," 12, 23n9, 280, 299, 308n6

Gómez, José Miguel, 35, 36
Gonzales v. Williams (1904), 3
González Echevarría, Roberto, 140, 141–42
González Rego, René, 285
González Ripoll, María Dolores, 62
Gosser Esquilín, Mary Ann, 18–19
Gosson, Renée K., 178, 188
Grito de Lares, 6
Grosfoguel, Ramón, 257
Guajiros (Cuban peasants), 35, 285, 286
Guerra, Lillian, 13–14, 98n11, 102, 149, 154n22
Guevara, Gema, 214
Guillén, Nicolás, 142, 143, 144
Güiro (percussion instrument), 234, 242, 243–44, 245–46

Habaneros (inhabitants of Havana), 21, 281–92
Haiti, 6, 19, 64, 177–91, 224; environmental degradation in, 177, 182, 184, 190; as focal point of environmental concerns, 181; migration to the Dominican Republic from, 181; migration to Puerto Rico from, 123, 124, 125, 126; migration to the United States from, 146; slave uprisings in, 180; as synecdoche for body of Antillean bird, 19, 177
Hall, Arthur D., 237
Hall, Stuart, 147, 148, 149, 153n20
Handley, George B., 178, 188
Haraway, Donna, 176, 178
Harlem, 101, 108, 109, 136, 150. *See also* East Harlem
Hay, John, 2
Helg, Aline, 35
Herédia, José María, 9, 24n9
Heteronormativity, 183, 211, 213, 218, 220
Hill, Robert, 237–38, 245–46, 248
Hip hop, 75, 148, 151, 153–54n21
Hispanic Caribbean: Afro-Asian dimensions of, 208; antiblackness in, 149; antiracism in, 154; and *Areíto*, 137, 138, 139, 145; Asian and queer characters in, 18, 212; Asian migrations to, 212; connections with African diaspora, 147; diasporas in New York City, 146, 153; gender relations in, 84; literary production in, 172; migration from, 295, 298, 308n3; miscegenation in, 226n5; mulatto and Black foundation of, 218; rural settings in, 86; sex work in, 86; sexual scandals in, 96; slavery in, 152n3; sociocultural transformations in, 83; traditional definitions of, 225
Hispaniola, 19, 176, 177, 180, 184, 190
Hispanophilia, 18, 212, 218, 222, 224, 225

Historical exiles. *See* "Golden Exiles"
Hoffnung-Garskof, Jesse, 15–16, 146, 152n3
Homoeroticism. *See* Same-sex desire
Hooker, Juliet, 211
Hospital, Carolina, 24n11
Hostos, Eugenio María de, 9, 23n7, 139
Hostosian National Independence Movement, 8

Illnesses and remedies, 90–94
Imagined Communities (Anderson), 222
Import-substitution industrialization, 14–15, 68
Independence movements, 1–2, 17–18, 101, 177; in Puerto Rico, 7, 8, 138, 140, 152n4, 164
Independent Party of Color (Cuba), 35, 38
Intersectionality, 4, 13, 146, 150, 257
Invitación al polvo (Ramos Otero), 210, 224
Iovino, Serenella, 178

Jacobson, Jenna Leving, 151n1
Jíbaros (Puerto Rican peasants), 40, 65, 237, 238, 244
Jiménez, Juan Ramón, 200, 205n5
Jiménez Román, Miriam, 149, 150
Johnson, Lyndon B., 58
Jones Act (1917), 251n1
Jottar, Berta, 264

Kahn, Douglas, 272
Kennedy, John F.: and Alliance for Progress, 55, 56; assassination of, 58n4; and Bay of Pigs invasion, 35; and Cuban Missile Crisis, 57, 58; and Muñoz Marín, 49, 52, 53; on U.S. military intervention in Cuba, 54
Knauer, Lisa Maya, 264
Knight, Franklin W., 23n4
Kubrick, Stanley, 274, 275–76
Kutzinski, Vera M., 153n18

La Cabaña (intellectual group), 199, 202–5
La Carreta (Marqués), 58, 154n25
La Fountain-Stokes, Lawrence, 211
La Liga (New York City), 100, 105, 107
La noche de los asesinos (Triana), 18, 159, 165–69, 173
Lagarde, Marcela, 205n1
Lalo, Eduardo, 138, 152n6
Lapidus, Benjamin, 20–21
Latin jazz, 20, 74, 260, 264
Latin music in New York City, 256–57, 261
Latinidad (Latinness), 17, 140

Latinx studies, 137, 139, 147–59
Laviera, Tato, 11, 146, 309n11
Lee Borges, José, 221, 226–27n9
Leinius, Johanna, 23n4
Lewis, Oscar, 95
Lewis, Ruth, 95
Lezama Lima, José, 192, 193, 195, 196, 205, 206n5
Lila, la mariposa (Ferrer), 18, 159, 169–71, 173n5
Lomas, Laura, 17–18, 151n1
López, Iraida, 24n11, 151n1
López, Kathleen, 219, 226n2
López-Calvo, Ignacio, 218
López Nieves, Luis, 136, 142
Lorde, Audre, 222
Los documentados (Arroyo Pizarro), 17, 121–34
"Los fundadores: Alfonso" (Casal), 18, 211–16, 226n6
Los soles truncos (Marqués), 18, 159, 160–65, 169, 170, 171
Ludmer, Josefina, 122, 124, 128, 133
Luna, Noel, 23n4

Maceo, Antonio, 100
Machado, Gerardo, 3
Macías, Rita, 257, 263
Madan, Cristóbal, 32
Malavet Vega, Pedro, 242
Manifest Destiny, 31
Manners, Robert, 87
Mariel exodus of 1980, 12, 24n10, 280; and Nuyorican musicians, 257, 260–64; musical impact of, 12, 20, 256–64
Marielitos. *See* Mariel exodus of 1980
Marín, Francisco "Pachín" Gonzalo, 23n7, 67, 103, 104, 138, 153n14
Maroonage, 64, 122
Marqués, René, 18, 57–58, 154n25, 159, 160–65, 173n2
Márquez, Roberto, 142, 143, 144–47, 148
Martí, José, 104; antiracist discourse of, 154n22; as architect of discourse of Cuban identity, 231; as author of "Nuestra América," 152n10; collaborated with New York–based clubs, 138; as contemporary of Rodríguez de Tió, 136; dies in battle, 103; dreams of integrating Cuba and Puerto Rico, 67; elected delegate of Club Las Dos Antillas, 100; exile as a theme in his work, 24n9; as leader of Cuba's independence movement, 101; as mistaken author of the poem "A Cuba," 210; quoted in *Areíto* magazine, 137; seeks refuge in the

United States, 9; silencing of race, 147–48; supported by Afro-Antilleans in New York City, 102, 114, 115
Martínez-Fernández, Luis, 65
Martínez Furé, Rogelio, 144, 154n22
Martínez Olivera, Manuel, 256, 262
Martínez-San Miguel, Yolanda, 18, 132, 308n5
Marxism, 8, 148, 257
Mayajigua (Cuba), 79, 82, 87, 88, 91, 93
McMurray, George, 165
Meehan, Kevin, 146
Memoirs of Bernardo Vega (Vega), 9, 53n11
Mendoza, Inés María, 20, 55, 192, 197–99, 202
Mestizaje, 226n5. *See also Mulataje*
Mi libro de Cuba (Rodríguez de Tió), 5, 209, 210
Mi novia preferida fue un bulldog francés (Rodríguez Iglesias), 17, 121–34
"Mi raza" (Martí), 107
Middleman (trading) minorities, 8, 22, 299–301, 306
Mignolo, Walter, 122
Migration, 1, 4, 8–9, 16, 276, 280–92, 295; Asian, 212; Chinese, 212, 214, 217, 219, 221, 223, 226n2, 226n8, 226–27n8, 301; from Cuba, 11, 12, 23–24n9, 24n11, 141, 308n9; from the Hispanic Caribbean, 298, 308n3; interisland, 124, 125; from Puerto Rico, 3, 16, 41, 68, 108, 152n11, 216, 226
Mills, C. Wright, 295
Mintz, Sidney W.: as author of *Worker in the Cane*, 15, 82, 83, 84, 85; fieldnotes of, 95; fieldwork in Puerto Rico of, 80, 81–82; as leading scholar in Caribbean anthropology, 81; letters from Taso to, 80, 81, 82, 90, 91, 101
Mirabal, Nancy Raquel, 102, 146, 257
Mistral, Gabriela, 197, 198, 226n5
Mixer, Knowlton, 239
Mohr, Nicholasa, 10, 150
Montero, Mayra, 18–19, 176–90
Montes Huidobro, Matías, 165, 169
Morúa Law of 1909, 35
Moscoso, Teodoro, 55
Mulataje, 212, 213, 226n5
Muñiz Varela, Carlos, 138, 152n7
Muñoz Marín, Luis, 43–58: as first elected governor of Puerto Rico, 36; delivers Godkin Lectures, 14, 43, 44, 48; growing integration of Puerto Rico into U.S. orbit under, 6–7; proclaims Puerto Rico's "peaceful revolution," 67; as promoter of Estado Libre Asociado, 28; response to nationalist uprising, 38; speeches of, 14, 43–57

Nationalism, 45, 48, 49; in Cuba, 6, 151, 218; in Puerto Rico, 6, 14, 67, 150, 218
Nationalist Party (Puerto Rico), 36, 37, 50, 197
Neglia, Erminio, 165, 168
Neocolonialism in Cuba, 32, 36, 42, 46, 72, 81, 82
New Rican Village, 259, 260
New York and the International Sound of Latin Music, 1940–1990 (Lapidus), 264, 265n1
Noel, Urayoán, 146
Northrop, Henry, 245
Norton, Albert James, 247, 248
Norton Anthology of Latino Literature (Stavans), 16
Nuclear holocaust, 14, 44, 51, 57, 58
"Nuestra América" (Martí), 152n10
Nuyorican drummers, 259, 260, 261, 262, 263
Nuyorican Poetry (Algarín and Piñero), 11, 146
Nuyorican Poets Café, 10–11, 23n8
Nuyorican writers, 10, 146, 148, 150

Ober, Frederick A., 236, 239–40
Ojeda Reyes, Félix, 23n7, 153n14
"One-and-a-half generation" (Rumbaut, Pérez Firmat), 12, 301–2, 308n10
Operation Bootstrap: connection with Estado Libre Asociado, 40; criticism of, 40; "Great Migration" under, 152–53n11; as model of government-led industrialization, 7, 37, 68, 81; and Moscoso, 55; and Muñoz Marín, 46; support for, 39; transformations under, 95
Operation Pedro Pan, 152n5, 153n13
Opperman, Serpil, 178
Orientales (inhabitants of eastern Cuba), 21, 281–93
Orientalism, 218, 219, 221
Orígenes (magazine), 193, 194, 196
Orishas, 150, 217–18, 258, 259, 262, 263. *See also Santería*
Orozco, Román, 258
Ortiz, Fernando, 195, 206n4
Ortiz López, Luis, 281, 282
Ortiz-Torres, Blanca, 21, 283
Orum, Thomas, 102
O'Sullivan, John, 31

Padilla, Heberto, 12, 24n10, 153n18, 307, 309n15
Padura, Leonardo, 16–17

"Página en blanco y staccato" (Ramos Otero), 18, 211–25
Palestinos. See *Orientales*
Pappademos, Melina, 102
Paravisini-Gebert, Lizabeth, 19, 177
Patria (newspaper), 103, 107
Patriarchal ideology: in Casal's "Los fundadores: Alfonso," 218–19, 221; exclusion of Black women, 127–28; in the Hispanic Caribbean, 225; in Marqués' *Los soles truncos*, 164, 171; in Montero's *Tú, la oscuridad*, 183; in Ramos Otero's "Página en blanco y staccato," 218–19; turning away from, 151
People of Puerto Rico, The (Steward et al.), 80
Perera, Hilda, 12
Pérez, Louis A., Jr., 32, 250
Pérez Firmat, Gustavo, 12, 301, 308n10
Picabia y Niebla, Juan Manuel (Manolo), 15, 79–96
Pietri, Pedro, 11, 146
"Pilgrims of Freedom," 9, 10, 23n7
Piñera, Virgilio, 226n1
Piñero, Miguel, 10, 11, 146
Plantation economy: demise in Haiti, 6; development in Cuba, 6, 33, 73; environmental impact of, 180–81; as part of "repeating island," 62, 180; in Puerto Rico, 65, 68
Platt, Oliver, 239
Platt Amendment: created siege mentality in Cuba, 34; imposed on Cuban Constitution of 1901, 2, 250; long-term impact of, 33, 36; repealed, 3; thwarted Cuban sovereignty, 6, 20
Plena (Puerto Rico), 242, 245
Popular Democratic Party, 39, 81, 198
Popular music in Cuba and Puerto Rico, 15, 74, 233–52, 308n5
Por qué . . . Cuentos negros de Cuba (Cabrera), 194, 195, 206n4
Portes, Alejandro, 308n6
Portuondo, Buenaventura, 103, 110
Postcoloniality, 3, 63, 147, 184, 212
Poyo, Gerald, 102
Pozo, Chano, 259
Prida, Dolores, 141
Prieto, Yolanda, 151n1
Pro Independence University Federation, 50
Prohías, Rafael, 141
Pro-Independence Movement, 7–8, 50, 300
Psychological space in theater, 18, 158–73
Puerto Rican exodus to the United States, 33–34, 76n1, 147, 298; during the "Great Migration," 23n6, 152–53n11, 216
Puerto Rican in New York and Other Sketches, A (Colón), 9
Puerto Rican Independence Party, 50
Puerto Rican Nation on the Move, The (Duany), 4, 296, 304
Puerto Rican Socialist Party, 7
Puerto Rican studies, 22, 137, 139, 152n5
"Puerto Rico Project, The," 81, 87, 97n3
Puertorriqueñidad (Puerto Ricanness): and Chinese-Cuban immigration, 227n9; exclusion of Puerto Rican migrants, 208n11; marginalization of Cuban immigrants, 304; in Ramos Otero's "Página en blanco y staccato," 213, 221, 222, 225

Queer perspectives on nationalist discourses, 18, 210, 211, 212, 218–22, 225

Race: according to Martí, 107, 115, 147–48; in Arroyo Pizarro and Rodríguez Iglesias' novels, 122; among Cuban and Puerto Rican migrants, 86n1; among diasporic Puerto Rican writers, 10; interconnectedness of, 4, 127, 150, 235, 243; and Mariel Cubans, 257; in Marxist theory, 148; race-conscious discourse in Cuba and Puerto Rico, 148, 154n22; race-consciousness in the diaspora, 148, 151; in republican Cuba, 35; in revolutionary Cuba, 146; and space, 102; Taso's silence on, 95; textual approach to, 102; in the United States, 103; in U.S. imperialist discourse, 32
Race War of 1912 (Cuba), 35, 149, 154n22
Racial segregation, 95, 102; in Harlem, 102, 109, 110, 111; in New York City, 108, 110, 114, 138, 142
Racialization: in Arroyo Pizarro's and Rodríguez Iglesias' novels, 17, 123, 130; of Caribbean immigrants in Puerto Rico, 125; of coloniality, 149; of Cuban diaspora, 141; of European immigrants, 31; of Latinx minorities, 141; of musical practices, 19, 234
Racism: "Black racism," 107; in Casal's "Los fundadores: Alfonso," 214; in East Harlem, 114–15; in prerevolutionary Cuba, 75, 148; in Puerto Rico, 75, 127; in revolutionary Cuba, 143, 150, 154n22, 281, 282; in the United States, 138, 149, 152n5, 153n11, 257. *See also* Antiblack racism

Ramos, Juan Antonio, 212
Ramos Otero, Manuel, 18, 209–26
Ramos Rosado, 127
Repeating Island, The (Benítez Rojo), 62, 63, 64, 187
Returning a Sound (Allora & Calzadilla), 21, 268–78
Reyes Rivera, Louis, 150
Reyes-Santos, Irmary (Alaí), 210
Rigdon, Susan, 95
Riis, Jacob, 108, 113
Ríos, Orlando "Puntilla," 256, 258, 259–61
Rius Rivera, Juan, 23n7, 64
Rivera Ortiz, Ángel, 304
Rivero, Eliana, 24n11
Rivero, Yeidy, 308n4
Rivière, Melisa, 75
Rodríguez, Abraham, Jr., 260, 261, 263
Rodríguez, Rosendo, 100, 103, 104, 106, 107
Rodríguez, Xiomara, 256, 263–64
Rodríguez Aldave, Alfonso, 193, 201, 202
Rodríguez Beltrán, María Elizabeth, 213
Rodríguez-Cancel, Mario A., 21, 283
Rodríguez de Tió, Lola, 18, 66, 75, 107, 147, 176, 300; dreams of independence of Cuba and Puerto Rico, 136; emotional attachment to both Puerto Rico and Cuba, 177; exiled in Cuba, 5; as part of "Pilgrims of Freedom," 23n7; promotes interisland solidarity, 7; rereading of, 210; seeks refuge in the United States, 9; support for Antillean Confederation, 225; writes poem "A Cuba," 64
Rodríguez Iglesias, Legna, 17, 121–34
Rodríguez Monegal, Emir, 153n18
Rojas, María Teresa de, 193, 194
Roosevelt, Franklin Delano, 58n2
Roosevelt, Theodore, 31–32
Rousseau, Jean-Jacques, 269, 275
Ruiz Belvis, Segundo, 9
Ruiz Sastre, Emilio F., 201
Rumba, 20, 258, 259, 260, 261, 262, 264
Rumba clave: Blen, blen blen (Falcón Paradí), 259, 263, 264
Rumbaut, Rubén G., 12, 301, 303, 308n8

Sagebien, Julia, 23n4
Saint-Domingue (Haiti), 6, 179, 180
Saldaño-Portillo, María Josefina, 154n23
Salsa music, 20, 71, 74, 264. *See also* Latin music in New York City
Same-sex desire, 128, 210, 221, 222, 257
Sanabria, Felix, 259, 260, 261–62, 263
Sánchez Korrol, Virginia, 10
Sanes, David, 268
Santería (Afro-Cuban religion), 127, 169, 212, 217, 258, 259, 262
Sarduy, Severo, 12, 218
Scarano, Francisco A., 14–15
Schaeffer, Pierre, 271
Schweitzer, Kenneth, 261
Schomburg, Arturo Alfonso: affiliated with La Liga, 107; interisland collaborations of, 138; photo of, 106; seeks refuge in New York City, 9; self-identifies as "Negro," 105; as secretary of Club Las Dos Antillas, 101, 104, 105; support for Martí, 101–2, 154n22; valorization of Black culture, 143
Section 936 (U.S. Internal Revenue Code), 73
Serra, Rafael: attends first meeting of Club Las Dos Antillas, 103; close ties to Portuondo, 103; collaborator of Martí, 154n22; collaborator of Figueroa, 102; influence on Cuban Revolutionary Party, 104; joins New York–based pro-independence clubs, 138; photos and accounts of La Liga, 105
Sex work, 81, 86–90, 94, 95–96
Sexual practices, 83–86, 89, 90, 92
Simal, Monica, 17
Socialism. *See* Communism
Soviet Union: alliances with Cuba, 53; and Cuban Communist Party, 39–49; central planning of economy in, 7; collapse of, 39–40, 72, 74; Cuba's dependence on, 7, 15, 39; Cubans' refusal to Sovietize, 71; during Cuban Missile Crisis, 57; launching of Sputnik satellite, 46; leadership of Eastern bloc, 70; philosophy of, 54; post-Soviet migrant wave from Cuba, 280; testing of atomic bomb by, 45
Spanglish, 144, 146, 306
Spanish Civil War, 20, 192, 193
Spanish-Cuban-American War, 2, 3, 6, 103, 143. *See also* War of 1898
Special Period in Times of Peace (Cuba), 72, 74
Spurr, David, 237
Stavans, Ilan, 16
Stephens, Michelle, 132

Steward, Julian H., 81
Stoever, Jennifer Lynn, 234
Sugarcane industry: boom in Puerto Rico, 65; and Cristóbal Madan, 31; damage to environment, 177; decline in Cuba, 73; during early twentieth century, 81; exports to U.S. consumer market, 2; foreseen by Columbus, 180; justification for U.S. military intervention in Cuba, 25; replaced by industrial economy in Puerto Rico, 68; role in Cuban economy, 6, 177, 235–36; Taso as worker in, 15, 83, 95; in Vieques, 216

Taínos, 1, 64, 136, 143, 269
Tarafa, Josefina, 20, 192, 193
Ten Years' War in Cuba, 2, 115n8, 219
Terry, Thomas, 248, 251
Testimonio (literary genre), 137, 140
Theatre of Cruelty (Artaud), 18, 158
Theatre of the Absurd, 18, 158, 166
Thomas, Piri, 10, 150, 153n12
Thompson, John, 96
Thompson, Lanny, 236, 239
Timmer, Nanne, 129, 131
Tirado, Modesto, 103–4
Toro Ortiz, Verónica, 304, 305
Torres, Daniel, 211
Torres, Jaime, 75
Torres, María de los Angeles, 152n5
Torres-Rodríguez, Laura, 218
Translation: and decolonization, 142–47, 151; of Duany's *The Puerto Rican Nation on the Move*, 305; of Fernández Retamar's "Caliban," 153n18; of Latinx literature, 13; of musical practices, 234
Transnationalism: in *Areíto*, 137; in business connections, 299; companies, 69; and diasporic cultures, 19; in the Hispanic Caribbean, 295, 298, 306, 307, 308n3; Puerto Rico as transnational nation, 4, 306; as theoretical framework, 125, 151
Treaty of Paris (1898), 5
Triana, José, 18, 159, 165–69, 173n2
Trujillo, Rafael Leónidas, 52, 55
Truman, Harry S., 37, 38, 55
Tú, la oscuridad (Montero), 18–19, 177–90
"Two wings of a bird" metaphor, 5, 64, 65, 66, 136, 178; applied to Cubans in Puerto Rico, 300; applied to cultural links between Cuba and Puerto Rico, 302; applied to popular music, 15, 74, 260; criticized by Arana Soto, 66; echoes in Caribbean translation, 147; extended to Haiti, 18, 19, 190; from an environmental perspective, 176, 177, 190; from the perspective of rural society, 96; quoted by Antilleans in New York City, 107; reinterpreted by Ramos Otero, 18, 210; among working-class immigrants, 16

Unincorporated territory, Puerto Rico as, 3, 6, 33
U.S. citizenship in Puerto Rico extended by Congress, 4, 33, 251n1
U.S. Congress: authorizes election of governor of Puerto Rico, 37; denies increased autonomy to Puerto Rico, 43; determines application of U.S. Constitution to Puerto Rico, 3; enacts Foraker Act, 251n1; enacts Jones Act, 251n1; grants U.S. citizenship to Puerto Ricans, 4; lack of effective representation of Puerto Rico in, 4, 33; Puerto Rican nationalist attack on, 38; ratifies Puerto Rico's Commonwealth formula, 45; reconsiders Section 936, 72–73
U.S. embargo (blockade) of Cuba, 7, 57, 69, 73, 137
U.S. imperialism, 31, 32, 40, 67
USS *Maine*, 2
U.S. military interventions: in the Caribbean, 305; in Cuba, 2–3, 31, 33, 35, 40, 54, 81, 249, 250; in Haiti, 181; in Puerto Rico, 3, 31, 40, 81, 152n10, 165, 249, 305
U.S. Supreme Court, 3

Van Middeldyk, Rudolph Adams, 38
Varela, Félix, 9
Vargas, Margarita, 161
Vega, Bernardo, 9, 10, 138, 143, 150, 153n11
Vientós Gastón, Nilita, 20, 197, 201
Vieques, 7, 268, 272, 273; U.S. Navy in, 21, 72, 268, 271, 272
Viera-Vega, Hugo R., 19–20
Villaronga Colón de Zayas, Elisabeth (Elí), 83, 84, 90
Voegelin, Salomé, 267, 277
Voodoo, 127, 182, 183, 187

Walcott, Derek, 121, 144
War of 1898, 6, 32, 250
Watson, Maida, 18
West-Durán, Alan, 21
Wet foot, dry foot policy, 151
White, Trumbull, 247, 248
Whiteness, 31, 32, 114, 148, 281, 300

Withers, Carl, 15, 80, 82, 88, 92, 97n4
Worker in the Cane (Mintz), 80, 83

Young Lords, 8
Yun, Lisa, 214

Zambrano, María, 20, 192–206
Zayas Alvarado, Anastacio (Taso), 15, 79–96
Zayas Alvarado, Tomasa, 84, 90
Zeuske, Michael, 102
Žižek, Slavoj, 274
Zurbano, Roberto, 149, 153n15, 154n22, 164n22